MATH

W9-CIG-788

Mc Graw Hill Education

connectED.mcgraw-hill.com

STEM McGraw-Hill is committed to providing instructional materials in Science, Technology, Engineering, and Mathematics (STEM) that give all students a solid foundation, one that prepares them for college and careers in the 21st century.

Send all inquiries to:
McGraw-Hill Education
STEM Learning Solutions Center
8787 Orion Place
Columbus, OH 43240

ISBN: 978-0-07-665690-5
MHID: 0-07-665690-X

Printed in the United States of America.

6 7 8 9 RMN 16

CONTENTS IN BRIEF

Organized by Focal Areas

Your assignment's due tomorrow...

but your book is in your locker!

NOW WHAT?

Even in crunch time, with ConnectED, we've got you covered!

With ConnectED, you have instant access to all of your study materials—anytime, anywhere. From homework materials to study guides—it's all in one place and just a click away. ConnectED even allows you to collaborate with your classmates and use mobile apps to make studying easy.

Resources built for you—available 24/7:

• Your eBook available wherever you are

• Personal Tutors and Self-Check Quizzes whenever you need them

• An Online Calendar with all of your due dates

• eFlashcard App to make studying easy

• A message center to stay in touch

Reimagine Learning

Go Online!
connectED.mcgraw-hill.com

Vocab
Learn about new vocabulary words.

Watch
Watch animations and videos.

Tutor
See and hear a teacher explain how to solve problems.

Tools
Explore concepts with virtual manipulatives.

Check
Check your progress.

eHelp
Get targeted homework help.

Worksheets
Access practice worksheets.

Chapter 1
Rational Numbers and the Coordinate Plane

Go to page 93 to learn about a 21st Century Career in Art!

Chapter 2
Multiply and Divide Rational Numbers

Go to page 187 to learn about a 21st Century Career in
Design!

Chapter 3
Operations
with Integers

Go to page 257 to learn about a 21st Century Career in
Astronomy!

Chapter 4
Understand Proportions

Go to page 341 to learn about a 21st Century Career in
Chemistry!

Chapter 5
Apply Proportions to Percent

Go to page 419 to learn about a 21st Century Career in **Movies!**

x

Chapter 6
Multiple Representations

Go to page 487 to learn about a 21st Century Career in
Atmospheric Science!

Chapter 7
Algebraic Expressions

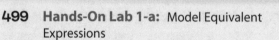

Go to page 577 to learn about a 21st Century Career in **Engineering!**

Chapter 8
Equations and Inequalities

Go to page 661 to learn about a 21st Century Career in
Music!

Chapter 9
Represent Geometry with Algebra

Go to page 767 to learn about a 21st Century Career in **Community Planning!**

Chapter 10
Statistical Measures and Displays

Go to page 871 to learn about a 21st Century Career in Environmental Science!

Chapter 11
Personal Financial Literacy

Texas Essential Knowledge and Skills, Grade 6

Track Your TEKS Progress

The knowledge and skills that you will learn this year are listed on these pages. Throughout the year, your teacher will ask you to rate how confident you feel about your knowledge of each one. Don't worry if you have no clue **before** you learn about them. You will rate your knowledge before and after you learn them. Your teacher will provide you with more instructions. Watch how your knowledge and skills grow as the year progresses!

😞 I have no clue.   😐 I've heard of it.   🙂 I know it!

6.1 Mathematical Process Standards	Before			After		
	😞	😐	🙂	😞	😐	🙂
The student uses mathematical processes to acquire and demonstrate mathematical understanding. The student is expected to:						
6.1(A) Apply mathematics to problems arising in everyday life, society, and the workplace;						
6.1(B) Use a problem-solving model that incorporates analyzing given information, formulating a plan or strategy, determining a solution, justifying the solution, and evaluating the problem-solving process and the reasonableness of the solution;						
6.1(C) Select tools, including real objects, manipulatives, paper and pencil, and technology as appropriate, and techniques, including mental math, estimation, and number sense as appropriate, to solve problems;						
6.1(D) Communicate mathematical ideas, reasoning, and their implications using multiple representations, including symbols, diagrams, graphs, and language as appropriate;						
6.1(E) Create and use representations to organize, record, and communicate mathematical ideas;						
6.1(F) Analyze mathematical relationships to connect and communicate mathematical ideas; and						
6.1(G) Display, explain, and justify mathematical ideas and arguments using precise mathematical language in written or oral communication.						

6.2 Number and Operations	Before			After		
The student applies mathematical process standards to represent and use rational numbers in a variety of forms. The student is expected to:	☹	😐	🙂	☹	😐	🙂
6.2(A) Classify whole numbers, integers, and rational numbers using a visual representation such as a Venn diagram to describe relationships between sets of numbers;						
6.2(B) Identify a number, its opposite, and its absolute value;						
6.2(C) Locate, compare, and order integers and rational numbers using a number line;						
6.2(D) Order a set of rational numbers arising from mathematical and real-world contexts; and						
6.2(E) Extend representations for division to include fraction notation such as a/b represents the same number as $a \div b$ where $b \neq 0$.						

6.3 Number and Operations	Before			After		
The student applies mathematical process standards to represent addition, subtraction, multiplication, and division while solving problems and justifying solutions. The student is expected to:	☹	😐	🙂	☹	😐	🙂
6.3(A) Recognize that dividing by a rational number and multiplying by its reciprocal result in equivalent values;						
6.3(B) Determine, with and without computation, whether a quantity is increased or decreased when multiplied by a fraction, including values greater than or less than one;						
6.3(C) Represent integer operations with concrete models and connect the actions with the models to standardized algorithms;						
6.3(D) Add, subtract, multiply, and divide integers fluently; and						
6.3(E) Multiply and divide positive rational numbers fluently.						

		Before			After		
6.4 Proportionality		☹	😐	☺	☹	😐	☺
The student applies mathematical process standards to develop an understanding of proportional relationships in problem situations. The student is expected to:							
6.4(A)	Compare two rules verbally, numerically, graphically, and symbolically in the form of $y = ax$ or $y = x + a$ in order to differentiate between additive and multiplicative relationships;						
6.4(B)	Apply qualitative and quantitative reasoning to solve prediction and comparison of real-world problems involving ratios and rates;						
6.4(C)	Give examples of ratios as multiplicative comparisons of two quantities describing the same attribute;						
6.4(D)	Give examples of rates as the comparison by division of two quantities having different attributes, including rates as quotients;						
6.4(E)	Represent ratios and percents with concrete models, fractions, and decimals;						
6.4(F)	Represent benchmark fractions and percents such as 1%, 10%, 25%, 33 1/3%, and multiples of these values using 10 by 10 grids, strip diagrams, number lines, and numbers;						
6.4(G)	Generate equivalent forms of fractions, decimals, and percents using real-world problems, including problems that involve money; and						
6.4(H)	Convert units within a measurement system, including the use of proportions and unit rates.						

		Before			After		
6.5 Proportionality		☹	😐	☺	☹	😐	☺
The student applies mathematical process standards to solve problems involving proportional relationships. The student is expected to:							
6.5(A)	Represent mathematical and real-world problems involving ratios and rates using scale factors, tables, graphs, and proportions;						
6.5(B)	Solve real-world problems to find the whole given a part and the percent, to find the part given the whole and the percent, and to find the percent given the part and the whole, including the use of concrete and pictorial models; and						
6.5(C)	Use equivalent fractions, decimals, and percents to show equal parts of the same whole.						

				Before			After	

6.6 Expressions, Equations, and Relationships

The student applies mathematical process standards to use multiple representations to describe algebraic relationships. The student is expected to:

		Before			After		
6.6(A)	Identify independent and dependent quantities from tables and graphs;						
6.6(B)	Write an equation that represents the relationship between independent and dependent quantities from a table; and						
6.6(C)	Represent a given situation using verbal descriptions, tables, graphs, and equations in the form $y = kx$ or $y = x + b$.						

6.7 Expressions, Equations, and Relationships

The student applies mathematical process standards to develop concepts of expressions and equations. The student is expected to:

		Before			After		
6.7(A)	Generate equivalent numerical expressions using order of operations, including whole number exponents and prime factorization;						
6.7(B)	Distinguish between expressions and equations verbally, numerically, and algebraically;						
6.7(C)	Determine if two expressions are equivalent using concrete models, pictorial models, and algebraic representations; and						
6.7(D)	Generate equivalent expressions using the properties of operations: inverse, identity, commutative, associative, and distributive properties.						

		Before			After		
6.8 **Expressions, Equations, and Relationships**		😞	😐	😊	😞	😐	😊
The student applies mathematical process standards to use geometry to represent relationships and solve problems. The student is expected to:							
6.8(A)	Extend previous knowledge of triangles and their properties to include the sum of angles of a triangle, the relationship between the lengths of sides and measures of angles in a triangle, and determining when three lengths form a triangle;						
6.8(B)	Model area formulas for parallelograms, trapezoids, and triangles by decomposing and rearranging parts of these shapes;						
6.8(C)	Write equations that represent problems related to the area of rectangles, parallelograms, trapezoids, and triangles and volume of right rectangular prisms where dimensions are positive rational numbers; and						
6.8(D)	Determine solutions for problems involving the area of rectangles, parallelograms, trapezoids, and triangles and volume of right rectangular prisms where dimensions are positive rational numbers.						

		Before			After		
6.9	**Expressions, Equations, and Relationships**	☹	😐	🙂	☹	😐	🙂
	The student applies mathematical process standards to use equations and inequalities to represent situations. The student is expected to:						
6.9(A)	Write one-variable, one-step equations and inequalities to represent constraints or conditions within problems;						
6.9(B)	Represent solutions for one-variable, one-step equations and inequalities on number lines; and						
6.9(C)	Write corresponding real-world problems given one-variable, one-step equations or inequalities.						

		Before			After		
6.10	**Expressions, Equations, and Relationships**	☹	😐	🙂	☹	😐	🙂
	The student applies mathematical process standards to use equations and inequalities to solve problems. The student is expected to:						
6.10(A)	Model and solve one-variable, one-step equations and inequalities that represent problems, including geometric concepts; and						
6.10(B)	Determine if the given value(s) make(s) one-variable, one-step equations or inequalities true.						

	Before			After		

6.11 Measurement and Data

The student applies mathematical process standards to use coordinate geometry to identify locations on a plane. The student is expected to:

Graph points in all four quadrants using ordered pairs of rational numbers.

6.12 Measurement and Data

The student applies mathematical process standards to use numerical or graphical representations to analyze problems. The student is expected to:

6.12(A) Represent numeric data graphically, including dot plots, stem-and-leaf plots, histograms, and box plots;

6.12(B) Use the graphical representation of numeric data to describe the center, spread, and shape of the data distribution;

6.12(C) Summarize numeric data with numerical summaries, including the mean and median (measures of center) and the range and interquartile range (IQR) (measures of spread), and use these summaries to describe the center, spread, and shape of the data distribution; and

6.12(D) Summarize categorical data with numerical and graphical summaries, including the mode, the percent of values in each category (relative frequency table), and the percent bar graph, and use these summaries to describe the data distribution.

6.13 Measurement and Data

The student applies mathematical process standards to use numerical or graphical representations to solve problems. The student is expected to:

6.13(A) Interpret numeric data summarized in dot plots, stem-and-leaf plots, histograms, and box plots; and

6.13(B) Distinguish between situations that yield data with and without variability.

			Before			After		
6.14	**Personal Financial Literacy**		☹	😐	🙂	☹	😐	🙂
The student applies mathematical process standards to develop an economic way of thinking and problem solving useful in one's life as a knowledgeable consumer and investor. The student is expected to:								
6.14(A)	Compare the features and costs of a checking account and a debit card offered by different local financial institutions;							
6.14(B)	Distinguish between debit cards and credit cards;							
6.14(C)	Balance a check register that includes deposits, withdrawals, and transfers;							
6.14(D)	Explain why it is important to establish a positive credit history;							
6.14(E)	Describe the information in a credit report and how long it is retained;							
6.14(F)	Describe the value of credit reports to borrowers and to lenders;							
6.14(G)	Explain various methods to pay for college, including through savings, grants, scholarships, student loans, and work-study; and							
6.14(H)	Compare the annual salary of several occupations requiring various levels of post-secondary education or vocational training and calculate the effects of the different annual salaries on lifetime income.							

Chapter 6
Multiple Representations

Texas Essential Knowledge and Skills

TEKS

Targeted TEKS

6.6 The student applies mathematical process standards to use multiple representations to describe algebraic relationships.

Mathematical Processes

6.1, 6.1(A), 6.1(B), 6.1(C), 6.1(D), 6.1(E), 6.1(F), 6.1(G)

Essential Question

HOW can you express a relationship between two quantities in different ways?

Math in the Real World

Zip lines can be used for entertainment or to access remote areas. The longest zip line in Texas is located at Lake Travis and is over 2,000 feet long.

On one zip line, the average speed is 44 ft/s. It takes 8 seconds to travel the length of the zip line. Fill in the table to find the distance.

Rate (ft/s)	×	Time (s)	=	Distance (ft)
44	×	1	=	
44	×	2	=	
44	×	3	=	
44	×	4	=	
44	×	5	=	
44	×	6	=	
44	×	7	=	
44	×	8	=	

Go Online!
www.connectED.mcgraw-hill.com

Watch Worksheets Vocab Tutor Tools Check

Vocabulary

additive relationship	independent quantity	sequence
arithmetic sequence	linear relationship	term
dependent quantity	multiplicative relationship	variable
geometric sequence		

Writing Math

Describe Data

When you *describe* something, you represent it in words.

Mark surveyed his class to find their favorite flavor of sugarless gum. Describe the data.

Favorite Flavor of Sugarless Gum	
Flavor	**Number**
Cinnamon	10
Peppermint	18
Watermelon	12

- Eight more people favor peppermint gum over cinnamon gum.

- The total number of people surveyed is 40.

These statements describe the data. What other ways can you

describe the data? _____

_____

_____

Describe the data below.

1.

Least Favorite "Bug"	
Kind	**Number**
Centipede	2
Cockroach	18
Spider	30

2.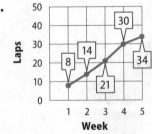

_____

_____

_____

_____

Your Turn! You will solve this problem in the chapter.

Quick Review

Review 6.2(C), 5.4(F)

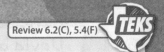

Example 1

Fill in the ◯ with <, >, or = to make a true statement.

71.238 ◯ 71.832

71.238   Use place value. Line up the digits.

71.832   Compare the tenths place. 2 < 8

So, 71.238 < 71.832.

Example 2

Simplify 4(7 + 5).

$4(7 + 5) = 4(12)$ Add.

$ = 48$ Multiply.

Quick Check

Check ✓

Compare Rational Numbers Fill in each ◯ with <, >, or =, to make the inequality true.

1. 302,788 ◯ 203,788

2. $5\frac{3}{4}$ ◯ $5\frac{7}{8}$

3. −8 ◯ 9

Show your work.

4. The table shows the number of bones in humans. Compare 300 and 206. _____

Bones in Humans	
Baby	300
Adult	206

Simplify Expressions Simplify.

5. 8(3 − 1) _____

6. 16(10 + 2) _____

7. 23(14 − 9) _____

8. A touchdown is worth 6 points. In the first game, a team scored 3 touchdowns. In the second game, the team scored 2 touchdowns. How many points did the team receive from touchdowns in those two games? _____

How Did You Do?

Which problems did you answer correctly in the Quick Check? Shade those exercise numbers below.

① ② ③ ④ ⑤ ⑥ ⑦ ⑧

FOLDABLES® Use the Foldable throughout this chapter to help you learn about multiple representations.

✂ cut on all dashed lines   ▭ fold on all solid lines   ▨ tape to page 490

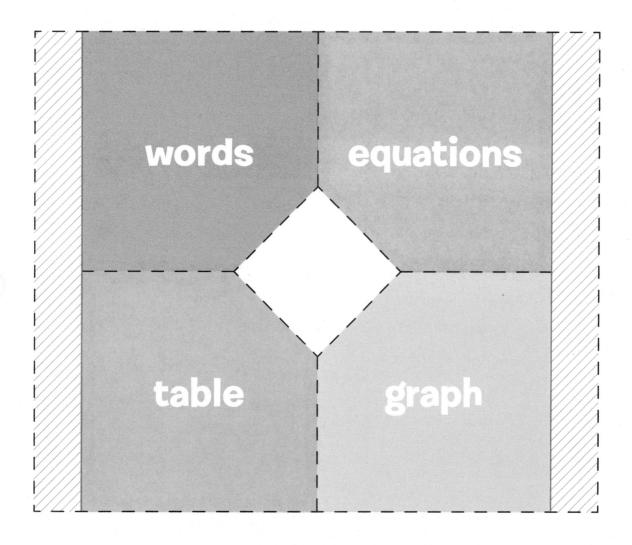

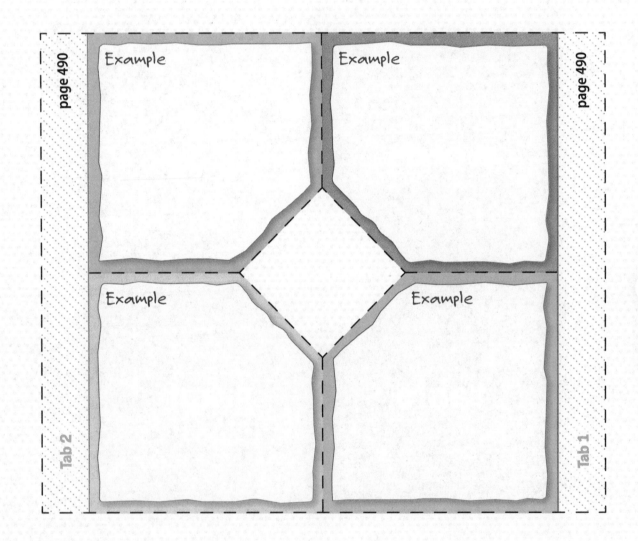

page 490

page 490

Example

Example

Example

Example

Tab 2

Tab 1

Algebraic Relationships: Tables

Launch the Lesson: Real World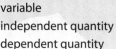

Watch

A ruby-throated hummingbird beats its wings about 52 beats per second. How can tables help you to determine the number of wing beats for 2, 6, or 20 seconds?

1. Make a table showing how many times the bird beats its wings in 2 seconds.

Number of Seconds (s)	s · 52	Wing Beats
2	2 · 52	

2. Make a table to show how many times it beats its wings in 6 seconds.

Number of Seconds (s)	s · 52	Wing Beats
6		

3. Make a table to show how many times it beats its wings in 20 seconds.

Number of Seconds (s)	s · 52	Wing Beats

4. A Giant Hummingbird beats its wings about 10 times per second. Make a table to show how many times the Giant Hummingbird beats its wings in 3 seconds.

Number of Seconds (s)	s · 10	Wing Beats

Which MP Mathematical Processes did you use?
Shade the circle(s) that applies.

Ⓐ Apply Math to the Real World.

Ⓑ Use a Problem-Solving Model.

Ⓒ Select Tools and Techniques.

Ⓓ Use Multiple Representations.

Ⓔ Organize Ideas.

Ⓕ Analyze Relationships.

Ⓖ Justify Arguments.

Texas Essential Knowledge and Skills

Targeted TEKS
6.6(A) Identify independent and dependent quantities from tables and graphs. *Also addresses 6.6(C).*

Mathematical Processes
6.1(A), 6.1(B), 6.1(D), 6.1(E), 6.1(F), 6.1(G)

Vocabulary
variable
independent quantity
dependent quantity

Essential Question
HOW can you express a relationship between two quantities in different ways?

Identify the Dependent Quantity

A **variable** is a symbol, usually a letter, used to represent an unknown number. On the previous page, the number of wing beats (output) depends on the number of seconds (input). A rule using a variable can be written to describe the relationship between each input and output. You can organize the input-output values and the rule in a table.

In an algebraic relationship, the input value is also known as the **independent quantity**, since it can be any number you choose. The value of the output depends on the input value, so the output value is known as the **dependent quantity**.

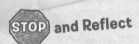

STOP and Reflect

What values were used for the independent quantity in Example 1? Answer below.

Tutor

Examples

1. The output is 7 more than the input. Complete a table for this relationship to identify the dependent quantities.

Use *x* for the input. The rule is *x* + 7. Add 7 to each input.

Input (x)	x + 7	Output
10		
12		
14		

→

Input (x)	x + 7	Output
10	10 + 7	17
12	12 + 7	19
14	14 + 7	21

2. The output is 5 times the input. Complete a table for this relationship to identify the dependent quantities.

Use *x* for the input . The rule is 5(*x*). Multiply each input by 5.

Input (x)	5(x)	Output
8		
10		
12		

→

Input (x)	5(x)	Output
8	5( )	
10	5( )	
12	5( )	

Got It? Do these problems to find out.

a.

Input (x)	x − 4	Output
4		
7		
10		

b.

Input (x)	3(x)	Output
0		
2		
5		

Identify the Independent Quantity

The input and output of a table can be represented as a set of ordered pairs, or a *relation*. The input represents the *x*-values, or independent quantities, and the output represents the *y*-values, or dependent quantities.

Example

Tutor

3. Identify the independent quantities for the table.

Input (*x*)	3(*x*)	Output
		6
		15
		21

Use the *work backward* strategy to determine the input. If the output is found by multiplying by 3, then the input is found by dividing by 3.

The independent quantities are 6 ÷ 3 or 2, 15 ÷ 3 or 5, and 21 ÷ 3 or 7.

> **Inverse Operations**
>
> Multiplication and division are inverse operations as well as addition and subtraction. Inverse operations "undo" each other.

Got It? Do these problems to find out.

c.

Input (*x*)	*x* − 2	Output
		9
		11
		13

d.

Input (*x*)	8(*x*)	Output
		16
		24
		32

Example

Tutor

4. The Gomez family is traveling at a rate of 70 miles per hour. The rule that represents this situation is 70(*x*), where *x* is the number of hours. Make a table to find how many hours they have driven at 140 miles, 280 miles, and 350 miles. Then graph the ordered pairs.

Input (*x*)	70(*x*)	Output (*y*)
2	70(2)	140
4	70(4)	280
5	70(5)	350

Divide each output by 70.

The missing independent quantities are 140 ÷ 70 or 2, 280 ÷ 70 or 4, and 350 ÷ 70 or 5.

The independent and dependent quantities are the ordered pairs (*x*, *y*). Plot each ordered pair on the graph.

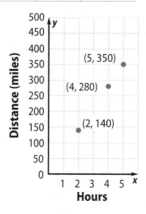

e.

Distance (miles): 60, 55, 50, 45, 40, 35, 30, 25, 20, 15, 10, 5, 0

Hours (x): 1 2 3 4 5

Got It? Do this problem to find out.

e. Briana bikes 12 miles per hour. The rule that represents this situation is 12(x), where x is the number of hours. Make a table to find how many hours she has biked when she has gone 12, 36, and 48 miles. Then graph the ordered pairs.

Input (x)	12(x)	Output (y)

Guided Practice

1. Isaiah is buying jelly beans. In bulk, they cost $3 per pound. The rule, 3(x) where x is the number of pounds, can be used to find the total cost of x pounds of jelly beans. Make a table to identify the dependent quantities, the total cost, of buying 2, 3, or 4 pounds of jelly beans. (Examples 1 and 2)

Pounds (x)	3(x)	Cost ($) (y)

2. Jasper hikes 4 miles per hour. The rule that represents this situation is 4(x), where x is the number of hours. Make a table to identify the independent quantities, how many hours he has hiked, when he has hiked 8, 12, and 20 miles. Then graph the ordered pairs. (Examples 3 and 4)

Hours (x)	4(x)	Miles (y)

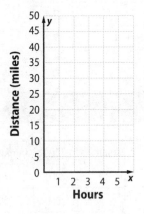

Distance (miles): 50, 45, 40, 35, 30, 25, 20, 15, 10, 5, 0

Hours (x): 1 2 3 4 5

3. **(?)** **Building on the Essential Question** How can a table help you identify the independent and dependent quantities?

_____

_____

_____

_____

Rate Yourself!

Are you ready to move on?
Shade the section that applies.

I have a few questions. | I'm ready to move on.

I have a lot of questions.

Find out online. Use the Self-Check Quiz.

Check ✓

FOLDABLES Time to update your Foldable!

Independent Practice

6.6(A), 6.6(C), 6.1(C)

MP **Select Tools and Techniques** **Complete each table.** (Examples 1–3)

1.

Input (x)	3(x)	Output
0		
3		
9		

2.

Input (x)	x − 4	Output
4		
8		
11		

3.

Input (x)	x + 2	Output
		2
		3
		8

4.

Input (x)	2(x)	Output
		14
		18
		30

5. Whitney has a total of 30 cupcakes for her guests. The rule, 30 ÷ x where x is the number of guests, can be used to find the number of cupcakes per guest. Make a table to identify the dependent quantities, the number of cupcakes each guest will get, if there are 6, 10, or 15 guests. Then graph the ordered pairs. (Examples 1 and 2)

Number of Guests (x)	30 ÷ x	Cupcakes per Guest (y)

6. Bella rollerblades 8 miles in one hour. The rule that represents this situation is 8(x), where x is the number of hours. Make a table to identify the independent quantities, how many hours she has skated, when she has traveled 16, 24, and 32 miles. Then graph the ordered pairs. (Examples 3 and 4)

Hours (x)	8(x)	Miles (y)

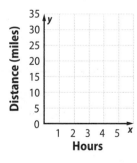

7. Find the Error Daniella is finding the dependent quantity when the rule is $10 \div x$ and the independent quantity is 2. Find her mistake and correct it.

_____

_____

_____

$2 \div 10 = 0.2$

 H.O.T. Problems Higher-Order Thinking

8. Analyze Around 223 million Americans keep containers filled with coins in their home. Suppose each of the 223 million people started putting their coins back into circulation at a rate of $10 per year. Create a table that shows the amount of money that would be recirculated in 1, 2, and 3 years.

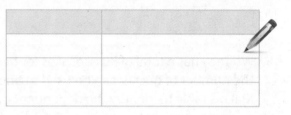

9. Analyze Explain how to identify the independent quantity given a rule and the dependent quantity.

_____

_____

10. Evaluate Given the rule $x + n$, describe the values of n for which the output value will be less than the input value. Justify your response.

_____

_____

11. Evaluate Compare and contrast the tables used in this lesson to ratio tables.

_____

_____

_____

12. Create Write and solve a real-world problem that can be represented by a rule and a table using division.

_____

_____

_____

_____

Multi-Step Problem Solving

13. Sandra places wooden sculptures on top of a 3-foot-tall stand. The table can be used to compare the height of a sculpture to the height including the stand. What is the total height, in inches, of a 5-foot-tall sculpture on a stand? **EE** **MP**

Ⓐ 8 in.   Ⓒ 60 in.

Ⓑ 10 in.   Ⓓ 96 in.

Height of Sculpture (ft) (x)	x + 3	Height on Stand (ft) (y)
2		
3		
5		

Use a problem-solving model to solve this problem.

1 Analyze

Read the problem. Circle the information you know. Underline what the problem is asking you to find.

2 Plan

What will you need to do to solve the problem? Write your plan in steps.

Step 1 Use the table to determine the height including the stand.

Step 2 Convert the height to inches by multiplying by 12.

3 Solve

Use your plan to solve the problem. Show your steps.

Height of Sculpture (ft) (x)	x + 3	Height on Stand (ft) (y)
2		
3		
5		

Read to Succeed!

There are 12 inches in 1 foot. To convert feet to inches, multiply by 12.

So, the height on the stand is ☐ feet. In inches, this is 8 × 12 or ☐ inches. Choice ☐ is correct. Fill in that answer choice.

4 Justify and Evaluate

How do you know your solution is accurate?

_____

_____

EE = Expressions, Equations, and Relationships   **MP** = Mathematical Processes

More **Multi-Step** Problem Solving

Use a problem-solving model to solve each problem.

14. Eduardo has a $5 coupon for groceries. The amount he owes can be found by subtracting 5 from the total cost of his groceries. He buys $42 worth of groceries and pays with a $50 bill. How much change does he receive? **EE** **N** **MP**

Cost of Groceries (x)	x − 5	Amount Owed (y)
$15		
$25		
$42		

Ⓐ $8

Ⓑ $13

Ⓒ $37

Ⓓ $82

15. Sam plays a trivia game. He earns 6 points for each question that he answers correctly. He creates a table to show this relationship. What is x when y = 30? **EE** **P** **MP**

Number of Correct Answers (x)	6(x)	Points Earned (y)
		6
		30

16. Catarina invites friends to come over for breakfast. She made 50 muffins. If there are x guests, then each guest can have 50 ÷ x muffins. She creates a table to show the relationship. If y = 2, what is x? **EE** **P** **MP**

Number of Guests (x)	50 ÷ (x)	Muffins per Guest (y)
		5
		2

17. If the side length of a square is x, then the perimeter of the square is 4x. Complete the table to find the perimeters for the squares with sides lengths as shown. Describe the relationship shown in the table. **EE** **MP**

Side Length (x)	4(x)	Perimeter (y)
$\frac{1}{3}$		
$\frac{1}{2}$		
$1\frac{1}{2}$		

N = Number and Operations   **P** = Proportionality   **EE** = Expressions, Equations, and Relationships   **MP** = Mathematical Processes

438 **Chapter 6** Multiple Representations

Copyright © McGraw-Hill Education

Algebraic Relationships: Rules

Copyright © McGraw-Hill Education   Nacivet/Photographer's Choice/Getty Images

Launch the Lesson: Vocabulary

A **sequence** is a list of numbers in a specific order. Each number in the list is called a **term** of the sequence.

Arithmetic sequences can be found by adding the same number to the previous term. In a **geometric sequence**, each term is found by multiplying the previous term by the same number.

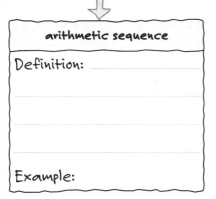

Compare arithmetic sequences and geometric sequences.

arithmetic sequence	geometric sequence
Definition:	Definition:
Example:	Example:

Texas Essential Knowledge and Skills

Targeted TEKS
6.6(A) Identify independent and dependent quantities from tables and graphs. *Also addresses 6.6(C).*

Mathematical Processes
6.1(A), 6.1(B), 6.1(D), 6.1(E), 6.1(F), 6.1(G)

Vocabulary
sequence
term
arithmetic sequence
geometric sequence

Essential Question
HOW can you express a relationship between two quantities in different ways?

Real-World Link

The China Palace sells lunch specials for \$6 with a delivery charge of \$5 per order. Fill in the table with the next three numbers in the sequence.

Specials	1	2	3	4	5	6	7
Cost (\$)	11	17	23	29			

Which MP **Mathematical Processes** did you use?
Shade the circle(s) that applies.

Ⓐ Apply Math to the Real World.   Ⓔ Organize Ideas.

Ⓑ Use a Problem-Solving Model.   Ⓕ Analyze Relationships.

Ⓒ Select Tools and Techniques.   Ⓖ Justify Arguments.

Ⓓ Use Multiple Representations.

Arithmetic and Geometric Sequences

Determining if a sequence is arithmetic or geometric can help you find the pattern. When you know the pattern, you can continue the sequence to find missing terms.

Examples

Tutor

1. Describe the relationship between the terms in the arithmetic sequence 7, 14, 21, 28, ... Then write the next three terms.

$$7, \quad 14, \quad 21, \quad 28, ...$$
$$+7 \quad +7 \quad +7$$

Each term is found by adding 7 to the previous term. Continue the pattern to find the next three terms.

$$28 + 7 = 35 \qquad 35 + 7 = 42 \qquad 42 + 7 = 49$$

The next three terms are 35, 42, and 49.

2. Describe the relationship between the terms in the geometric sequence 2, 4, 8, 16, ... Then write the next three terms.

$$2, \quad 4, \quad 8, \quad 16, ...$$
$$\times 2 \quad \times 2 \quad \times 2$$

Even though each term can be found by adding the previous term ($2 + 2 = 4, 4 + 4 = 8$, etc.), the sequence is not arithmetic because the difference between each term is not the same.

Each term is found by multiplying the previous term by two. Continue the pattern to find the next three terms.

$$16 \times 2 = 32 \qquad 32 \times 2 = 64 \qquad 64 \times 2 = 128$$

The next three terms are 32, 64, and 128.

Got It? Do these problems to find out.

a. 0, 15, 30, 45, ...   b. 4.5, 4, 3.5, 3, ...

c. 1, 3, 9, 27, ...   d. 3, 6, 12, 24, ...

Show your work.

a. _____

b. _____

c. _____

d. _____

Determine a Rule from a Table

A sequence can also be shown in a table. The table gives both the position of each term in the list and the value of the term.

List

8, 16, 24, 32, ...

Table

Position	1	2	3	4
Value of Term	8	16	24	32

You can write an algebraic expression to describe a sequence. The value of each term can be described in relation to its position in the sequence.

In the table above, the position can be considered the independent quantity, and the value of the term as the dependent quantity.

Tutor

Example

3. **Use words and symbols to describe the value of each term in relation to its position. Then find the value of the tenth term.**

Position	1	2	3	4	n
Value of Term	3	6	9	12	▨

Notice that the value of each term is 3 times its position number. So, the value of the term in position n is $3(n)$.

Now find the value of the tenth term.

$3(n) = 3(10)$ Replace n with 10.

$= 30$ Multiply.

Position	Multiply by 3	Value of Term
1	1×3	3
2	2×3	6
3	3×3	9
4	4×3	12
n	$n \times 3$	$3(n)$

The value of the tenth term in the sequence is 30.

> **Work Backward**
> You can check your rule by working backward. Divide each term by 3 to check the position.

Got It? Do these problems to find out.

Use words and symbols to describe the value of each term in relation to its position. Then find the value of the eighth term.

e.

Position	2	3	4	5	n
Value of Term	12	18	24	30	▨

f.

Position	3	4	5	6	n
Value of Term	7	8	9	10	▨

Show your work.

e. _____

f. _____

Example

4. The table shows the number of necklaces Ari can make, based on the number of hours she works. Write a rule to find the number of necklaces she can make in *x* hours.

Notice that the dependent quantities 4, 8, 12, … are four times the number of hours. So, the rule is 4(*x*).

To test the rule 4(*x*), use the *guess, check, and revise* strategy.

Row 1: $4(x) = 4(1) = 4$

Row 2: $4(x) = 4(2) = 8$

Row 3: $4(x) = 4(3) = 12$

The rule 4(*x*) represents the table.

Hours (*x*)	Number of Necklaces
1	4
2	8
3	12
x	■

STOP and Reflect

Find the rule for the following sequence:

5, 10, 15, 20. . . .

Guided Practice

1. Describe the relationship between the terms in the sequence 13, 26, 52, 104, … Then write the next three terms in the sequence. (Examples 1 and 2)

_____

2. Use words and symbols to describe the value of each term in relation to its position. Then find the value of the fifteenth term in the sequence. (Example 3)

Position	1	2	3	4	*n*
Value of Term	2	4	6	8	■

_____

3. The table at the right shows the fee for overdue books at a library, based on the number of weeks the book is overdue. Write a rule to find the fee for a book that is *x* weeks overdue. (Example 4) _____

Weeks Overdue (*x*)	Fee ($)
1	0.50
2	1.00
3	1.50
4	2.00
x	■

4. **?** **Building on the Essential Question** What is the difference between an arithmetic sequence and a geometric sequence? _____

_____

_____

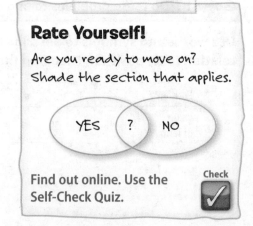

Rate Yourself!

Are you ready to move on? Shade the section that applies.

YES ? NO

Find out online. Use the Self-Check Quiz.

Check ✓

Independent Practice

6.6(A), 6.6(C), 6.1(F) TEKS

Use words and symbols to describe the value of each term in relation to its position. Then find the value of the twelfth term in the sequence. (Examples 1–3)

1.

Position	3	4	5	6	n
Value of Term	12	13	14	15	▣

_____

_____

2.

Position	2	3	4	5	n
Value of Term	24	36	48	60	▣

_____

_____

3. Describe the relationship between the terms in the sequence 6, 18, 54, 162, ... Then write the next three terms in the sequence. (Example 2)

_____

_____

4. The table shows the amount it costs to rock climb at an indoor rock climbing facility, based on the number of hours. What is the rule to find the amount charged to rock climb for x hours? Explain. (Example 4)

Time (x)	Amount ($)
1	8
2	16
3	24
4	32
x	▣

_____

_____

MP Analyze Relationships Determine how the next term in each sequence can be found. Then find the next two terms in the sequence.

5. 4, 16, 28, 40, ...

_____

6. 1.5, 3.9, 6.3, 8.7, ...

_____

7. $2\frac{1}{4}, 2\frac{3}{4}, 3\frac{1}{4}, 3\frac{3}{4}, ...$

_____

Determine the missing number in each sequence.

8. 30, _____, 19, $13\frac{1}{2}$, ...

9. 43.8, 36.7, _____, 22.5, ...

10. MP Analyze Relationships Describe the relationship between the terms in the sequence 9, 7, 5, 3, ... using two different rules that use integers.

_____

_____

Determine whether each sequence is arithmetic or geometric. Then find the next two terms in the sequence.

11. 1, 6, 36, 216

_____

_____

12. 0.75, 1.75, 2.75, 3.75

_____

_____

13. 0, 13, 26, 39

_____

_____

14. Jay is stacking cereal boxes to create a store display. The number of boxes in each row is shown in the table. Is the pattern an example of an arithmetic sequence or a geometric sequence? Explain. How many boxes will be in row 5?

Row	Number of Boxes
1	4
2	6
3	8
4	10
5	■

_____

_____

_____

 H.O.T. Problems Higher-Order Thinking

15. Create Create a sequence in which $1\frac{1}{4}$ is added to each number.

_____

16. Analyze Use words and symbols to generalize the relationship of each term in relation to its position. Then determine the value of the term when $n = 100$.

Position	1	2	3	4	5	n
Value of Term	1	4	9	16	25	■

_____

_____

17. Analyze What is the rule that can be used to determine the value of the missing term in the sequence at the right? Justify your response.

Position, (x)	Value of Term
1	1
2	5
3	9
4	13
5	17
x	■

_____

_____

Multi-Step Problem Solving

18. Autumn and Bennett painted signs for a school campaign. The table shows the total number of signs painted, based on the number of hours spent painting. How many more signs did Autumn paint than Bennett after 6 hours?

Hours	Autumn	Bennett
1	6	4
2	9	6
3	12	8
4	15	10

Use a problem-solving model to solve this problem.

1 Analyze

Read the problem. Circle the information you know. Underline what the problem is asking you to find.

2 Plan

What will you need to do to solve the problem? Write your plan in steps.

Step 1 Determine the rule for each person.

Step 2 Use the rule to determine the number of signs made at 6 hours.

Step 3 Subtract to determine how many more signs Autumn painted.

> **Read to Succeed!**
> After determining the algebraic rule for each person, test your rule by using the independent and dependent quantities from the table.

3 Solve

Use your plan to solve the problem. Show your steps.

Autumn: $3(x) + 3$ Bennett: $2(x) + 2$

$3(\boxed{}) + 3 = \boxed{}$ $2(\boxed{}) + 2 = \boxed{}$

So, Autumn painted $\boxed{} - \boxed{}$ or $\boxed{}$ more signs. Complete the grid.

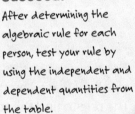

4 Justify and Evaluate

How do you know your solution is accurate?

_____

_____

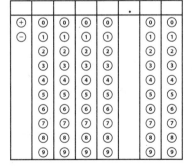

EE = Expressions, Equations, and Relationships   **MP** = Mathematical Processes

More Multi-Step Problem Solving

Use a problem-solving model to solve each problem.

19. The table shows the number of boxes Sandra and Charles can fill with canned food during a food drive, based on the number of hours worked. How many more boxes can Charles fill than Sandra after 7 hours? **EE** **MP**

Hours	Sandra	Charles
1	4	8
2	7	16
3	10	24
4	13	32

20. The table shows the number of miles David and Bailey ran each of the last six days. How many more miles did David run than Bailey on the sixth day? **EE** **MP**

Days	David	Bailey
1	1.10	5.0
2	2.20	4.1
3	3.30	3.2
4	4.40	2.3
5	?	?
6	?	?

21. The table shows the amount it costs to ride a go-kart, based on the number of hours. The rule to find the total cost is $a(x) + b$. What is the sum of a and b? **EE** **MP**

Time (x)	Amount ($)
$1\frac{1}{2}$	13
2	15
3	19
5	27

22. The table shows two rules. Describe each rule. What is the relationship between Rule 1 and Rule 2? **EE** **MP**

Position	Rule 1: Value of Term	Rule 2: Value of Term
1	1	1
2	4	8
3	9	27
4	16	64

EE = Expressions, Equations, and Relationships   **MP** = Mathematical Processes

Algebraic Relationships: Equations

 ## Launch the Lesson: Vocabulary

Texas Essential Knowledge and Skills

Targeted TEKS
6.6(B) Write an equation that represents the relationship between independent and dependent quantities from a table. *Also addresses 6.6(C).*

Mathematical Processes
6.1(A), 6.1(B), 6.1(D), 6.1(E), 6.1(F), 6.1(G)

A **linear relationship** is an algebraic relationship whose graph is a line.

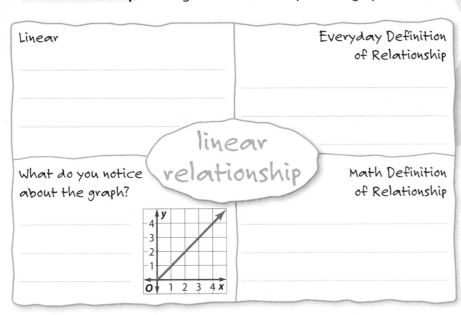

Linear	Everyday Definition of Relationship
linear relationship	
What do you notice about the graph?	Math Definition of Relationship

Vocabulary
linear relationship

Essential Question
HOW can you express a relationship between two quantities in different ways?

 ## Real-World Investigation

The table shows the amount of money Carli earns based on the number of hours she babysits.

1. Write a sentence that describes the relationship between the number of hours she babysits and her earnings.

Hours Babysitting	Earnings ($)
1	6
2	12
3	18
4	24

Which MP **Mathematical Processes** did you use?
Shade the circle(s) that applies.

Ⓐ Apply Math to the Real World.

Ⓑ Use a Problem-Solving Model.

Ⓒ Select Tools and Techniques.

Ⓓ Use Multiple Representations.

Ⓔ Organize Ideas.

Ⓕ Analyze Relationships.

Ⓖ Justify Arguments.

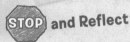

STOP and Reflect

In the equation $d = 36t$, where d is the distance traveled and t is the time, which quantity is independent and which is dependent? Explain below.

Write an Equation to Represent a Relationship

You can use an equation to represent an algebraic relationship. The input, or independent variable, represents the x-value, and the output, or dependent variable, represents the y-value. An equation represents the relationship between the independent and dependent quantities.

Tutor

Example

1. Write an equation to represent the relationship between the independent and dependent quantities shown in the table.

Input, x	1	2	3	4	5
Output, y	9	18	27	36	45

Input, x	Multiply by 9	Output, y
1	1 × 9	9
2	2 × 9	18
3	3 × 9	27
4	4 × 9	36
5	5 × 9	45

$\big)$ +9
$\big)$ +9
$\big)$ +9
$\big)$ +9

The value of y is equal to 9 times the value of x. So, the equation that represents the relationship is $y = 9(x)$.

Got It? Do this problem to find out.

 Show your work.

a. Write an equation to represent the relationship between the independent and dependent quantities shown in the table.

Input, x	1	2	3	4	5
Output, y	16	32	48	64	80

a. _____

Represent Linear Relationships Using Graphs

You can also graph a relationship. If the graph is a line, the relationship is then called a *linear relationship*. When graphing the relationship, the independent quantity is the x-coordinate and the dependent quantity is the y-coordinate.

$$\left(\begin{array}{cc} \textit{independent} & \textit{dependent} \\ \textit{quantity} & , & \textit{quantity} \end{array} \right) \longrightarrow (x, y)$$

Example

Tutor

2. **Represent the relationship $y = 2(x)$ with a graph.**

Step 1 Make a table of ordered pairs. Select any three values for x. Substitute these values for x to find y.

x	2(x)	y	(x, y)
0	2(0)	0	(0, 0)
1	2(1)	2	(1, 2)
2	2(2)	4	(2, 4)

Step 2 Graph each ordered pair. Draw a line through each point.

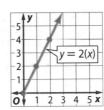

$y = 2(x)$

Show your work.

Got It? Do these problems to find out.

b. $y = x + 1$

c. $y = 3(x)$

b.

c.

Examples

Real World

Tutor

Martino constructed the graph shown, which shows the height of his cactus after several weeks of growth.

3. **Represent the relationship with a table.**

Input, x	Output, y
1	2
2	4
3	6

Cactus Height

The three independent quantities are 1, 2, and 3. The corresponding dependent quantities are 2, 4, and 6.

4. **Write an equation from the graph that could be used to find the height y of the cactus after x weeks.**

Since the dependent quantities increase by 2, the equation includes $2(x)$. So, the equation is $y = 2(x)$.

Magazines (x)	Total (y)

d. _____

Got It? Do this problem to find out.

d. The graph shows the total amount y that you spend if you buy x magazines. Represent the relationship with a table. Write an equation from the graph that could be used to find the total amount y if you buy x magazines.

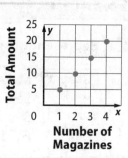

Total Amount

Number of Magazines

Guided Practice

1. Write an equation to represent the relationship between the independent and dependent quantities shown in the table. *(Example 1)*

Input (x)	0	1	2	3	4
Output (y)	0	4	8	12	16

_____

2. Represent the relationship $y = x + 3$ with a graph. *(Example 2)*

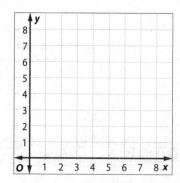

3. The graph below shows the number of inches of rainfall x equivalent to inches of snow y. Represent the relationship with a table. Write an equation from the graph that can be used to find the total inches of snow y equivalent to inches of rain x. *(Examples 3 and 4)*

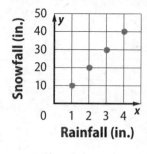

Snowfall (in.)

Rainfall (in.)

Rain (x)	Snow (y)

_____

4. **Building on the Essential Question** How are ordered pairs of a relationship used to create the graph of the relationship?

_____

_____

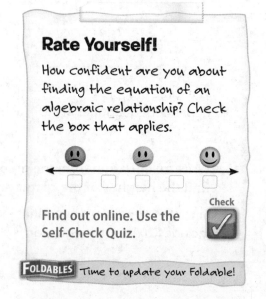

Rate Yourself!

How confident are you about finding the equation of an algebraic relationship? Check the box that applies.

Find out online. Use the Self-Check Quiz.

Check

FOLDABLES Time to update your Foldable!

Independent Practice

6.6(B), 6.6(C), 6.1(D) **TEKS**

Write an equation to represent each relationship between the independent and dependent quantities. (Example 1)

1.

Input (x)	1	2	3	4	5
Output (y)	6	12	18	24	30

_____

2.

Input (x)	0	1	2	3	4
Output (y)	0	15	30	45	60

_____

Represent each relationship with a graph. (Example 2)

3. $y = x + 4$

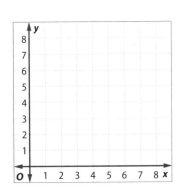

4. $y = 2(x)$

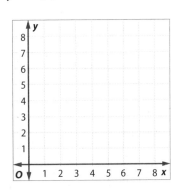

5. $y = 0.5(x)$

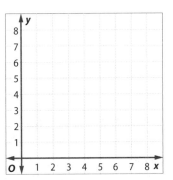

6. The graph shows the charges for a health club in a month. Represent the relationship with a table. Write an equation that can be used to find the total charge y for the number of x classes.

(Examples 3 and 4)

Input (x)				
Output (y)				

_____

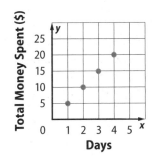

7. The graph shows the amount of money Pasha spent on lunch. Represent the relationship with a table. Write an equation that can be used to find the money spent y for any number of days x.

(Examples 3 and 4)

Input (x)				
Output (y)				

_____

8. **MP Use Multiple Representations** The table shows the area of a square with the given side length.

Side Length (x)	Area of Square (y)
0	0
1	1
2	4
3	9
4	16

   a. **Variables** Write an equation that could represent the table.

   _____

   b. **Graphs** Represent the relationship with a graph.

   c. **Words** Is this a linear relationship? Explain.

   _____

🔥 H.O.T. Problems   Higher-Order Thinking

9. **Create** Write about a real-world situation that can be represented by the equation $y = 7(x)$. Be sure to explain what the variables represent in the situation. _____

   _____

10. **Create** Write an equation to represent the relationship in the table. _____

Input (x)	6	8	10	12	14	16
Output (y)	0	1	2	3	4	5

11. **Create** Write an equation that represents the relationship between the independent and dependent quantities shown in the table. _____

Input (x)	1	2	3	4
Output (y)	3	5	7	9

12. **Analyze** The inverse of a relationship can be found by switching the coordinates in each ordered pair. Make a table for the input and output values of $y = x + 3$. Then, find the equation of the inverse of $y = x + 3$.

   _____

Multi-Step Problem Solving

13. Kya's take-home pay, y, on a given day equals her earnings, x, minus $3 for parking. The relationship can be represented by the equation $y = x - 3$. Make a table of values and plot the ordered pairs. Which ordered pair will NOT be on the graph? **EE** **MP**

ⓐ (70, 67)

ⓑ (51, 54)

ⓒ (82, 79)

ⓓ (93, 90)

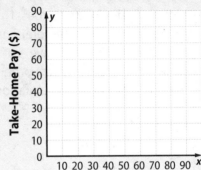

Use a problem-solving model to solve this problem.

1 Analyze

Read the problem. Circle the information you know.
Underline what the problem is asking you to find.

2 Plan

What will you need to do to solve the problem? Write your plan in steps.

Step 1 Make a table to show the independent and dependent quantities.

Step 2 Write and graph the ordered pairs.

3 Solve

Use your plan to solve the problem. Show your steps.

x	$x - 3$	y

Read to Succeed!

Use the x-coordinates in the table to check the y-coordinates of the answer choices.

The ordered pair (51, 54) is not on the graph. So, choice _____ is correct.
Fill in that answer choice.

4 Justify and Evaluate

How do you know your solution is accurate?

_____

_____

EE = Expressions, Equations, and Relationships   **MP** = Mathematical Processes

Use a problem-solving model to solve each problem.

14. Antonio is buying tomatoes. The equation $y = 3(x)$ represents the total number of tomatoes that he will have, y, if he buys x packs of tomatoes. Which ordered pairs will be on the graph of this equation? **EE** **MP**

Ⓐ (0, 0), (3, 1), (9, 3)

Ⓑ (0, 0), (1, 3), (3, 9)

Ⓒ (0, 3), (1, 4), (3, 10)

Ⓓ (0, 0), (2, 6), (3, 6)

15. The table shows the amount of commission, y, that Fernando earns compared to his weekly sales, x. If the equation for this situation is $y = ax$, what is the value of a? **EE** **P** **MP**

Sales (x)	Commission (y)
$250	$75
$175	$52.50
$80	$24

16. The graph compares the number of snow cones purchased to the total cost of the snow cones. If the equation for the situation is $y = ax$, what is the value of a? As the number of snow cones increases, does the total cost increase or decrease? **EE** **P** **MP**

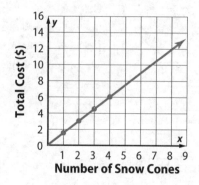

17. The perimeter of a rectangle is 30. The dimensions are unknown. Write an equation that gives the length, y, in terms of the width, x. Complete the table of values to help you. **EE** **MP**

Width (x)	Length (y)

P = Proportionality   **EE** = Expressions, Equations, and Relationships   **MP** = Mathematical Processes

Splitting Up

Blue-green algae is a type of bacteria that can double its population by splitting up to four times in one day.

If it grows at this rate, would the number of bacteria be over 1,000 within a week?

Mathematical Process
6.1(B) Use a problem-solving model that incorporates analyzing given information, formulating a plan or strategy, determining a solution, justifying the solution, and evaluating the problem-solving process and the reasonableness of the solution.

Targeted TEKS 6.6(C)

Analyze *What are the facts?*

Blue-green algae can double its population up to four times in one day.

I know how to multiply.

Plan *What is your strategy to solve this problem?*

Make a table to display and organize the information.

Solve *How can you apply the strategy?*

Follow the pattern to find the total number of bacteria during the second day.

Day Number	Number of Times Split	Total Number of Bacteria	
1	0	1	← ×2
1	1	2	← ×2
1	2		← ×2
1	3		← ×2
1	4		← ×2
2	5		← ×2
2	6		← ×2

Continue the pattern. The number of bacteria would be 128, 256, 512, 1,024, 2,048, and 4,096. The number of bacteria is greater than 1,000 during Day 3.

Justify and Evaluate

Use information from the problem to check your answer.

_____

_____

Game On!

Miguel and Lauren are testing two versions of a new video game. In Miguel's version he receives 24 points at the start of the game, plus 1 point for each level he completes. In Lauren's version she receives 18 points at the start of the game, and 2 points for each level she completes.

At what level will they both have the same number of points?

Analyze

Read the problem. What are you being asked to find?

I need to find _____.

Underline key words and values in the problem.
What information do you know?

Miguel starts with ☐ points and earns ☐ point for each level.

Lauren starts with ☐ points and earns ☐ points for each level.

Plan

Choose a problem-solving strategy.

I will use the _____ strategy.

Solve

Use your problem-solving strategy to solve the problem.

	Start	Level 1	Level 2	Level 3	Level 4	Level 5	Level 6
Miguel							
Lauren							

So, Miguel and Lauren will have the same score after completing

Level ☐.

Justify and Evaluate

Use information from the problem to check your answer.

_____

_____

Multi-Step Problem Solving

Work with a small group to solve the following problems. Show your work on a separate piece of paper.

1. Geometry

Determine how many cubes are used in each step.

Make a table to find the number of cubes in the seventh step.

2. Car Rental

Anne Marie needs to rent a car for 9 days to take on vacation. The cost of renting a car is $66 per day, $15.99 for insurance, and $42.50 to fill up the gas tank.

Determine the total cost of her rental car, if she fills the gas tank once.

3. Numbers

The difference between two whole numbers is 14. Their product is 1,800.

Determine the two numbers.

Use any strategy!

4. Money

The admission for a fair is $6 for adults, $4 for children, and $3 for senior citizens. Twelve people paid a total of $50 for admission.

If 8 children attended, how many adults and senior citizens attended?

Vocabulary Check

1. Define *sequence*. Give an example of an arithmetic and geometric sequence.
   TEKS 6.6(A), 6.1(G)

_____

_____

Key Concept Check

2. Complete the graphic organizer by giving an algebraic table, rule, and
   equation for the real-world situation. **TEKS** 6.6(C), 6.1(E)

   Charlie can run 1 mile in 11 minutes.

Algebraic Table	Algebraic Rule	Algebraic Equation

3. Arnold reads an average of 21 pages each day. Write an equation to represent

   the number of pages, *p*, read after any number of days, *d*. **TEKS** 6.6(B), 6.1(B) _____

Multi-Step Problem Solving

4. The table shows the cost of renting an inner tube to use at the Wave-a-Rama
   Water Park. Suppose an equation of the form $y = ax$ is written for the data
   in the table. What is the value of *a*? **EE** **MP**

Input (x)	Cost (y)
2	$11.00
3	$16.50
4	$22.00

   Ⓐ 5   Ⓒ 6

   Ⓑ 5.5   Ⓓ 6.5

EE = Expressions, Equations, and Relationships   **MP** = Mathematical Processes

Multiple Representations

Launch the Lesson: Real World

Texas Essential Knowledge and Skills

Targeted TEKS
6.6(C) Represent a given situation using verbal descriptions, tables, graphs, and equations in the form $y = kx$ or $y = x + b$. *Also addresses 6.6(A), 6.6(B).*

Mathematical Processes
6.1(A), 6.1(B), 6.1(D), 6.1(E), 6.1(F), 6.1(G)

A group of friends are going to the museum. Each friend must pay an admission price of $9. What equation can be used to represent the situation?

Total Cost of Admission

Number of Friends (n)	Total Cost ($)
1	9
2	
3	
4	

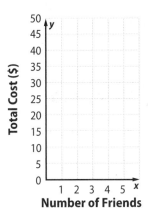

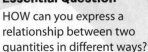

Essential Question

HOW can you express a relationship between two quantities in different ways?

1. Complete the table and graph the ordered pairs (number of friends, total cost).

2. Describe the graph.

   _____

3. Write an equation to find the cost of *n* tickets.

   _____

4. Identify the independent and dependent quantities.

   _____

   _____

   _____

Which MP **Mathematical Processes** did you use?
Shade the circle(s) that applies.

(A) Apply Math to the Real World.

(B) Use a Problem-Solving Model.

(C) Select Tools and Techniques.

(D) Use Multiple Representations.

(E) Organize Ideas.

(F) Analyze Relationships.

(G) Justify Arguments.

Represent Relationships Using Verbal Descriptions and Equations

Words   A runner's distance in a marathon is equal to 8 miles per hour times the number of hours.

Equation $d = 8(t)$

Verbal descriptions and equations can be used to describe relationships. For example, when a rate is expressed in words, it can be written as an equation with variables. When you write an equation, determine what variables to use to represent different quantities.

Examples

Tutor

1. The drama club is holding a bake sale. They are charging $5 for each pie they sell. Write an equation to find the total amount earned *t* for selling *p* pies.

> **Words**   Total earned equals $5 times the number of pies sold.
>
> **Variable**   Let *t* represent the total earned and *p* represent the number of pies sold.
>
> **Equation** $t = 5 \cdot p$

So, the equation is $t = 5(p)$.

2. In a science report, Mia finds that the average adult breathes 14 times each minute when not active. Write an equation to find the total breaths *b* a non-active person takes in *m* minutes.

Let *b* represent the total breaths and *m* represent the number of minutes.

The number of total breaths equals 14 times the number of minutes. So, the equation is $b = 14(m)$.

Got It? Do these problems to find out.

a. _____

b. _____

a. A mouse can travel 8 miles per hour. Write an equation to find the total distance *d* a mouse can travel in *h* hours.

b. Samantha can make 36 cookies each hour. Write an equation to find the total number of cookies *c* that she can make in *h* hours.

Represent Relationships Using Tables and Graphs

Table

Time (h)	Distance (mi)
0	0
1	8
2	16

Graph

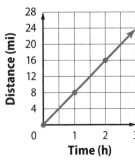

Tables and graphs can also be used to represent relationships.

 Examples

Tutor

The Student Council is holding a car wash to raise money. They are charging $7 for each car they wash.

3. Write an equation and make a table to show the relationship between the number of cars washed c and the total amount earned t.

Using the assigned variables, the total earned t equals $7 times the number of cars washed c. So, the equation is $t = 7(c)$.

Cars Washed, c	$7(c)$	Total Earned ($), t
1	1×7	7
2	2×7	14
3	3×7	21
4	4×7	28

STOP and Reflect

Do the input and output values in Example 3 form a ratio table? Explain.

4. Graph the ordered pairs. Analyze the graph and identify the independent and dependent quantities.

The ordered pairs (c, t) are (1, 7), (2, 14), (3, 21), and (4, 28). Graph the ordered pairs.

The graph is linear because the amount earned increases by $7 for each car washed.

The independent quantity is c, the number of cars washed. The dependent quantity is t, the total earned.

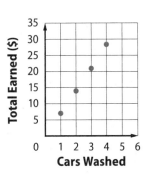

c. _____

d. _____

Got It? Do these problems to find out.

While in normal flight, a bald eagle flies at an average speed of 30 miles per hour.

c. Write an equation and make a table to show the relationship between the total distance *d* that a bald eagle can travel in *h* hours.

d. Graph the ordered pairs. Analyze the graph and identify the independent and dependent quantities.

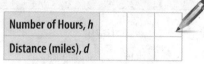

Number of Hours, *h*			
Distance (miles), *d*			

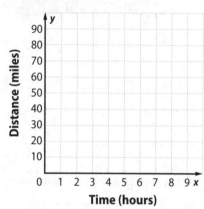

Guided Practice

1. The school cafeteria sells lunch passes that allow a student to purchase any number of lunches in advance for $3 per lunch. (Examples 1–4)

   a. Write an equation to find *t*, the total cost in dollars for a lunch pass with *n* lunches. _____

Number of Lunches, *n*			
Total Cost ($), *t*			

   b. Make a table to show the relationship between the number of lunches *n* and the cost *t*.

   c. Graph the ordered pairs. Analyze the graph and identify the independent and dependent quantities.

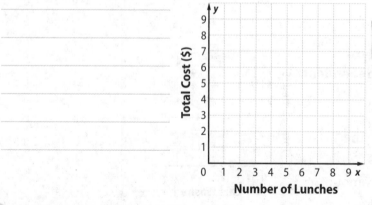

2. **Building on the Essential Question** Why do you represent relationships in different ways?

_____

_____

Independent Practice

6.6(C), 6.6(A), 6.6(B) 6.1(A), 6.1(D) TEKS

1. An African elephant eats 400 pounds of vegetation each day. (Examples 1–4)

   a. Write an equation to find *v*, the number of pounds of vegetation

   an African elephant eats in *d* days. _____

   b. Make a table to show the relationship between the number of pounds *v* an African elephant eats in days *d*.

   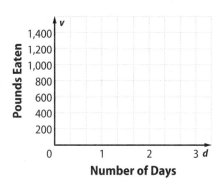

Number of Days, *d*			
Pounds Eaten, *v*			

   c. Graph the ordered pairs. Analyze the graph and identify the independent and dependent quantitites.

   _____

   _____

   _____

   _____

2. MP **Apply Math to the Real World** Refer to the graphic novel frame below for Exercises a–c.

   a. The total cost of a ticket and the online fee for one ticket is $32.25. Let *f* represent the cost of ordering each ticket online. Write an equation that could be used to find the cost of ordering each ticket online.

   _____

   b. Solve the equation from part a. _____

   c. Another friend wants to go to the concert. What is the total cost of ordering three tickets online?

   _____

3. Maurice earns $1.75 for each chore he completes.

a. Write an equation to find t, the total amount earned for c chores in

one week. _____

_____

b. Make a table to show the relationship between the number of chores completed c and the total amount earned t in one week for 1, 2, and 3 chores.

Number of Chores, c			
Total Earned ($), t			

c. Graph the ordered pairs.

d. How much will Maurice earn if he completes 5 chores

in one week? _____

e. Identify the independent and dependent quantities.

_____

_____

_____

H.O.T. Problems Higher-Order Thinking

4. Analyze What would the graph of $y = x$ look like? Name three

ordered pairs that lie on the line. _____

_____

5. Evaluate Boards 4 U charges $10 per hour to rent a snowboard while Slopes charges $12 per hour. Will the cost to rent snowboards at each place ever be the same for the same number of hours after zero hours? If so, for what number of hours?

_____

6. Create Write a real-world problem in which you could graph a relationship.

_____

_____

7. Analyze A movie rental club charges a one-time fee of $25 to join and $2 for every movie rented. Write an equation that represents the cost of joining the club and renting any number of movies.

_____

_____

Multi-Step Problem Solving

8. Brian's baseball team is hosting a tournament to help raise money to buy new uniforms. Each team pays $100 to compete, but some of the money will be used to pay for uniforms. Use the table to help you find the amount of money raised for uniforms if 6 teams compete.

(P) (EE) (MP)

Number of Teams Competing	Money for Uniforms ($)
1	50
2	100
3	

Ⓐ $50 Ⓒ $300

Ⓑ $250 Ⓓ $600

Use a problem-solving model to solve this problem.

1 Analyze

Read the problem. Circle the information you know.
Underline what the problem is asking you to find.

2 Plan

What will you need to do to solve the problem? Write your plan in steps.

Step 1 Determine the rule that represents the situation.

Step 2 Use the rule to determine the amount of money raised if 6 teams compete.

3 Solve

Use your plan to solve the problem. Show your steps.

Each dependent quantity is [ ] times the independent quantity.

The rule is $y =$ [ ].

So, the amount raised when 6 teams compete is 50([ ]) or $[ ].

Choice [ ] is correct. Fill in that answer choice.

Read to Succeed!

Looking for a pattern in the table is another strategy.

4 Justify and Evaluate

How do you know your solution is accurate?

_____

_____

_____

(P) = Proportionality (EE) = Expressions, Equations, and Relationships (MP) = Mathematical Processes

More Multi-Step Problem Solving

Use a problem-solving model to solve each problem.

9. Felicia has an alarm system for her home. She paid $80 to have the alarm installed, and pays $45.50 each month. How much does she spend on the alarm system in the first year?

Number of Months	Total Cost ($)
1	125.50
2	171

Ⓐ $125.50

Ⓑ $216.50

Ⓒ $626.00

Ⓓ $1,005.50

10. At a craft store, Georgina buys several packs of beads. The equation $y = 1.50x$ represents her total cost y if she buys x packs of beads. If the data are graphed, what is the value of x in $(x, 16.50)$? Ⓟ Ⓝ MP

11. Montel is playing a math game. He earns points for every correct answer. The points on the graph represent the number of questions he answered correctly x, to his total score y. If the point $(7, y)$ is on the graph, what is y? Ⓟ EE MP

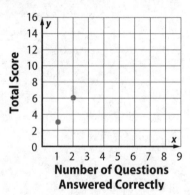

12. Three friends are throwing a party at a park. They decide to rent a climbing wall for the party. The equation $y = 150x$ represents the total cost y for renting the wall for x hours. If they rented the wall for 5 hours and they split the cost equally, how much does each friend owe? Ⓟ EE MP

Ⓝ = Number and Operations   Ⓟ = Proportionality   EE = Expressions, Equations, and Relationships   MP = Mathematical Processes

466   Chapter 6 Multiple Representations

Additive Relationships: $y = x + a$

Targeted TEKS
6.6(C) Represent a given situation using verbal descriptions, tables, graphs, and equations in the form $y = kx$ or $y = x + b$. *Also addresses 6.4(A), 6.6(B).*

Mathematical Processes
6.1(A), 6.1(B), 6.1(D), 6.1(E), 6.1(F), 6.1(G)

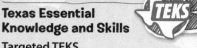

Texas Essential Knowledge and Skills

 Launch the Lesson: Real World

Manuel has a $20 gift card to an electronics store and some money in his savings account. He can buy an item that is $20 more than the amount in his savings account. Make a table to represent the amounts in his savings account and the amounts he can spend.

1. Complete the table.

2. Graph the ordered pairs (amount in savings, total Manuel can spend).

3. Describe the graph.

_____

_____

Amount in Savings Account ($)	Total Manuel Can Spend ($)
50	
60	
70	
80	

Vocabulary
additive relationship

_____

Essential Question
HOW can you express a relationship between two quantities in different ways?

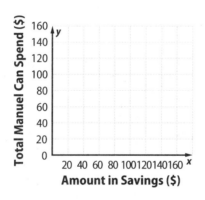

Total Manuel Can Spend ($) (y-axis: 0, 20, 40, 60, 80, 100, 120, 140, 160)
Amount in Savings ($) (x-axis: 20 40 60 80 100 120 140 160)

4. Write an equation to find how much he can spend with x dollars

   in savings. _____

5. What operation is represented in this relationship? _____

Which **MP** Mathematical Processes did you use?
Shade the circle(s) that applies.

Ⓐ Apply Math to the Real World.

Ⓑ Use a Problem-Solving Model.

Ⓒ Select Tools and Techniques.

Ⓓ Use Multiple Representations.

Ⓔ Organize Ideas.

Ⓕ Analyze Relationships.

Ⓖ Justify Arguments.

Determine Additive Relationships

Additive relationships compare the independent and dependent quantities of a relationship using addition. Additive relationships can be represented as tables, graphs, and equations in the form $y = x + a$, where a is any rational number.

Tutor

Examples

Determine if each relationship is an additive relationship. Explain.

1. Each output is 4 more than the input. Since the equation that represents the table is $y = x + 4$, the relationship is additive.

Input (x)	4	5	6
Output (y)	8	9	10

2. Each output is three times the input. Since the relationship cannot be written in the form $y = x + a$, it is not an additive relationship.

Input (x)	3	5	7
Output (y)	9	15	21

3. Each y-value is four times the x-value. Since the relationship cannot be written in the form $y = x + a$, it is not an additive relationship.

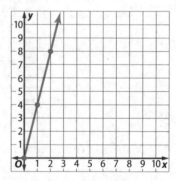

 Show your work.

Got It? Do these problems to find out.

Determine if each relationship is an additive relationship. Explain.

a.

Input (x)	11	13	15
Output (y)	20	22	24

b.

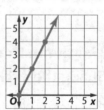

a. _____

b. _____

Multiple Representations of Additive Relationships

You can represent additive relationships using verbal descriptions, tables, graphs, and equations in the form $y = x + a$, where a is any rational number.

 Real World

Tutor

Example

4. Isaiah has 28 more songs downloaded on his MP3 player than Melanie.

   a. **Make a table to show the relationship between the number of songs y Isaiah has on his MP3 player and the number of songs x on Melanie's MP3 player.**

Number of Songs on Melanie's MP3 Player (x)	10	20	30
Number of Songs on Isaiah's MP3 Player (y)	38	48	58

   Isaiah has 28 more songs, so add 28 to each x-value.

   b. **Graph the ordered pairs. Analyze the graph.**

   Use the ordered pairs (10, 38), (20, 48), and (30, 58).

   The points appear to lie in a straight line. The line will not pass through the origin.

   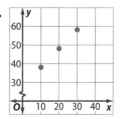

   c. **Write an equation to find the number of songs y on Isaiah's MP3 player given the number of songs x on Melanie's MP3 player.**

   Since each y-value is 28 more than the x-value, the equation is $y = x + 28$.

Got It? Do this problem to find out.

 Show your work.

c. **Financial Literacy** A store marks up the cost of shoes when it receives them from the manufacturer. It charges $6 more than the cost to make them. Make a table to show the relationship between the cost x of making the shoes and the price y the store charges. Graph the relationship and analyze the graph. Write an equation to represent the relationship.

c. _____

Example

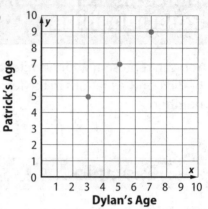

5. The graph shows the relationship between the ages of Dylan and Patrick. Make a table and write an equation to represent the relationship. Write a verbal description to represent the relationship.

To make a table of the graph, use the ordered pairs.

Each y-value is 2 more than the x-value, so the equation is $y = x + 2$. The relationship shows that Patrick is two years older than Dylan.

Dylan's Age (x)	3	5	7
Patrick's Age (y)	5	7	9

Guided Practice

1. Determine if the relationship shown in the table is an additive relationship. Explain. (Examples 1–3)

Input (x)	6	8	10
Output (y)	18	24	30

_____

_____

2. The table shows the relationship between the savings account balances of two sisters. Write an equation to represent the relationship and graph the relationship. Write a verbal description to represent the relationship.
(Examples 4 and 5)

Alejandra's Account Balance (x) ($)	20	25	30
Valentina's Account Balance (y) ($)	35	40	45

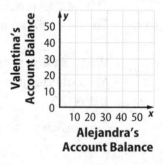

_____

_____

3. (?) **Building on the Essential Question** How can you determine if a relationship is an additive relationship by its graph? _____

_____

_____

_____

Rate Yourself!

Are you ready to move on?
Shade the section that applies.

YES   ?   NO

Find out online. Use the Self-Check Quiz.

Check ✓

Independent Practice

6.4(A), 6.6(C), 6.1(D)

Determine if each relationship is an additive relationship. Explain. (Examples 1–3)

1.

Input (x)	Output (y)
4	5
7	9
10	13

2.

Input (x)	Output (y)
1	9
4	12
7	15

3.

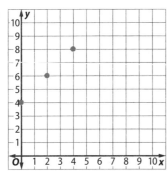

4.

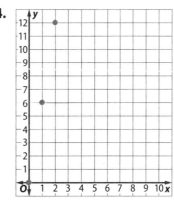

5. **MP** **Use Multiple Representations** Kelly started running around a track two laps before Anne. They are running at the same speed. (Examples 4 and 5)

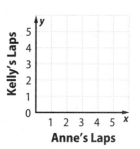

Number of Laps Anne Ran (x)			
Number of Laps Kelly Ran (y)			

   a. Table Make a table to show the relationship between the number of laps y Kelly ran and the number of laps x Anne ran.

   b. Graph Graph the ordered pairs. Analyze the graph.

   _____

   _____

   c. Equation Write an equation to find the number of laps y Kelly has run given the number of laps x Anne has run. _____

   d. Verbal Description Describe the relationship between the quantities.

   _____

6. **MP Use Multiple Representations** The graph shows the total amount Deshawn earns given how much he earns doing lawn work.

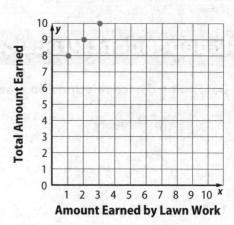

Amount Earned by Lawn Work

a. **Table** Make a table to show the relationship between the total amount y Deshawn earns and the amount x he earns by doing lawn work.

Amount Earned by Lawn Work ($) ($x$)			
Total Amount Earned ($) ($y$)			

b. **Equation** Write an equation to find the total amount y Deshawn earns given the amount x he earns by doing lawn work.

_____

c. **Verbal Description** Explain the relationship.

_____

_____

Determine if each relationship is an additive relationship. Explain.

7.

Input (x)	0.5	1.5	4.5
Output (y)	7.25	8.25	11.25

_____

_____

_____

8.

Input (x)	2.6	3.4	4.2
Output (y)	2.86	3.74	4.62

_____

_____

_____

H.O.T. Problems   Higher-Order Thinking

9. **Evaluate** Is $y = x$ an additive relationship? Explain. _____

_____

10. **Create** Write a real-world problem in which you make a table of values and write an equation to represent an additive relationship. _____

_____

_____

Multi-Step Problem Solving

11. Lin made 20 more cookies than Doralina. Complete the table showing the relationship. Which equation represents the relationship shown in the table? **EE** **MP**

Doralina (x)	Lin (y)
20	40
25	45
	50
	55
	60

Ⓐ $y = 20x$

Ⓑ $y = x + 20$

Ⓒ $y = x - 20$

Ⓓ $y = 20 \div x$

Use a problem-solving model to solve this problem.

1 Analyze

Read the problem. Circle the information you know. Underline what the problem is asking you to find.

2 Plan

What will you need to do to solve the problem? Write your plan in steps.

Step 1 Complete the table by subtracting 20 from each y-value.

Step 2 Determine the rule using the independent and dependent quantities.

Read to Succeed!

The phrase "20 more" means to add. So, use the inverse operation of addition to find how many cookies Doralina makes.

3 Solve

Use your plan to solve the problem. Show your steps.

Since each y-value is 20 more than the x-value, the equation is $y = \boxed{}$.

So, choice $\boxed{}$ is correct. Fill in that answer choice.

Doralina (x)	Lin (y)
20	40
25	45
	50
	55
	60

4 Justify and Evaluate

How do you know your solution is accurate?

_____

_____

EE = Expressions, Equations, and Relationships   **MP** = Mathematical Processes

More Multi-Step Problem Solving

Use a problem-solving model to solve each problem.

12. A music store prices its guitars by charging $250 more than the cost to make them. Complete the table below and choose the equation that represents the relationship.

Cost to Produce (x)	Price (y)
$250	$500
$300	
$350	
$400	
$450	

- Ⓐ $y = 250x$
- Ⓑ $y = x - 250$
- Ⓒ $y = 250x + 250$
- Ⓓ $y = x + 250$

13. Samantha and Rodney each have some baseball cards. They have different amounts of cards, but buy the same number of cards each week. When Samantha has 150 cards, Rodney has y cards. If he sells all his cards for $0.25 each, how much does he make, in dollars? **EE** **N** **MP**

Number of Samantha's Cards (x)	Number of Rodney's Cards (y)
50	60
70	80
90	100
110	120

14. The table below represents an additive relationship. If $y = 2\frac{1}{6}$, then what is $2x$, to the nearest hundredth? **P** **N** **MP**

x	y
$\frac{1}{3}$	$\frac{8}{15}$
$\frac{3}{4}$	$\frac{19}{20}$

15. When Sammy goes to the local smoothie café, he always buys a $5 smoothie, plus something else. His total cost can always be found by using the equation $y = x + 5$. Graph this equation. He buys a sandwich for $7 and a smoothie. If he pays with a $20 bill, how much change does he receive, in dollars? **P** **N** **MP**

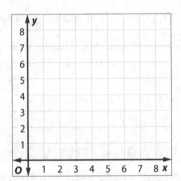

EE = Expressions, Equations, and Relationships **P** = Proportionality **N** = Number and Operations **MP** = Mathematical Processes

474 **Chapter 6** Multiple Representations

Multiplicative Relationships: $y = ax$

  Launch the Lesson: Real World

Leann is training for a marathon. She knows that each kilometer she runs is approximately equal to 0.62 mile. About how many miles does she run if she runs 5 kilometers?

1. Complete the table.

Kilometers (x)	Miles (y)
1	
2	
3	
4	

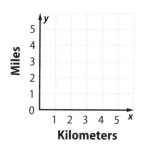

2. Graph the ordered pairs (kilometers, miles).

3. Use the graph to predict the number of miles she runs if she runs 5 kilometers. _____

4. Write an equation to represent how many miles y she runs if she runs x kilometers. _____

Which **MP** Mathematical Processes did you use?
Shade the circle(s) that applies.

Ⓐ Apply Math to the Real World.

Ⓔ Organize Ideas.

Ⓑ Use a Problem-Solving Model.

Ⓕ Analyze Relationships.

Ⓒ Select Tools and Techniques.

Ⓖ Justify Arguments.

Ⓓ Use Multiple Representations.

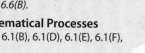 **Texas Essential Knowledge and Skills**

Targeted TEKS
6.6(C) Represent a given situation using verbal descriptions, tables, graphs, and equations in the form $y = kx$ or $y = x + b$. *Also addresses 6.4(A), 6.6(B).*

Mathematical Processes
6.1(A), 6.1(B), 6.1(D), 6.1(E), 6.1(F), 6.1(G)

Vocab

Vocabulary
multiplicative relationship

Essential Question
HOW can you express a relationship between two quantities in different ways?

Determine Multiplicative Relationships

Multiplicative relationships use multiplication to compare the independent and dependent quantities of a relationship. Multiplicative relationships can be represented as tables, graphs, and equations in the form $y = ax$, where a is any rational number.

Tutor

Examples

Determine if each relationship is a multiplicative relationship. Explain.

1. Each output is twice the input. Since the equation that represents the table is $y = 2x$, the relationship is multiplicative.

Input (x)	7	8	9
Output (y)	14	16	18

2. Each output is 4 more than the input. Since the relationship cannot be written in the form $y = ax$, it is not a multiplicative relationship.

Input (x)	3	5	8
Output (y)	7	9	12

> **Additive Relationships**
>
> In Example 2, since the relationship can be written in the form $y = x + 4$, it is an additive relationship.

3. Each y-value is found by multiplying by $\frac{1}{4}$. Since the relationship can be written as $y = \frac{1}{4}x$, it is a multiplicative relationship.

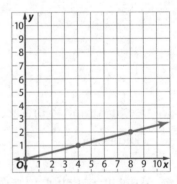

Got It? Do these problems to find out.

Determine if each relationship is a multiplicative relationship. Explain.

a.

Input (x)	2	4	6
Output (y)	−6	−12	−18

b.

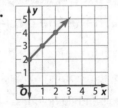

a. _____

b. _____

Compare Additive and Multiplicative Relationships

You can compare two algebraic relationships verbally, numerically, graphically, and symbolically in the form of $y = ax$ or $y = x + a$ in order to differentiate between additive and multiplicative relationships.

Example

Tutor

4. On one Web site, you can download songs for $2 each. Another Web site charges a fee of $10 more than the number of songs downloaded.

a. **Make a table for each Web site to show the relationship between the number of songs downloaded x and the total cost y. Compare the tables.**

First Site:

Number of Songs (x)	1	2	3
Total Cost (y)	2	4	6

Second Site:

Number of Songs (x)	1	2	3
Total Cost (y)	11	12	13

The first table shows a ratio table since $\frac{1}{2} = \frac{2}{4} = \frac{3}{6}$. Because these are equivalent ratios, the first table shows a proportional relationship. The second table does not.

b. **Graph the ordered pairs. Analyze the graphs.**

Use the ordered pairs from each table.

Each set of points appears to form a line. The first set of points passes through the origin while the other set does not. The first set is also steeper than the second set.

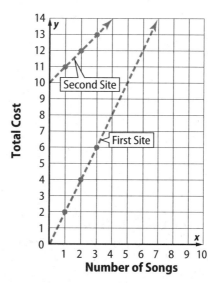

c. **Write an equation for each relationship. Compare the equations.**

For the first Web site, the dependent quantities are 2 times the independent quantities. So, the relationship can be written in the form $y = 2x$. It is a multiplicative relationship.

In the table for the second Web site, the dependent quantities are 10 more than the independent quantities. The relationship can be written in the form $y = x + 10$. It is an additive relationship.

Got It? Do this problem to find out.

c. Abigail charges $5 for one hour of babysitting per child. Cheyenne charges $8 per hour more than the number of children. Compare the relationships by making a table and writing an equation for each.

c. _____

Guided Practice

1. Determine if the relationship is a multiplicative relationship. Explain. (Examples 1–3)

Input (x)	9	11	15
Output (y)	63	77	105

_____

_____

2. The graph shows the relationship between the number of laps Samantha and Rebecca each swim and the length of time it takes each to swim those laps. Write an equation and a verbal description of each relationship. Compare the relationships. (Example 4)

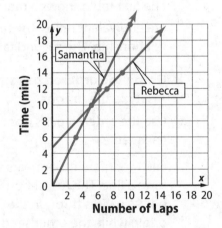

_____

_____

_____

_____

_____

3. ❓ **Building on the Essential Question** How is the graph of a multiplicative relationship different from the graph of an additive relationship? _____

_____

_____

Independent Practice

6.4(A), 6.6(C), 6.1(D) TEKS

Determine if each relationship is a multiplicative relationship.
Explain. (Examples 1–3)

1.

Input (x)	5	8	11
Output (y)	7.5	12	16.5

_____

_____

_____

2.

Input (x)	2	7	13
Output (y)	5	10	16

_____

_____

_____

3. **MP Use Multiple Representations** Kodi makes and decorates custom cupcakes. She sells one dozen for $15.99. Shellie sells cupcakes for $14.99 more than the number of dozens of cupcakes. (Example 4)

a. Table Make a table for each person to show the relationship between the cost y of the cupcakes given the number of dozens x sold.

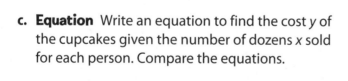

Kodi			
Number of Dozens (x)			
Cost ($) (y)			

Shellie			
Number of Dozens (x)			
Cost ($) (y)			

b. Graph Graph the ordered pairs from each table. Compare the graphs.

_____

_____

_____

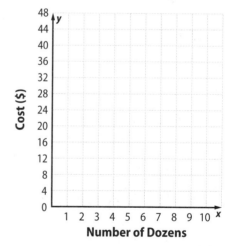

c. Equation Write an equation to find the cost y of the cupcakes given the number of dozens x sold for each person. Compare the equations.

_____

_____

_____

d. Verbal Description Describe the relationship between the quantities.

_____

_____

_____

_____

4. **MP Use Multiple Representations** A checking account is overdrawn when a check is written for more than the balance in the account. The table shows the total amount in fees given the number of times a checking account is overdrawn for two different banks.

Number of Times Overdrawn (x)	Bank A Fee ($) (y)	Bank B Fee ($) (y)
1	15	26
2	30	27
3	45	28

a. **Graph** Graph each relationship on the coordinate grid. Compare the graphs.

_____

_____

_____

b. **Equation** Write an equation to find the total fee y given the number of times x the account is overdrawn. Compare the equations.

_____

_____

Total Fee ($) — y-axis labeled 0, 10, 20, 30, 40, 50
Number of Times Overdrawn — x-axis labeled 1 2 3 4 5

c. **Verbal Description** Explain the relationships.

_____

_____

_____

Write a verbal description and equation for each multiplicative relationship.

5.

Input (x)	4	9	20
Output (y)	6	13.5	30

_____

_____

6.

Input (x)	15	24	36
Output (y)	10	16	24

_____

_____

H.O.T. Problems Higher-Order Thinking

7. **Analyze** How is the graph of $y = 3x$ different from the graph of $y = \frac{1}{3}x$?

_____

_____

8. **Create** Write a real-world problem in which you write an equation with $a < 1$ to represent a multiplicative relationship.

_____

_____

Multi-Step Problem Solving

9. Jack is comparing the cost of buying notebooks at two different online stores. Store A charges $2.25 each with no shipping charge, and Store B charges $1.00 each plus $2.00 shipping on each order. Complete the table to find out how much more it would cost to buy 5 notebooks from Store A than Store B. **P** **EE** **MP**

Number of Notebooks	Cost at Store A	Cost at Store B
1		
2		
3		
4		
5		

   Ⓐ $3.00

   Ⓑ $4.25

   Ⓒ $7.00

   Ⓓ $11.25

Use a problem-solving model to solve this problem.

1 Analyze

**Read the problem. Circle the information you know.
Underline what the problem is asking you to find.**

2 Plan

What will you need to do to solve the problem? Write your plan in steps.

Step 1   Complete the chart that shows the cost at each store.

Step 2   Subtract to determine how much more 5 notebooks cost from Store A than Store B.

Read to Succeed!
The phrase "how much more" indicates subtraction.

3 Solve

Use your plan to solve the problem. Show your steps.

Complete the table based on the situation.

Store A charges $ [ ] for 5 notebooks.

Store B charges $ [ ]. So, Store A is

$ [ ] − $ [ ] or $ [ ] more than Store B.

Choice [ ] is correct. Fill in that answer choice.

Number of Notebooks	Cost at Store A	Cost at Store B
1		
2		
3		
4		
5		

4 Justify and Evaluate

How do you know your solution is accurate?

_____

P = Proportionality   **EE** = Expressions, Equations, and Relationships   **MP** = Mathematical Processes

More Multi-Step Problem Solving

Use a problem-solving model to solve each problem.

10. Yoko is comparing the prices of headphones at two different stores. Store A charges $6.25 more than the number of sets of headphones. Store B charges $3.00 per set of headphones. How much more would Yoko spend on 5 sets of headphones at Store B than Store A? **P** **EE** **MP**

Sets of Headphones	Cost at Store A	Cost at Store B
3		
4		
5		
6		
7		

Ⓐ $0.25

Ⓑ $3.75

Ⓒ $7.75

Ⓓ $11.25

11. Three stores have different prices for CDs. Store 1 charges $12.00 per CD, Store 2 charges $10.00 per CD, and Store 3 charges $9.00 per CD. Graph each multiplicative relationship. Which store has the steepest slope? **P** **EE** **MP**

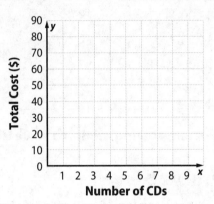

12. A store usually sells a package of 5 pairs of socks for $10.00. They are on sale for 50% off. The relationship between the number of packages and price is graphed. What is the *y*-coordinate when the *x*-coordinate is 0? **P** **EE** **MP**

13. One store sells baskets for $2.50 each. Another sells the same baskets for $3.00 more than the number of baskets bought. For the price to be the same at each store, how many baskets would need to be purchased? Explain your answer. **P** **EE** **MP**

P = Proportionality   **EE** = Expressions, Equations, and Relationships   **MP** = Mathematical Processes

Graphing Technology: Compare Algebraic Relationships

INQUIRY HOW can I select tools to compare additive and multiplicative relationships?

Jupiter is the largest planet in our solar system. The weight of an object on Jupiter is 2.36 times that of its weight on Earth. An object on Saturn weighs 1.06 times that of the object on Earth. If a dog weighs 35 pounds on Earth, how much more does it weigh on Jupiter than on Saturn?

Texas Essential Knowledge and Skills

Targeted TEKS
6.4(A) Compare two rules verbally, numerically, graphically, and symbolically in the form of $y = ax$ or $y = x + a$ in order to differentiate between additive and multiplicative relationships. *Also addresses 6.6(C).*

Mathematical Processes
6.1(C), 6.1(D), 6.1(E), 6.1(F)

Hands-On Activity 1

A graphing calculator can be used to graph relationships. You can compare multiple relationships at once by graphing them on the same coordinate grid. Before graphing equations, the viewing window must be set and any existing equations cleared from the list.

Step 1 Clear any existing equations by pressing Y= and CLEAR for each line.

Step 2 Set the viewing window by pressing WINDOW and setting the Xmin and Ymin to 0. This will have the origin be at the bottom left. The Xmax and Ymax should be set to 200. The scale of each axis, Xscl and Yscl, should be set to 10 each.

Step 3 Enter the equation for Jupiter on the $Y_1 =$ line and the equation for Saturn on the $Y_2 =$ line.

Jupiter: 2 · 3 6 X,T,θ,n

Saturn: 1 · 0 6 X,T,θ,n

Step 4 Press GRAPH to view the graphs of both relationships. By using the TRACE button, you can use the arrows to follow along each of the graphs and compare the corresponding ordered pairs.

At 35 pounds, a dog on Jupiter would weigh 82.6 pounds. On Saturn, the dog would weigh 37.1 pounds. It would weigh 82.6 – 37.1, or 45.5, more pounds.

Hands-On Activity 2

You can graph additive and multiplicative relationships on the same coordinate grid to compare and contrast them.

Step 1   Clear any existing equations and set the viewing window to an Xmin and Ymin of 0 and Xmax and Ymax of 10. The scale for each axis is 1.

Step 2   Enter each equation.

Y_1: $y = 3x$ [Y=] [3] [X,T,θ,n] [ENTER]

Y_2: $y = x + 3$ [X,T,θ,n] [+] [3]

Step 3   Graph the equations by pressing [GRAPH]. Use the [TRACE] function to compare the graphs. Notice the equation is given for the graph you are tracing.

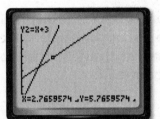

$y = 3x$ crosses the y-axis at $\left(\boxed{}, \boxed{}\right)$.

$y = x + 3$ crosses the y-axis at $\left(\boxed{}, \boxed{}\right)$.

Step 4   Press [2nd] [TABLE] to see a list of inputs and outputs for each equation.

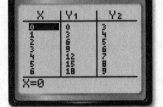

1. When x is 2, what is the value of each equation? How much greater is Y_1 than Y_2?

_____

2. When x is 6, how much greater is Y_1 than Y_2?

_____

3. When x is 15, how much greater is Y_1 than Y_2?

_____

4. Which equation's table represents a ratio table? Justify your response.

_____

_____

Investigate

Collaborate

Work with a partner. Use technology to graph each equation on the same coordinate grid. Make a table of values for each equation.

5. $Y_1 = 4.5x$

$Y_2 = x + 4.5$

X	Y_1	Y_2

a. When x is 3, how much greater is Y_1 than Y_2?

_____

b. When x is 50, how much greater is Y_1 than Y_2?

_____

c. Compare the graphs of Y_1 and Y_2. _____

_____

_____

_____

6. $Y_1 = \left(\dfrac{2}{3}\right)x$

$Y_2 = x + \left(\dfrac{2}{3}\right)$

X	Y_1	Y_2

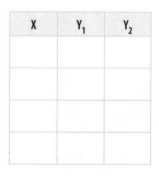

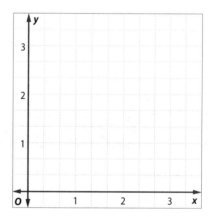

a. Within the first quadrant, will the two graphs intersect? Justify your response.

_____

_____

_____

_____

b. Compare the graphs of Y_1 and Y_2. _____

_____

_____

_____

7. **MP Organize Ideas** Refer to Exercises 5 and 6. Which relationships are additive? multiplicative?

_____

8. **MP Analyze Relationships** How is the table of a multiplicative relationship similar to and different from the table of an additive relationship?

_____

_____

_____

9. **MP Analyze Relationships** How is the graph of a multiplicative relationship similar to and different from the graph of an additive relationship?

_____

_____

_____

10. **MP Analyze Relationships** How is the equation of a multiplicative relationship similar to and different from the equation of an additive relationship?

_____

_____

_____

Create

On Your Own

11. **MP Apply Math to the Real World** Write a real-world problem in which you would compare two multiplicative relationships.

_____

_____

_____

_____

12. **INQUIRY** HOW can I select tools to compare additive and multiplicative relationships?

_____

Meteorologist

Have you ever wondered how forecasters can predict severe storms such as hurricanes before they occur? Keeping track of changes in air pressure is one method that they use. Meteorologists study Earth's air pressure, temperature, humidity, and wind velocity. They use complex computer models to process and analyze weather data and to make accurate forecasts. In addition to understanding the processes of Earth's atmosphere, meteorologists must have a solid background in mathematics, computer science, and physics.

Mathematical Process
6.1(A) Apply mathematics to problems arising in everyday life, society, and the workplace.
Targeted TEKS 6.6(C)

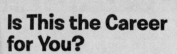

Is This the Career for You?

Are you interested in a career as a meteorologist? Take some of the following courses in high school.

- ◆ Algebra
- ◆ Calculus
- ◆ Earth and Its Environment
- ◆ Environmental Science
- ◆ Physics

College & Career
READINESS

Explore college and careers at ccr.mcgraw-hill.com

The Pressure is On!

Use the information in the diagram and the table to solve each problem.

1. The temperature of the ocean at the end of the first month was 74°F. At the end of the second month, it was 76°F. Write an equation to represent the relationship if the temperature increases at the same rate. After how many months is the temperature where it needs to be for hurricane formation?

2. The depth of the water that is at least 80°F was 120 feet by the end of the first month. By the end of the second month, the depth of the warm water was 145 feet. Write an equation to represent the relationship if the depth of the warm water extended at the same rate. After how many months is the depth of the warm water where it needs to be for hurricane formation?

3. Air pressure decreases during a storm. The first hour, the pressure was 1,040 millibars. The second hour, the air pressure was 1,025 millibars. The third hour, it was at 1,010 millibars. Write an equation to represent the relationship if the air pressure dropped at a steady rate. At what hour was the air pressure the same as that of Hurricane Katrina?

4. After a hurricane makes landfall, the air pressure begins to rise. One hour after landfall, the air pressure was 954 millibars. Three hours after landfall, the air pressure was 990 millibars. Write an equation to represent the relationship if the air pressure rose at a steady rate.

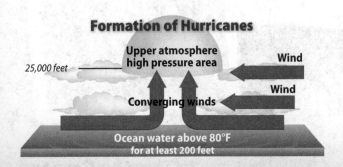

Formation of Hurricanes

25,000 feet

Upper atmosphere high pressure area

Wind

Wind

Converging winds

Ocean water above 80°F for at least 200 feet

Top 5 Most Intense Hurricanes at Landfall in the U.S.		
Rank	Hurricane	Pressure (millibars)
1	Florida Keys, (Labor Day), 1935	892
2	Hurricane Camille, 1969	909
3	Hurricane Katrina, 2005	920
4	Hurricane Andrew, 1992	922
5	Texas (Indianola), 1886	925

TEKS Career Project

It's time to update your career portfolio! Interview a meteorologist at a local television station. Be sure to ask what he or she likes most about being a meteorologist and what is most challenging. Include all the interview questions and answers in your portfolio. Prepare a brief oral presentation and present it to your classmates. As others are presenting, listen carefully to their presentations. At the end, ask any clarifying questions.

What skills would you need to improve to succeed in this career?

Chapter Review

Vocabulary Check

 Work with a partner to complete the crossword puzzle using the vocabulary list at the beginning of the chapter. Seek clarification of each vocabulary term as needed.

Across

1. each number in a sequence
4. an algebraic relationship whose graph is a line
6. the output value of an equation
7. the input value of an equation

Down

2. an algebraic relationship that can be written in the form $y = ax$
3. a list of numbers in a specific order
5. an algebraic relationship that can be written in the form $y = x + a$

Use Your FOLDABLES

Collaborate

Use your Foldable to help review the chapter. Share your Foldable with a partner and take turns summarizing what you learned in this chapter, while the other partner listens carefully. Seek clarification of any concepts, as needed. **TEKS** 6.1(E)

Tape here

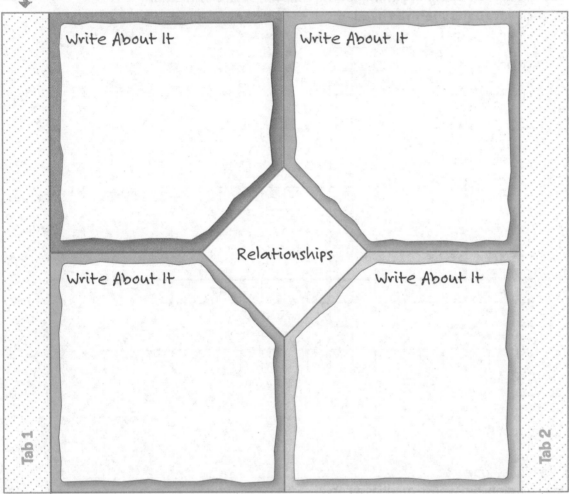

Write About It

Write About It

Relationships

Write About It

Write About It

Tab 1

Tab 2

Got it?

Circle the correct term or number to complete each sentence. **TEKS** 6.6(B), 6.6(C)

1. The next number in the sequence 12, 15, 18, 21, . . . is (24, 27).

2. The output of a relationship is the (independent, dependent) quantity.

3. A(n) (arithmetic, geometric) sequence can be found by multiplying each previous term by the same number.

4. The input of a relationship is the (independent, dependent) quantity.

5. A(n)(additive relationship, multiplicative relationship) can be written in the form $y = x + a$.

6. The table shows the cost for buying student movie tickets online at Movies Inc. Movies-4-U charges a one-time fee of $3 plus $6.50 for each ticket bought online. If you need to buy 6 student tickets online, which theater offers a better deal? Show the steps you used and justify your solution. **P** **EE** **MP**

Movies Inc.	
Number of Tickets	Cost ($)
2	15.00
3	22.50
4	30.00
5	37.50

1 Analyze

2 Plan

3 Solve

4 Justify and Evaluate

Got it?

7. A baker is making cupcakes for a wedding. She has already decorated 48 cupcakes. The table shows the rate at which she can decorate cupcakes. Suppose in 5 hours she needs to have 150 cupcakes decorated. Working at this rate, will she make her goal? Show the steps you used and justify your solution. **P** **EE** **MP**

Time (min)	Cupcakes Decorated
15	6
30	12
45	18

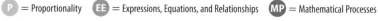 **P** = Proportionality   **EE** = Expressions, Equations, and Relationships   **MP** = Mathematical Processes

Reflect

Use what you learned about multiple representations to complete the graphic organizer.

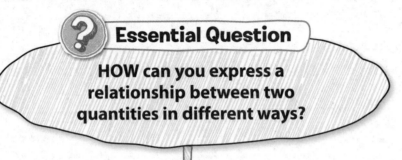

Essential Question

HOW can you express a relationship between two quantities in different ways?

Table	Equation	Graph
What does it mean?	What does it mean?	What does it mean?
Example	Example	Example

 Answer the Essential Question. HOW can you express a relationship between two quantites in different ways? Verbally share your response with a partner, seeking and providing clarification as needed.

Chapter 7
Algebraic Expressions

Texas Essential Knowledge and Skills

Targeted TEKS

6.7 The student applies mathematical process standards to develop concepts of expressions and equations.

Mathematical Processes
6.1, 6.1(A), 6.1(B), 6.1(C), 6.1(D), 6.1(E), 6.1(F), 6.1(G)

Essential Question

HOW is it helpful to write numbers in different ways?

Math in the Real World

Tramways From Ranger Peak, accessible by the Wyler Aerial Tramway, a visitor can view 7,000 square miles across three states and two nations. Circle the expression below that is equivalent to 7,000.

$$7 \times 10^1$$

$$7 \times 10^2$$

$$7 \times 10^3$$

Go Online!
www.connectED.mcgraw-hill.com

Watch
Worksheets
Vocab
Tutor
Tools
Check

What Tools Do You Need?

Vocabulary

algebra	Distributive Property	numerical expression
algebraic expression	equivalent expressions	order of operations
Associative Properties	evaluate	perfect square
base	exponent	powers
coefficient	factor the expression	prime factorization
Commutative Properties	factor tree	prime number
composite number	Identity Properties	properties
constant	Inverse Properties	term
defining the variable	like terms	variable

Reading Math

Meaning of Division Look for these other meanings when you are solving a word problem.

- **To share:**
  Zach and his friend are going to share 3 apples equally. How many apples will each boy have?

- **To take away equal amounts:**
  Isabel is making bookmarks from a piece of ribbon. Each bookmark is 6.5 centimeters long. How many bookmarks can she make from a piece of ribbon that is 26 centimeters long?

- **To find how many times greater:**
  The Nile River, the longest river on Earth, is 4,160 miles long. The Rio Grande River is 1,900 miles long. About how many times as long is the Nile than the Rio Grande?

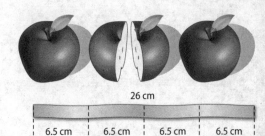

26 cm

6.5 cm | 6.5 cm | 6.5 cm | 6.5 cm

Nile River 4,160 mi

Rio Grande 1,900 mi | Rio Grande 1,900 mi

Practice

Identify the meaning of division shown in each problem. Then solve the problem.

1. The Jackson family wants to buy a flat-screen television that costs $1,200. They plan to pay in six equal payments. What will be the amount of each payment?

2. A full-grown blue whale can weigh 150 tons. An adult African elephant weights about 5 tons. How many times as great does a blue whale weigh than an African elephant?

Quick Review

Review 6.3(E), 5.3(K) **TEKS**

Example 1

Multiply $5 \times 5 \times 5 \times 5$.

5 is used as a factor four times.

$5 \times 5 \times 5 \times 5 = 625$

Example 2

Find $3\frac{7}{8} - 1\frac{1}{2}$.

$$3\frac{7}{8} = \quad 3\frac{7}{8}$$

$$-1\frac{1}{2} = -1\frac{4}{8} \quad \text{Rename using the LCD, 8.}$$

$$\overline{\quad\quad\quad 2\frac{3}{8}} \quad \text{Subtract.}$$

Quick Check

Check

Number Patterns **Multiply.**

Show your work.

1. $7 \times 7 \times 7 =$ _____

2. $2 \times 2 \times 2 =$ _____

3. $9 \times 9 \times 9 \times 9 =$ _____

Fractions **Add or subtract. Write in simplest form.**

4. $\frac{4}{5} - \frac{1}{2} =$ _____

5. $\frac{8}{9} + \frac{2}{3} =$ _____

6. $3\frac{1}{10} - 2\frac{5}{6} =$ _____

7. What fraction more of the coupon books did Jabar sell than Guto?

_____

Coupon Book Sales	
Student	Fraction of Total Sales
Guto	$\frac{1}{12}$
Holly	$\frac{3}{40}$
Jabar	$\frac{2}{15}$

How Did You Do?

Which problems did you answer correctly in the Quick Check? Shade those exercise numbers below.

① ② ③ ④ ⑤ ⑥ ⑦

 Use the Foldable throughout this chapter to help you learn about properties.

✂ cut on all dashed lines   ⬜ fold on all solid lines   tape to page 580

Properties of Addition

Commutative	Associative	Identity
+	**+**	**+**
X	**X**	**X**
Commutative	Associative	Identity

Properties of Multiplication

FOLDABLES®

Use the Foldable throughout this chapter to help you learn about properties.

✂ cut on all dashed lines   ✄ fold on all solid lines   tape to page 580

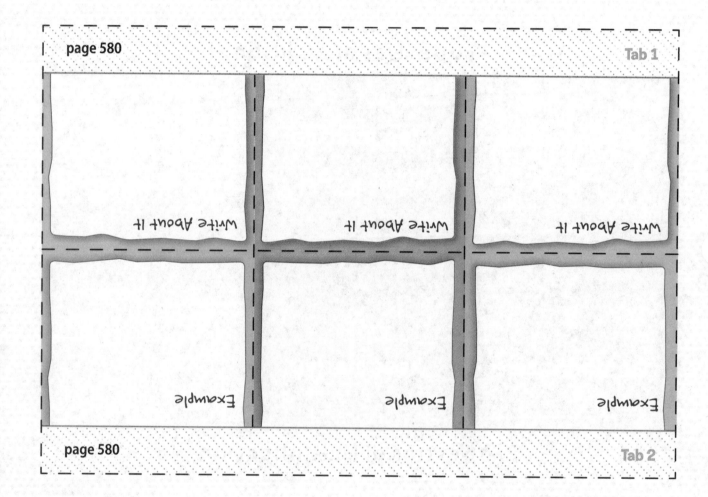

page 580   Tab 1

Write About It   Write About It   Write About It

Example   Example   Example

page 580   Tab 2

Model Equivalent Expressions

INQUIRY How can I use multiple representations to generate equivalent expressions?

Fitness Fortress recycles plastic water bottles. On Saturday, 8 bottles were placed in the bins. On Sunday, 8 more bottles were recycled.

Texas Essential Knowledge and Skills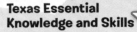

Targeted TEKS
6.7(C) Determine if two expressions are equivalent using concrete models, pictorial models, and algebraic representations.

Mathematical Processes
6.1(C), 6.1(D), 6.1(E), 6.1(G)

Hands-On Activity 1

You can use an expression to represent the number of bottles that were recycled. An *expression* consists of a combination of numbers and operations. Each *term* of an expression is separated by a plus or minus sign. *Equivalent expressions* have the same value.

Step 1 Use a pictorial model, such as a bar diagram, to represent the number of bottles recycled on Saturday. Use a second bar diagram to represent the number of bottles recycled on Sunday.

| Saturday | **8 bottles** |
| Sunday | **8 bottles** |

Step 2 The addition expression $8 + 8$ represents the total.

How many terms are in the expression? ☐

Step 3 The multiplication expression 2×8 also represents the total. Is 2×8 equivalent to $8 + 8$? _____

How many terms are in the expression? ☐

Investigate

Collaborate

Work with a partner. Rewrite each sum as an equivalent product. Then determine if the expressions are equivalent.

1. $14 + 14 =$ _____

Are the expressions

equivalent? _____

2. $92 + 92 + 92 =$ _____

Are the expressions

equivalent? _____

Hands-On Activity 2

Some expressions can be written as the product of a sum. For example,
$2 \times (3 + 4)$ represents the product of 2 and the sum of 3 and 4.
The expression $2 \times (3 + 4)$ can also be thought of as the product of two *factors*.

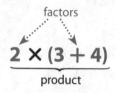

Melina and Kendrick are selling tins of cashews for a school fundraiser.
Melina sold 5 tins on Monday and 5 tins on Tuesday. Kendrick sold 4 tins
Monday and 4 tins on Tuesday.

Step 1   Use a pictorial model. Divide and label each bar diagram to represent the amount sold each day.

Monday [ ]

Tuesday [ ]

Step 2   Write an expression involving a sum of four terms to represent the total amount sold.

☐ + ☐ + ☐ + ☐

Step 3   Complete the expression below involving the product of a sum to represent the total amount sold.

$2 \times \left(☐ + ☐ \right)$

3. Determine if the expressions in Steps 2 and 3 are equivalent. Justify your response using the pictorial model.

_____

Investigate

Collaborate

4. Draw a pictorial model to represent the expression
$19 + 56 + 19 + 56$. Then determine if the
expression is equivalent to $2 \times (19 + 56)$.
Justify your response using your model.

_____

Investigate

Determine if each pair of expressions are equivalent by a drawing a pictorial model. Justify your response using your model.

5. $2 \times (3 + 1)$ and $3 + 1 + 3 + 1$

6. $2 \times (5 + 2)$ and $2 + 5 + 2$

7. $3 \times (11 + 15)$ and $11 + 15 + 11 + 15 + 11 + 15$

8. $2 \times (6 + 8)$ and $6 + 6 + 6 + 8$

9. $3 \times (1 + 2)$ and 3×2

10. $2 \times (4 + 3)$ and $3 + 3 + 4 + 4$

Work with a partner to match each description to the correct expression.
The first one is already done for you.

Description		Expression
11.	This expression is a sum of two terms.	a. $(1 + 2) \times 2$
12.	This expression can be thought of as a product of two factors. One of the factors is the sum of 6 and 4.	b. $6 + 6$
13.	This expression can be thought of as a product of two factors. One of the factors is the sum of 1 and 2.	c. $14 \div 7$
14.	This expression is the quotient of 14 and 7.	d. $(6 + 4) \times 2$

15. **MP Analyze Relationships** Consuela wrote the expression $2 \times (31 + 47)$. She states that the expression is a product and that the expression $(31 + 47)$ is a factor. Marcus states that the expression $(31 + 47)$ is a sum of two terms. Who is correct? Explain. _____

_____

_____

Create
On Your Own

16. **MP Select Tools and Techniques** Write an expression that is the sum of six terms that can also be written as an equivalent expression with two terms.

_____

17. **MP Apply Math to the Real World** Write two equivalent expressions and a real-world problem for the situation modeled to the right.

4 pounds	6 pounds
4 pounds	6 pounds

_____

_____

_____

18. **INQUIRY** HOW can I use multiple representations to generate equivalent expressions?

_____

_____

Powers and Exponents

Texas Essential Knowledge and Skills

Targeted TEKS
6.7(A) Generate equivalent numerical expressions using order of operations, including whole number exponents and prime factorization.

Mathematical Processes
6.1(A), 6.1(B), 6.1(F)

 ## Launch the Lesson: Vocabulary

A product of like factors can be written in exponential form using an exponent and a base. The **base** is the number used as a factor. The **exponent** tells how many times a base is used as a factor.

1. Fill in the boxes with the words *factors*, *exponent*, and *base*.

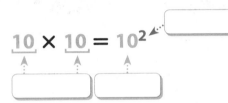

$$10 \times 10 = 10^2$$

2. Give an example of an exponent.

_____

3. Write the definition of *exponent* in your own words.

_____

_____

Vocabulary
base
equivalent expressions
exponent
powers
perfect square

Essential Question
HOW is it helpful to write numbers in different ways?

 ## Real-World Link

MP3 players come in different storage sizes, such as 2GB, 4GB, or 16GB, where GB means gigabyte. One gigabyte is equal to $10 \times 10 \times 10 \times 10 \times 10 \times 10 \times 10 \times 10 \times 10$ bytes.

What is this number written with exponents? [ ]

Which MP Mathematical Processes did you use?
Shade the circle(s) that applies.

Ⓐ Apply Math to the Real World.   Ⓔ Organize Ideas.

Ⓑ Use a Problem-Solving Model.   Ⓕ Analyze Relationships.

Ⓒ Select Tools and Techniques.   Ⓖ Justify Arguments.

Ⓓ Use Multiple Representations.

Equivalent Expressions Using Exponents

Numbers expressed using exponents are called **powers**. For example, 100 is a power of 10 because it can be written as 10^2. Numbers like 100 are **perfect squares** because they are the squares of whole numbers.

 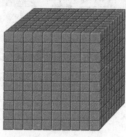

$10 \times 10 = 100$
$10^2 = 100$

$10 \times 10 \times 10 = 1,000$
$10^3 = 1,000$

Perfect cubes are numbers with three identical whole number factors such as $4 \times 4 \times 4 = 64$. So, the number 64 is a perfect cube.

You can generate equivalent expressions using whole number exponents. **Equivalent expressions** have the same value.

Examples

Tutor

For each of the following, generate an equivalent expression using an exponent.

1. $6 \times 6 \times 6 \times 6$

$6 \times 6 \times 6 \times 6 = 6^4$ 6 is used as a factor four times.

2. $4 \times 4 \times 4$

The factor $\boxed{}$ is the base.

The factor is multiplied $\boxed{}$ times.

The exponent is $\boxed{}$.

So, $4 \times 4 \times 4$ can be written as _____.

Show your work.

Got It? Do these problems to find out.

For each of the following, generate an equivalent expression using an exponent.

a. _____

b. _____

    a. $7 \times 7 \times 7 \times 7$

    b. $9 \times 9 \times 9 \times 9 \times 9 \times 9 \times 9$

Equivalent Expressions Using Products

To write powers as equivalent products, determine the base and the exponent. The base of 10^2 is 10 and the exponent is 2. To read powers, consider the exponent. The power 10^2 is read as *ten squared* and 10^3 is read as *ten cubed*.

Examples

Tutor

3. Express 5^2 as a product of the same factor. Then determine the value.

The base is 5. The exponent is 2. So, 5 is used as a factor two times.

$5^2 = 5 \times 5$ Write 5^2 as a product.

$\quad = 25$ Multiply 5 by itself.

4. Express 1.5^3 as a product of the same factor. Then determine the value.

The base is 1.5. The exponent is 3. So, 1.5 is used as a factor three times.

$1.5^3 = 1.5 \times 1.5 \times 1.5$ Write 1.5^3 as a product.

$\quad = 3.375$ Multiply.

5. Express $\left(\dfrac{1}{2}\right)^3$ as a product of the same factor. Then determine the value.

The base is $\dfrac{1}{2}$. The exponent is 3. So $\dfrac{1}{2}$ is used as a factor three times.

$\left(\dfrac{1}{2}\right)^3 = \dfrac{1}{2} \times \dfrac{1}{2} \times \dfrac{1}{2}$ Write $\left(\dfrac{1}{2}\right)^3$ as a product.

$\quad = \dfrac{1}{8}$ Multiply.

Notation

In Example 5, the fraction $\dfrac{1}{2}$ is set in parentheses to note that the entire fraction is the base.

$\left(\dfrac{1}{2}\right)^3 = \dfrac{1}{2} \times \dfrac{1}{2} \times \dfrac{1}{2} = \dfrac{1}{8}$

Without the parentheses, it is understood that only the numerator of the fraction is the base.

$\dfrac{1^3}{2} = \dfrac{1 \times 1 \times 1}{2} = \dfrac{1}{2}$

Got It? Do these problems to find out.

Express each power as a product of the same factor. Then determine the value.

c. 10^5 **d.** 2.1^2 **e.** $\left(\dfrac{1}{4}\right)^2$

Show your work.

c. _____

d. _____

e. _____

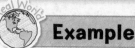 **Example**

6. **STEM** The zoo has an aquarium that holds around 7^4 gallons of water. About how many gallons of water does the aquarium hold?

$7^4 = 7 \times 7 \times 7 \times 7$ Write 7^4 as a product.

     $= 2,401$ Multiply.

So, the aquarium holds about 2,401 gallons of water.

Got It? Do this problem to find out.

Show your work.

f. _____

f. **STEM** Michigan has more than 10^4 inland lakes. Determine the value of 10^4.

Guided Practice

Generate an equivalent expression using an exponent. (Examples 1 and 2)

1. $8 \times 8 \times 8 =$ _____

 Show your work.

2. $1 \times 1 \times 1 \times 1 \times 1 =$ _____

Express each power as a product of the same factor. Then determine the value. (Examples 3–5)

3. $\left(\dfrac{1}{7}\right)^3 =$

_____

4. $2^5 =$

_____

5. $1.4^2 =$

_____

6. Coal mines have shafts that can be as much as 7^3 feet deep. About how many feet deep into Earth's crust are these shafts? (Example 6)

_____

_____

7. (?) **Building on the Essential Question** How can you generate equivalent expressions using exponents?

_____

_____

_____

Rate Yourself!

How confident are you about powers and exponents? Shade the ring on the target.

I'm on target.

I need help.

Find out online. Use the Self-Check Quiz.

Check

Independent Practice

6.7(A), 6.1(A), 6.1(B), 6.1(F) **TEKS**

Generate an equivalent expression using an exponent. (Examples 1 and 2)

1. $6 \times 6 =$

2. $1 \times 1 \times 1 =$

3. $5 \times 5 \times 5 \times 5 \times 5 \times 5 =$

Show your work.

4. $12 \times 12 =$

5. $27 \times 27 \times 27 \times 27 =$

6. $15 \times 15 \times 15 =$

Express each power as a product of the same factor. Then determine the value. (Examples 3–5)

7. $6^4 =$

8. $0.5^3 =$

9. $\left(\frac{1}{8}\right)^2 =$

10. **MP** **Analyze Relationships** A byte is a basic unit of measurement for information storage involving computers. (Example 6)

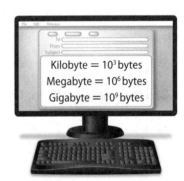

Kilobyte = 10^3 bytes
Megabyte = 10^6 bytes
Gigabyte = 10^9 bytes

a. A kilobyte is equal to 10^3 bytes. Express 10^3 as a product of the same factor. Then determine the value.

_____

_____

b. A megabyte is equal to 10^6 bytes. Express 10^6 as a product of the same factor. Then determine the value.

_____

_____

c. How many more bytes of information are in a

gigabyte than a megabyte? _____

_____

Determine the value of each expression.

11. $0.5^4 + 1 =$

_____

12. $3.2^3 \times 10 =$

_____

13. $10.3^3 + 8 =$

_____

 H.O.T. Problems Higher-Order Thinking

14. Analyze Write a power whose value is greater than 1,000.

_____

15. Analyze Use the table to solve.

a. Describe the pattern for the powers of 2.

Write the values of 2^1 and 2^0 in the table. _____

_____

_____

b. Describe the pattern for the powers of 4.

Write the values of 4^1 and 4^0 in the table. _____

Powers of 2	Powers of 4	Powers of 10
$2^4 = 16$	$4^4 = 256$	$10^4 = 10,000$
$2^3 = 8$	$4^3 = 64$	$10^3 = 1,000$
$2^2 = 4$	$4^2 = 16$	$10^2 = 100$
$2^1 =$	$4^1 =$	$10^1 =$
$2^0 =$	$4^0 =$	$10^0 =$

_____

_____

c. Describe the pattern for the powers of 10. Write the values of 10^1 and 10^0 in

the table. _____

_____

d. Create Write a rule for finding the value of any base with an exponent of 0.

_____

_____

16. Analyze Multiplication is defined as repeated addition. Use the word
repeated to define exponential form. Justify your reasoning.

_____

_____

_____

17. Create Find $(-3)^2$ and $(-3)^3$. Write a rule for finding the sign of the value of

a negative integer with an even or odd exponent. _____

_____

_____

Multi-Step Problem Solving

18. Delmar is studying the reproduction rate of a specific type of bacteria. He places 3 cells in a petri dish and records the number of bacteria over time. He notices a pattern, which is shown in the table. Predict the number of bacteria in the petri dish after 25 hours. Express the answer using exponents. Then evaluate to determine the number of bacteria.

Number of Hours	Number of Bacteria
5	3×3
10	$3 \times 3 \times 3$
15	$3 \times 3 \times 3 \times 3$
20	$3 \times 3 \times 3 \times 3 \times 3$

   Ⓐ 3^6; 729   Ⓑ 6^3; 216   Ⓒ 3^5; 243   Ⓓ 3^6; 18

Use a problem-solving model to solve this problem.

1 Analyze

Read the problem. Circle the information you know. Underline what the problem is asking you to find.

2 Plan

What will you need to do to solve the problem? Write your plan in steps.

Step 1   Determine the pattern in the table.

Step 2   Express the answer using an exponent based on the pattern and evaluate.

3 Solve

Use your plan to solve the problem. Show your steps.

Every 5 hours, the number of bacteria triples. So, the number

of bacteria after 25 hours is $3 \times 3 \times 3 \times 3 \times 3 \times 3$ or 3^6.

Since $3^6 = \boxed{}$, choice $\boxed{}$ is correct. Fill in that answer choice.

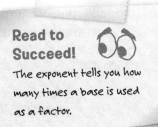

Read to Succeed!
The exponent tells you how many times a base is used as a factor.

4 Justify and Evaluate

How do you know your solution is accurate?

_____

_____

_____

 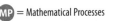

More Multi-Step Problem Solving

Use a problem-solving model to solve each problem.

19. Lilly is studying the reproduction rate of fleas. She places 2 fleas in an enclosed habitat and records the number of eggs each day. She notices a pattern, which is shown in the table. Predict the number of eggs in the habitat on the 5th day. Express the answer using exponents. Then evaluate to determine the number of eggs. **EE** **N** **MP**

Number of Days	Number of Eggs
1	5×5
2	$5 \times 5 \times 5$
3	$5 \times 5 \times 5 \times 5$
4	$5 \times 5 \times 5 \times 5 \times 5$

Ⓐ 6^5; 7,776

Ⓑ 5^5; 3,125

Ⓒ 5^6; 15,625

Ⓓ 6^6; 46,656

20. Elena has a fish tank that holds 2^5 gallons of water. How many fluid ounces of water does the fish tank hold? **EE** **P** **N** **MP**

21. Faith is turning 12 this year. She asks her parents to give her $1 on her birthday and to double that amount for her next birthday. If she continues with this pattern, how much money will Faith get on her 20th birthday? **EE** **N** **MP**

Birthday	Amount ($)
12th	2^0
13th	2^1
14th	2^2
15th	2^3

22. In any cube, the length, width, and height each have the same measure. The volume of the cube below can be found by calculating a^3, where a is the length of a side. Suppose a is 8 inches. How many gallons of water would the cube hold if 231 cubic inches is equal to 1 gallon? Round the answer to the nearest tenth of a gallon. List the steps you used to find your answer. **EE** **N** **P** **MP**

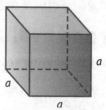

EE = Expressions, Equations, and Relationships   **N** = Number and Operations   **P** = Proportionality   **MP** = Mathematical Processes

Prime Factorization

Texas Essential Knowledge and Skills

Targeted TEKS
6.7(A) Generate equivalent numerical expressions using order of operations, including whole number exponents and prime factorization.

Mathematical Processes
6.1(A), 6.1(B), 6.1(F)

 Launch the Lesson: Vocabulary

A whole number that has exactly two factors, 1 and itself, is a **prime number**. A number greater than 1 with more than two factors is a **composite number**.

$1 \times 13 = 13$ $1 \times 9 = 9$ and $3 \times 3 = 9$

prime   composite

Draw a line matching each number with its list of factors. Circle the prime numbers.

1. 50   1, 31

2. 23   1, 2, 3, 4, 6, 8, 12, 16, 24, 48

3. 48   1, 2, 5, 10, 25, 50

4. 100   1, 23

5. 31   1, 2, 4, 5, 10, 20, 25, 50, 100

Vocabulary
prime number
composite number
prime factorization
factor tree

Essential Question
HOW is it helpful to write numbers in different ways?

 Real-World Link

Texas has 254 counties, more than any other state. What are the factors of 254? Is 254 prime or composite? Explain.

_____

_____

Which MP Mathematical Processes did you use? Shade the circle(s) that applies.

Ⓐ Apply Math to the Real World.   Ⓔ Organize Ideas.

Ⓑ Use a Problem-Solving Model.   Ⓕ Analyze Relationships.

Ⓒ Select Tools and Techniques.   Ⓖ Justify Arguments.

Ⓓ Use Multiple Representations.

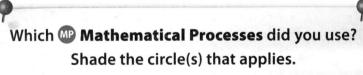

Identify Prime and Composite Numbers

Whole numbers are either prime or composite. Zero and 1 are neither prime nor composite.

Examples

Tutor

State whether each number is *prime*, *composite*, or *neither*. Explain.

1. **35**   Factors of 35: 1, _____ , _____ , 35

Since 35 has more than two factors, it is a _____ number.

....

2. **17**   Factors of 17: 1, _____

Since 17 has exactly _____ factors, it is a _____ number.

Got It? Do these problems to find out.

State whether each number is *prime*, *composite*, or *neither*. Explain.

a. 55   **b.** 130   **c.** 19

Show your work.

a. _____

b. _____

c. _____

Equivalent Expressions Using Prime Factorization

Every composite number can be written as a product of prime numbers. This is called its **prime factorization**. A **factor tree** is a diagram that can be used to find the prime factorization of a number. You can generate equivalent expressions using prime factorization.

Examples

Tutor

Generate an equivalent expression using prime factorization.

3. **120**

Write the number being factored at the top.

Choose a pair of factors.

Continue to factor until only prime numbers remain.

The prime factorization of 120 is 2 × 2 × 2 × 3 × 5,

or ☐ × ☐ × ☐.

So, 120 = 2^3 × 3 × 5.

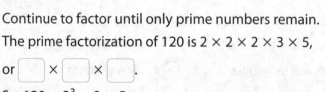

4. **36**

Write the number being factored at the top.

Choose a pair of factors.

Continue to factor until prime numbers remain.

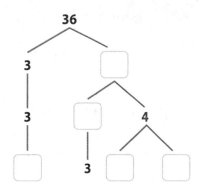

The prime factorization of 36 is 2 × 2 × 3 × 3, or $\boxed{}$ × $\boxed{}$.

So, $36 = 2^2 \times 3^2$.

5. **−70**

To factor a negative integer, use −1 as a factor. Since −70 = −1 × 70, factor 70 and include −1 in the prime factorization.

The prime factorization of −70 is −1 × 2 × 5 × 7.

So, −70 = −1 × 2 × 5 × 7.

6. **−1,260**

The prime factorization of −1,260 is

−1 × $\boxed{}$ × $\boxed{}$ × $\boxed{}$ × $\boxed{}$.

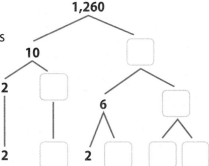

So, $-1{,}260 = -1 \times 2^2 \times 3^2 \times 5 \times 7$.

Got It? Do these problems to find out.

d. 63   **f.** 60

e. −16   **g.** −800

Show your work.

d. _____

e. _____

f. _____

g. _____

Example

7. **STEM** The table shows the number of cells after a cell divides into 2 for various numbers of splits. How many cells are there after 8 splits?

Number of Splits	Number of Cells after Splits
1	2
2	4
3	8
4	16
5	32

Look for a pattern in the number of cells after splits.

$2 = 2 \times 1$

$4 = 2 \times 2$ or 2^2

$8 = 2 \times 2 \times 2$ or 2^3

$16 = $ _____ or ____

$32 = $ _____ or ____

The number of splits tells how many times to use 2 as a factor.

So, the number of cells after 8 splits is _____ or _____ cells.

Guided Practice

State whether each number is *prime, composite,* or *neither.* (Examples 1 and 2)

1. 51 _____

2. 23 _____

Generate an equivalent expression using prime factorization for each number. (Examples 3–6)

3. 75 = _____

4. 42 = _____

5. −90 = _____

6. A mockingbird has about 28 different songs it sings. Generate an equivalent expression using prime factorization for the number 28. (Example 7)

_____

_____

7. (?) **Building on the Essential Question** Explain why the factor tree for a number can have different forms, but the prime factorization will always be the same.

_____

_____

_____

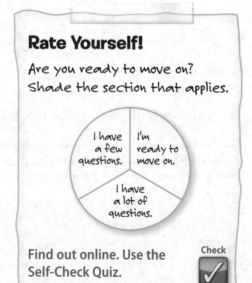

Rate Yourself!

Are you ready to move on?
Shade the section that applies.

I have a few questions.

I'm ready to move on.

I have a lot of questions.

Find out online. Use the Self-Check Quiz.

Check ✓

Independent Practice

6.7(A), 6.1(F), 6.1(G) **TEKS**

State whether each number is *prime*, *composite*, or *neither*. (Examples 1 and 2)

1. 47 _____

2. 2 _____

3. 99 _____

4. 31 _____

5. 1 _____

6. 35 _____

Generate an equivalent expression using prime factorization for each number. (Examples 3–6)

7. 66 = _____

8. 120 = _____

9. −48 = _____

10. 56 = _____

11. −126 = _____

12. 500 = _____

13. Penelope has 300 different types of beads she uses when decorating dresses. Generate an equivalent expression using prime factorization for the number 300. (Example 7)

_____

14. There are about 1,265 school districts in the state of Texas. Generate an equivalent expression using prime factorization for the number 1,265.

_____

15. All odd numbers greater than or equal to 7 can be expressed as the sum of three prime numbers. Which three prime numbers have a sum of 37? Justify your answer.

_____

16. Melanie bought bags of colored sand that each cost the same. She spent a total of $24. Find three possible costs per bag and the number of bags that she could have purchased.

_____

_____

17. **Use Multiple Representations** Draw three different possible factor trees to find the prime factorization of 300.

 H.O.T. Problems Higher-Order Thinking

18. Analyze Select two prime numbers that are greater than 50 but less than 100. _____

19. Analyze _Twin primes_ are two prime numbers that are consecutive odd integers such as 3 and 5, 5 and 7, and 11 and 13. Determine all of the twin primes that are less than 100. _____

_____

20. Evaluate A _counterexample_ is an example that shows a statement is not true. Write a counterexample for the statement below. Explain your reasoning.

All even numbers are composite numbers.

_____

_____

21. Analyze Complete the table by finding the value of the powers of 9 and the prime factorizations of the products. Look for a pattern in the prime factorizations. Determine the prime factorization of each mentally.

a. $9^7 =$ _____   **b.** $9^{10} =$ _____

Power	Value	Prime Factorization
9^1	9	3×3 or 3^2
9^2	81	$3 \times 3 \times 3 \times 3$ or 3^4
9^3		
9^4		

Multi-Step Problem Solving

22. The table shows the number of raffle tickets collected at a county fair during a three-day period. The prime factorization of the sum of raffle tickets was found. What is the greatest prime number in the prime factorization? (EE) (N) (MP)

Day	Raffle Tickets
Friday	250
Saturday	510
Sunday	100

Use a problem-solving model to solve this problem.

1 Analyze

Read the problem. Circle the information you know.
Underline what the problem is asking you to find.

2 Plan

What will you need to do to solve the problem? Write your plan in steps.

Step 1   Determine the sum of raffle tickets collected.

Step 2   Determine the prime factorization of the sum.

Read to Succeed!
Use a factor tree to find the prime factorization of a number.

3 Solve

Use your plan to solve the problem. Show your steps.

The total number of raffle tickets collected is $250 + 510 + 100$

or ⬚. The prime factorization of ⬚ is ⬚ × ⬚ × ⬚.

So, the greatest prime number in the prime factorization is ⬚.

Complete the grid.

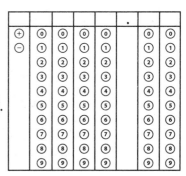

4 Justify and Evaluate

How do you know your solution is accurate?

_____

_____

_____

(EE) = Expressions, Equations, and Relationships   (N) = Number and Operations   (MP) = Mathematical Processes

Use a problem-solving model to solve each problem.

23. The table shows the number of hot dogs, pizza slices, and cheese sandwiches sold at a sporting event. The prime factorization of the sum of items sold was found. Each term of the prime factorization has the same exponent. What is that exponent? **EE** **MP**

Food	Number Sold
Hot Dog	144
Pizza Slice	42
Cheese Sandwich	30

24. The prime factorization of -160 is $-1 \times 2^a \times 5^b$. What is the sum of $a + b$? **EE** **MP**

25. Determine the area of the rectangle. Express the number of square feet as a prime factorization. Which factor in this expression occurs exactly two times? **EE** **MP**

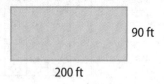

90 ft

200 ft

26. The rectangle shown below is an Olympic-sized pool at a training facility. What is an equivalent expression for the prime factorization of a smaller pool that has an area one-half the area of the Olympic-size pool? Explain. **EE** **MP**

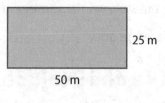

25 m

50 m

EE = Expressions, Equations, and Relationships   **MP** = Mathematical Processes

Lesson 3

Order of Operations

 Launch the Lesson: Real World

The table shows the cost of different snacks at a concession stand at the school hockey game. How much do 3 boxes of popcorn and 4 hot dogs cost?

Item	Price ($)
Popcorn	2
Juice or Soda	1
Hot Dog	4

1.  = $ ☐

2.  = $ ☐

3. Find the total cost of buying 3 boxes of popcorn and 4 hot dogs.

_____

4. What two operations did you use in Exercises 1–2? Explain how to find the answer to Exercise 3 using these operations.

_____

_____

_____

Which MP **Mathematical Processes did you use?**
Shade the circle(s) that applies.

Ⓐ Apply Math to the Real World.　　Ⓔ Organize Ideas.

Ⓑ Use a Problem-Solving Model.　　Ⓕ Analyze Relationships.

Ⓒ Select Tools and Techniques.　　Ⓖ Justify Arguments.

Ⓓ Use Multiple Representations.

Texas Essential Knowledge and Skills

Targeted TEKS
6.7(A) Generate equivalent numerical expressions using order of operations, including whole number exponents and prime factorization.

Mathematical Processes
6.1(A), 6.1(B), 6.1(F), 6.1(G)

Vocab

Vocabulary
numerical expression
order of operations

Essential Question

HOW is it helpful to write numbers in different ways?

Order of Operations

1. Simplify the expressions inside grouping symbols, like parentheses.
2. Find the value of all powers.
3. Multiply and divide in order from left to right.
4. Add and subtract in order from left to right.

A **numerical expression** like $3 \times 2 + 4 \times 4$ is a combination of numbers and operations. The **order of operations** tells you which operation to perform first so that everyone finds the same value for an expression.

You can generate equivalent numerical expressions using the order of operations.

Tutor

Examples

Generate an equivalent expression for each using the order of operations.

1. $14 - 5 + 3$

There are no grouping symbols or powers.

There are no multiplication or division symbols.

Add and subtract in order from left to right.

$14 - 5 + 3 = 9 + 3$ Subtract 5 from 14 first.

$ = 12$ Add 9 and 3.

2. $7 + 10 \times 2$

There are no grouping symbols or powers.

Multiply before adding.

$7 + 10 \times 2 = 7 + 20$ Multiply 10 and 2.

$ = 27$ Add 7 and 20.

Show your work.

Got It? Do these problems to find out.

a. _____

b. _____

a. $18 + 5 \times 2$

b. $27 \div 3 \times 1$

Parentheses and Exponents

You can generate equivalent expressions using the order of operations, including parentheses and exponents.

Expressions inside grouping symbols, such as parentheses, are simplified first. Follow the order of operations inside parentheses. For example, in the expression $3 + (4^2 + 5)$, you will need to find the value of the power, 4^2, before you can add the expression inside the parentheses.

 STOP and Reflect

Why is it important to have the order of operations?

Tutor

Examples

Generate an equivalent expression for each using the order of operations.

3. $36 \div 4 + 20 \times (3 + 5)$

$$
\begin{aligned}
36 \div 4 + 20 \times (3 + 5) &= 36 \div 4 + 20 \times 8 && \text{Add 3 and 5.} \\
&= 9 + 20 \times 8 && \text{Divide 36 by 4.} \\
&= 9 + 160 && \text{Multiply 20 by 8.} \\
&= 169 && \text{Add 9 and 160.}
\end{aligned}
$$

4. $4 \times 5^2 + 7$

$$
\begin{aligned}
4 \times 5^2 + 7 &= 4 \times 25 + 7 && \text{Find } 5^2. \\
&= 100 + 7 && \text{Multiply 4 and 25.} \\
&= 107 && \text{Add 100 and 7.}
\end{aligned}
$$

5. $5 + (8^2 - 2) \times 2$

$$
\begin{aligned}
5 + (8^2 - 2) \times 2 &= 5 + \left(\boxed{} - 2 \right) \times 2 && \text{Simplify the exponent.} \\
&= 5 + \boxed{} \times 2 && \text{Simplify inside parentheses.} \\
&= 5 + \boxed{} && \text{Multiply.} \\
&= \boxed{} && \text{Add.}
\end{aligned}
$$

Show your work.

c. _____

d. _____

> **Got It?** Do these problems to find out.
>
> **c.** $21 \times (4 + 1) \div 3 - 10$ **d.** $24 \div (2^3 + 4)$

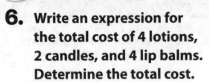

Example

6. Write an expression for the total cost of 4 lotions, 2 candles, and 4 lip balms. Determine the total cost.

Cost of Items			
Item	Lotion	Candle	Lip balm
Cost ($)	4	8	3

$4 \times \$4 + 2 \times \$8 + 4 \times \$3$

$= 4^2 + 2 \times 8 + 4 \times 3$

$= 16 + 2 \times 8 + 4 \times 3$ Simplify 4^2 to find the cost of the lotions.

$= 16 + 16 + 4 \times 3$ Multiply 2 and 8 to find the cost of the candles.

$= 16 + 16 + 12$ Multiply 4 and 3 to find the cost of the lip balms.

$= 44$

The total cost of the items is $44.

 Show your work.

Got It? Do this problem to find out.

e. _____

e. Alexis and 3 friends are at the mall. Each person buys a pretzel for $4, sauce for $1, and a drink for $2. Write an expression for the total and determine the total cost.

Guided Practice

Generate an equivalent expression for each using the order of operations.
(Examples 1–5)

1. $8 - 3 + 9 =$ _____

2. $(16 + 7) \times 2 + 3 =$ _____

3. $7^2 + 6 \div 3 =$ _____

Show your work.

4. Financial Literacy Tickets to the Children's Museum of Houston cost $8 for adults and children and $7 for seniors. Write an expression to find the total cost of 5 adult tickets and 2 senior tickets. Then determine the total cost. (Example 6)

_____

_____

5. **Building on the Essential Question** How can you generate equivalent numerical expressions using the

order of operations? _____

_____

_____

Rate Yourself!

How well do you understand order of operations? Circle the image that applies.

Clear   Somewhat Clear   Not So Clear

Find out online. Use the Self-Check Quiz.

Check

Independent Practice

6.7(A), 6.1(F), 6.1(G) TEKS

Generate an equivalent expression for each using the order of operations.

(Examples 1–5)

1. $7 + 3 - 2 =$ _____

 Show your work.

2. $42 - 21 + 17 =$ _____

3. $5 + 7 \times (6 + 2) =$ _____

4. $52 - 3^3 \div 9 =$ _____

5. $48 \div 12 + 5 \times (9 - 2) =$ _____

6. $9^2 - 7 \times 3 =$ _____

7. $2 \times (7^2 - 15) + 11 =$ _____

8. $4 + 6^2 \times (18 - 13) \div 18 + 9 =$ _____

9. Financial Literacy Tyree and four friends go to the movies. Each person buys a movie ticket for $9, a snack for $6, and a drink for $4. Write an expression for the total cost of the trip to the movies. Then determine the total cost. (Example 6)

_____

_____

10. Financial Literacy The Molina family went to a concert together. They purchased 4 concert tickets for $25 each, 3 T-shirts for $15 each, and a poster for $10. Write an expression for the total cost. Then determine the total cost.

_____

_____

11. **Select Tools and Techniques** A wholesaler sells rolls of fruit snacks in two sizes of bags. The table shows the number of rolls that come in each bag. Write an expression that could be used to determine the number of rolls in 3 large bags and 2 small bags. Then determine the number of rolls.

Bag	Number of Rolls
Large	10
Small	5

12. **Find the Error** Luis is finding $9 - 6 + 2$. Determine his mistake and correct it.

$9 - 6 + 2 = 9 - 8$
$= 1$

 H.O.T. Problems Higher-Order Thinking

13. **Analyze** Use the expression $34 - 12 \div 2 + 7$.

a. Place parentheses in the expression so that the value of the expression is 18.

b. Place parentheses in the expression to find a value other than 18. Then find the value of the new expression.

14. **Create** Write an expression with a value of 12. It should contain four numbers and two different operations.

15. **Evaluate** Which expression does *not* belong with the other three? Justify your response.

$6^2 - 9$ 3^3 $(5 + 4)^2 \div 3$ $4 \times 5 + 9$

16. **Analyze** Place parentheses, if needed, to make each statement true.

a. $7 + 3 \times 2 + 4 = 25$

b. $8^2 \div 4 \times 8 = 2$

c. $16 + 8 - 5 \times 2 = 14$

Multi-Step Problem Solving

17. An art store sells art kits that include crayons and a sketch pad. The table shows the number of crayons and sketch pad pages in each art kit size. A school buys 30 small, 10 large, and 24 medium art kits. Then they return 18 medium art kits. How many crayons do they have in all?

Art Kit Size	Number of Crayons	Sketch Pad Pages
Small	16	20
Medium	24	40
Large	68	100

Ⓐ 3,240   Ⓒ 1,736

Ⓑ 2,560   Ⓓ 1,304

Use a problem-solving model to solve this problem.

1 Analyze

Read the problem. Circle the information you know. Underline what the problem is asking you to find.

2 Plan

What will you need to do to solve the problem? Write your plan in steps.

Step 1 Write an expression to represent the situation.

Step 2 Evaluate the expression.

3 Solve

Use your plan to solve the problem. Show your steps.
The school bought a total of 30 small, 6 medium, and 10 large kits.

(30 × ⬜) + (6 × ⬜) + (10 × ⬜) = ⬜

So, the school has ⬜ crayons. Choice ⬜ is correct. Fill in that answer choice.

Read to Succeed!

When evaluating the expression, remember to follow the order of operations. Perform the operations in the parentheses first then add.

4 Justify and Evaluate

How do you know your solution is accurate?

_____

_____

_____

 = Expressions, Equations, and Relationships   = Mathematical Processes

Use a problem-solving model to solve each problem.

18. The table shows the chocolate chip cookies in each container type. Yesterday, the bakery sold 4 tubs, 10 baskets, and 12 boxes. However, 3 of the boxes were returned. How many total cookies were sold by the end of the day? Ⓝ ⒺⒺ ⓂⓅ

Container Type	Chocolate Chip Cookies
Basket	16
Box	36
Tub	48

Ⓐ 160   Ⓒ 432

Ⓑ 192   Ⓓ 676

19. The table shows the number of salt and yogurt pretzels that come in different sized boxes. A store orders 3 small boxes and 5 large boxes and then sells them at $2.00 per salt pretzel and $2.50 per yogurt pretzel. How much will the store make if they sell all the pretzels? Ⓝ ⒺⒺ ⓂⓅ

Box Size	Salt Pretzel	Yogurt Pretzel
Small	36	12
Large	48	24

20. A luxury line of furniture at a store sells couches for $4,000, reclining chairs for $2,040, and loveseats for $2,800. This luxury line went on sale where the price of each piece of furniture was divided by 4. During the sale, how much would 2 couches, 1 reclining chair, and 3 loveseats cost? Ⓝ ⒺⒺ ⓂⓅ

21. Determine the value of the expression below. Explain your answer. ⒺⒺ ⓂⓅ

$$\frac{120 - (3^3 - 36 \div 2)^2}{10 + 3(10 - 6) - 27 \div 3}$$

Ⓝ = Number and Operations   ⒺⒺ = Expressions, Equations, and Relationships   ⓂⓅ = Mathematical Processes

Algebraic Expressions

Launch the Lesson: Vocabulary

Algebra is a language of symbols, including variables. A **variable** is a symbol, usually a letter, used to represent a number.

Scan the lesson to complete the graphic organizer.

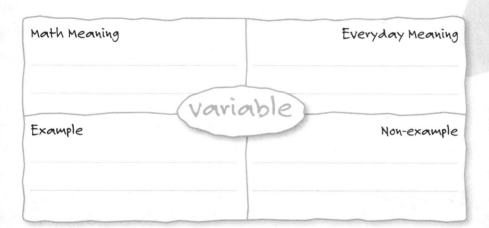

Math Meaning	Everyday Meaning
variable	
Example	Non-example

Texas Essential Knowledge and Skills

Targeted TEKS
Preparation for 6.7(D) Generate equivalent expressions using the properties of operations such as the inverse, identity, commutative, associative, and distributive properties.

Mathematical Processes
6.1(A), 6.1(B), 6.1(F), 6.1(G)

Vocab

Vocabulary
algebra
algebraic expression
evaluate
variable

Essential Question
HOW is it helpful to write numbers in different ways?

Real-World Investigation

A box contains an unknown number of markers. There are 2 markers outside the box. The total number of markers is represented by the bar diagram below.

unknown number of markers	2 markers

1. Suppose there are 14 markers in the box. Find the total number of markers. Explain your answer. _____

Which MP **Mathematical Processes** did you use?
Shade the circle(s) that applies.

Ⓐ Apply Math to the Real World.
Ⓑ Use a Problem-Solving Model.
Ⓒ Select Tools and Techniques.
Ⓓ Use Multiple Representations.
Ⓔ Organize Ideas.
Ⓕ Analyze Relationships.
Ⓖ Justify Arguments.

Evaluate One-Step Expressions

Algebraic expressions contain at least one variable and at least one operation. For example, the expression $n + 2$ represents *the sum of an unknown number and two*.

> Any letter can be used as a variable. ·····▸ $n + 2$

The letter x is often used as a variable. To avoid confusion with the symbol $\times$, there are other ways to show multiplication.

$$5 \cdot x \qquad 5(x) \qquad 5x$$

$$\uparrow \qquad\qquad \uparrow \qquad\qquad \uparrow$$

$$5 \text{ times } x \qquad 5 \text{ times } x \qquad 5 \text{ times } x$$

The variables in an expression can be replaced with any number. Once the variables have been replaced, you can **evaluate**, or find the value of, the algebraic expression.

Tutor

Examples

1. Evaluate $16 + b$ if $b = 25$.

$\quad 16 + b = 16 + 25 \qquad$ Replace b with 25.

$\qquad\quad\ = 41 \qquad\qquad$ Add 16 and 25.

2. Evaluate $x - y$ if $x = 64$ and $y = 27$.

$\quad x - y = 64 - 27 \qquad$ Replace x with 64 and y with 27.

$\qquad\quad = 37 \qquad\qquad$ Subtract 27 from 64.

3. Evaluate $6x$ if $x = \frac{1}{2}$.

$\quad 6x = 6 \cdot \frac{1}{2} \qquad$ Replace x with $\frac{1}{2}$.

$\qquad = 3 \qquad\quad$ Multiply 6 and $\frac{1}{2}$.

> Show your work.

Got It? Do these problems to find out.

Evaluate each expression if $a = 6$, $b = 4$, and $c = \frac{1}{3}$.

    a. $a + 8$ **b.** $a - b$ **c.** $a \cdot b$ **d.** $9c$

a. _____

b. _____

c. _____

d. _____

Evaluate Multi-Step Expressions

To evaluate multi-step expressions, replace each variable with the correct value and follow the order of operations.

Examples

Tutor

4. Evaluate $5t + 4$ if $t = 3$.

$$5t + 4 = 5 \cdot 3 + 4 \qquad \text{Replace } t \text{ with 3.}$$
$$= 15 + 4 \qquad \text{Multiply 5 and 3.}$$
$$= 19 \qquad \text{Add 15 and 4.}$$

5. Evaluate $4x^2$ if $x = \frac{1}{8}$.

$$4x^2 = 4 \cdot \left(\frac{1}{8}\right)^2 \qquad \text{Replace } x \text{ with } \frac{1}{8}.$$
$$= 4 \cdot \frac{1}{64} \qquad \text{Simplify } \left(\frac{1}{8}\right)^2.$$
$$= \frac{1}{16} \qquad \text{Multiply.}$$

6. Evaluate $10a + 7$ if $a = \frac{1}{5}$.

$$10a + 7 = 10\left(\dfrac{\boxed{}}{\boxed{}}\right) + 7 \qquad \text{Replace } a \text{ with } \frac{1}{5}.$$

$$= \boxed{} + 7 \qquad \text{Multiply 10 and } \frac{1}{5}.$$

$$= \boxed{} \qquad \text{Add.}$$

Got It? Do these problems to find out.

Evaluate each expression if $d = 12$ and $e = \frac{1}{3}$.

e. $2d - 5$

f. $50 - 3d$

g. $9e^2$

Show your work.

e. _____

f. _____

g. _____

Copyright © McGraw-Hill Education

Example

7. Khalil is wrapping a gift for his sister's birthday. The box has side lengths that are $\frac{1}{2}$ foot. Use the expression $6s^2$, where s represents the length of a side, to determine the surface area of the box he is wrapping. Express your answer in square feet.

$$6s^2 = 6 \cdot \left(\frac{1}{2}\right)^2 \qquad \text{Replace } s \text{ with } \frac{1}{2}.$$

$$= 6 \cdot \frac{1}{4} \qquad \text{Simplify } \left(\frac{1}{2}\right)^2.$$

$$= \frac{6}{4} \text{ or } 1\frac{1}{2} \qquad \text{Multiply.}$$

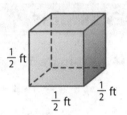

$\frac{1}{2}$ ft $\frac{1}{2}$ ft $\frac{1}{2}$ ft

So, the surface area of the box is $1\frac{1}{2}$ square feet.

Guided Practice

Evaluate each expression if $m = 4$, $z = 9$, and $r = \frac{1}{6}$. (Examples 1–6)

1. $3 + m$ _____

2. $z - m$ _____

3. $12r$ _____

Show your work.

4. $4m - 2$ _____

5. $60r - 4$ _____

6. $3r^2$ _____

7. The amount of money that remains from a $20 bill after Malina buys 4 party favors for p dollars each is $20 - 4p$. Determine the amount remaining if each favor

cost $3. (Example 7) _____

8. ? **Building on the Essential Question** How are numerical expressions and algebraic expressions different?

_____

_____

_____

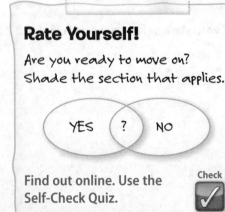

Rate Yourself!

Are you ready to move on?
Shade the section that applies.

YES   ?   NO

Find out online. Use the Self-Check Quiz.

Check ✓

Independent Practice

Preparation for 6.7(D), 6.1(A), 6.1(F)

Evaluate each expression if $m = 2$, $n = 16$, and $p = \frac{1}{3}$. (Examples 1–6)

1. $m + 10$ _____

2. $n \div 4$ _____

3. $m + n$ _____

4. $6m - 1$ _____

Show your work.

5. $3p$ _____

6. $12p$ _____

7. $12m - 4$ _____

8. $9p^2$ _____

9. A paper recycling bin has the dimensions shown. Use the expression s^3, where s represents the length of a side, to determine the volume of the bin. Express your answer in cubic meters. (Example 7)

_____

$\frac{1}{2}$ m $\frac{1}{2}$ m $\frac{1}{2}$ m

10. **MP** **Apply Math to the Real World** Refer to the graphic novel frame below for Exercises a–b.

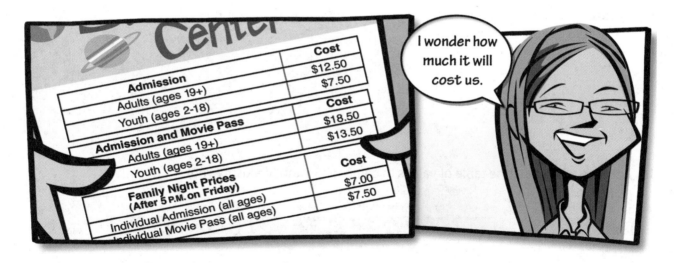

Admission	Cost
Adults (ages 19+)	$12.50
Youth (ages 2-18)	$7.50
Admission and Movie Pass	Cost
Adults (ages 19+)	$18.50
Youth (ages 2-18)	$13.50
Family Night Prices (After 5 P.M. on Friday)	Cost
Individual Admission (all ages)	$7.00
Individual Movie Pass (all ages)	$7.50

I wonder how much it will cost us.

a. What is the total cost for one individual admission and one individual movie pass on Family Night? _____

b. The expression $14.50x$ can be used to find the total cost for x tickets on Family Night for admission and the movie. What is the cost for 3 tickets?

_____

11. Financial Literacy Julian earns $13.50 per hour. His company deducts 23% of his pay each week for taxes. Julian uses the expression 0.77(13.50h) to compute his earnings after taxes for the hours h he works. What will be his earnings after taxes, if he works 40 hours? _____

Evaluate each expression if $x = 3$, $y = 12$, and $z = 8$.

12. $4z + 8 - 6$ _____

13. $7z \div 4 + 5x$ _____

14. $y^2 \div (3z)$ _____

15. **Analyze Relationships** To find the area of a trapezoid, use the expression $\frac{1}{2}h(b_1 + b_2)$, where h represents the height, b_1 represents the length of the top base, and b_2 represents the length of the bottom base. What is the area of the trapezoidal table? _____

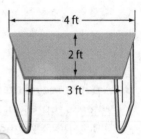

4 ft

2 ft

3 ft

H.O.T. Problems Higher-Order Thinking

16. Analyze Isandro and Yvette each have a calculator. Yvette starts at 100 and subtracts 7 each time. Isandro starts at zero and adds 3 each time. If they press the keys at the same time, will their displays ever show the same number?

If so, what is the number? _____

17. Create Provide an example of a numerical expression and an example of an algebraic expression. Explain.

_____

_____

_____

18. Analyze Complete the table of values to compare $5n$ and 5^n. Justify your response.

n	1	2	3	4
$5n$				
5^n				

_____

_____

_____

_____

Multi-Step Problem Solving

19. The table shows the dimensions of three picture frame sizes available at a framing shop. What is the total perimeter, in inches, of two small frames and three large frames? The perimeter of a rectangle is $2\ell + 2w$, where ℓ is the length and w is the width.

Picture Frame Size	Length (in.)	Width (in.)
Small	3	5
Medium	5	7
Large	8	10

Use a problem-solving model to solve this problem.

1 Analyze

Read the problem. Circle the information you know. Underline what the problem is asking you to find.

2 Plan

What will you need to do to solve the problem? Write your plan in steps.

Step 1 Determine the perimeter of a small frame and a large frame.

Step 2 Determine the total perimeter for the five frames.

> **Read to Succeed!**
> Remember that 2ℓ is the same as $2 \times \ell$ and $2w$ is $2 \times w$.

3 Solve

Use your plan to solve the problem. Show your steps.

The perimeter of a small frame is 2(___) + 2(___) or ___ inches.

The perimeter of a large frame is 2(___) + 2(___) or ___ inches.

The total perimeter of the five frames is 2(16) + 3(36) or ___ inches.

Complete the grid.

4 Justify and Evaluate

How do you know your solution is accurate?

_____

_____

_____

More Multi-Step Problem Solving

Use a problem-solving model to solve each problem.

20. The table shows different dog carrier sizes available at a pet store. What is the total perimeter, in feet, of one large, two extra-small, and three medium dog carriers? Represent the situation with an expression. **EE** **MP**

Carrier Size	Length (in.)	Width (in.)
Extra-Small	19	13
Small	24	18
Medium	30	19
Large	36	23

21. Gabby is going to cover her ruler shown below with construction paper for an art project. The area of the ruler can be found using the expression ℓw, where ℓ is the length and w is the width of the rectangle. What is the area, in square inches, of the construction paper needed if 4 rulers are used in her art project? Represent the situation with an expression. **EE** **MP**

1 in.

12 in.

22. Calvin is filling a sandbox with sand. The volume of the sandbox can be found using the expression ℓwh where ℓ is the length, w is the width, and h is the height. What is the volume, in cubic inches, of two of these sandboxes? Represent the situation with an expression. *(Hint: There are $12 \times 12 \times 12$ cubic inches in a cubic foot.)* **EE** **MP**

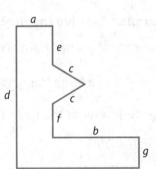

$\frac{1}{2}$ ft

2 ft

2 ft

23. Write an expression for the perimeter of the irregular-shaped figure shown below. Explain. **EE** **MP**

a

e

c

d

c

f

b

g

EE = Expressions, Equations, and Relationships   **MP** = Mathematical Processes

Model and Write Algebraic Expressions

INQUIRY HOW can bar diagrams help me write expressions in which letters stand for numbers?

Kevin has 6 more baseball cards than Elian. Write an algebraic expression to represent the number of baseball cards Kevin has.

What do you know? _____

_____

What do you need to know? _____

_____

Texas Essential Knowledge and Skills

Targeted TEKS
Preparation for 6.9(A) Write one-variable, one-step equations and inequalities to represent constraints or conditions within problems.

Mathematical Processes
6.1(C), 6.1(D), 6.1(E), 6.1(F), 6.1(G)

Hands-On Activity 1

Algebraic expressions are similar to numerical expressions.

Step 1 Elian has an unknown number of baseball cards c. Use a bar diagram to show Elian's cards.

Elian | **c cards** |

Step 2 Kevin has 6 more baseball cards than Elian. Complete the bar diagram below to show how many baseball cards Kevin has.

Kevin | **c cards** | [ ] **cards** |

So, Kevin has [ ] + [ ] baseball cards.

Recall that the terms of an expression are separated by addition or subtraction signs.

1. How many terms are in the expression? [ ]

2. Does the expression represent a *sum, difference, product,* or *quotient*?

_____

Hands-On Activity 2

Sam sent 10 fewer messages in July than in August. Write an algebraic expression to represent the number of text messages Sam sent in July.

Step 1   Sam sent an unknown number of messages *m* in August. Label the bar diagram to represent the messages Sam sent in August.

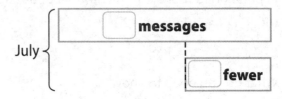

August [*m* messages]

Step 2   Sam sent 10 fewer messages in July. Label the bar diagram to show the messages Sam sent in July.

July { [ ] **messages** 　 [ ] **fewer**

So, Sam sent [ ] − 10 messages in July.

3. How many terms are in the expression? [ ]

4. Does the expression represent a *sum, difference, product,* or *quotient*?

Hands-On Activity 3

A bottlenose dolphin can swim *d* miles per hour. Humans swim one-third as fast as dolphins. Write an algebraic expression that could be used to determine how fast humans can swim.

Step 1   Dolphins can swim an unknown number of miles per hour *d*. Use a bar diagram to represent the speed a dolphin swims.

Dolphins [*d* **miles per hour**]

Step 2   Humans swim one-third as fast as dolphins. Divide and shade a second bar diagram to represent the speed humans can swim.

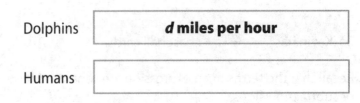

Dolphins [*d* **miles per hour**]

Humans [   ]

So, humans can swim [ ] ÷ [ ] miles per hour.

5. How many terms are in the expression? [ ]

6. Does the expression represent a *sum, difference, product,* or *quotient*?

Investigate

Collaborate

Work with a partner. Write a real-world problem and algebraic expression for each situation modeled.

7.

Year 1	*p* people	
Year 2	*p* people	43 people

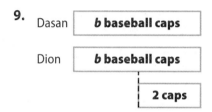
Show your work.

8.

Bag of Apples	*p* pounds	
Bag of Oranges		

9.

Dasan	*b* baseball caps	
Dion	*b* baseball caps	
		2 caps

10.

Kent	*m* square miles	
Ames	*m* square miles	
		12

11.

Harry	*m* minutes			
Janice				

12.

Sixth Grade	*h* inches	
Seventh Grade	*h* inches	2 inches

Analyze and Reflect

Work with a partner to complete the table. The first one is done for you.

	Algebraic Expression	Word Phrase	Model	
	$t + 8$	the sum of a number and 8	t	8
13.	$r - 4$			
14.	$5w$			
15.	$\dfrac{c}{3}$			
16.	$7 + m$			

17. **MP Analyze Relationships** Write an algebraic expression that represents

a number y divided by 10. _____

Create

18. **MP Select Tools and Techniques** Write a real-world situation and an algebraic expression that is represented by the bar diagram.

w	w	w	3

_____

_____

19. **INQUIRY** HOW can bar diagrams help me write expressions in which letters stand for numbers?

_____

_____

Write Algebraic Expressions

Launch the Lesson: Real World

Watch ▷

Missouri has 8 major commercial airports. California has 24 major commercial airports. Let's investigate how to compare quantities using the four operations.

1. Alabama has 4 fewer airports than Missouri.

   a. Underline the key math word in the problem.

   b. Circle the operation you would use to determine how many airports are located in Alabama. Explain.

$$+ \qquad - \qquad \times \qquad \div$$

_____

_____

2. California has three times as many airports as Georgia.

   a. Underline the key math word in the problem.

   b. Circle the operation would you use to find how many airports Georgia has. Explain.

$$+ \qquad - \qquad \times \qquad \div$$

_____

_____

_____

3. Missouri has two times as many airports as Ohio. How many airports does Ohio have?

$$8 \bigcirc 2 = \underline{\qquad}$$

Missouri or Bust!

Which ⓂⓅ **Mathematical Processes** did you use?
Shade the circle(s) that applies.

Ⓐ Apply Math to the Real World.

Ⓔ Organize Ideas.

Ⓑ Use a Problem-Solving Model.

Ⓕ Analyze Relationships.

Ⓒ Select Tools and Techniques.

Ⓖ Justify Arguments.

Ⓓ Use Multiple Representations.

Texas Essential Knowledge and Skills TEKS

Targeted TEKS
Preparation for 6.9(A) Write one-variable, one-step equations and inequalities to represent constraints or conditions within problems.

Mathematical Processes
6.1(A), 6.1(B), 6.1(F), 6.1(G)

Vocab

Vocabulary 🔤
defining the variable

Essential Question ❓
HOW is it helpful to write numbers in different ways?

Write Phrases as Algebraic Expressions

To write verbal phrases as algebraic expressions, follow the steps below. In the second step, **defining the variable**, choose a variable and decide what it represents.

Words	Describe the situation. Use only the most important words.
Variable	Choose a variable to represent the unknown quantity.
Expression	Translate your verbal phrase into an algebraic expression.

Tutor

Examples

Write each phrase as an algebraic expression.

1. *eight dollars more than Ryan earned*

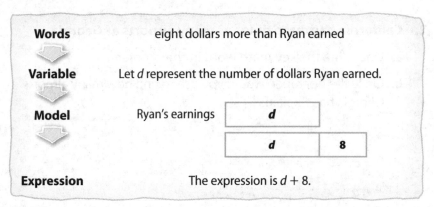

Words	eight dollars more than Ryan earned
Variable	Let *d* represent the number of dollars Ryan earned.
Model	Ryan's earnings
Expression	The expression is $d + 8$.

2. *ten dollars less than the original price*

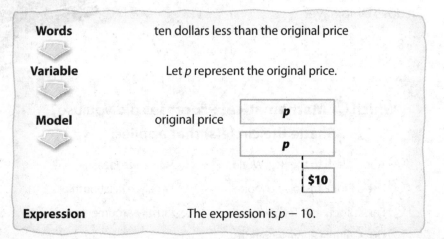

Words	ten dollars less than the original price
Variable	Let *p* represent the original price.
Model	original price
Expression	The expression is $p - 10$.

Less Than

You can write *ten more than a number* as either $10 + p$ or $p + 10$. But *ten less than a number* can only be written as $p - 10$.

3. *four times the number of gallons*

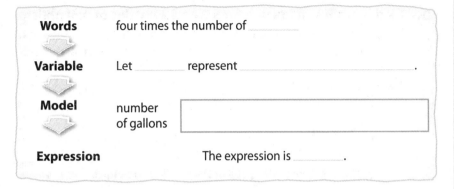

Words	four times the number of _____
Variable	Let _____ represent _____.
Model	number of gallons [_____]
Expression	The expression is _____ .

Show your work.

a. _____

Got It? Do these problems to find out.

a. four points fewer than the Bulls scored

b. 12 times the number of feet

c. the total cost of a shirt and an $8 pair of socks

b. _____

c. _____

Write Two-Step Expressions

Two-step expressions contain two different operations.

Example

Tutor

4. Write the phrase *5 less than 3 times the number of points* as an algebraic expression.

Words	5 less than 3 times the number of points
Variable	Let *p* represent the number of points.
Model	number of points

p	*p*	*p*
		5

Expression	The expression is $3p - 5$.

Got It? Do this problem to find out.

d. Write the phrase *$3 more than four times the cost of a pretzel* as an algebraic expression.

d. _____

Tutor

Example

5. Terri bought a magazine for $5, and 2 bottles of nail polish. Write an expression to represent the total amount she spent. Then find the total amount if each bottle of nail polish cost $3.

Step 1 The nail polish costs an unknown amount. Use d to represent the cost of the nail polish.

Step 2 She bought 2 bottles of polish plus a magazine.

total amount	d dollars	d dollars	$5

The expression is $2 \times d + 5$ or $2d + 5$.

$$2d + 5 = 2(3) + 5 \qquad \text{Replace } d \text{ with 3.}$$
$$= 6 + 5 \qquad \text{Multiply.}$$
$$= 11 \qquad \text{Add.}$$

So, the total amount is $11.

Guided Practice

Define a variable and write each phrase as an algebraic expression. (Examples 1–4)

1. four times more money than Elliot saved _____

2. half as many pages as George read _____

3. the width of a box that is 4 inches less than the length _____

4. the cost of 5 CDs and a $12 DVD _____

_____

5. Shoko bought a box of popcorn for $3.50 and three medium drinks. Define a variable and write an expression to represent the total amount they spent. Then find the total amount if one drink costs $1.50. (Example 5)

_____

_____

6. **Building on the Essential Question** How can writing phrases as algebraic expressions help you solve problems?

_____

_____

_____

Rate Yourself!

☐ I understand how to write algebraic expressions.

▶▶ Great! You're ready to move on!

☐ I still have some questions about writing algebraic expressions.

📖 No problem! Go online to access a Personal Tutor.

Check ✓

Independent Practice

Preparation for 6.9(A), 6.1(D) | TEKS

Define a variable and write each phrase as an algebraic expression.
(Examples 1–4)

1. six feet less than the width

_____

2. 6 hours more per week than Theodore studies

_____

3. six years less than Tracey's age

_____

4. 2 less than one-third of the points that the Panthers scored

_____

5. The United States House of Representatives has 35 more members than four times the number of members in the United States Senate. Define a variable and write an expression to represent the number of members in the House of Representatives. Then find the number of members in the House of Representatives, if there are 100 members in the Senate. (Example 5)

_____

_____

6. **MP Use Multiple Representations** Dani uses the table to help her convert measurements when she is sewing.

Number of feet	3	6	9	12
Number of yards	1	2	3	4

a. Words Describe the relationship between the number of feet and the number of yards.

_____

b. Symbols Write an expression for the number of yards in f feet.

_____

c. Numbers Determine the number of yards in 63 feet.

_____

7. **MP Analyze Relationships** An inch is equal to about 2.54 centimeters. Write an expression which estimates the number of centimeters in x inches. Then estimate the number of centimeters in 12 inches.

8. **Financial Literacy** A Euro was equal to about 1.2 American dollars on a recent day. Write an expression which estimates the number of dollars in *x* Euros.

   Then estimate the number of American dollars equal to 25 Euros. _____

9. Justin is 2 years older than one-third Marcella's age. Aimee is four years younger than 2 times Justin's age. Define a variable and write an expression to represent Justin's age. Then find Justin's age and Aimee's age if Marcella is

   63 years old. _____

10. **Find the Error** Elisa is writing an algebraic expression for the phrase *5 less than a number*. Determine her mistake and correct it.

5 − n

 H.O.T. Problems Higher-Order Thinking

11. **Analyze** Wendy earns $2 for every table she serves plus 20% of the total customer order. Define a variable and write an expression to represent the amount of money she earns for one table.

12. **Analyze** If *n* represents the amount of songs stored on an MP3 player, analyze the meaning of the expressions $n + 7$, $n - 2$, $4n$, and $n \div 2$.

13. **Create** Write a real-world situation that requires two operations. Define a variable and write an algebraic expression to represent the situation.

14. **Analyze** Which of the following algebraic expressions cannot represent the phrase *half of a number x*? _____

$$x \div 2 \qquad \frac{1}{2}x \qquad 2x \qquad 0.5x$$

Multi-Step Problem Solving

15. The cost of tickets at a movie theater is shown in the table. Write an expression to represent the total cost of tickets using the variables in the table. Then use the expression to find the total ticket cost in dollars for 2 adults, 3 children, and 1 senior.

Type of Ticket	Number of Tickets	Cost ($)
Adult	a	8
Child	c	5
Senior	s	6

  Ⓐ $a + c + s$; $6

  Ⓑ $(8 + 5 + 6)(a + c + s)$; $114

  Ⓒ $8a + 5c + 6s$; $37

  Ⓓ $8a + 5c + 6s$; $19

Use a problem-solving model to solve this problem.

1 Analyze

Read the problem. Circle the information you know.
Underline what the problem is asking you to find.

2 Plan

What will you need to do to solve the problem? Write your plan in steps.

  Step 1   Represent the situation with an expression.

  Step 2   Substitute the values given and evaluate.

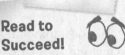

Read to Succeed!

Follow the order of operations when evaluating expressions. Multiply first then add.

3 Solve

Use your plan to solve the problem. Show your steps.

The cost of a adult tickets is ☐ , c child tickets is ☐ , and s senior tickets is ☐ .

The total for any number of tickets is ☐ + ☐ + ☐ .

So, the total for 2 adults, 3 children, and 1 senior is $8(2) + 5(3) + 6(1)$ or ☐ .

Choice ☐ is correct. Fill in that answer choice.

4 Justify and Evaluate

How do you know your solution is accurate?

_____

_____

_____

EE = Expressions, Equations, and Relationships   **MP** = Mathematical Processes

More Multi-Step Problem Solving

Use a problem-solving model to solve each problem.

16. Shelby is attending classes at a university that charges $175 per credit, plus an application fee of $45. Write an expression that represents the total cost of tuition based on the number of credits c. Then use the expression to determine the tuition amount if Shelby plans on taking 14 credits.

    Ⓐ $45c + 175$; $805

    Ⓑ $175c + 45$; $2,495

    Ⓒ $(175 + 45)c$; $3,080

    Ⓓ $\dfrac{175}{c} + 45$; $57.50

17. Michael is working on his budget and decides to allocate a percentage of each paycheck as described in the circle graph. Write an expression to determine the total amount he would deposit in the bank b. How much does he deposit if his check is $800?

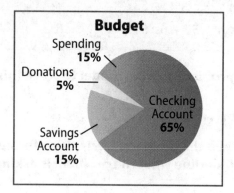

18. Brad is designing an A-frame house and needs to include angle measures on the diagram below. The sum of angles 1, 2, and 3 is 180°. The sum of angles 3 and 4 is 180°. The measure of angle 1 is 50° and the measure of angle 2 is 20°. Write an equation that can be used to find the measure of angle 4.

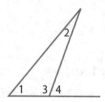

19. Write an expression to find the area of the shaded region.

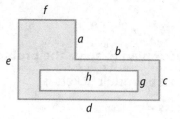

N = Number and Operations   P = Proportionality   FL = Personal Financial Literacy   EE = Expressions, Equations, and Relationships   MP = Mathematical Processes

546 **Chapter 7** Algebraic Expressions

Volleyball

At a volleyball tournament, the players lined up at the podium. Pat stood before Deirdre. Lani stood next to last. Iris stood between Melanie and Lani. Sofia stood after Daniela, and Gabrielle stood before Melanie. Kiara stood after Lani, and Deirdre stood before Daniela. Sofia stood between Daniela and Gabrielle.

In what order did the teammates stand?

Mathematical Process
6.1(B) Use a problem-solving model that incorporates analyzing given information, formulating a plan or strategy, determining a solution, justifying the solution, and evaluating the problem-solving process and the reasonableness of the solution.

Targeted TEKS 6.7(A)

Analyze *What are the facts?*

- There are 9 teammates.
- The names of the teammates are Pat, Deirdre, Lani, Iris, Melanie, Sofia, Daniela, Gabrielle, and Kiara.

Plan *What is your strategy to solve this problem?*

Act it out by using strips of paper with each name on them.

Solve *How can you apply the strategy?*

On each of 9 pieces of paper, write the name of a teammate. Based on each clue listed, arrange the strips of paper in the order in which the teammates are standing. Keep moving the names around until the order of teammates matches the clues.

Pat	Gabrielle
Deirdre	Melanie
Daniela	Iris
Sofia	Lani
	Kiara

The order that the teammates stood is _____, _____, _____, _____,

_____, _____, _____, _____, _____.

Justify and Evaluate *Does the answer make sense?*

Read through each clue to determine if the order matches.

Stand Up

A group of 32 people counted off by 1s, beginning with the number 1. Each person who counted a number that was a multiple of 2 stood up. Then the people who were seated counted off by 1s again. Each person who counted a number that was a multiple of 2 this time stood up.

How many people are still seated?

 Analyze

Read the problem. What are you being asked to find?

I need to _____.

 Plan

Choose a problem-solving strategy.

I will use the _____ strategy.

 Solve

Use your problem-solving strategy to solve the problem.

 Justify and Evaluate

Use information from the problem to check your answer.

_____

_____

_____

Multi-Step Problem Solving

Work with a small group to solve the following problems. Show your work on a separate piece of paper.

1. Teams

Twenty-four students will be divided into four equal-size teams. Each student will count off, beginning with the number 1 as the first team.

If Nate is the eleventh student to count off, to which team number will he be assigned?

2. Savings

Dakota has $5.38 in her savings account. Each week she adds $2.93.

How much money does Dakota have after 5 weeks? after n weeks?

3. Vacations

The tourism board surveyed people on their favorite vacation cities. Half of the people said Houston, $\frac{1}{4}$ said Dallas, $\frac{1}{8}$ said San Antonio, $\frac{1}{16}$ responded Corpus Christi, $\frac{1}{32}$ said Galveston, and the rest said Amarillo.

If 22 people said Amarillo, how many people responded Houston?

Birth Months		
June	July	April
March	July	June
October	May	August
June	April	October
May	October	April
September	December	January

Use any strategy!

4. School

The birth months of the students in Miss Desimio's geography class are shown.

What is the difference in the percentage of students born in June than in August? Round to the nearest whole percent.

Vocabulary Check

1. Define *powers*. Provide an example of a power with an exponent of 2.
   TEKS 6.7(A), 6.1(F)

Key Concept Check

2. Complete the graphic organizer by giving a verbal expression and drawing a model for the algebraic expression shown. **TEKS** Preparation for 6.9(A), 6.1(E)

Algebraic Expression	$x + 7$
Words	
Model	

3. **MP Analyze Relationships** Tia is 8 years younger than her sister Annette. Annette is y years old. Write an algebraic expressions that describes Tia's age.

   TEKS Preparation for 6.9(A), 6.1(B)

Multi-Step Problem Solving

4. The prices of different types of chocolates are shown. Which of the following expressions can be used to find the cost of 2 white chocolates, 3 mint chocolates, and 1 dark chocolate, all for 20% off? **EE MP**

   Ⓐ $0.20(2 \times 3.95 + 3 \times 4.25 + 1 \times 5.99)$

   Ⓑ $0.20(2 + 3.95 \times 3 + 4.25 \times 1 + 5.99)$

   Ⓒ $0.80(2 \times 3.95 + 3 \times 4.25 + 1 \times 5.99)$

   Ⓓ $0.80(2 + 3.95 \times 3 + 4.25 \times 1 + 5.99)$

Chocolate!

White Chocolate .. $3.95
Mint Chocolate..... $4.25
Dark Chocolate..... $5.99

EE = Expressions, Equations, and Relationships   **MP** = Mathematical Processes

Launch the Lesson: Real World

Angelica and Nari are baking cookies for a bake sale fundraiser. Angelica baked 6 sheets with 10 cookies each and Nari baked 10 sheets with 6 cookies each. How many cookies did each girl bake?

1. How many total cookies did Angelica bake?

6 ◯ 10 = ☐

2. How many total cookies did Nari bake?

10 ◯ 6 = ☐

3. What do you notice about your answers for Exercises 1 and 2?

_____

_____

4. What do these exercises suggest about the order in which factors are multiplied?

_____

_____

  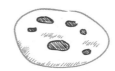

Which MP **Mathematical Processes did you use?**
Shade the circle(s) that applies.

Ⓐ Apply Math to the Real World.   Ⓔ Organize Ideas.

Ⓑ Use a Problem-Solving Model.   Ⓕ Analyze Relationships.

Ⓒ Select Tools and Techniques.   Ⓖ Justify Arguments.

Ⓓ Use Multiple Representations.

Texts Essential Knowledge and Skills

Targeted TEKS
6.7(D) Generate equivalent expressions using the properties of operations such as the inverse, identity, commutative, associative, and distributive properties.

Mathematical Processes
6.1(A), 6.1(B), 6.1(F), 6.1(G)

Vocab

Vocabulary
properties
Commutative Properties
Associative Properties
Identity Properties
Inverse Properties

Essential Question

HOW is it helpful to write numbers in different ways?

Equivalent Expressions Using Properties

Commutative Properties	The order in which two numbers are added or multiplied does not change their sum or product.

$$7 + 9 = 9 + 7 \qquad\qquad 4 \cdot 6 = 6 \cdot 4$$
$$a + b = b + a \qquad\qquad a \cdot b = b \cdot a$$

Associative Properties	The way in which three numbers are grouped when they are added or multiplied does not change their sum or product.

$$3 + (9 + 4) = (3 + 9) + 4 \qquad 8 \cdot (5 \cdot 7) = (8 \cdot 5) \cdot 7$$
$$a + (b + c) = (a + b) + c \qquad a \cdot (b \cdot c) = (a \cdot b) \cdot c$$

Identity Properties	The sum of an addend and 0 is the addend. The product of a factor and 1 is the factor.

$$13 + 0 = 13 \qquad\qquad 7 \cdot 1 = 7$$
$$a + 0 = a \qquad\qquad a \cdot 1 = a$$

Inverse Properties	The sum of an addend and its additive inverse is 0. The product of a factor and its multiplicative inverse is 1.

$$6 + (-6) = 0 \qquad\qquad 6 \cdot \frac{1}{6} = 1$$
$$a + (-a) = 0 \qquad\qquad a \cdot \frac{1}{a} = 1$$

Properties are statements that are true for any number. The expressions 6×10 and 10×6 are equivalent expressions because they have the same value.

Examples

Tutor

Determine whether the two expressions are equivalent. If so, tell what property is applied. If not, explain why.

1. $15 + (5 + 8)$ **and** $(15 + 5) + 8$

The numbers are grouped differently. They are equivalent by the Associative Property.

$$15 + (5 + 8) = 28 \qquad\qquad (15 + 5) + 8 = 28$$

Use an $=$ sign to compare the expressions.

So, $15 + (5 + 8) = (15 + 5) + 8$.

2. $(20 - 12) - 3$ **and** $20 - (12 - 3)$

The expressions are not equivalent because the Associative Property is not true for subtraction.

$$(20 - 12) - 3 = 5 \qquad\qquad 20 - (12 - 3) = 11$$

Use the $\neq$ sign to show the expressions are not equivalent.

So, $(20 - 12) - 3 \neq 20 - (12 - 3)$.

Determine whether the two expressions are equivalent. If so, identify the properties that are applied. If not, explain why.

3. **34 + 0 and 34**

The expressions are equivalent by the Identity Property.
So, $34 + 0 = 34$.

- -

4. **20 ÷ 5 and 5 ÷ 20**

The expressions are not equivalent because the Commutative Property does not hold for division.
So, $20 \div 5 \neq 5 \div 20$.

Division

The Commutative Property does not hold for division. To prove this, simplify the expressions in Example 4,

$20 \div 5 = 4$

$5 \div 20 = \frac{1}{4}$

Since 4 is not equal to $\frac{1}{4}$, expressions are not equivalent.

Show your work.

Got It? Do these problems to find out.

a. $5 \times (6 \times 3)$ and $(5 \times 6) \times 3$ **b.** $27 \div 3$ and $3 \div 27$

c. $(18 + 13) - 13$ and 18 **d.** $(2 \times 6) \times \frac{1}{6}$ and 2

a. _____

b. _____

c. _____

d. _____

Generate Equivalent Expressions

Properties can also be used to generate equivalent expressions and to solve problems.

Real World Example   Tutor

5. **In a recent season, the Kansas Jayhawks had 15 guards, 4 forwards, and 3 centers on their roster. Generate two equivalent expressions using the Associative Property that can be used to find the total number of players on their roster.**

The Associative Property states that the grouping of numbers when they are added does not change the sum, so $15 + (4 + 3)$ is equivalent to $(15 + 4) + 3$.

Got It? Do this problem to find out.

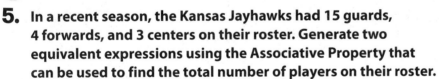

e. **Financial Literacy** Brandi earned $7 babysitting and $12 cleaning out the garage. Generate two equivalent expressions using the Commutative Property that can be used to find the total amount she earned.

e. _____

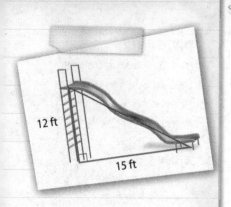

12 ft

15 ft

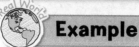 **Example**

6. The area of a triangle can be found using the expression $\frac{1}{2}bh$, where b is the base and h is the height. Use properties to find the area of the triangle shown at the left.

$$\frac{1}{2}bh = \frac{1}{2}(15)(12)$$ Replace b with 15 and h with 12.

$$= \frac{1}{2}(12)(15)$$ Commutative Property

$$= 6(15)$$ Multiply. $\frac{1}{2} \times 12 = 6$

$$= 90 \text{ square feet}$$ Multiply.

The area of the triangle is 90 square feet.

Show your work.

Got It? Do this problem to find out.

f. _____

f. **Financial Literacy** Vickie earned $6 an hour while working 11 hours over the weekend. She put $\frac{1}{3}$ of what she earned in a savings account. Find how much she put into the account.

Guided Practice

Determine whether the two expressions are equivalent. If so, tell what property is applied. If not, explain why. (Examples 1–4)

1. $(35 + 17) + 43$ and $35 + (17 + 43)$ _____

2. $(25 - 9) - 5$ and $25 - (9 - 5)$ _____

3. 59×1 and 59 _____

4. At a gymnastics meet, a gymnast scored an 8.95 on the vault and a 9.2 on the uneven bars. Generate two equivalent expressions that could be used to find her total score. (Example 5) _____

5. Nadia bought suntan lotion for $12, sunglasses for $15, and a towel for $18. Use the Associative Property to mentally find the total of her purchases. (Example 6)

_____

_____

6. **(?)** **Building on the Essential Question** How can using properties help you to generate equivalent expressions?

_____

_____

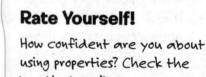

Rate Yourself!

How confident are you about using properties? Check the box that applies.

Find out online. Use the Self-Check Quiz.

Check ✓

Independent Practice

6.7(D), 6.1(F)

Determine whether the two expressions are equivalent. If so, tell what property is applied. If not, explain why. (Examples 1–4)

1. $(8 + 27) + 52$ and $8 + (27 + 52)$ _____

_____

2. $(3 \cdot 6) \cdot 9$ and $3 \cdot (6 \cdot 9)$ _____

_____

3. $72 - (63 - 8)$ and $(72 - 63) - 8$ _____

_____

4. $36 \div (12 \div 3)$ and $(36 \div 12) \div 3$ _____

_____

5. $0 + 32$ and 0 _____

_____

6. **STEM** Find the perimeter of the triangle shown using the Associative Property. (Example 6)

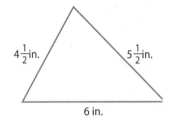

$4\frac{1}{2}$ in. $5\frac{1}{2}$ in.

6 in.

7. Each day, about 75,000 people visit Paris, France. Use the Commutative Property to generate two equivalent expressions that could be used to find the number of people that visit over a 5-day period. (Example 5)

_____

_____

Use one or more properties to rewrite each expression as an equivalent expression that does not use parentheses.

8. $(y + 1) + 4 =$ _____

9. $(8 \cdot r) \cdot \frac{1}{8} =$ _____

Determine the value of x that makes a true statement.

10. $24 + x = 24$ _____

11. $17 + x = 3 + 17$ _____

12. **MP Analyze Relationships** The graphic shows the driving distance between certain cities in Florida.

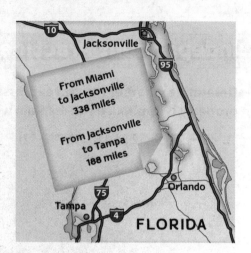

a. Write a number sentence that compares the mileage from Miami to Jacksonville to Tampa, and the mileage from Tampa to Jacksonville to Miami.

_____

_____

b. Refer to part a. Name the property that is illustrated by this sentence.

_____

_____

H.O.T. Problems Higher-Order Thinking

13. **Create** Write two equivalent expressions that illustrate the Associative Property of Addition.

_____

_____

14. **Evaluate** Determine whether $(18 + 35) \times 4 = 18 + 35 \times 4$ is *true* or *false*. Explain.

_____

_____

_____

15. **Analyze** A *counterexample* is an example showing that a statement is not true. Provide a counterexample to the following statement.

Division of whole numbers is commutative.

_____

_____

16. **Analyze** Do $(4 + 9) + 5 = (9 + 4) + 5$ and $(4 + 9) + 5 = 4 + (9 + 5)$ illustrate the same property? Justify your response.

_____

_____

_____

17. **Evaluate** How can the Associative Property be used to mentally find $48 + 82$?

_____

_____

Multi-Step Problem Solving

18. Marla calculated the sum $1 + 2 + 3 + 4 + 5 + \ldots + 12 + 13 + 14$ by performing the additions shown in the table and then multiplying 15×7. What property did Marla use to make the addition problem easier to compute? **EE** **MP**

Addends	Sum
1 + 14	15
2 + 13	15
3 + 12	15
4 + 11	15
5 + 10	15
6 + 9	15
7 + 8	15

(A) Commutative Property of Addition

(B) Commutative Property of Multiplication

(C) Associative Property of Addition

(D) Associative Property of Multiplication

Use a problem-solving model to solve this problem.

1 Analyze

Read the problem. Circle the information you know.
Underline what the problem is asking you to find.

2 Plan

What will you need to do to solve the problem? Write your plan in steps.

Step 1 Determine the pattern shown in the table.

Step 2 Determine the property used.

Read to Succeed!

The Commutative Property says the order in which two numbers are added or multiplied does not matter. The Associative Property says the grouping of the numbers when added or multiplied does not matter.

3 Solve

Use your plan to solve the problem. Show your steps.
When Marla reordered the addends, she used the first and last, second and second-to-last addend, and so on. When reordering the addends, she used the Commutative Property of Addition.

So, choice ____ is correct. Fill in that answer choice.

4 Justify and Evaluate

How do you know your solution is accurate?

_____

_____

_____

EE = Expressions, Equations, and Relationships   **MP** = Mathematical Processes

More Multi-Step Problem Solving

Use a problem-solving model to solve each problem.

19. The table shows the number of students that chose different sports based on gender. Kevin wants to determine the total number of boys surveyed. Which of the following expressions uses the Associative Property to help him mentally determine the sum? **EE** **MP**

Sport	Number of Girls	Number of Boys
Basketball	14	11
Football	2	19
Lacrosse	7	5
Soccer	13	12
Swimming	12	13

- Ⓐ $14 + 2 + 7 + 13 + 12$
- Ⓑ $(11 + 19) + [5 + (12 + 13)]$
- Ⓒ $(11 + 5) + (19 + 12 + 13)$
- Ⓓ $2(13) + 2(12)$

20. The table shows pairs of equivalent expressions. Which expression does not model one of the different properties of number operations? **N** **EE** **MP**

$9 + 7 = 7 + 9$	$9 + 0 = 9$
$10 + 10 = 5 + 15$	$(8 + 6) + 0 = 8 + (6 + 0)$
$0 \times 8 = 8 \times 0$	$8 \times 1 = 8$

21. Four students were each given 48 blocks to arrange to make a rectangular prism. For two of these students, the length and width model the Commutative Property. What is the product of the length and width that they used? **N** **EE** **MP**

Student	Length	Width	Height
Lucy	12	4	1
Jose	4	4	3
Maria	3	4	4
Tony	4	12	1

22. How could you use the Commutative and Associative Properties to quickly find the value of the expression $28 + (9^2 + 72)$? **N** **EE** **MP**

The Distributive Property

Launch the Lesson: Real World

 TEKS

Texas Essential Knowledge and Skills

Targeted TEKS
6.7(D) Generate equivalent expressions using the properties of operations such as the inverse, identity, commutative, associative, and distributive properties.

Mathematical Processes
6.1(A), 6.1(B), 6.1(F), 6.1(G)

Three friends went to a baseball game. Each ticket cost $20 and all three friends bought a baseball hat for $15 each. How can I find the total spent using two different ways?

1. What does the expression $3(20 + 15)$ represent?

3 represents: _____

20 represents: _____

15 represents: _____

2. Evaluate the expression in Exercise 1.

$(20 + 15) = \boxed{}$

$\boxed{} \times \boxed{} = \boxed{}$

3. What does the expression $3 \times 20 + 3 \times 15$ represent?

3×20 represents: _____

3×15 represents: _____

4. Evaluate the expression $3 \times 20 + 3 \times 15$.

$3 \times 20 = \boxed{}$

$3 \times 15 = \boxed{}$

$\boxed{} + \boxed{} = \boxed{}$

5. What do you notice about the answers to Exercises 2 and 4?

_____

_____

Vocabulary

Distributive Property
factor the expression

Essential Question

HOW is it helpful to write numbers in different ways?

Which MP Mathematical Processes did you use? Shade the circle(s) that applies.

Ⓐ Apply Math to the Real World.

Ⓑ Use a Problem-Solving Model.

Ⓒ Select Tools and Techniques.

Ⓓ Use Multiple Representations.

Ⓔ Organize Ideas.

Ⓕ Analyze Relationships.

Ⓖ Justify Arguments.

Distributive Property

Words	To multiply a sum by a number, multiply each addend by the number outside the parentheses.

Example	Numbers	Algebra
	$2(7 + 4) = 2 \times 7 + 2 \times 4$	$a(b + c) = ab + ac$

Work Zone

The expressions $3(20 + 15)$ and $3 \times 20 + 3 \times 15$ show how the **Distributive Property** combines addition and multiplication.

Tutor

Example

1. Determine $9 \times 4\frac{1}{3}$ mentally using the Distributive Property.

$$9 \times 4\frac{1}{3} = 9\left(4 + \frac{1}{3}\right) \qquad \text{Write } 4\frac{1}{3} \text{ as } 4 + \frac{1}{3}.$$

$$= 9(4) + 9\left(\frac{1}{3}\right) \qquad \text{Distributive Property}$$

$$= 36 + 3 \qquad \text{Multiply.}$$

$$= 39 \qquad \text{Add.}$$

Show your work.

Got It? Do these problems to find out.

a. _____

Determine each product mentally. Show the steps you used.

   a. $5 \times 2\frac{3}{5}$ **b.** $12 \times 2\frac{1}{4}$ **c.** 2×3.6

b. _____

c. _____

Tools Tutor

Example

2. Generate an expression equivalent to $2(x + 3)$ using the Distributive Property.

$$2(x + 3) = 2(x) + 2(3) \qquad \text{Distributive Property}$$

$$= 2x + 6 \qquad \text{Multiply.}$$

d. _____

Got It? Do these problems to find out.

e. _____

Generate an equivalent expression using the Distributive Property.

   d. $8(x + 3)$ **e.** $5(9 + x)$ **f.** $2(x + 3)$

f. _____

Tutor

Example

3. **Fran is making a pair of earrings and a bracelet for four friends. Each pair of earrings uses 4.5 centimeters of wire and each bracelet uses 13 centimeters. Generate two equivalent expressions and then find how much total wire is needed.**

Using the Distributive Property, 4(4.5) + 4(13) and 4(4.5 + 13) are equivalent expressions.

$$4(4.5) + 4(13) = 18 + 52 \qquad 4(4.5 + 13) = 4(17.5)$$
$$= 70 \qquad\qquad\qquad = 70$$

So, Fran needs 70 centimeters of wire.

Got It? Do this problem to find out.

Show your work.

g. Each day, Martin lifts weights for 10 minutes and runs on the treadmill for 25 minutes. Generate two equivalent expressions and then find the total minutes that Martin exercises in 7 days.

g. _____

Factor an Expression

When numeric or algebraic expressions are written as a product of their factors, the process is called **factoring the expression**.

Tutor

Example

4. **Factor 12 + 8 to generate an equivalent expression.**

$$12 = \boxed{2} \cdot \boxed{2} \cdot 3$$ Write the prime factorization of 12 and 8.
$$8 = \boxed{2} \cdot \boxed{2} \cdot 2$$ Circle the common factors.

The GCF of 12 and 8 is 2 · 2 or 4.

Write each term as a product of the GCF and its remaining factor. Then use the Distributive Property to *factor out* the GCF.

$$12 + 8 = \mathbf{4}(3) + \mathbf{4}(2)$$ Rewrite each term using the GCF.
$$= \mathbf{4}(3 + 2)$$ Distributive Property

So, 12 + 8 = 4(3 + 2).

> **Prime Factorization**
>
> The prime factorization of an algebraic expression contains both the prime factors and any variable factors. For example, the prime factorization of 6x is 2 · 3 · x.

Got It? Do these problems to find out.

Factor each expression to generate an equivalent expression.

h. 9 + 21   **i.** 14 + 28   **j.** 80 + 56

h. _____

i. _____

j. _____

Example

5. Factor $3x + 15$ to generate an equivalent expression.

$3x = \boxed{3} \cdot x$ Write the prime fractorization of 15 and $3x$.

$15 = \boxed{3} \cdot 5$ Circle the common factors.

The GCF of $3x$ and 15 is 3.

$3x + 15 = 3(x) + 3(5)$ Rewrite each term using the GCF.

$= 3(x + 5)$ Distributive Property

So, $3(x + 5) = 3x + 15$.

Show your work.

k. _____

l. _____

m. _____

Got It? Do these problems to find out.

Factor each expression to generate an equivalent expression.

k. $16 + 4x$ **l.** $7x + 42$ **m.** $36x + 30$

Guided Practice

1. Determine $9 \times 8\frac{2}{3}$ mentally. Show the steps you used. (Example 1) _____

Generate an equivalent expression using the Distributive Property. (Example 2)

2. $3(x + 1) =$ _____   **3.** $5(x + 8) =$ _____   **4.** $4(x + 6) =$ _____

Show your work.

Factor each expression to generate an equivalent expression. (Examples 4 and 5)

5. $25 + 60 =$ _____   **6.** $4x + 40 =$ _____

7. Financial Literacy Six friends are going to the state fair. The cost of one admission is $9.50, and the cost for one ride on the Ferris wheel is $1.50. Generate two equivalent expressions and then determine the total cost. (Example 3)

_____

_____

8. **Building on the Essential Question** How can the Distributive Property help you to generate equivalent

expressions? _____

_____

_____

Rate Yourself!

How well do you understand the Distributive Property? Circle the image that applies.

Clear   Somewhat Clear   Not So Clear

Find out online. Use the Self-Check Quiz.

Check ✓

Independent Practice

6.7(D), 6.1(D), 6.1(F)

Determine each product mentally. Show the steps you used. (Example 1)

1. $9 \times 44 =$

2. $4 \times 5\frac{1}{8} =$

3. $7 \times 3.8 =$

Show your work. ➡

_____

Generate an equivalent expression using the Distributive Property. (Example 2)

4. $8(x + 7) =$ _____

5. $6(11 + x) =$ _____

6. $8(x + 1) =$ _____

7. **MP Analyze Relationships** A coyote can run up to 43 miles per hour while a rabbit can run up to 35 miles per hour. Generate two equivalent expressions and then determine how many more miles a coyote can run in six hours than a rabbit at these rates. (Example 3)

_____

_____

Factor each expression to generate an equivalent expression. (Examples 4 and 5)

8. $8 + 16 =$ _____

9. $54 + 24 =$ _____

10. $63 + 81 =$ _____

11. $11x + 55 =$ _____

12. $32 + 16x =$ _____

13. $77x + 21 =$ _____

14. **MP Analyze Relationships** A video game costs $29.35 at one store and $32.79 at another store. Generate two equivalent expressions and then find how much more 4 video games cost at the second store.

_____

15. **MP** **Apply Math to the Real World** Refer to the graphic novel frame below for Exercises a–b.

	Cost
Admission	
Adults (ages 19+)	$12.50
Youth (ages 2-18)	$7.50
Admission and Movie Pass	**Cost**
Adults (ages 19+)	$18.50
Youth (ages 2-18)	$13.50
Family Night Prices	**Cost**
(After 5 P.M. on Friday)	
Individual Admission (all ages)	$7.00
Individual Movie Pass (all ages)	$7.50

I wonder what's the cheapest.

a. Generate two equivalent expressions that demonstrate the Distributive Property for the cost of *x* tickets for admission and movie passes on Family Night. _____

b. Is it less expensive for a youth to pay regular admission with a movie pass or go on Family Night? Explain. _____

🔥 H.O.T. Problems   Higher-Order Thinking

16. Analyze Evaluate the expression 0.1(3.7) mentally. Justify your response using the Distributive Property. _____

17. Create Generate two equivalent expressions involving decimals that illustrate the Distributive Property. _____

18. Evaluate A friend rewrote the expression 5(x + 2) as 5x + 2. Write a few sentences to your friend explaining the error. Then, rewrite the expression 5(x + 2) correctly. _____

19. Evaluate Explain why 3(5x) does not equal (3 · 5)(3 · x). _____

Name _____

Multi-Step Problem Solving

20. Wen is buying bottles of apple juice and wants to mentally calculate how much they will cost. He buys 5 bottles of juice at $2.15 each. Which of the following shows equivalent expressions using the Distributive Property? How much change will he receive from $20? **EE** **MP**

Ⓐ $5(2.15) = 5(2) + 0.15$; $10.75

Ⓑ $5(2.15) = 5(2) - 0.15$; $9.25

Ⓒ $5(2.15) = 5(2) + 5(0.15)$; $9.25

Ⓓ $5(2.15) = 5(2) - 5(0.15)$; $10.75

Use a problem-solving model to solve this problem.

1 Analyze

Read the problem. Circle the information you know.
Underline what the problem is asking you to find.

2 Plan

What will you need to do to solve the problem? Write your plan in steps.

Step 1   Generate equivalent expressions using the Distributive Property.

Step 2   Determine the total spent and subtract from $20 to find the change he will receive.

3 Solve

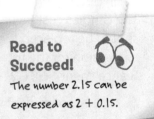

Read to Succeed!
The number 2.15 can be expressed as 2 + 0.15.

Use your plan to solve the problem. Show your steps.

Five bottles of apple juice will cost 5(⬚). An equivalent

expression, using the Distributive Property, is $5(2) + 5(0.15)$.

The total spent would be $⬚. Wen will receive $20.00 − $⬚ or

$⬚ in change.

So, choice ⬚ is correct. Fill in that answer choice.

4 Justify and Evaluate

How do you know your solution is accurate?

_____

_____

More Multi-Step Problem Solving

Use a problem-solving model to solve each problem.

21. Cole is connecting 3 benches to make one long bench. Each bench has a length of $5\frac{1}{2}$ feet. Which of the following show equivalent expressions using the Distributive Property?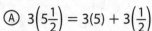

Ⓐ $3\left(5\frac{1}{2}\right) = 3(5) + 3\left(\frac{1}{2}\right)$

Ⓑ $3\left(5\frac{1}{2}\right) = 3(5) - 3\left(\frac{1}{2}\right)$

Ⓒ $3\left(5\frac{1}{2}\right) = 3(5) + \left(\frac{1}{2}\right)$

Ⓓ $3\left(5\frac{1}{2}\right) = 5(3) + 5\left(\frac{1}{2}\right)$

22. The total area of two rectangles can be calculated using different methods. What number can be substituted for x so that each expression will show the total area of the two rectangles? **EE** **MP**

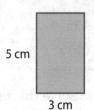
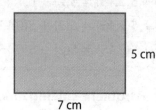

5 cm   5 cm

3 cm   7 cm

$$x(3 + 7) = x(3) + x(7)$$

23. Elijah bought 5 more candles, c, than Bianca. The candles cost $2 each. What number should be replaced for x to give an equivalent expression for the total amount Elijah and Bianca spent? **EE** **MP**

$$2c + 2(c + 5) = xc + 10$$

24. Corbin needs to buy 8 notebooks that cost $3.75 each. Two friends show a shortcut for mentally calculating the total price. Evaluate each student's method. **EE** **MP**

Juanita	$8(3 + 0.75)$
Joe	$8(4 - 0.25)$

INQUIRY HOW can I use multiple representations to determine if two expressions are equivalent?

Derrick and his friends bought tickets for the dirt bike rally. The cost of each ticket was x dollars. Derrick bought 2 tickets on Saturday and 3 tickets on Sunday. They paid $4 for parking. The expression $2x + 4 + 3x$ represents the total cost in dollars of the dirt bike rally.

Texas Essential Knowledge and Skills

Targeted TEKS
6.7(C) Determine if two expressions are equivalent using concrete models, pictorial models, and algebraic representations. *Also addresses: 6.7(A), 6.7(D).*

Mathematical Processes
6.1(C), 6.1(D), 6.1(E), 6.1(F), 6.1(G)

Hands-On Activity

Tools

You can use concrete models and algebraic representations to determine equivalent expressions.

Generate an expression equivalent to $2x + 4 + 3x$ using algebra tiles.

Step 1 Choose tiles to represent each addend. Use ☐ x-tiles to model $2x$, ☐ 1-tiles to model 4, and ☐ x-tiles to model $3x$.

Step 2 Find the like terms, or the terms that are similar. The like terms are ☐ and ☐ because they are both x-tiles. There are a total of ☐ x-tiles and four 1-tiles.

Step 3 Draw the algebra tiles in the space at the right, placing all like terms together.

Step 4 Generate an equivalent expression using addition to combine the like terms. Add $2x$ and $3x$.

So, $2x + 4 + 3x =$ ☐ $+$ ☐ .

Rearrange the algebra tiles to determine if $2x + 4 + 3x$ is equivalent to $4x + x + 4$.

Are they equivalent expressions? _____

Investigate

Work with a partner. Generate an equivalent expression using algebra tiles. Draw algebra tile models to represent each expression.

1. $x + 4x + x =$ _____

2. $4x + 7 + 2x =$ _____

3. $2(x + 2) =$ _____

4. Determine if the expressions $x + 1 + 3x$ and $4x + 1$ are equivalent using algebra tiles and algebraic representations. Draw your algebra tiles below. _____

On Your Own

Create

5. **MP Select Tools and Techniques** Maggie is x years old. Her brother Demarco is 4 years older than her. Anna is 3 times as old as Demarco. Generate two equivalent expressions that represent Anna's age. Explain.

_____

_____

_____

6. **INQUIRY** HOW can I use multiple representations to determine if two expressions are equivalent?

_____

_____

_____

Simplify Expressions

Texas Essential Knowledge and Skills

Targeted TEKS
6.7(D) Generate equivalent expressions using the properties of operations such as the inverse, identity, commutative, associative, and distributive properties.

Mathematical Processes
6.1(A), 6.1(B), 6.1(F), 6.1(G)

 Launch the Lesson: Vocabulary

When addition or subtraction signs separate an algebraic expression into parts, each part is called a **term**. The numerical factor of a term that contains a variable is called the **coefficient**. A term without a variable is called a **constant**. **Like terms** are terms that contain the same variables, such as x, $2x$, and $3x$.

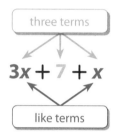

three terms

The three terms are $3x$, 7, and x.

$$3x + 7 + x$$

The terms $3x$ and x are like terms because they have the same variable, x.

like terms

The constant is 7.

Label the graphic organizer below.

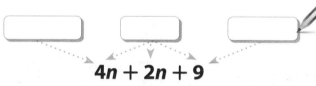

$$4n + 2n + 9$$

Vocabulary

term
coefficient
constant
like terms

Essential Question

HOW is it helpful to write numbers in different ways?

 Real-World Investigation

Andrew's mother gave him a computer game and $10 for his birthday. His aunt gave him two computer games and $5. The expression $x + 10 + 2x + 5$, where x represents the cost of each game, can be used to represent Andrew's birthday gifts.

1. What is the coefficient of the term $2x$? ☐

2. How many terms are in the expression $x + 10 + 2x + 5$? ☐

Which MP Mathematical Processes did you use?
Shade the circle(s) that applies.

Ⓐ Apply Math to the Real World.   Ⓔ Organize Ideas.

Ⓑ Use a Problem-Solving Model.   Ⓕ Analyze Relationships.

Ⓒ Select Tools and Techniques.   Ⓖ Justify Arguments.

Ⓓ Use Multiple Representations.

Simplify Expressions with One Variable

To simplify an algebraic expression, use properties to generate an equivalent expression that has no like terms and no parentheses.

Numbers	Variables
$3 + 3 = 2(3)$ or 6	$x + x = 2x$

Tutor

Example

1. **Simplify the expression $-4(6x)$.**

$$-4(6x) = -4 \cdot (6 \cdot x) \qquad \text{Parentheses indicate multiplication.}$$
$$= (-4 \cdot 6) \cdot x \qquad \text{Associative Property}$$
$$= -24x \qquad \text{Multiply } -4 \text{ and } 6.$$

 Show your work.

Got It? Do these problems to find out.

Simplify each expression.

a. _____

b. _____

    a. $(3 \cdot x) \cdot 11$ **b.** $x + x + x$ **c.** $7x + 8 + x$

c. _____

 Real World

Example

Tutor

2. **Three friends will pay \$$x$ each for admission to the museum plus \$1 each to view the mummy exhibit. A fourth friend will pay admission but will not view the mummy exhibit. Write and simplify an expression that represents the total cost.**

The expression $3(x + 1) + x$ represents the total cost.

cost of admission and exhibit for three friends — cost of admission for the fourth friend

$$3(x + 1) + x = 3x + 3 + x \qquad \text{Distributive Property}$$
$$= 3x + x + 3 \qquad \text{Commutative Property}$$
$$= 4x + 3 \qquad \text{Combine like terms.}$$

So, the total cost is \$$4x$ + \$3.

Got It? Do this problem to find out.

d. _____

    d. Write and simplify an expression for the total cost of six friends to go to the museum if only four friends view the mummy exhibit.

Simplify Expressions with Two Variables

Properties can be used to simplify or to factor expressions with two variables.

Compare the effects of operations on numbers to the effects of operations on variables.

Numbers	Variables
$3 + 3 + 4 = 2(3) + 4$	$x + x + y = 2x + y$

Examples

Tutor

3. **Simplify the expression $(14y + x) + 22y$.**

$$
\begin{aligned}
(14y + x) + 22y &= (x + 14y) + 22y && \text{Commutative Property} \\
&= x + (14y + 22y) && \text{Associative Property} \\
&= x + 36y && \text{Combine like terms.}
\end{aligned}
$$

4. **Simplify $4(2x + y)$ using the Distributive Property.**

$$
\begin{aligned}
4(2x + y) &= 4(2x) + 4(y) && \text{Distributive Property} \\
&= 8x + 4y && \text{Multiply.}
\end{aligned}
$$

5. **Factor $27x + 18y$.**

Step 1 Find the GCF of $27x$ and $18y$.

$27x = 3 \cdot ③ \cdot ③ \cdot x$ Write the prime factorization of $27x$ and $18y$.
$18y = 2 \cdot ③ \cdot ③ \cdot y$ Circle the common factors.

The GCF of $27x$ and $18y$ is $3 \cdot 3$ or 9.

Step 2 Write each term as a product of the GCF and its remaining factors. Then use the Distributive Property to *factor out* the GCF.

$$
\begin{aligned}
27x + 18y &= 9(3x) + 9(2y) && \text{Rewrite each term using the GCF.} \\
&= 9(3x + 2y) && \text{Distributive Property}
\end{aligned}
$$

Got It? Do these problems to find out.

e. Simplify $3x + 9y + 2x$.

f. Simplify $7(3x + y)$.

g. Factor $12x + 8y$.

Show your work.

e. _____

f. _____

g. _____

Example

Tutor

6. The farmer's market sells fruit baskets. Each basket has 3 apples and 1 pear. Use *a* to represent the cost of each apple and *p* to represent the cost of each pear. Write and simplify an expression that represents the total cost of 5 baskets.

Use the expression $3a + p$ to represent the cost of each basket.

Use $5(3a + p)$ to represent the cost of 5 baskets.

Use the Distributive Property to rewrite $5(3a + p)$.

$5(3a + p) = 5(3a) + 5(p)$ Distributive Property

$\qquad\qquad = 15a + 5p$ Multiply.

So, the total cost of five baskets is $15a + 5p$.

Guided Practice

Simplify each expression. (Examples 1, 3, and 4)

Show your work.

1. $5(6x) = $ _____

2. $2x + 5y + 7x = $ _____

3. $4(2x + 5y) = $ _____

4. Factor $35x + 28y$. (Example 5) _____

5. Mikayla bought five skirts at \$*x* each. Three of the five skirts came with a matching top for an additional \$9 each. Write and simplify an expression that represents the total cost of her purchase. (Example 2)

_____

6. The gift bag from Claire Cosmetics includes 5 bottles of nail polish and 2 tubes of lip gloss. Use *p* to represent the cost of each bottle of nail polish and *g* to represent the cost of each tube of lip gloss. Write and simplify an expression that represents the total cost of 8 gift bags. (Example 6)

_____

7. **(?)** **Building on the Essential Question** How can properties help to generate equivalent algebraic expressions?

_____

_____

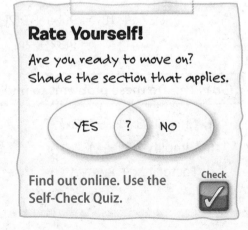

Rate Yourself!

Are you ready to move on?
Shade the section that applies.

YES   ?   NO

Find out online. Use the Self-Check Quiz.

Check ✓

Independent Practice

6.7(D), 6.1(C) TEKS

Simplify each expression. (Examples 1, 3, and 4)

1. $x + 4x + 6x =$ _____

Show your work.

2. $3x + 4x + 5x =$ _____

3. $-9(5x) =$ _____

4. $3x + 8y + 13x =$ _____

5. $7(3x + 5y) =$ _____

6. $3x + 6x + 2x =$ _____

Factor each expression. (Example 5)

7. $24x + 18y =$ _____

8. $16x + 40y =$ _____

9. Eight friends went to a hockey game. The price of admission per person was $x. Four of the friends paid an extra $6 each for a player guide book. Write and simplify an expression that represents the total cost. (Example 2)

10. Gabriella is x years old. Her sister, Felicia, is six years older than she is. Their mother is twice as old as Felicia. Their aunt, Tanya, is x years older than their mother. Write and simplify an expression that represents Tanya's age in years. (Example 2)

11. A DVD box set includes 3 thriller movies and 2 comedies. Use t to represent the cost of each thriller and c to represent the cost of each comedy. Write and simplify an expression that represents the total cost of 6 box sets. (Example 6)

12. A fall candle gift set has 4 vanilla candles and 6 pumpkin spice candles. Use v to represent the cost of each vanilla candle and p to represent the cost of each pumpkin candle. Write and simplify an expression that represents the total cost of 4 sets. (Example 6)

Determine the value of *y* that makes each equation true for all values of *x*.

13. $3x + 6x = yx$ _____

14. $x + 5 + 11x = 12x + y$ _____

15. MP **Select Tools and Techniques** Pizza Palace charges $*x* for a large cheese pizza and an additional fee based on the number of toppings ordered.

Pizza Palace Prices	
Pizza	**Price ($)**
large cheese	*x*
add 1 topping	add $0.75
add 2 toppings	add $1.50
add 3 toppings	add $2.25
add 4 toppings	add $3.00

   a. Two large cheese pizzas and three large pepperoni pizzas are ordered. Write and simplify an expression that represents the total cost. _____

   b. Write and simplify an expression that represents the total cost of eight large pizzas, if two are cheese and six have four toppings each.

   _____

   c. Elsa orders three large cheese pizzas, a large pepperoni and mushroom pizza, and a large green pepper and onion pizza. Write and simplify an expression that represents the total cost.

   _____

H.O.T. Problems Higher-Order Thinking

16. Create Generate an expression that, when simplified, is equivalent to 15*x* + 7. _____

17. Analyze Explain why the expressions $y + y + y$ and $3y$ are equivalent.

_____

_____

Analyze For Exercises 18 and 19, simplify each expression.

18. $7x + 5(x + 3) + 4x - x - 2$ _____

19. $6 + 2(x - 8) + 3x - 11 + x$ _____

20. Analyze The algebraic expression shown below is missing two whole-number constants. Determine the constants so that the expression simplifies to 14*x* + 11. _____

$$4x + 8(x + \blacksquare) + \blacksquare + 2x$$

Multi-Step Problem Solving

21. When buying frozen yogurt, there are many choices for the toppings. Which simplified expression represents the price of 2 cones with fruit and 3 cones with candy and syrup? **EE MP**

(A) $5x + 2.25$

(B) $5x + 5.75$

(C) $2x + 2$

(D) $2x + 4.50$

Frozen Yogurt	Price ($)
Cone	x
Candy Topping	add $0.75
Syrup Topping	add $0.50
Fruit Topping	add $1.00

Use a problem-solving model to solve this problem.

1 Analyze

Read the problem. Circle the information you know. Underline what the problem is asking you to find.

2 Plan

What will you need to do to solve the problem? Write your plan in steps.

Step 1   Determine the expressions for each type of cone.

Step 2   Combine like terms to simplify the expressions.

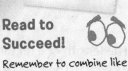

Read to Succeed!
Remember to combine like terms when simplifying expressions. Like terms have the same variable.

3 Solve

Use your plan to solve the problem. Show your steps.

Two cones with fruit: $2(x + 1.00) = \boxed{} + \boxed{}$

Three cones with candy and syrup: $3(x + 0.75 + 0.50) = \boxed{} + \boxed{}$

Adding the two expressions and simplifying results in $\boxed{} + \boxed{}$.

Choice $\boxed{}$ is correct. Fill in that answer choice.

4 Justify and Evaluate

How do you know your solution is accurate?

_____

_____

_____

EE = Expressions, Equations, and Relationships   **MP** = Mathematical Processes

More Multi-Step Problem Solving

Use a problem-solving model to solve each problem.

22. At a taco stand, chicken tacos are available with a choice of 3 different toppings. Which simplified expression represents the price of 2 tacos with cheese and lettuce, and 1 taco with cheese, lettuce, and sour cream?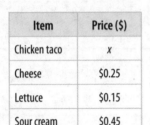

Item	Price ($)
Chicken taco	x
Cheese	$0.25
Lettuce	$0.15
Sour cream	$0.45

Ⓐ $2x + 0.40$

Ⓑ $3x + 1.25$

Ⓒ $3x + 1.65$

Ⓓ $3x + 2.55$

23. Treven and Dylan each bought fruit at the market. Treven bought 3 pears and 7 apples. Dylan bought 4 pears and 9 apples and spent $3.00 on oranges. If p represents the cost of each pear and a represents the cost of each apple, the expression below represents the total cost. What is the value of x? **EE MP**

$$xp + 16a + 3$$

24. The length of a rectangle is x feet more than its width. The area of the rectangle is $5x + 25$. What is the width of the rectangle? **EE MP**

25. Julian asked x students about their favorite color, and displayed the results in the circle graph. Claire thinks that the same number of people voted for orange and red as did green and purple. Write three equal expressions that show that she is correct. **EE P MP**

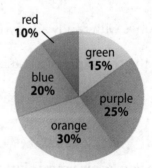

N = Number and Operations   **P** = Proportionality   **EE** = Expressions, Equations, and Relationships   **MP** = Mathematical Processes

576   **Chapter 7** Algebraic Expressions

Water Slide Engineer

Do you love riding the twisting, plunging slides at water parks? Do you have ideas to make them more fun and exciting? If so, you should think about a career designing water slides! Water slide engineers apply engineering principles, the newest technology, and creativity to design water slides that are both innovative and safe. These engineers design the winding flumes that riders slide down and the pumping systems that allow the slides to have the appropriate flow of water.

Mathematical Process
6.1(A) Apply mathematics to problems arising in everyday life, society, and the workplace.
Targeted TEKS 6.7(D)

Is This the Career for You?

Are you interested in a career as a water slide engineer? Take some of the following courses in high school.

◆ Algebra
◆ Computer-Aided Drafting
◆ Engineering Calculus
◆ Engineering Technology
◆ Physics

Explore college and careers at ccr.mcgraw-hill.com

It's a Slippery Ride!

Use the information in the table to solve each problem.

1. The table shows the relationship between the number of minutes and the gallons of water pumped out on The Black Hole. Generate an expression to determine the number of gallons pumped out for any number of minutes.

Number of Minutes (*m*)	Water Pumped Out (*g*)
3	3,000
6	6,000
9	9,000

2. Refer to the fact about Big Thunder. Define a variable. Then generate an expression that could be used to find the number of feet that riders travel in any number of seconds.

3. Generate two equivalent expressions that could be used to find the number of gallons of water pumped out of the Crush 'n' Gusher after 90 seconds. Then determine the number of gallons pumped in 90 seconds.

4. Explain how you could use the Distributive Property to find how many gallons of water are pumped out of The Black Hole in $2\frac{1}{2}$ minutes.

Water Slides	
Water Slide, Park	**Fact**
Big Thunder, Rapids Water Park	At the steepest drop, riders travel about 30 feet per second.
The Black Hole, Wet 'n Wild	Riders plummet 500 feet as water is pumped out at 1,000 gallons per minute.
Crush 'n' Gusher, Typhoon Lagoon	The water jet nozzle on each slide pumps out about 23 gallons of water per second.
Gulf Scream, Adventure Island	Riders hurl down a 210-foot slide at 25 miles per hour.

 **Career Project**

It's time to update your career portfolio!
Find three water slides in your state. Use a spreadsheet to compare several features of the slides, such as the longest drop, total length, and gallons of water pumped. Describe how you, as a water slide engineer, would have designed the slides differently. Prepare a brief oral presentation and present it to your classmates. As others are presenting, listen carefully to their presentations. At the end, ask any clarifying questions.

List several challenges associated with this career.

Chapter Review

Vocabulary Check

Work with a partner to complete the crossword puzzle using the vocabulary list at the beginning of the chapter. Seek clarification of each term as needed.

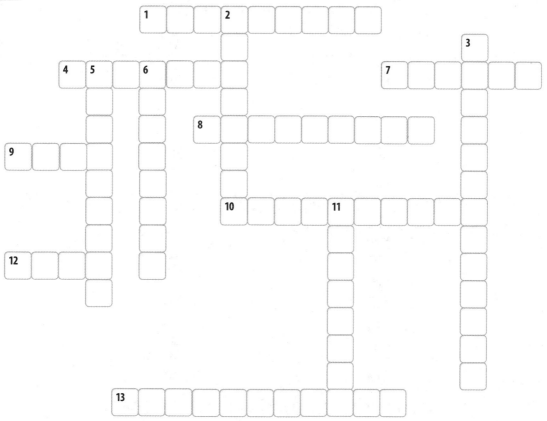

Across

1. an expression which combines variables, numbers, and at least one operation
4. a mathematical language of symbols, including variables
7. numbers expressed using exponents
8. an expression which combines numbers and operations
9. in a power, the number used as a factor
10. expressions that have the same value
12. each part of an algebraic expression separated by a plus or minus sign
13. the numerical factor of a term that contains a variable

Down

2. to find the value of an algebraic expression
3. number with a square root that is a whole number
5. terms that contain the same variables to the same power
6. in a power, the number that tells how many times the base is used as a factor
11. a symbol used to represent a number

Use Your FOLDABLES

Use your Foldable to help review the chapter. Share your Foldable with a partner and take turns summarizing what you learned in this chapter, while the other partner listens carefully. Seek clarification of any concepts, as needed. **TEKS** 6.1(E)

Tape here

Tab 1	Properties of Addition	
Example	Example	Example
Write About It	Write About It	Write About It
Tab 2	Properties of Multiplication	

Tape here

Got it?

Match each expression with the equivalent expression. **TEKS** 6.7(D)

1. $2(6x + 6)$

2. $16x - 8$

3. $3(x - 2)$

4. $3(4x + 4)$

5. $2x + 6$

6. $4(x + 3)$

a. $2(x + 3)$

b. $4x + 12$

c. $12x + 12$

d. $3x - 6$

e. $8(2x - 1)$

f. $2x + 8$

Multi-Step Problem Solving

7. Marcy sent a text message to three friends. Those 3 friends each send the text message to three friends, and so on. Marcy sending the message to three friends is considered Round 1. How many additional text messages will have been sent by Round 5? Show the steps you used and justify your solution. **EE** **MP**

1 Analyze

2 Plan

3 Solve

4 Justify and Evaluate

_____

_____

_____

Got it?

8. Cameron bought 16 party hats priced at 4 for $1.60 and 16 goodie bags priced at 4 for $5. How much did Cameron spend in all, not including tax? Show the steps you used and justify your solution. **EE** **MP**

_____

_____

_____

EE = Expressions, Equations, and Relationships   **MP** = Mathematical Processes

Reflect

Use what you learned about expressions to complete the graphic organizer.

TEKS 6.1(D), 6.1(F), 6.1(G)

 Essential Question

HOW it is helpful to write numbers in different ways?

Expression	Variable	Write a real-world example. What does the variable represent?
$17x$	x	Each ticket to the school play costs $17. The variable x represents the number of tickets purchased.
$9 + y$		
$23 - p$		
$\frac{d}{4}$		
$\frac{3}{5}c$		

Answer the Essential Question HOW is it helpful to write numbers in different ways? Verbally share your response with a partner, seeking and providing clarification as needed.

Chapter 8

Equations and Inequalities

Texas Essential Knowledge and Skills

Targeted TEKS

6.9 The student applies mathematical process standards to use equations and inequalities to represent situations. *Also addresses 6.7, 6.10.*

Mathematical Processes

6.1, 6.1(A), 6.1(B), 6.1(C), 6.1(D), 6.1(E), 6.1(F), 6.1(G)

Essential Question

HOW are symbols, such as $<$, $>$, and $=$, useful?

Math in the Real World

Desert Life Texas horned lizards, the state reptile, are mostly found in southwest Texas. The lizard uses the intense sunlight to create Vitamin D and during the winter, it hibernates underground.

A male horned lizard can be as much as 3.7 inches in length, while a female can be as much as 4.5 inches in length. Compare 3.7 inches and 4.5 inches.

Male   **Female**

[ ] $<$ [ ]

What Tools Do You Need?

Vocabulary

Addition Property of Equality

Division Property of Equality

equals sign

equation

inequality

inverse operations

Multiplication Property of Equality

solution

solve

Subtraction Property of Equality

Studying Math

Simplify the Problem Read the problem carefully to determine what information is needed to solve the problem.

Step 1   **Read the problem.**

Kylie wants to order several pairs of running shorts from an online store. They cost $14 each, and there is a one-time shipping fee of $7. What is the total cost of buying any number of pairs of shorts?

Step 2   **Rewrite the problem to make it simpler. Keep all of the important information but use fewer words.**

Kylie wants to buy some _____ that cost _____ each plus a shipping fee of _____. What is the total cost for any number of pairs of shorts?

Step 3   **Rewrite the problem using even fewer words. Write a variable for the unknown.**

The total cost of *x* shorts is _____ + _____.

Step 4   **Translate the words into an expression.**

_____

Use the method above to write an expression for each problem.

1. Akira is saving money to buy a bicycle. He has already saved $80 and plans to save an additional $5 each week. Find the total amount he has saved after any number of weeks.

2. A taxi company charges $1.50 per mile plus a $10 fee. What is the total cost of a taxi ride for any number of miles?

Your Turn! You will solve this problem in the chapter.

Review 5.3(K) **TEKS**

Example 1

Find 1.37 − 0.75.

$$\begin{array}{r} {}^{0\ 1}\\ \cancel{1}.37 \\ -\ 0.75 \\ \hline 0.62 \end{array}$$

Line up the decimal points.

Subtract.

Example 2

Find $\dfrac{3}{4} - \dfrac{5}{9}$.

The LCD of $\dfrac{3}{4}$ and $\dfrac{5}{9}$ is 36.

Write the problem.	Rename using the LCD, 36.		Subtract the numerators.

$$\dfrac{3}{4} \rightarrow \dfrac{3 \times 9}{4 \times 9} = \dfrac{27}{36} \rightarrow \dfrac{27}{36}$$
$$-\dfrac{5}{9} \rightarrow \dfrac{5 \times 4}{9 \times 4} = -\dfrac{20}{36} \rightarrow -\dfrac{20}{36}$$
$$\dfrac{7}{36}$$

Quick Check

Check ✓

Subtract Decimals Find each difference.

Show your work.

1. 2.34 − 1.23 = _____

2. 1.26 − 0.78 = _____

3. 3.65 − 0.96 = _____

Subtract Fractions Find each difference. Write in simplest form.

4. $\dfrac{7}{8} - \dfrac{1}{4} =$ _____

5. $\dfrac{5}{6} - \dfrac{1}{2} =$ _____

6. $\dfrac{3}{5} - \dfrac{2}{7} =$ _____

7. Pamela ran $\dfrac{7}{10}$ mile on Tuesday and $\dfrac{3}{8}$ mile on Thursday. How much farther did she run on Tuesday?

_____

How Did You Do?

Which problems did you answer correctly in the Quick Check? Shade those exercise numbers below.

① ② ③ ④ ⑤ ⑥ ⑦

FOLDABLES® Use the Foldable throughout this chapter to help you learn about equations and inequalities.

✂ cut on all dashed lines   ▭ fold on all solid lines   ▨ tape to page 664

equations and inequalities

Models   Symbols

addition (+)

Models   Symbols

subtraction (−)

Models   Symbols

multiplication (×) and division (÷)

FOLDABLES®

Use the Foldable throughout this chapter to help you learn about equations and inequalities.

✂ cut on all dashed lines   ▭ fold on all solid lines   ▨ tape to page 664

page 664   Tab 4

Write About It

page 664   Tab 3

Write About It

page 664   Tab 2

Write About It

page 664   Tab 1

Write About It

Equations

 Launch the Lesson: Vocabulary

An **equation** is a mathematical sentence showing two expressions are equal. An equation contains an **equals sign**, =.

Equation
Verbal Definition
Numeric and Algebraic Examples

Expression
Verbal Definition
Numeric and Algebraic Examples

How are an equation and an expression similar?

How are an equation and an expression different?

 Real-World Link

Anna bought a package of 6 pairs of socks. She writes the equation below to find how much she paid per pair. Circle the *solution* of the equation.

$$6x = \$9$$

$0.50 $1.50 $2.00

Which MP Mathematical Processes did you use?
Shade the circle(s) that applies.

Ⓐ Apply Math to the Real World.   Ⓔ Organize Ideas.

Ⓑ Use a Problem-Solving Model.   Ⓕ Analyze Relationships.

Ⓒ Select Tools and Techniques.   Ⓖ Justify Arguments.

Ⓓ Use Multiple Representations.

Texas Essential Knowledge and Skills

Targeted TEKS
6.10(B) Determine if the given value(s) make(s) one-variable, one-step equations or inequalities true. *Also addresses 6.7(B), 6.9(B).*

Mathematical Processes
6.1(A), 6.1(B), 6.1(D), 6.1(F)

Vocabulary
equation
equals sign
solve
solution

Essential Question ❓
HOW are symbols, such as <, >, and =, useful?

Determine Values that Make Addition and Subtraction Equations True

When you replace a variable with a value that results in a true sentence, you **solve** the equation. That value for the variable is the **solution** of the equation because it makes the equation true.

$$2 + x = 9$$

$$2 + 7 = 9$$

The value for the variable that results in a true sentence is 7. So, 7 is the solution.

$$9 = 9$$ This sentence is true.

Examples

Tutor

STOP and Reflect

How can you check if your solution to an equation is correct?

1. Determine if 3, 4, or 5 makes the equation $a + 7 = 11$ true.

Value of a	$a + 7 \stackrel{?}{=} 11$	Are Both Sides Equal?
3	$3 + 7 \stackrel{?}{=} 11$ $10 \neq 11$	no
4	$4 + 7 \stackrel{?}{=} 11$ $11 = 11$	yes ✔
5	$5 + 7 \stackrel{?}{=} 11$ $12 \neq 11$	no

The value 4 makes the equation true. So, the solution is 4.

2. Solve $g - 7 = 3$ mentally.

$g - 7 = 3$ **Think** What number minus 7 equals 3?

$10 - 7 = 3$ You know that $10 - 7 = 3$ is a true equation.

$3 = 3$

The solution is 10.

3. The total cost of a pair of skates and kneepads is $63. The skates cost $45. Use the *guess, check, and revise* strategy to solve the equation $45 + k = 63$ to find k, the cost of the kneepads.

Use the *guess, check, and revise* strategy.

Try 14.

$45 + k = 63$

$45 + 14 \stackrel{?}{=} 63$

$59 \neq 63$

Try 16.

$45 + k = 63$

$45 + 16 \stackrel{?}{=} 63$

$61 \neq 63$

Try 18.

$45 + k = 63$

$45 + 18 \stackrel{?}{=} 63$

$63 = 63$ ✔

So, the kneepads cost $18.

Got It? Do these problems to find out.

a. Determine if 4, 5, or 6 makes the equation $c + 8 = 13$ true.

b. Solve $9 - x = 2$ mentally.

c. The difference between an ostrich's speed and a chicken's speed is 31 miles per hour. An ostrich can run at a speed of 40 miles per hour. Use mental math or the *guess, check, and revise* strategy to solve the equation $40 - c = 31$ to find c, the speed a chicken can run.

a. _____

b. _____

c. _____

Determine Values that Make Multiplication and Division Equations True

Multiplication and division equations can be solved mentally in a similar way to addition and subtraction equations.

Tutor

Examples

4. **Determine if 3, 4, or 5 makes the equation $18 = 6z$ true.**

Value of z	$18 \stackrel{?}{=} 6z$	Are Both Sides Equal?
3	$18 \stackrel{?}{=} 6 \cdot 3$ $18 = 18$	yes ✔
4	$18 \stackrel{?}{=} 6 \cdot 4$ $18 \neq 24$	no
5	$18 \stackrel{?}{=} 6 \cdot 5$ $18 \neq 30$	no

The value 3 makes the equation true. So, the solution is 3.

5. **Solve $16 \div s = 8$ mentally.**

$16 \div s = 8$ **Think** 16 divided by what number equals 8?

$16 \div 2 = 8$ You know that $16 \div 2 = 8$ is a true equation.

$ 8 = 8$

The solution is 2.

Show your work.

Got It? Do these problems to find out.

d. Determine if 2, 3, or 4 makes the equation $4n = 16$ true.

e. Solve $-24 \div w = -8$ mentally.

d. _____

e. _____

Example

Tutor

6. Mason bought 72 sticks of gum. There are 8 sticks of gum in each package. Use the *guess, check, and revise* strategy to solve the equation $8 \cdot p = 72$ to find p, the number of packages Mason bought.

Use the *guess, check, and revise* strategy.

Try 7.	Try 8.	Try 9.
$8 \cdot p = 72$	$8 \cdot p = 72$	$8 \cdot p = 72$
$8 \cdot 7 \stackrel{?}{=} 72$	$8 \cdot 8 \stackrel{?}{=} 72$	$8 \cdot 9 \stackrel{?}{=} 72$
$56 \neq 72$	$64 \neq 72$	$72 = 72$ ✓

So, Mason bought 9 packages of gum.

Guided Practice

Determine if the given value(s) make(s) each equation true. (Examples 1 and 4)

1. $9 + w = 17$; 7, 8, 9 _____

Show your work.

2. $8 \div c = 8$; 0, 1, 2 _____

Solve each equation mentally. (Examples 2 and 5)

3. $x - 11 = 23$ _____

4. $4x = -32$ _____

5. Mississippi and Georgia have a total of 22 electoral votes. Mississippi has 6 electoral votes. Use mental math or the *guess, check, and revise* strategy to solve the equation $6 + g = 22$ to find g, the number of electoral votes Georgia has. (Example 3)

_____

6. Riley and her sister collect stickers. Riley has 220 stickers in her sticker collection. Her sister has 55 stickers in her collection. Riley has how many times as many stickers as her sister? Use mental math or the *guess, check, and revise* strategy to solve the equation $55x = 220$. (Example 6)

_____

7. ❓ **Building on the Essential Question** Distinguish verbally between expressions and equations. _____

_____

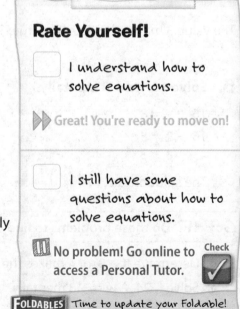

Rate Yourself!

☐ I understand how to solve equations.

▶▶ Great! You're ready to move on!

☐ I still have some questions about how to solve equations.

📖 No problem! Go online to access a Personal Tutor.

Check ✓

FOLDABLES Time to update your Foldable!

Independent Practice

6.10(B), 6.7(B), 6.1(F) TEKS

Determine if the given value(s) make(s) each equation true. (Examples 1 and 4)

1. $29 + d = 54$; 24, 25, 26 _____

2. $35 = 45 - n$; 10, 11, 12 _____

Show
your
work.

3. $6w = 30$; 5, 6, 7 _____

4. $x \div 7 = 3$; 20, 21, 22 _____

Solve each equation mentally. (Examples 2 and 5)

5. $m + 4 = 17$ _____

6. $10t = 90$ _____

7. $22 \div y = -2$ _____

MP **Analyze Relationships** For Exercises 8–10, solve using mental math or the *guess, check, and revise* strategy. (Examples 3 and 6)

8. One season, the Cougars won 20 games. They played a total of 25 games. Use the equation $20 + g = 25$ to find g, the number of games the team lost.

_____

9. Five friends earn a total of $50 doing yard work in their neighborhood. Each friend earns the same amount. Use the equation $5f = 50$ to find f, the

amount that each friend earns. _____

10. Last year, 700 students attended Walnut Springs Middle School. This year, there are 665 students. Use the equation $700 - d = 665$ to find d, the decrease in the number of students from last year to this year.

_____

11. Distinguish between expressions and equations numerically, by providing an example of a numerical expression and an example of a numerical equation.

_____

_____

12. Distinguish between expressions and equations algebraically, by providing an example of an algebraic expression and an example of an algebraic equation.

_____

_____

13. Charlie ran 5 miles in 51.5 minutes. Use the equation $5r = 51.5$ to find r, the average rate he ran.

_____

_____

 H.O.T. Problems Higher-Order Thinking

14. Analyze What 3 consecutive even numbers added together equal 42? Use the equation $n + (n + 2) + (n + 4) = 42$ to help you solve.

_____

_____

15. Create Give an example of an equation that has a solution of 5.

_____

_____

16. Evaluate Tell whether the statement below is _always, sometimes,_ or _never_ true. Explain your reasoning.

> Equations like $a + 4 = 8$ and $4 - m = 2$ have exactly one solution.

_____

_____

Evaluate Tell whether each statement is _true_ or _false_. Then explain your reasoning.

17. In $m + 8$, the variable m can have any value.

_____

_____

18. In $m + 8 = 12$, the variable m can have any value and be a solution.

_____

_____

Multi-Step Problem Solving

19. Sandi bought a sandwich and a milkshake. She spent $12 in all. The equation $s + 4.25 = 12$ can be used to determine the cost of the sandwich. Which of the following is the solution to the equation? **EE** **MP**

Item	Cost ($)
Sandwich	s
Milkshake	4.25

Ⓐ $7.75

Ⓑ $8.75

Ⓒ $16

Ⓓ $16.25

Use a problem-solving model to solve this problem.

1 Analyze

**Read the problem. Circle the information you know.
Underline what the problem is asking you to find.**

2 Plan

What will you need to do to solve the problem? Write your plan in steps.

Step 1 Test each answer choice to determine if a true number sentence is created.

3 Solve

Use your plan to solve the problem. Show your steps.

$7.75 + 4.25 = 12$ ✓

$8.75 + 4.25 \neq 12$ ✗

$16 + 4.25 \neq 12$ ✗

$16.25 + 4.25 \neq 12$ ✗

Since ☐ $+ 4.25 = 12$, choice ☐ is correct. Fill in that answer choice.

Read to Succeed!
Substitute each answer choice for s and add to determine if the number sentence is true.

4 Justify and Evaluate

How do you know your solution is accurate?

_____

_____

_____

EE = Expressions, Equations, and Relationships   **MP** = Mathematical Processes

More Multi-Step Problem Solving

Use a problem-solving model to solve each problem.

20. Kaleena paid $26.25 to rent a kayak for 3 hours. The equation $3x = 26.25$ can be used to determine the amount she paid per hour. Which of the following is the solution to the equation? **EE** **N** **MP**

(A) $8.66

(B) $8.75

(C) $23.25

(D) $29.25

21. Shalah went to the grocery store with $50 in cash and bought the items shown in the table. In the equation $s + x = 50$, s represents the amount she spent, and x represents the amount she had left. Does she have $14.25, $28.50, or $35.75 left? **EE** **N** **MP**

Item	Milk	Eggs	Ham
Cost	$3.25	$2.50	$8.50

22. Kirsten had 65 inches of wire. After she used some for a project, she had 14 inches left. The equation $x + 14 = 65$ can be used to determine the amount of wire that she used in inches. Did she use 79, 51, or 37 inches of wire? Plot the solution on the number line. **EE** **N** **MP**

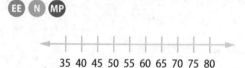

35 40 45 50 55 60 65 70 75 80

23. George made 12 ounces of rice. He had 4 ounces left after he finished eating. Use *guess, check, and revise* strategy to solve the equation $12 - r = 4$ to find r, the number of ounces of rice that he ate. Then convert your answer to find how many cups of rice George ate. **EE** **N** **MP**

r	$12 - r = 4$	Are Both Sides Equal?
5		
6		
7		
8		

Write Equations and Represent Solutions

 Launch the Lesson: Vocabulary

Texas Essential Knowledge and Skills

Targeted TEKS
6.9(A) Write one-variable, one-step equations and inequalities to represent constraints or conditions within problems. *Also addresses 6.9(B), 6.9(C).*

Mathematical Processes
6.1(A), 6.1(B), 6.1(D), 6.1(F)

Write key words that indicate each operation in the graphic organizer.

Addition	Subtraction
Multiplication	Division

Essential Question
HOW are symbols, such as <, >, and =, useful?

 Real-World Link

Neptune has 12 more moons than Earth. Circle the expression that represents the situation.

$e + 12$ $e - 12$ $e \times 12$ $e \div 12$

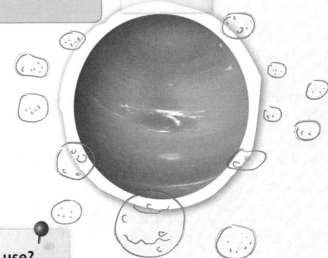

Which MP Mathematical Processes did you use?
Shade the circle(s) that applies.

Ⓐ Apply Math to the Real World.   Ⓔ Organize Ideas.

Ⓑ Use a Problem-Solving Model.   Ⓕ Analyze Relationships.

Ⓒ Select Tools and Techniques.   Ⓖ Justify Arguments.

Ⓓ Use Multiple Representations.

Write Equations

You can write an equation to represent constraints or conditions within real-world problems.

Examples

Tutor

Write an equation for each real-world problem.

1. An orange and a cup of juice are 210 Calories. An orange has 90 Calories. How many Calories does a cup of juice have?

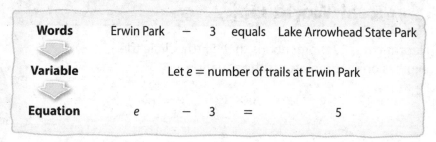

| Words | orange | and | juice | equal | 210 Calories |

Variable Let j = Calories in juice

| Equation | 90 | + | j | = | 210 |

The equation is $90 + j = 210$.

2. Lake Arrowhead State Park has 3 less hiking trails than Erwin Park. Lake Arrowhead State Park has 5 hiking trails. How many trails does Erwin Park have?

| Words | Erwin Park | − | 3 | equals | Lake Arrowhead State Park |

Variable Let e = number of trails at Erwin Park

| Equation | e | − | 3 | = | 5 |

The equation is $e - 3 = 5$.

3. Seven tickets to the Children's Museum of Brownsville cost $35. How much does one ticket cost?

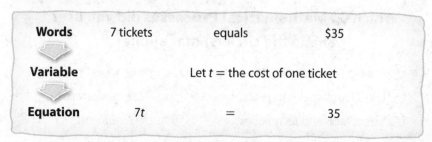

| Words | 7 tickets | equals | $35 |

Variable Let t = the cost of one ticket

| Equation | $7t$ | = | 35 |

The equation is $7t = 35$.

4. Ground beef is being divided into 4 hamburgers. Each burger is 6 ounces. How many ounces of beef are there altogether?

Words	ground beef divided into 4 burgers equals 6 ounces each
Variable	Let h = the total amount of beef
Equation	$h \div 4 = 6$

The equation is $h \div 4 = 6$.

Got It? Do these problems to find out.

Define a variable and write an equation for each situation.

a. A checking account had a balance of $-\$40$. A deposit was made and the balance is now $-\$25$. What was the deposit amount?

b. When first planted, a cotton plant's roots grow about 3 inches per week. A cotton plant's roots are about 18 inches long. For how many weeks have they been growing?

a. _____

b. _____

Represent Solutions to Equations on Number Lines

You can represent solutions for equations on number lines.

Tutor

Examples

Represent the solution to each equation on a number line.

5. $x + 7 = 13$

Think: What plus 7 equals 13? 6

Locate 6 on a number line.

6. $-8w = 32$

Think: What times -8 equals 32? -4

Locate -4 on a number line.

Got It? Do these problems to find out.

c. $r - 7 = 10$ **d.** $z \div (-9) = -9$

c. _____

d. _____

Write Real-World Problems for Equations

Given an equation, you can write a corresponding real-world problem.

 Example

 Tutor

7. Write a real-world problem that can be represented by the equation $-8x = -48$.

The temperature dropped 8 degrees each hour. After so many hours, the temperature had dropped 48 degrees. For how many hours did the temperature drop?

Guided Practice

Define a variable and write an equation for each real-world problem.
(Examples 1–4)

1. Manny earned a total of 15 points on two quizzes. He earned 8 points on the first quiz. How many points did he earn on the second quiz?

_____

2. Each of the bracelets that Veronica made has 45 beads. She made 4 bracelets. How many total beads did she use?

_____

Represent the solution to each equation on a number line. (Examples 5 and 6)

3. $m - 3 = 11$

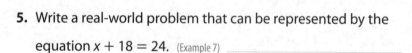

4. $r \div (-5) = 6$

5. Write a real-world problem that can be represented by the equation $x + 18 = 24$. (Example 7) _____

_____

_____

6. **Building on the Essential Question** How does defining a variable help you write an equation to represent a real-world problem? _____

_____

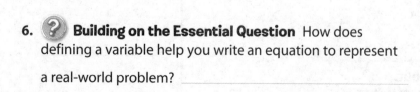
Rate Yourself!

How confident are you about writing and graphing equations? Shade the face that applies.

Find out online. Use the Self-Check Quiz.

Check

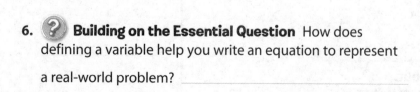

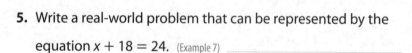

Independent Practice

6.9(A), 6.9(B), 6.9(C), 6.1(F) TEKS

Define a variable and write an equation for each real-world problem. (Examples 1–4)

1. The Marriott Rivercenter in San Antonio, Texas has a main roof height of 441 feet. With the additional height of antennas, the structure is 546 feet tall. What is the height of the antennas?

   _____

2. The average heart rate of a cat is one-third that of a hamster's heart rate. The average heart rate of a cat is 150 beats per minute. What is the average heart rate of a hamster? _____

3. The temperature dropped 3 degrees per hour for a total decrease of 51 degrees. For how many hours did the temperature drop?

   _____

4. The number of sandwiches needed for a family reunion is 15 less than the number needed for a company picnic. The number of sandwiches needed for a family reunion is 35. How many are needed for a company picnic?

   _____

Represent the solution to each equation on a number line. (Examples 5 and 6)

5. $-5w = 45$

6. $c - 7 = -12$

7. $n \div 6 = 8$

8. $p + (-9) = -13$

9. Write a real-world problem that can be represented by the equation

   $7w = 17.15$. (Example 7) _____

   _____

   _____

10. Write a real-world problem that can be represented by the equation

    $f + 5 = -9$. _____

    _____

11. A store marks up the price of a sweater by $7.35. The total cost of a sweater is $25.65. How much does the store pay for the sweater? Define a variable and write an equation to represent the real-world problem.

12. **Find the Error** Alex raised $138.75 for his school's Walk-A-Thon. He donated $14.50 of his own money and wrote the equation $d - 14.50 = 138.75$ to find out how much was donated by others. Determine his mistake and correct it.

H.O.T. Problems Higher-Order Thinking

13. **Analyze** Write two different equations that can be used to represent the following real-world problem.

    Carter picked 4.4 more pounds of strawberries than Gabrielle. Carter picked 7.2 pounds of strawberries. How many pounds did Gabrielle pick?

14. **Create** Write a real-world problem and equation with the following solution.

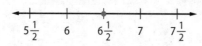

$$5\frac{1}{2} \quad 6 \quad 6\frac{1}{2} \quad 7 \quad 7\frac{1}{2}$$

15. **Analyze** Explain how you would represent the solution to $-17 - x = -9$ on a number line. Then represent the solution.

16. **Create** Write a real-world problem that can be represented by the equation $(m - 2.7) + 4.1 = 13.5$.

Multi-Step Problem Solving

17. Jacob has a gift card for a music store. He used it to make a
$40 purchase, and now has $35 left on it. Which equation
represents the amount that was initially on Jacob's gift card? **EE** **MP**

    Ⓐ $g + 40 = 35$ Ⓒ $g - 40 = 35$

    Ⓑ $g + 35 = 40$ Ⓓ $40 - 35 = g$

Use a problem-solving model to solve this problem.

1 Analyze

Read the problem. Circle the information you know.
Underline what the problem is asking you to find.

2 Plan

What will you need to do to solve the problem? Write your plan in steps.

  Step 1   Determine a variable.

  Step 2   Write the equation that represents the situation.

Read to Succeed!

The amount left is the difference. So, it is by itself in the equation.

3 Solve

Use your plan to solve the problem. Show your steps.

Let $g =$ the amount originally on the card.

Jacob had an amount on the card and $_____ was subtracted from it,

leaving $_____ .

So, ▢ − ▢ = ▢ .

Choice _____ is correct. Fill in that answer choice.

4 Justify and Evaluate

How do you know your solution is accurate?

_____

_____

_____

EE = Expressions, Equations, and Relationships   **MP** = Mathematical Processes

More Multi-Step Problem Solving

Use a problem-solving model to solve each problem.

18. Montell gets $10.50 each week for doing yard work for his neighbors. He has earned $63 so far. Write and solve an equation to find how many weeks it took for him to earn that amount.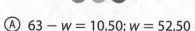

- Ⓐ $63 - w = 10.50; w = 52.50$
- Ⓑ $w - 10.50 = 63; w = 73.5$
- Ⓒ $63w = 10.50; w = 4$
- Ⓓ $10.50w = 63; w = 6$

19. Craig owes the bank $9.50. After he deposits some money, his account balance is $16.25. How much did he deposit in the bank? Write and solve an equation. Plot the solution on the number line.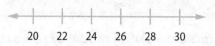

<!-- number line: 20 22 24 26 28 30 -->

---

20. Chandra is buying music for $1 per song. She uses a coupon that lets her get two songs for the price of one. She ends up spending $14. Write and solve a multiplication equation to solve for *s*, the number of songs she bought. Plot the solution on the number line.

<!-- number line: 20 21 22 23 24 25 26 27 28 29 30 -->

---

21. Use the clues to write and solve equations. What is the value of *x*?

Five increased by *x* is the same as *b* less than *a*. The product of two-tenths and *a* is three. The quotient of *b* and one-half is four.

EE = Expressions, Equations, and Relationships   **P** = Proportionality   **N** = Number and Operations   **MP** = Mathematical Processes

604   Chapter 8 Equations and Inequalities

Model and Solve Addition and Subtraction Equations

Texas Essential
Knowledge and Skills

Targeted TEKS
6.10(A) Model and solve one-variable, one-step equations and inequalities that represent problems, including geometric concepts. *Also addresses 6.9(A), 6.9(B), 6.9(C).*

Mathematical Processes
6.1(C), 6.1(D), 6.1(E), 6.1(G)

INQUIRY HOW can I select tools to model and solve addition and subtraction equations?

Zack gave 5 trading cards to his sister. Now he has 41 cards. How many cards did he have originally?

What do you know? _____

_____

What do you need to find? _____

_____

Hands-On Activity 1

Step 1 Define a variable. Use the variable *c* to represent the number of cards Zack had originally.

Step 2 Use a bar diagram to help write the equation.

original number of cards, *c*	
├------- 41 cards ------┤	5 cards ┤

The total length of the diagram shows _____.

The number 41 represents _____.

The number 5 represents _____.

 $\Box - \Box = \Box$

Step 3 Work backward. Rewrite the equation as an addition sentence and solve.

 $\Box + \Box = \Box$

So, Zack originally had $\Box$ trading cards.

Step 4 Represent the solution on a number line. Locate 46 on a number line.

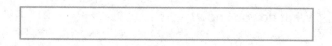

Investigate

Work with a partner. Write and solve a subtraction equation using a bar diagram.

1. Mariska gave her friend Elise 8 beads and was left with 37 beads. How many did she have originally?

2. Clinton has $12 after buying a snack at the mall. The snack cost $5. How much money did Clinton have originally?

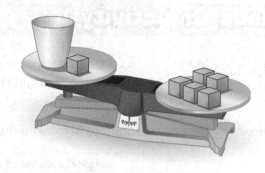

Hands-On Activity 2

Watch Tools

An equation is like a balance. The quantity on the left side of the equals sign is balanced with the quantity on the right.

To solve an addition equation using cups and counters, subtract the same number of counters from each side of the mat so that the equation remains balanced.

Solve $x + 1 = 5$ using cups and counters.

Step 1   Model the equation. Use a cup to represent x.

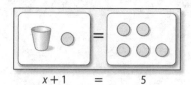

$$x + 1 \quad = \quad 5$$

Step 2   Use the model above. Cross out 1 counter from each side so that the cup is by itself.

Step 3   There are ☐ counters remaining on the right side, so $x = $ ☐.

So, the solution is ☐.

Step 4   Represent the solution on a number line.

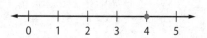

Investigate

Collaborate

Work with a partner. Solve each equation using cups and counters. Draw cups and counters to show your work.

3. $1 + x = 8$

$x =$ _____

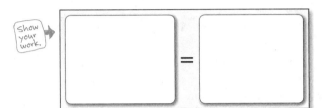

4. $x + 2 = 7$

$x =$ _____

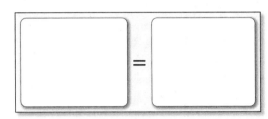

5. $3 + x = 6$

$x =$ _____

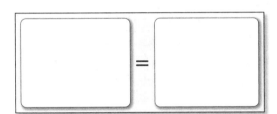

6. $x + 5 = 7$

$x =$ _____

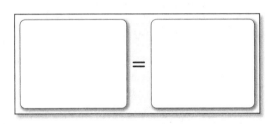

Work with a partner. Write a real-world problem that can be represented by the equation. Solve each addition equation using the model of your choice.

7. $9 = x + 3$

_____

_____

_____

8. $4 + x = 6$

_____

_____

_____

9. Terrell bought an MP3 player. He spent the rest of his money on an Internet music subscription for $25.95. If he started with $135, how much was the MP3 player? Write and solve an equation using a bar diagram. _____

Analyze and Reflect

Collaborate

Work with a partner to complete the table. The first one is done for you.

	Addition Equation	Subtraction Sentence	Solution
	$x + 1 = 3$	$3 - 1 = x$	$x = 2$
10.	$y + 9 = 12$		
11.	$47 = 17 + v$		
12.	$100 + c = 129$		
13.	$h + 89.4 = 97.4$		

14. (MP) **Analyze Relationships** Write a rule that you can use to solve an addition equation without using models. _____

_____

_____

15. How can the number family 3, 4, 7 help you to solve the equation $3 + x = 7$?

_____

_____

_____

Create

On Your Own

16. (MP) **Select Tools and Techniques** Write a real-world problem for the equation modeled below. Then write the equation and solve.

|-------------- 6 weeks --------------|
length of vacation, v	**2 weeks**

_____

_____

_____

17. **INQUIRY** HOW can I select tools to model and solve addition and subtraction equations?

_____

_____

_____

Solve Addition and Subtraction Equations

Launch the Lesson: Real World   Watch

On the second hole of miniature golf, it took Anne 3 putts to sink the golf ball. Her score is now 5. She represents this situation with cups and counters. What was Anne's score on the first hole?

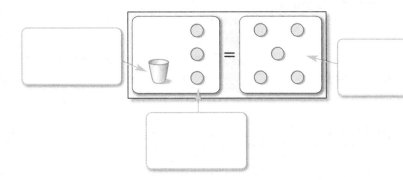

1. Fill in the boxes above using the phrases below.
   • Her score on the first hole is unknown.
   • Her score is now 5.
   • She scored a 3 on the second hole.

2. Write the addition equation shown in the figure.

   _____

3. Explain how to solve the equation.

   _____

4. What was Anne's score on the first hole? ☐

Texas Essential Knowledge and Skills

Targeted TEKS
6.10(A) Model and solve one-variable, one-step equations and inequalities that represent problems, including geometric concepts. *Also addresses 6.9(A), 6.9(B), 6.9(C).*

Mathematical Processes
6.1(A), 6.1(B), 6.1(D), 6.1(F)

Vocabulary Vocab

inverse operations

Subtraction Property of Equality

Addition Property of Equality

Essential Question

HOW are symbols, such as $<$, $>$, and $=$, useful?

Which MP Mathematical Processes did you use?
Shade the circle(s) that applies.

(A) Apply Math to the Real World.

(B) Use a Problem-Solving Model.

(C) Select Tools and Techniques.

(D) Use Multiple Representations.

(E) Organize Ideas.

(F) Analyze Relationships.

(G) Justify Arguments.

Subtraction Property of Equality

Words   If you subtract the same number from each side of an equation, the two sides remain equal.

Examples

Numbers	Algebra
$5 = 5$	$x + 2 = 3$
$-3 = -3$	$-2 = -2$
$2 = 2$	$x = 1$

You can use **inverse operations** to solve equations. Inverse operations *undo* each other. For example, to solve an addition equation, use subtraction. When you solve an equation by subtracting the same number from each side of the equation, you are using the **Subtraction Property of Equality.**

Watch Tutor

Example

Checking Solutions
You should always check your solution. You will know immediately whether your solution is correct or not.

1. **Ruben and Tariq have 245.5 downloaded minutes of music. If Ruben has 132 minutes, how many belong to Tariq? Write and solve an addition equation to determine how many minutes belong to Tariq.**

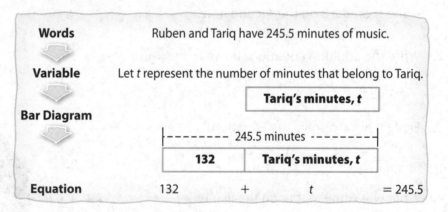

Words	Ruben and Tariq have 245.5 minutes of music.
Variable	Let *t* represent the number of minutes that belong to Tariq.

Bar Diagram

Tariq's minutes, *t*

|--------- 245.5 minutes ---------|

132	Tariq's minutes, *t*

| **Equation** | 132 | + | *t* | = 245.5 |

$$132 + t = 245.5 \quad \text{Write the equation.}$$
$$-132 \quad = -132 \quad \text{Subtract 132 from each side.}$$
$$t = 113.5 \quad \text{Simplify.}$$

So, 113.5 minutes belong to Tariq.

Check $132 + 113.5 = 245.5$ ✓

 Show your work.

Got It? Do this problem to find out.

a. Suppose Ruben had 147.5 minutes of the 245.5 that were downloaded. Write and solve an addition equation to determine how many minutes belong to Tariq.

a. _____

Addition Property of Equality

Words If you add the same number to each side of an equation, the two sides remain equal.

Examples

Numbers	Algebra
$5 = 5$	$x - 2 = 3$
$+3 = +3$	$+2 = +2$
$8 = 8$	$x = 5$

When you solve an equation by adding the same number to each side of the equation, you are using the **Addition Property of Equality.**

Tutor

Example

2. **STEM** At age 25, Gherman Titov of Russia was the youngest person to travel into space. This is 52 years less than the oldest person to travel in space, John Glenn. How old was John Glenn? Write and solve a subtraction equation.

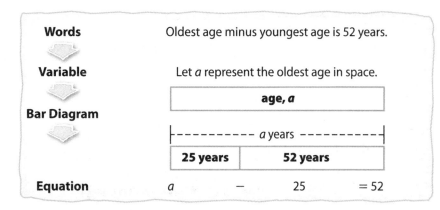

Words	Oldest age minus youngest age is 52 years.
Variable	Let *a* represent the oldest age in space.

age, *a*

|---- *a* years ----|
| **25 years** | **52 years** |

| Equation | $a \quad - \quad 25 \quad = 52$ |

$$a - 25 = 52 \qquad \text{Write the equation.}$$
$$\underline{+25 = +25} \qquad \text{Add 25 to each side.}$$
$$a \quad = \quad 77 \qquad \text{Simplify.}$$

John Glenn was 77 years old.

Check $77 - 25 = 52$ ✓

Show your work.

Got It? Do this problem to find out.

b. Georgia's height is 4 inches less than Sienna's height. Georgia is 58 inches tall. Write and solve a subtraction equation to find Sienna's height.

b. _____

Example

3. **Write a real-world problem that can be represented by the equation $w + 181 = 379$.**

The equation is an addition equation. The variable w can represent the weight of an average female gorilla.

A male gorilla weighs 379 pounds on average. This is 181 pounds more than the weight of the average female gorilla. What is the weight of an average female gorilla?

Guided Practice

Solve each equation. Check your solution. (Examples 1 and 2)

1. $y + 7 = -10$ _____

2. $4 = e - 8$ _____

3. A board that measures 19.5 meters in length is cut into two pieces. One piece measures 7.2 meters. Write and solve an equation to find the length of the other piece. (Example 1)

_____

4. Catherine studied 1.25 hours for her science test. This was 0.5 hour less than she studied for her algebra test. Write and solve a subtraction equation to find how long she studied for her algebra test. (Example 2)

_____

5. Write a real-world problem that can be represented by the equation $x + 26 = 43$. (Example 3)

_____

_____

_____

6. (?) **Building on the Essential Question** How can the Subtraction Property of Equality be used to solve addition equations?

_____

_____

Rate Yourself!

How confident are you about solving addition and subtraction equations? Shade the ring on the target.

I'm on target.

I need help.

Find out online. Use the Self-Check Quiz.

Check

FOLDABLES Time to update your Foldable!

Independent Practice

Solve each equation. Check your solution. (Examples 1 and 2)

1. $c + 3 = 6$ _____

2. $-9 = -2 + x$ _____

3. $a - 2.1 = 5.8$ _____

Show your work.

4. Zacarias and Paz together have $756.80. If Zacarias has $489.50, how much does Paz have? Write and solve an addition equation to find how much money belongs to Paz. (Example 1) _____

5. A CD costs $14.95. This is $7.55 less than the cost of a DVD. Write and solve a subtraction equation to find the cost of the DVD. (Example 2)

6. Write a real-world problem that can be represented by the equation $a - 6 = 15$. (Example 3)

7. **MP** **Apply Math to the Real World** Refer to the graphic novel frame below for Exercises a–b.

a. If Mei has already earned 30 points, write and solve an addition equation to determine the number of points she still needs.

b. Suppose Julie has already earned 36 points. Write and solve an addition equation to find the number of points she still needs to earn the pizza party.

Solve each equation. Check your solution.

8. $a + \frac{1}{10} = \frac{5}{10}$ _____

9. $m + \frac{1}{3} = \frac{2}{3}$ _____

10. $s - \frac{1}{3} = \frac{7}{9}$ _____

11. Alejandra spent her birthday money on a video game that costs $24, a controller for $13, and a memory card for $16. The total tax was $3. Write and solve a subtraction equation to determine how much money Alejandra gave the cashier if she received $4 in change.

_____

 H.O.T. Problems Higher-Order Thinking

12. Create Write two different addition equations that have 12 as the solution.

_____

_____

13. Analyze In the equation $x + y = 5$, the value for x is a whole number greater than 2 but less than 6. Determine the possible solutions for y.

_____

14. Evaluate Identify the equation that does not belong with the other three. Explain your reasoning.

$6 + x = 9$	$15 = x + 12$	$x + 9 = 11$	$7 + x = 10$

_____

_____

15. Create Write a real-world problem that could be represented by $d - 32.73 = 64.31$.

_____

_____

16. Analyze Another type of subtraction equation is $16 - b = 7$. Explain how you would solve this equation. Then solve it.

_____

_____

Multi-Step Problem Solving

17. A bookstore has a sale on mysteries. The table shows the cost of each book format. Abigail has $70 to spend. She bought two paperbacks, one hardcover, and one audio book. Which addition equation can be used to determine how much more money Abigail still has to spend?

Book	Cost ($)
Hardcover	19
Paperback	8
E-book	10
Audio Book	25

(A) $70 + 60 = x$

(C) $70 + x = 60$

(B) $60 + x = 70$

(D) $52 + 70 = x$

Use a problem-solving model to solve this problem.

1 Analyze

Read the problem. Circle the information you know.
Underline what the problem is asking you to find.

2 Plan

What will you need to do to solve the problem? Write your plan in steps.

Step 1 Determine how much Abigail spent.

Step 2 Write an equation to represent the situation.

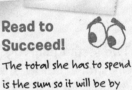

Read to Succeed!
The total she has to spend is the sum so it will be by itself in the equation.

3 Solve

Use your plan to solve the problem. Show your steps.

Abigail spent 2($ ⬚) + $ ⬚ + $ ⬚ , or $ ⬚ .

Let x = the amount she has left.

So, ⬚ + x = ⬚ . Choice ⬚ is correct. Fill in that answer choice.

4 Justify and Evaluate

How do you know your solution is accurate?

_____

_____

_____

EE = Expressions, Equations, and Relationships   **MP** = Mathematical Processes

More Multi-Step Problem Solving

Use a problem-solving model to solve each problem.

18. Kisho has $45 to spend at a pizza shop for a pizza party. The table shows the cost of each size of pizza. He bought four small pizzas and one large pizza. Which addition equation can be used to determine how much more money he still has to spend? **EE** **MP**

Pizza Size	Cost ($)
Small	5
Medium	8
Large	10
Extra Large	15

(A) $x + 45 = 30$

(B) $x - 30 = 45$

(C) $x + 30 = 45$

(D) $x - 45 = 30$

19. A grocery store is having a "two for the price of one" sale for several items. The cost of these items is shown in the table. Davion bought two boxes of cereal and two loaves of bread. He also paid $0.39 in tax. The equation $x - (4.50 + 1.99 + 0.39) = 13.12$ can be used to determine how much money he gave the cashier. Determine how much money, in dollars, Davion gave the cashier if he received $13.12 in change. **EE** **MP**

Item	Cost ($)
Bread	1.99
Cereal	4.50
Orange Juice	3.00

20. Two rectangular rugs in Winona's bedroom are shown below. The larger rug is 32 square feet bigger than the smaller rug. The equation $x + 32 = 35$ can be used to find the area of the smaller rug. What is the width of the smaller rug, in feet? **EE** **MP**

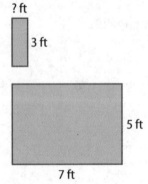

21. What value of x makes the following equation true? Write a real-world problem that could be modeled with this equation. **EE** **MP**

$$x - \frac{1}{8} = \frac{1}{12}$$

EE = Expressions, Equations, and Relationships   **MP** = Mathematical Processes

Model and Solve Multiplication and Division Equations

INQUIRY HOW can I select tools to model and solve multiplication and division equations?

In 3 days, Nicole ran a total of 12 miles. She ran the same amount each day. How much did she run each day?

What do you know? _____

_____

What do you need to find? _____

Texas Essential Knowledge and Skills TEKS

Targeted TEKS
6.10(A) Model and solve one-variable, one-step equations and inequalities that represent problems, including geometric concepts. *Also addresses 6.9(A), 6.9(C).*

Mathematical Processes
6.1(C), 6.1(D), 6.1(E), 6.1(G)

Hands-On Activity 1

Solve $3x = 12$. Check your solution.

Step 1 Model the equation. Use one cup to represent each x.

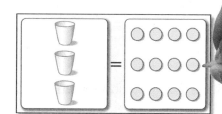

Step 2 Use the model above. Divide the 12 counters equally by circling 3 groups. There are ▢ counters in each group.

So, the solution is ▢.

Step 3 Represent the solution on a number line.

Graph 4 on a number line.

0 1 2 3 4 5 6

Check $3\,\boxed{} = 12$ Write the original equation.

$3(\boxed{}) \overset{?}{=} 12$ Replace x with your solution.

$\boxed{} = 12$ Is the sentence true? _____

Hands-On Activity 2

Four friends decided to split the cost of season concert tickets equally.
Each person paid $35. Find the total cost of the season concert tickets.

Step 1   Define a variable. Use the variable c to represent the total cost of the tickets.

Step 2   Use a bar diagram to help write the equation.

total cost, c			
amount each person pays	amount each person pays	amount each person pays	amount each person pays

$\vdash$---- $35 ----$\dashv$

The total length of the diagram shows _____.

The number 35 represents _____.

There are four equal sections because _____.

$\boxed{} \div \boxed{} = \boxed{}$

Step 3   Rewrite the equation as a multiplication sentence and solve.

$\boxed{} \times \boxed{} = c$

So, the total cost of the season tickets was $\$\boxed{}$.

Step 4   Represent the solution, 140, on a number line.

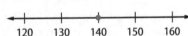

120   130   140   150   160

Investigate

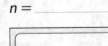
Collaborate

Work with a partner. Solve each equation using cups and counters.

1. $4n = 8$

Show your work. ➡ $n =$ _____

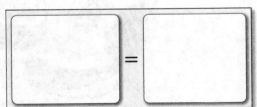

2. $3x = 9$

$x =$ _____

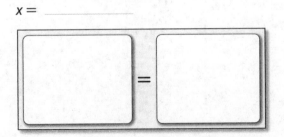

 Investigate

Work with a partner. Write and solve a division equation using a bar diagram. Represent the solution on a number line.

3. Three teachers went to a conference. They shared the cost of gasoline *g* equally. Each teacher paid $38.50. Draw a bar diagram to find the total cost of gasoline.

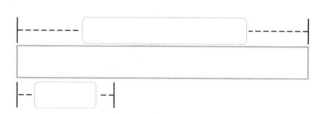

4. Silvia has completed 8 math exercises *e*. This is one-fourth of the assignment. How many exercises were assigned?

Define a variable. Then write and solve a multiplication equation using a bar diagram. Represent the solution on a number line.

5. The average lifespan of a horse is 40 years, which is five times longer than the average lifespan of a guinea pig. Use the bar diagram below to find the average lifespan of a guinea pig. Label each section of the diagram.

6. Kosumi is saving an equal amount each week for 4 weeks to buy a $40 video game. Use the bar diagram below to find how much he is saving each week. Label each section of the diagram.

Analyze and Reflect

Collaborate

Work with a partner to complete the table. The first one is done for you.

Multiplication Equation	Coefficient	Variable	Product	Division Sentence	Solution
$7g = 14$	7	g	14	$14 \div 7 = g$	$g = 2$
7. $21 = 3y$					$y =$
8. $5m = 45$					$m =$
9. $48 = 8d$					$d =$

10. **MP Analyze Relationships** Write a rule for solving equations like $2x = 24$ without using models. Use a related division sentence to explain your answer.

_____

_____

11. **MP Use Multiple Representations** Write and solve an equation to represent the situation modeled at the right.

_____

Create

On Your Own

12. **MP Use Multiple Representations** Write a real-world problem for the equation modeled below. Then write the equation and solve.

	$12		
c	c	c	c

_____

_____

13. **INQUIRY** HOW can I select tools to model and solve multiplication and division equations?

_____

_____

_____

_____

Solve Multiplication and Division Equations

  Launch the Lesson: Real World Watch

Leslie spends $5 a month on snacks at school, which is one-fourth of her monthly allowance. Complete the questions below to find Leslie's monthly allowance.

1. Draw a bar diagram to represent $5 as one-fourth of Leslie's monthly allowance.

2. What is Leslie's monthly allowance? ☐

3. What operation did you use to find Leslie's allowance?

_____

4. How can you check your answer to determine if it is accurate?

_____

Texas Essential Knowledge and Skills

Targeted TEKS
6.10(A) Model and solve one-variable, one-step equations and inequalities that represent problems, including geometric concepts. *Also addresses 6.8(C), 6.8(D), 6.9(A), 6.9(B), 6.9(C).*

Mathematical Processes
6.1(A), 6.1(B), 6.1(D), 6.1(F)

Vocab

Vocabulary
Division Property of Equality
Multiplication Property of Equality

Essential Question ❓
HOW are symbols, such as <, >, and =, useful?

Which ⓂⓅ **Mathematical Processes did you use? Shade the circle(s) that applies.**

Ⓐ Apply Math to the Real World.

Ⓔ Organize Ideas.

Ⓑ Use a Problem-Solving Model.

Ⓕ Analyze Relationships.

Ⓒ Select Tools and Techniques.

Ⓖ Justify Arguments.

Ⓓ Use Multiple Representations.

Division Property of Equality

Words	If you divide each side of an equation by the same nonzero number, the two sides remain equal.

Examples

Numbers	Algebra
$18 = 18$	$3x = 12$
$\dfrac{18}{6} = \dfrac{18}{6}$	$\dfrac{3x}{3} = \dfrac{12}{3}$
$3 = 3$	$x = 4$

Work Zone

When you solve an equation by dividing both sides of the equation by the same number, you are using the **Division Property of Equality**.

Real World

Example Tutor

1. The sixth-grade class at Reading Middle School is building a rectangular greenhouse that is six feet long. The area of the floor is 24 square feet. How wide is the greenhouse?

STOP and Reflect

What is the coefficient in the equation in Example 1?

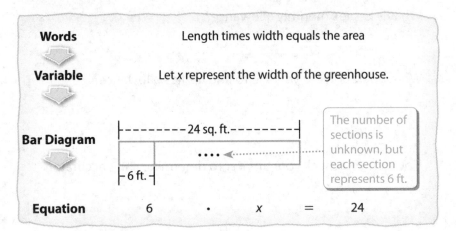

Words	Length times width equals the area
Variable	Let x represent the width of the greenhouse.
Bar Diagram	24 sq. ft. / 6 ft. — The number of sections is unknown, but each section represents 6 ft.
Equation	$6 \cdot x = 24$

$6x = 24$ Write the equation.

$\dfrac{6x}{6} = \dfrac{24}{6}$ Divide each side by 6.

$x = 4$ Simplify.

Check $6 \times 4 = 24$ ✓

The greenhouse is 4 feet wide.

 Show your work.

Got It? Do this problem to find out.

a. In 2004, Pen Hadow and Simon Murray walked 680 miles to the South Pole. The trip took 58 days. Suppose they traveled the same distance each day. Write and solve a multiplication equation to find about how many miles they traveled each day to the nearest whole number.

a. _____

Multiplication Property of Equality

Key Concept

Words If you multiply each side of an equation by the same nonzero number, the two sides remain equal.

Examples

Numbers	Algebra
$3 = 3$	$\dfrac{x}{4} = 7$
$3(6) = 3(6)$	$\dfrac{x}{4}(4) = 7(4)$
$18 = 18$	$x = 28$

When you solve an equation by multiplying each side of the equation by the same number, you are using the **Multiplication Property of Equality**.

Example

Tutor

2. The weight of an object on the Moon is one-sixth that of its weight on Earth. If an object weighs 35 pounds on the Moon, write and solve a division equation to find its weight on Earth.

Words Weight of object on Earth divided by 6 equals weight on Moon.

Variable Let w represent the weight of the object on Earth.

Bar Diagram

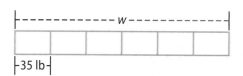

Equation $\dfrac{w}{6}$ = 35

$\dfrac{w}{6} = 35$ Write the equation.

$\dfrac{w}{6}(6) = 35(6)$ Multiply each side by 6.

$w = 210$ $6 \times 35 = 210$

The object weighs 210 pounds on Earth.

Got It? Do this problem to find out.

b. Nathan picked a total of 60 apples in $\dfrac{1}{3}$ hour. Write and solve a division equation to find how many apples Nathan could pick in 1 hour.

 Show your work.

b. _____

Division Equations

In Example 2, dividing by 6 is the same as multiplying by $\frac{1}{6}$.

$\dfrac{w}{6} = \dfrac{1}{6}w$

So, the equation can also be solved with the multiplicative inverse of $\frac{1}{6}$.

$\dfrac{1}{6}w = 35$

$6 \cdot \dfrac{1}{6}w = 35 \cdot 6$

$w = 210$

Example

Tutor

3. Write a real-world problem that can be represented by the equation $\frac{r}{8.5} = 16$. Solve the equation and represent the solution on a number line.

Carla is buying ribbon for costumes. She wants to divide the ribbon into 8.5-inch pieces for 16 costumes. What length of ribbon should Carla buy?

Let r represent the length of ribbon Carla should buy.

$$\frac{r}{8.5} = 16 \qquad \text{Write the equation.}$$

$$(8.5)\frac{r}{8.5} = 16(8.5) \qquad \text{Multiply each side by 8.5.}$$

$$r = 136 \qquad 8.5 \times 16 = 136$$

Carla should buy 136 inches of ribbon. Graph the solution.

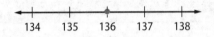
```
134   135   136   137   138
```

Guided Practice

1. The length of an object in feet is equal to 3 times its length in yards. The length of a waterslide is 48 feet. Write and solve a multiplication equation to find the length of the waterslide in yards. (Example 1) _____

2. Chen is buying a ham. He wants to divide it into 6.5-ounce servings for 12 people. Write and solve a division equation to find what size ham Chen should buy.

(Example 2) _____

3. Write a real-world problem that can be represented by the equation $\frac{s}{11} = 2$. Solve the equation and graph the solution on a number line. (Example 3) _____

_____

_____

4. **?** **Building on the Essential Question** When solving an equation, why is it necessary to perform the same operation on each side of the equal sign? _____

_____

_____

Rate Yourself!

How well do you understand solving multiplication and division equations? Circle the image that applies.

Clear   Somewhat   Not So
            Clear   Clear

Find out online. Use the Self-Check Quiz.

Check ✓

FOLDABLES Time to update your Foldable!

Independent Practice

Solve each equation. Check your solution. (Examples 1 and 2)

Show your work.

1. $4g = 24$ _____

2. $-5d = 30$ _____

3. $-4.7 = \dfrac{g}{-3.2}$ _____

Write and solve an equation to solve each problem. Represent the solution on a number line. (Examples 1 and 2)

4. A jewelry store is selling a set of 4 pairs of gemstone earrings for $58, including tax. What is the cost of one pair of earrings?

_____

5. Sophia is buying party favors. She has a budget of $2.75 a person for 6 people. How much can Sophia spend on party favors?

_____

6. Write a real-world problem that can be represented by the equation $8.6r = 34.4$. Solve the equation. (Example 3)

_____

_____

7. **MP** **Apply Math to the Real World** Refer to the graphic novel frame below for Exercises a–b.

a. If Mei has earned 30 points, write and solve a multiplication equation to find how many more books she needs to read. _____

b. Suppose Mei has read 7 books. Write and solve a division equation to find the number of points she has earned. _____

Solve each equation. Check your solution.

8. $39 = 1\frac{3}{10}b$ _____

9. $\frac{1}{2}e = \frac{1}{4}$ _____

10. $\frac{2}{5}g = \frac{3}{5}$ _____

11. Find the Error Noah is solving $5x = 75$. Determine his mistake and correct it.

_____

_____

12. **STEM** An average person's heart beats about 103,680 times a day. Write and solve an equation to find about how many times the average person's heart beats in one minute.

_____

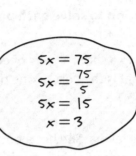
$5x = 75$
$5x = \frac{75}{5}$
$5x = 15$
$x = 3$

H.O.T. Problems Higher-Order Thinking

13. Evaluate Identify the equation that does not belong with the other three. Explain your reasoning.

$5x = 20$	$4b = 7$	$8w = 32$	$12y = 48$

_____

14. Analyze Explain how you know that the equations $\frac{1}{4} = 2x$ and $\frac{1}{4} \div x = 2$ have the same solution. Then, find the solution.

_____

_____

_____

15. Create Write a division equation that has a solution of 42.

_____

16. Create Write a real-world problem that can be represented with the equation $\frac{16}{c} = 8$. Then solve the equation.

_____

_____

_____

Multi-Step Problem Solving

17. The table shows the number of miles Diego and some friends traveled each day and the amount of time it took. Which equation can be used to determine the average speed, r, at which they traveled? What property would you use to solve the equation?

Day	Distance (miles)	Time (hours)
1	110	1.9
2	90	1.5
3	105	1.8
4	120	2.1

Ⓐ $425 = \frac{7.3}{r}$; Multiplication Property of Equality

Ⓑ $425 = 7.3r$; Division Property of Equality

Ⓒ $425 = r + 7.3$; Subtraction Property of Equality

Ⓓ $425 = r - 7.3$; Addition Property of Equality

Use a problem-solving model to solve this problem.

1 Analyze

**Read the problem. Circle the information you know.
Underline what the problem is asking you to find.**

2 Plan

What will you need to do to solve the problem? Write your plan in steps.

Step 1 Write an equation to represent the situation.

Step 2 Determine the property used to solve the equation.

> **Read to Succeed!**
> When solving problems dealing with distance, rate, and time, the equation is $d = rt$, where d is the distance, r is the rate, and t is the time.

3 Solve

Use your plan to solve the problem. Show your steps.

The group drove a total of 425 miles in 7.3 hours.

$d = r \cdot t$ Distance, rate, time equation

_____ $= r \cdot$ _____   Substitute known values.

To solve the equation, you would use the _____ Property of Equality.

Choice _____ is correct. Fill in that answer choice.

4 Justify and Evaluate

How do you know your solution is accurate?

_____

_____

Ⓟ = Proportionality   ⒺⒺ = Expressions, Equations, and Relationships   Ⓜ Ⓟ = Mathematical Processes

More Multi-Step Problem Solving

Use a problem-solving model to solve each problem.

18. The table shows the distance Catrell biked each day and his rate. Which equation can be used to determine the average time, t, he spent riding his bike each day? What property would you use to solve the equation? (EE) (P) (MP)

Day	Distance (miles)	Rate (miles/hour)
1	15	10
2	18	12
3	21	14
4	24	16

(A) $78 = \dfrac{t}{52}$; Division Property of Equality

(B) $78 = 52t$; Multiplication Property of Equality

(C) $78 = \dfrac{t}{52}$; Multiplication Property of Equality

(D) $78 = 52t$; Division Property of Equality

19. The model below shows the relationship between a gallon and pints. Use the model to write an equation to determine the number of pints given the gallons. Use the equation to convert $\dfrac{2}{3}$ gallon into pints. Round the answer to the nearest tenth. (EE) (P) (N) (MP)

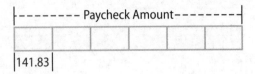

20. Linh decides to put $\dfrac{1}{6}$ of her paycheck into her savings account. Use the model below to write an equation that represents the amount of her paycheck in terms of the amount put into savings. Then use the equation to determine the amount of her paycheck. (EE) (N) (MP)

Paycheck Amount

141.83					

21. In the diagram below, $\angle ABC$ is divided into 4 angles of equal measure and $m\angle ABC = 140°$. Write and solve two equations that can be used to find the degree measure of $\angle EBF$. Identify any properties of equalities that you used to solve either equation. (EE) (N) (MP)

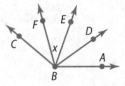

EE = Expressions, Equations, and Relationships   **P** = Proportionality   **N** = Number and Operations   **MP** = Mathematical Processes

628   Chapter 8 Equations and Inequalities

Guess, Check, and Revise

Mathematical Process
6.1(B) Use a problem-solving model that incorporates analyzing given information, formulating a plan or strategy, determining a solution, justifying the solution, and evaluating the problem-solving process and the reasonableness of the solution.

Targeted TEKS 6.9(A)

Smart Money

Damian received $100 for his birthday to pay for guitar lessons. The gift money was in $20 bills and $10 bills. When he paid for his lesson, he gave his teacher 8 bills.

How many $20 bills and how many $10 bills did Damian receive?

Analyze *What are the facts?*

- Damian received 8 bills that add up to $100.
- The money was in $20 bills and $10 bills.

Plan *What is your strategy to solve this problem?*

Make a guess until you find an answer that makes sense for the problem.

Solve *How can you apply the strategy?*

Use addends that have a sum of 8 to find the number of $20 and $10 bills.

Number of $20 bills	Number of $10 bills	Total Amount	Compare to $100
1	7	1($20) + 7($10) = $	
2	6	2($20) + 6($10) = $	
3	5	3($20) + 5($10) = $	
4	4	4($20) + 4($10) = $	

Justify and Evaluate *Does the answer make sense?*

The other combinations are either less than or greater than $100.

Anime Adventure

A bookstore sells used graphic novels in packages of 5 and new graphic novels in packages of 3.

If Amy buys a total of 16 graphic novels, how many packages of new and used graphic novels did she buy?

Analyze

Read the problem. What are you being asked to find?

I need to find _____

_____.

<u>Underline</u> **key words and values in the problem.**
What information do you know?

The _____ novels come in packages of ☐ and the _____

novels come in packages of ☐. Amy buys ☐ graphic novels.

Plan

Choose a problem-solving strategy.

I will use the _____ strategy.

Solve

Use your problem-solving strategy to solve the problem. Make a guess.

Justify and Evaluate

Use information from the problem to check your answer.

Make a list of multiples of 3 and a list of multiples of 5. Look for a combination of these multiples that add up to 16.

Multi-Step Problem Solving

Work with a small group to solve the following problems. Show your work on a separate piece of paper.

1. Quizzes

On a science quiz, Ivan earned 18 points. There are six problems worth 2 points each and two problems worth 4 points each.

Determine the number of problems of each type Ivan answered correctly.

2. Numbers

Kathryn is thinking of four numbers from 1 through 9 with a sum of 18. Each number is used only once.

Determine the numbers.

3. Equations

Use the symbols +, −, ×, or ÷ to make the following equation true. Use each symbol only once.

$$3 \ \blacksquare \ 4 \ \blacksquare \ 6 \ \blacksquare \ 1 = 18$$

Use any strategy!

4. Money

Nathaniel is saving money to buy a new graphics card for his computer that costs $260.

If he is saving $18 a month and already has $134, in how many more months will he have enough money for the graphics card?

Vocabulary Check

1. Define *equation*. Give an example of an equation and an example of an expression. Use a variable in each example. **TEKS** 6.7(B), 6.1(B)

Key Concept Check

2. Complete the graphic organizer by giving key words that indicate the given type of equation, an example of the type of equation, and the operation used to solve the equation. **TEKS** 6.10(A), 6.1(E)

Type	Key Words	Example	Operation Used to Solve
Addition			
Subtraction			
Multiplication			
Division			

3. The difference between the water levels for high and low tide was 3.6 feet. Write and solve an equation to find the water level at high tide. **TEKS** 6.9(A), 6.1(B) _____

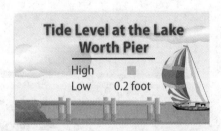

Tide Level at the Lake Worth Pier

High   ▪
Low   0.2 foot

Multi-Step Problem Solving

4. If $-9.8x = -14.7$, what is the value of $8(x - 9.2)$? **EE** **MP**

   Ⓐ 1.5   Ⓒ −61.6

   Ⓑ −7.7   Ⓓ −85.6

EE = Expressions, Equations, and Relationships   **MP** = Mathematical Processes

Model Inequalities

INQUIRY HOW can I select tools and techniques to model inequalities?

In saltwater fishing, any flounder that is caught may be kept if it is greater than or equal to 12 inches long. Any flounder shorter than that must be released back into the water. Pat caught a flounder that is 14 inches long. He wants to know if he can keep the fish.

Texas Essential Knowledge and Skills

Targeted TEKS
6.10(A) Model and solve one-variable, one-step equations and inequalities that represent problems, including geometric concepts.

Mathematical Processes
6.1(C), 6.1(D), 6.1(E), 6.1(G)

Hands-On Activity

An *inequality* is a mathematical sentence that compares quantities. An inequality like $x < 7$ or $x > 5$ can be written to express how a variable compares to a number.

Step 1 Label the minimum length of flounders that may be kept.

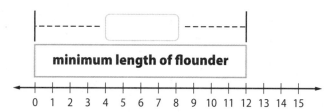

Step 2 Label the length of the flounder Pat caught on the top bar diagram.

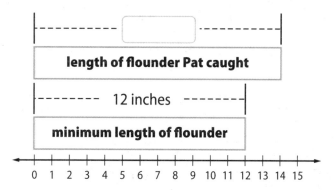

The bar representing Pat's fish is _____ than the bar representing the minimum length that can be kept.

So, Pat _____ keep the fish.

Investigate

MP Select Tools and Techniques Work with a partner. Draw bar diagrams to solve each problem.

1. For flights within the United States, luggage must be no more than 50 pounds. Imelda's luggage weighs 53 pounds. Can she take the luggage on her flight? _____

2. Byron needs at least 20 minutes between the end of his soccer practice and the start of his dentist appointment. His practice ends at 4:30 and his appointment is at 5:00. Does he have enough time? _____

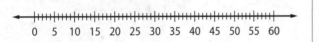

0 5 10 15 20 25 30 35 40 45 50 55 60

0 2 4 6 8 10 12 14 16 18 20 22 24 26 28 30

3. **MP Analyze Relationships** Which inequality is used when the situation involves a "minimum"? Explain.

_____

_____

_____

4. **MP Analyze Relationships** Which inequality is used when the situation involves a "maximum"? Explain.

_____

_____

_____

Create

5. **MP Analyze Relationships** Write a rule for determining possible values of a variable in an inequality. _____

_____

_____

_____

6. **INQUIRY** HOW can I select tools and techniques to model inequalities?

_____

_____

_____

Lesson 5

Inequalities

 Launch the Lesson: Vocabulary

An **inequality** is a mathematical sentence that compares quantities.

Definition	Symbols

 inequality

Example	Nonexample

Texas Essential Knowledge and Skills

Targeted TEKS
6.10(B) Determine if the given value(s) make(s) one-variable, one-step equations or inequalities true.

Mathematical Processes
6.1(A), 6.1(B), 6.1(D), 6.1(F)

Vocabulary
inequality

Essential Question
HOW are symbols, such as $<$, $>$, and $=$, useful?

Real-World Investigation

Compare the following using $<$ or $>$.

1. the score after 2 goals is ◯ the score after 3 goals

2. the cost to download 10 songs is ◯ the cost to download 2 songs

3. the outside temperature in summer is ◯ the outside temperature in winter

4. the height of a 1st grade student is ◯ the height of a 6th grade student

5. the time to eat lunch is ◯ the time to brush your teeth

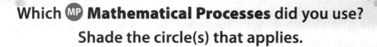 **Which MP Mathematical Processes did you use?**
Shade the circle(s) that applies.

Ⓐ Apply Math to the Real World.   Ⓔ Organize Ideas.

Ⓑ Use a Problem-Solving Model.   Ⓕ Analyze Relationships.

Ⓒ Select Tools and Techniques.   Ⓖ Justify Arguments.

Ⓓ Use Multiple Representations.

Inequalities

Symbols	<	>	≤	≥
Words	• is less than • is fewer than	• is greater than • is more than	• is less than or equal to • is at most	• is greater than or equal to • is at least
Examples	$3 < 5$	$8 > 4$	$7 \le 10$	$12 \ge 9$

Inequalities can be solved by determining if given values of the variables make the inequality true.

Tutor

Example

1. **Of the given values 6, 7, or 8, determine which value(s) make(s) the inequality $f + 2 < 9$ true.**

Replace f with each of the given values.

$f + 2 < 9$	Write the inequality.
$6 + 2 \overset{?}{<} 9$	Replace f with 6.
$8 < 9$ ✓	This is a true statement.

$f + 2 < 9$	Write the inequality.
$7 + 2 \overset{?}{<} 9$	Replace f with 7.
$9 < 9$ ✗	This is not a true statement.

$f + 2 < 9$	Write the inequality.
$8 + 2 \overset{?}{<} 9$	Replace f with 8.
$10 < 9$ ✗	This is not a true statement.

Since the number 6 is the only value that makes a true statement, 6 is a solution of the inequality.

Got It? Do this problem to find out.

a. Of the given values 8, 9, or 10, determine which value(s) make(s) the inequality $n - 3 > 6$ true.

Work Zone

Show your work.

a. _____

Determine Solutions of an Inequality

Since an inequality uses greater than and less than symbols, one-variable inequalities have infinitely many solutions. For example, any rational number greater than 4 will make the inequality $x > 4$ true.

Once you have determined if a given value makes an inequality true, you have determined a solution to that inequality.

Tutor

Examples

Is the given value a solution of the inequality?

2. $x + 3 > 9, x = 4$

$x + 3 > 9$ Write the inequality.

$4 + 3 \overset{?}{>} 9$ Replace x with 4.

$\qquad 7 \not> 9$ Simplify.

Since 7 is not greater than 9, 4 is not a solution.

3. $12 \le 18 - y, y = 6$

$12 \le 18 - y$ Write the inequality.

$12 \overset{?}{\le} 18 - 6$ Replace y with 6.

$12 \le 12$ Simplify.

Since $12 = 12$, 12 is a solution.

4. $17 \ge 11 + x, x = 8$

$17 \ge 11 + x$ Write the inequality.

$17 \overset{?}{\ge} 11 + \boxed{}$ Replace x with $\boxed{}$.

$17 \not\ge \boxed{}$ Simplify.

Since $\boxed{}$ is not greater than or equal to $\boxed{}$, $\boxed{}$ is not a solution.

> **Got It?** Do these problems to find out.

b. $a + 7 > 15, a = 9$ **c.** $22 \le 15 + b, b = 6$

d. $n - 4 < 6, n = 10$ **e.** $12 \ge 5 + g, g = 7$

STOP and Reflect

Name two solutions of the inequality $12 > 6 + y$.

Show your work.

b. _____

c. _____

d. _____

e. _____

 Tutor

Example

5. Luisa works at a gift shop. She receives a bonus if she makes more than 20 balloon bouquets in a month. Which months did Luisa receive a bonus? Use the inequality $b > 20$, where b represents the number of balloon bouquets made each month, to solve.

Balloon Sales	
Month	Number Sold
July	25
August	12
September	18
October	32

Use the *guess*, *check*, and *revise* strategy.

Try 25.	Try 12.	Try 18.	Try 32.
$b > 20$	$b > 20$	$b > 20$	$b > 20$
$25 > 20$ Yes	$12 > 20$ No	$18 > 20$ No	$32 > 20$ Yes

So, Luisa received a bonus in July and October.

Guided Practice

Determine if the given value(s) make(s) each inequality true. (Example 1)

1. $9 + a < 17; 7, 8, 9$ _____

2. $b - 10 > 5; 14, 15, 16$ _____

 Show your work.

Is the given value a solution of the inequality? (Examples 2–4)

3. $x - 5 < 5, x = 15$

_____

4. $32 \geq 8n, n = 3$

_____

5. If the bakery sells more than 45 bagels in a day, they make a profit. Use the inequality $b > 45$ to determine which days the bakery made a profit. (Example 5)

Day	Number of Bagels Sold
Monday	18
Tuesday	25
Wednesday	21
Thursday	36
Friday	50
Saturday	48
Sunday	40

6.  **Building on the Essential Question** How can mental math help you find solutions to inequalities?

_____

_____

Rate Yourself!

☐ I understand how to solve inequalities.

▶▶ Great! You're ready to move on!

☐ I still have some questions about solving inequalities.

📖 No problem! Go online to access a Personal Tutor. Check ✓

Independent Practice

6.10(B), 6.1(F) TEKS

Determine if the given value(s) make(s) each inequality true. (Example 1)

1. $1 + f < 7; 5, 6, 7$ _____

Show your work.

2. $g - 3 > 4; 6, 7, 8$ _____

Is the given value a solution of the inequality? (Examples 2–4)

3. $q - 2 > 16, q = 20$ _____

4. $t - 7 < 10, t = 28$ _____

5. The table shows the number of different types of roller coasters in the United States. An amusement park wants to build a new roller coaster. They will only build a roller coaster if there are less than 10 of that type in the United States. Use the inequality $r < 10$, where r is the number of a certain type of roller coaster, to determine which type(s) will be built. (Example 5)

_____

_____

Type	Number
Sit down (steel)	460
Sit down (wood)	111
Inverted	42
Flying	9
Stand up	7
Suspended	5

6. The table shows the number of different types of movies in Lavar's collection. He wants to buy a new movie to add to his collection. He only wants to buy a movie if he already has more than 15 movies of that type. Use the inequality $m > 15$, where m is the number of the type of movie, to determine which type(s) he will buy. (Example 5)

_____

Movie Type	Number
Action	18
Comedy	24
Drama	12
Thriller	15

7. The number of text messages Lelah sent each month is shown in the table. She can send no more than 55 messages each month without being charged. Use the inequality $t \leq 55$, where t is the number of text messages in a month, to determine in which months she exceeded her limit. If each additional text costs $0.25, how much was Lelah charged from January to April?

_____

_____

Month	Text Messages
Jan.	56
Feb.	57
Mar.	55
Apr.	51

8. **MP Analyze Relationships** Use one-variable equations and inequalities to fill in the graphic organizer.

	Equation	Inequality
Example		
Number of Solutions		

 H.O.T. Problems Higher-Order Thinking

9. **Analyze** State three numbers that are solutions to the inequality $x + 1 \leq 5$.

_____

10. **Evaluate** If $x = 2$, is the following inequality *true* or *false*? Explain.

$$\frac{112}{8} + x \geq 15 + 4x - 7$$

_____

_____

11. **Analyze** If $a > b$ and $b > c$, what is true about the relationship between a and c? Explain your reasoning.

_____

_____

_____

12. **Evaluate** Explain why inequalities of the form $x > c$ or $x < c$, where c is any rational number, have infinitely many solutions.

_____

_____

_____

13. **Analyze** Analyze the relationship between the inequalities in each pair of inequalities below. Write the integers that are solutions to both inequalities in each pair.

a. $y > 4$ and $y \leq 6$ _____

b. $x \geq -3$ and $x < 0$ _____

c. $m < 5$ and $m > 3$ _____

d. $r < -1$ and $r > 0$ _____

Download more Extra Practice at **connectED.mcgraw-hill.com.**

Multi-Step Problem Solving

14. Some friends each hope to attend a festival that costs $65. To earn money, they mowed lawns. Use the inequality $f + s \geq 65$, where f is the Friday earnings and s is the Saturday earnings, to determine who earned enough money to go to the festival.

	Friday	Saturday
Cody	$30	$10
Dominic	$60	$0
Emir	$45	$10
Fernando	$20	$55

Ⓐ Cody   Ⓒ Emir

Ⓑ Dominic   Ⓓ Fernando

Use a problem-solving model to solve this problem.

1 Analyze

Read the problem. Circle the information you know.
Underline what the problem is asking you to find.

2 Plan

What will you need to do to solve the problem? Write your plan in steps.

Step 1   Substitute the values for f and s in the inequality.

Step 2   Determine whether the inequality is true.

> **Read to Succeed!**
>
> The inequality $\geq$ means greater than or equal to, so sums must be greater than or equal to 65 for the inequality to be true.

3 Solve

Use your plan to solve the problem. Show your steps.

Cody	Dominic	Emir	Fernando
$30 + 10 \geq 65$	$60 + 0 \geq 65$	$45 + 10 \geq 65$	$20 + 55 \geq 65$
☐ ≥ 65	☐ ≥ 65	☐ ≥ 65	☐ ≥ 65

Since $75 \geq 65$, _____ earned enough money. Choice ☐ is correct.
Fill in that answer choice.

4 Justify and Evaluate

How do you know your solution is accurate?

_____

_____

_____

EE = Expressions, Equations, and Relationships   **MP** = Mathematical Processes

More Multi-Step Problem Solving

Use a problem-solving model to solve each problem.

15. The classmates below each have a cell phone plan that allows 200 text messages per month. Use the inequality $a + b > 200$, where a is the number of texts during Week 1 and b is the number of texts during Week 2, to determine who is already over their monthly budget of 200 texts. **EE** **MP**

	Week 1	Week 2
Olivia	25	50
Anna	150	10
Sierra	125	110
Vanesa	100	100

Ⓐ Olivia

Ⓑ Anna

Ⓒ Sierra

Ⓓ Vanesa

16. Rafael has more than 5 feet of wire. He uses 1.5 feet for a project. In the inequality $x + 1.5 > 5$, x represents the amount of wire that Rafael has left, in feet. What is the minimum number of inches he has left? **EE** **P** **MP**

17. Hannah's backpack can hold no more than 30 pounds. She has a laptop that weighs 7 pounds and books that weigh 5 pounds each. What is the maximum number of books that Hannah can carry in her backpack? **EE** **MP**

18. If $x < 11$ and $x \geq 4$, what are the possible whole number values of x? **EE** **MP**

EE = Expressions, Equations, and Relationships   **P** = Proportionality   **MP** = Mathematical Processes

642   **Chapter 8** Equations and Inequalities

Write Inequalities and Represent Solutions

 Launch the Lesson: Real World

Texas Essential Knowledge and Skills

Targeted TEKS
6.9(A) Write one-variable, one-step equations and inequalities to represent constraints or conditions within problems. *Also addresses 6.9(B), 6.9(C).*

Mathematical Processes
6.1(A), 6.1(B), 6.1(D), 6.1(F)

Look at the situations below. Circle the numbers that are possible answers in each situation.

1. Jessica spent more than $5 at the arcade.

   1 2 3 4 5 6 7 8 9 10 11 12 13 14 15

2. Less than 6 people rang the bell on the mallet game.

   1 2 3 4 5 6 7 8 9 10 11 12 13 14 15

3. There were less than 10 people in line for the Ferris wheel.

   1 2 3 4 5 6 7 8 9 10 11 12 13 14 15

4. It costs more than 6 tokens to ride the bumper cars.

   1 2 3 4 5 6 7 8 9 10 11 12 13 14 15

5. There are less than 8 lemonade stands.

   1 2 3 4 5 6 7 8 9 10 11 12 13 14 15

6. There are more than 12 different flavors of taffy.

   1 2 3 4 5 6 7 8 9 10 11 12 13 14 15

7. Describe any patterns you see in Exercises 1–6.

Essential Question
HOW are symbols, such as <, >, and =, useful?

ping!

Which 🔵**MP** **Mathematical Processes did you use?**
Shade the circle(s) that applies.

Ⓐ Apply Math to the Real World.

Ⓑ Use a Problem-Solving Model.

Ⓒ Select Tools and Techniques.

Ⓓ Use Multiple Representations.

Ⓔ Organize Ideas.

Ⓕ Analyze Relationships.

Ⓖ Justify Arguments.

Write Inequalities

You can write an inequality to represent constraints or conditions within real-world problems.

To do so, you must first define a variable.

Tutor

Examples

Write an inequality for each constraint or condition.

1. **You must be over 12 years old to ride the go-karts.**

Words	Your age	is over	12.
Variable		Let $a =$ your age.	
Inequality	a	$>$	12

The inequality is $a > 12$.

STOP and Reflect

Which inequality symbol represents "is at most"?

2. **A pony is less than 14.2 hands tall.**

Words	A pony	is less than	14.2.
Variable		Let $p =$ the height of the pony	
Inequality	p	$<$	14.2

The inequality is $p < 14.2$.

3. **You must be at least 16 years old to have a driver's license.**

Words	Your age	is at least	16 years.
Variable		Let $a =$ your age.	
Inequality	a	$\geq$	16

The inequality is $a \geq 16$.

Got It? Do these problems to find out.

Write an inequality for each constraint or condition.

a. You must be older than 13 to play in the basketball league.

b. To use one stamp, your domestic letter must weigh under 3.5 ounces.

c. You must be at least 18 years old to vote.

a. _____

b. _____

c. _____

Represent an Inequality on the Number Line

Inequalities can be represented, or graphed, on a number line. Sometimes, it is impossible to show all the values that make an inequality true. The graph helps you see the values that make the inequality true.

Tutor

Examples

Represent each inequality on a number line.

4. $n > 9$

Place an open dot at 9. Then draw a line and an arrow to the right.

The open dot means the number 9 is *not* included in the graph.

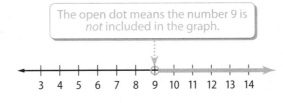

The values that lie on the line make the sentence true. All numbers greater than 9 make the sentence true.

> **Graphing Inequalities**
>
> When inequalities are represented on a number line, an open dot means the number is not included ($<$ or $>$) and a closed dot means it is included ($\leq$ or $\geq$).

5. $n \leq 10$

Place a closed dot at 10. Then draw a line and an arrow to the left.

The closed dot means the number 10 *is* included in the graph.

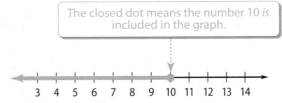

All numbers 10 and less make the sentence true.

Got It? Do these problems to find out.

d. $a < 15$

e. $b \geq 7$

Example

6. Write a real-world problem that can be represented by the inequality $s \leq 25$. Represent the solution on a number line.

Traffic on a residential street can travel at speeds of no more than 25 miles per hour.

Place a closed dot at 25. Then draw a line and an arrow to the left. All numbers 25 and less make the sentence true.

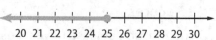

Guided Practice

Write an inequality for each constraint or condition. (Examples 1–3)

1. The movie will be no more than 90 minutes in length. _____

2. The mountain is at least 985 feet tall. _____

Represent each inequality on a number line. (Examples 4 and 5)

3. $a \leq 6$

4. $b > -4$

5. Write a real-world problem that can be represented by the inequality $b \leq 40$. Represent the solution on a number line.

(Example 6) _____

_____

6. (?) **Building on the Essential Question** How can graphing an inequality help to solve it? _____

_____

Rate Yourself!

How confident are you about writing and graphing inequalities? Shade the ring on the target.

I'm on target.

I need help.

Find out online. Use the Self-Check Quiz.

Check

Independent Practice

Write an inequality for each constraint or condition. (Examples 1–3)

1. Swim practice will be no more than 35 laps. _____

2. Kevin ran for less than 5 miles. _____

3. The occupancy of the room must be less than 437 people. _____

Represent each inequality on a number line. (Examples 4 and 5)

4. $f > -1$

5. $x \leq 5$

6. $y \geq -4$

7. Write a real-world problem that can be represented by the inequality $s < 20$. Represent the solution on a number line. (Example 6)

8. **MP Analyze Relationships** Fill in the information in the table. The first is done for you.

Symbol	Words	Open or closed dot on number line?
>	greater than	open dot
	greater than or equal to	
	less than	
≤		

9. **Find the Error** Mei is writing an inequality for the expression *at least 10 hours of community service*. Determine her mistake and correct it.

_____

_____

_____

_____

$c \leq 10$

 H.O.T. Problems Higher-Order Thinking

10. **Evaluate** Name three solutions of the inequality $w \leq \frac{4}{5}$. Then justify

your response using a number line. _____

<----------------------------------->

11. **Analyze** Explain the difference between graphing an inequality with a closed dot and one with an open dot. Use examples to support your reasoning.

_____

_____

_____

_____

_____

12. **Analyze** Analyze the relationship between the inequalities in each pair of inequalities below. Represent the solution that satisfies the pair of inequalities.

a. $x > 5$ and $x < 8$ <+——+——+——+——+——+——+——+——+>

b. $y \geq -2$ and $y < 7$ <+——+——+——+——+——+——+——+——+>

13. **Analyze** Write an inequality to represent each graph.

a.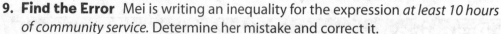
   2   3   4   5   6   7   _____

   b.
   −10 −9 −8 −7 −6 −5 −4 −3   _____

Multi-Step Problem Solving

14. The table shows the heights of 5 people and whether they were allowed to ride a certain roller coaster. Let *a* represent a person's height in inches. Which inequality represents the heights, in inches, of people allowed to ride this roller coaster? **EE P MP**

Height	Allowed
5 ft 7 in.	Yes
5 ft 3 in.	Yes
4 ft 6 in.	Yes
4 ft 5 in.	No
4 ft 3 in.	No

Ⓐ $a > 46$

Ⓑ $a > 54$

Ⓒ $a \geq 54$

Ⓓ $a < 54$

Use a problem-solving model to solve this problem.

1 Analyze

Read the problem. Circle the information you know. Underline what the problem is asking you to find.

2 Plan

What will you need to do to solve the problem? Write your plan in steps.

Step 1 Determine the minimum height allowed on the roller coaster. Convert the height to inches.

Step 2 Write an inequality that represents the situation.

Read to Succeed!
When the term "minimum" is used, the inequality is greater than or equal to.

3 Solve

Use your plan to solve the problem. Show your steps.

The minimum height that was allowed on the roller coaster was ☐ ft ☐ in. Heights shorter than that were not allowed on the roller coaster.

☐ feet ☐ inches = ☐ inches

So, $a \geq$ ☐. Choice ☐ is correct. Fill in that answer choice.

4 Justify and Evaluate

How do you know your solution is accurate?

_____

_____

_____

EE = Expressions, Equations, and Relationships   **P** = Proportionality   **MP** = Mathematical Processes

More Multi-Step Problem Solving

Use a problem-solving model to solve each problem.

15. The table shows the resting heart rate of different people and whether or not it was considered elevated. Let h represent the heart rate in beats per minute. Which inequality represents the heart rates that are considered elevated? **EE** **MP**

Heart Rate (bpm)	Result
62	Normal
79	Normal
100	Normal
101	Elevated
105	Elevated

    Ⓐ $h \leq 100$

    Ⓑ $h > 101$

    Ⓒ $h < 100$

    Ⓓ $h \geq 101$

16. Lorenzo solved the following inequality $x + 3 < 10$ and graphed the solution on a number line. The graph contained the values -3, 2.4, 0, and 7. Which of these values is incorrect? Explain. **EE** **MP**

17. Marcus has $50 in his wallet. He buys 2 CDs that costs $12 each and wants to buy posters that cost $6 each. The inequality $p \leq 4$ represents the number of posters he can buy. Represent the solutions of the inequality on the number line. **EE** **MP**

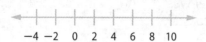

18. Marianna wants to run at least 6.2 miles to train for a quarter-marathon. The inequality $m \geq 6.2$, where m is the number of miles she has run, represents the runs where she met her goal. Represent the solutions of the inequality on the number line. **EE** **MP**

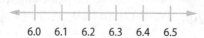

EE = Expressions, Equations, and Relationships   **MP** = Mathematical Processes

Model and Solve One-Step Inequalities

INQUIRY HOW can I select tools to model and solve one-step inequalities?

In a recent Kentucky Derby, the total weight a horse could carry was less than 126 pounds. A jockey weighs a certain number of pounds and his equipment weighs 9 pounds. How much could the jockey weigh?

What do you know? _____

_____

What do you need to find? _____

Texas Essential Knowledge and Skills

Targeted TEKS
6.10(A) Model and solve one-variable, one-step equations and inequalities that represent problems, including geometric concepts. *Also addresses 6.9(A), 6.9(B), 6.9(C).*

Mathematical Processes
6.1(C), 6.1(D), 6.1(E), 6.1(G)

Hands-On Activity

You already learned that you can add or subtract the same quantity to each side of an equation when solving it. This is also true for inequalities.

Step 1   You can represent the situation with an inequality.

$$x + 9 < 126$$

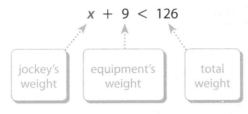

jockey's weight   equipment's weight   total weight

Step 2   Model and solve the inequality $x + 9 < 126$ using a bar diagram. Place a dashed line on 126.

Step 3   The symbol is <, so a box is drawn to the left of 126.

Step 4   The bar represents $x +$ ☐.
Label the bar diagram.

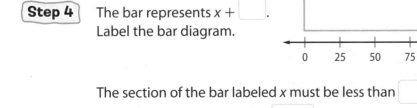

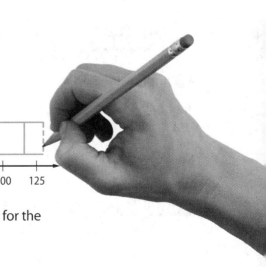

The section of the bar labeled x must be less than ☐ for the inequality to be true. So, $x <$ ☐.

Investigate

Work with a partner to solve each problem by using a model.

1. Regina sent x text messages before lunch. She sent another 4 messages after lunch. She sent less than 7 messages today. How many text messages could she have sent before lunch? Write your answer as an inequality. _____

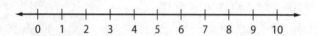

2. A player with five personal fouls cannot stay in the game. Dylan has already earned two personal fouls. How many more personal fouls x could he earn and still stay in the game? Write your answer as an inequality. _____

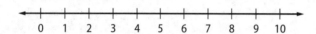

Work with a partner to solve by using the *guess, check, and revise* strategy. Find the least or greatest number that makes the inequality true.

3. $x - 5 \leq 1$ _____

4. $x + 3 \geq 8$ _____

Analyze and Reflect

5. MP Analyze Relationships Explain how you could solve the inequality $x + 7 \leq 12$ using the *guess, check, and revise* strategy. Then solve.

_____

_____

Create

6. MP Apply Math to the Real World Write and solve a word problem using the inequality $x + 6 \leq 25$. _____

_____

_____

7. INQUIRY HOW can I select tools to model and solve one-step inequalities?

_____

_____

Solve One-Step Inequalities

 Launch the Lesson: Real World

Texas Essential Knowledge and Skills

Targeted TEKS
6.10(A) Model and solve one-variable, one-step equations and inequalities that represent problems, including geometric concepts. *Also addresses 6.9(A), 6.9(B), 6.9(C).*

Mathematical Processes
6.1(A), 6.1(B), 6.1(D), 6.1(F)

The graph shows the number of home runs that the top hitters on the baseball team hit last season.

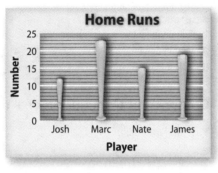

Essential Question
HOW are symbols, such as $<$, $>$, and $=$, useful?

1. Write an inequality that compares the number of home runs James hit to the number of home runs Marc hit.

   _____ $<$ _____

Determine if the inequality you wrote in Exercise 1 remains true after each operation. Explain.

2. Multiply each side of the inequality by 4.

   _____

3. Multiply each side of the inequality by -4.

   _____

4. How could you rewrite the inequality in Exercise 3 so that it was a true statement?

   _____

Which MP Mathematical Processes did you use?
Shade the circle(s) that applies.

Ⓐ Apply Math to the Real World.   Ⓔ Organize Ideas.

Ⓑ Use a Problem-Solving Model.   Ⓕ Analyze Relationships.

Ⓒ Select Tools and Techniques.   Ⓖ Justify Arguments.

Ⓓ Use Multiple Representations.

Use Addition and Subtraction Properties to Solve Inequalities

Work Zone

Words When you add or subtract the same number from each side of an inequality, the inequality remains true.

Example

$$5 < 9$$
$$+4 \quad +4$$
$$\overline{9 < 13}$$

$$11 > 6$$
$$-3 \quad -3$$
$$\overline{8 > 3}$$

These properties are also true for $\leq$ and $\geq$.

Tutor

Examples

1. **Solve $x + 7 \geq 10$. Represent the solution on a number line.**

$x + 7 \geq 10$	Write the inequality.
$\underline{-7 \quad -7}$	Subtract 7 from each side.
$x \quad \geq 3$	Simplify.

The solution is $x \geq 3$. To graph it, draw a closed dot at 3 and draw an arrow to the right on the number line.

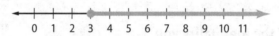

> **Integers**
>
> When adding or subtracting integers, remember to follow the rules for when a sum or difference is positive or negative.
>
> $-9 + 3 = -6$

2. **Solve $x - 3 < -9$. Represent the solution on a number line.**

$x - 3 < -9$	Write the inequality.
$\underline{+3 \quad +3}$	Add 3 to each side.
$x \quad < -6$	Simplify.

The solution is $x < -6$. To graph it, draw an open dot on -6 and draw an arrow to the left on the number line.

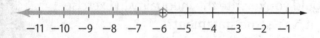

Show your work.

Got It? Do these problems to find out.

a. $n + 2 \leq -5$

b. $y - 3 > 9$

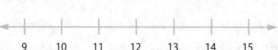

a. _____

b. _____

Use Multiplication and Division Properties to Solve Inequalities

Key Concept

Words	When you multiply or divide each side of an inequality by the same *positive* number, the inequality remains true.
	When you multiply or divide each side of an inequality by the same *negative* number, the inequality symbol must be reversed for the inequality to remain true.

Example

$5 < 10$ $16 > 12$

$5 \times 2 < 10 \times 2$ $\dfrac{16}{-2} < \dfrac{12}{-2}$

$10 < 20$ $-8 < -6$

Examples

Tutor

3. **Solve $-5x \le 45$. Represent the solution on a number line.**

$-5x \le 45$ Write the inequality.

$\dfrac{-5x}{-5} \le \dfrac{45}{-5}$ Divide each side by -5.

$x \ge -9$ Simplify. Reverse the inequality symbol.

The solution is $x \ge -9$.

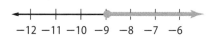
$-12 \quad -11 \quad -10 \quad -9 \quad -8 \quad -7 \quad -6$

---

4. **Solve $\dfrac{x}{8} > 3$. Represent the solution on a number line.**

$\dfrac{x}{8} > 3$ Write the inequality.

$\dfrac{x}{8}(8) > 3(8)$ Multiply each side by 8.

$x > 24$ Simplify.

The solution is $x > 24$.

$21 \quad 22 \quad 23 \quad 24 \quad 25 \quad 26 \quad 27$

Got It? Do these problems to find out.

c. $10x < 80$

$5 \quad 6 \quad 7 \quad 8 \quad 9 \quad 10 \quad 11$

d. $\dfrac{x}{-6} \ge -7$

$39 \quad 40 \quad 41 \quad 42 \quad 43 \quad 44 \quad 45$

Show your work.

c. _____

d. _____

Checking Solutions
You can check your solutions by substituting numbers into the inequality and testing to verify that it holds true.

Example

5. Write and solve a real-world problem that can be represented by the inequality $7c \leq 42$. Represent the solution on a number line.

The symbol $\leq$ means at most or no more than.

Laverne is making bags of party favors for each of the 7 friends attending her birthday party. She does not want to spend more than $42 on the party favors. What is the maximum cost for each party favor bag?

$7c \leq 42$ Write the inequality.

$\dfrac{7c}{7} \leq \dfrac{42}{7}$ Divide each side by 7.

$c \leq 6$ Simplify.

Each bag is, at most, $6.

Guided Practice

Solve each inequality. Represent the solution on a number line. (Examples 1–4)

1. $h - 6 \geq 13$ _____

2. $-5y > -30$ _____

Show your work.

3. Johanna's parents give her $10 per week for lunch money. She cannot decide whether she wants to buy or pack her lunch. If a hot lunch at school costs $2, write and solve an inequality to find the maximum number of times per week Johanna can buy her lunch. (Examples 1–4)

_____

4. Write and solve a real-world problem that can be represented by the inequality $9p \leq 45$. Represent the

solution on a number line. (Example 5) _____

_____

5. (?) **Building on the Essential Question** How is solving an inequality similar to solving an equation?

_____

_____

Rate Yourself!

Are you ready to move on?
Shade the section that applies.

YES   ?   NO

Find out online. Use the Self-Check Quiz.

Check ✓

Independent Practice

6.9(A), 6.9(B), 6.9(C), 6.10(A), 6.1(A)

Solve each inequality. Represent the solution on a number line. (Examples 1–4)

1. $-2 + y \leq -3$ _____

2. $w - 1 < 4$ _____

Show your work.

⟵——————————————⟶

⟵——————————————⟶

3. $7x > 56$ _____

4. $\dfrac{d}{-3} \leq -2$ _____

⟵——————————————⟶

⟵——————————————⟶

5. Write and solve a real-world problem that can be represented by the inequality $0.1x \leq 5.00$. Represent the solution on a number line. (Example 5)

⟵——————————————⟶

_____

_____

_____

6. **MP** **Apply Math to the Real World** Refer to the graphic novel frame below for Exercises a–b.

a. Suppose David has $65 to spend on his ticket and some shirts. He already spent $32.25 on his ticket and fee. Write an inequality that could be used to find the maximum number of shirts he can buy.

_____

b. What is the maximum number of shirts he can buy? _____

Solve each inequality. Represent the solution on a number line.

7. $p - \frac{7}{12} > \frac{3}{10}$ _____

8. $f + 0.3 < -1.7$ _____

 H.O.T. Problems Higher-Order Thinking

9. **Create** Write a word problem that would have the solution $p \leq 21$.

_____

_____

_____

10. **Evaluate** Explain the difference between the solutions to $-6x \geq 36$ and $6x \geq 36$.

_____

_____

_____

_____

11. **Evaluate** Does the order of the quantities in an inequality matter? Explain.

_____

_____

12. **Create** Write a real-world problem and an inequality that can be represented by the number line below.

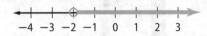

_____

_____

_____

13. **Create** Write an inequality that can be solved using division, where the inequality symbol is not reversed.

_____

Multi-Step Problem Solving

14. The table shows the costs of different size sandwiches at a sandwich shop. Ava has $30 to spend. She spends $5.25 on drinks and buys two Club sandwiches. Write and solve an inequality to find the maximum number of foot long sandwiches she can buy. **EE** **MP**

Sandwich Size	Cost ($)
Club	2.75
6-inch	4.00
Foot long	6.25

Use a problem-solving model to solve this problem.

1 Analyze

Read the problem. Circle the information you know. Underline what the problem is asking you to find.

2 Plan

What will you need to do to solve the problem? Write your plan in steps.

Step 1 Write an inequality to represent the situation.

Step 2 Solve the inequality.

> **Read to Succeed!**
> The term "maximum" means that all values that make the inequality true will be less than the given value.

3 Solve

Use your plan to solve the problem. Show your steps.

Let x represent the number of foot long sandwiches she can buy.

$\$ \boxed{} + 2(\$ \boxed{}) + \boxed{} \; x \; \leq \; \$ \boxed{}$

drinks   club sandwiches   foot long sandwiches   total she can spend

$5.25 + 2(2.75) + 6.25x \leq 30$ Write the inequality.

$\boxed{} + 6.25x \leq 30$ Simplify the constants.

$6.25x \leq \boxed{}$ Subtract.

$x \leq \boxed{}$ Divide.

The greatest whole number that is a solution to the inequality is $\boxed{}$. Complete the grid.

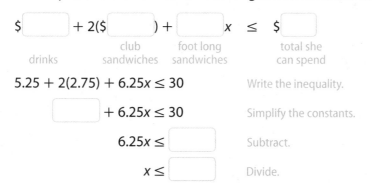

4 Justify and Evaluate

How do you know your solution is accurate?

_____

_____

EE = Expressions, Equations, and Relationships   **MP** = Mathematical Processes

More **Multi-Step** Problem Solving

Use a problem-solving model to solve each problem.

15. The table shows the costs of different bed sheet sizes at a home interior store. Phong has $100.25 to spend. He spends $45 on a blanket, and he buys one twin sheet for his brother. Write and solve an inequality to find the maximum number of full sheets he can buy. **EE** **MP**

Sheet Size	Cost ($)
Twin	9.99
Full	10.50
Queen	20
King	28.50

16. The rectangle below represents a table top that Lakita wants to cover with tiles. Each tile has an area of 7 square inches. To find the maximum number of tiles that will fit the table top, Lakita wants to use the inequality $7x \leq y$. What is the value of y? What is the maximum number of tiles she can use? **EE** **MP**

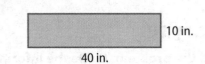

10 in.

40 in.

17. Jamal wants to sell at least 50 tickets for a school raffle. He sells 10 tickets to his family. His dad is going to take at least $\frac{1}{2}$ of the remaining tickets to sell at work. Write and solve an inequality to find the minimum number of tickets his dad will take to work. Represent the solution on the number line. **EE** **MP**

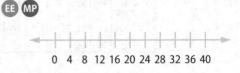

18. Write a word problem for the one-step inequality $3x \leq 15$. **EE** **MP**

_____

_____

_____

_____

21ST CENTURY CAREER

Sound Engineer

Do you enjoy using electronics to make music sound better? If so, you might want to explore a career in sound engineering. Sound engineers, or audio technicians, prepare the sound equipment for recording sessions and live concert performances. They are responsible for operating consoles and other equipment to control, replay, and mix sound from various sources. Sound engineers adjust the microphones, amplifiers, and levels of various instrument and voice tones so that everything sounds great together.

Mathematical Process
6.1(A) Apply mathematics to problems arising in everyday life, society, and the workplace.
Targeted TEKS 6.9(A)

Is This the Career for You?

Are you interested in a career as a sound engineer? Take some of the following courses in high school.

- ◆ Algebra
- ◆ Electronic Technology
- ◆ Music and Computers
- ◆ Physics
- ◆ Sound Engineering

College & Career READINESS

Explore college and careers at ccr.mcgraw-hill.com

Amping the Band!

Use the information in the table and the diagram to solve each problem.

1. In the diagram, the distance between the microphones is 6 feet. This is 3 times the distance d from each microphone to the sound source. Write an equation that represents this situation. _____

2. Solve the equation that you wrote in Exercise 1. Explain the solution. _____

3. The distance from the microphone to the acoustic guitar sound hole is about 11 inches less than what it should be. Write an equation that models this situation. _____

4. Solve the equation that you wrote in Exercise 3. Explain the solution. _____

5. The microphone is about 9 times farther from the electric guitar amplifier than it should be to produce a natural, well-balanced sound. Write and solve an equation to find how far from the amplifier the microphone should be placed. _____

Microphone Mistakes		
Sound Source	**Location of Microphone**	**Resulting Sound**
Acoustic guitar	3 inches from sound hole	very bassy
Electric guitar amplifier	36 inches from amp	thin, reduced bass

6 ft

TEKS Career Project

It's time to update your career portfolio! Go to the *Occupational Outlook Handbook* online and research careers in sound engineering. Make a list of the advantages and disadvantages of working in that field. Prepare a brief oral presentation and present it to your classmates. As others are presenting, listen carefully to their presentations. At the end, ask any clarifying questions.

_____

_____

List several challenges associated with this career.

• _____
• _____
• _____
• _____

Chapter Review

Vocabulary Check

Vocab
abc

Work with a partner to write the correct term for each clue in the crossword puzzle. Seek clarification of each term as needed.

Across

6. operations that undo each other

Down

1. a combination of numbers, variables, and at least one operation

2. property of equality used to solve multiplication equations

3. property of equality used to solve subtraction equations

4. replace a variable with a value that results in a true sentence

5. a symbol of equality

6. a mathematical sentence that compares quantities

7. mathematical sentence showing two expressions are equal

8. the value of a variable that makes an equation true

Key Concept Check ☑ Check

Use Your FOLDABLES

Use your Foldable to help review the chapter. Share your Foldable with a partner and take turns summarizing what you learned in this chapter, while the other partner listens carefully. Seek clarification of any concepts, as needed. **TEKS** 6.1(E)

Tape here

Tab 4

Tab 3

Tab 2

Tab 1

Models   Symbols

Got it?

Match each equation with its solution. **TEKS** 6.10(A)

1. $8x = 128$ **a.** $x > 68$

2. $13 + x = 29$ **b.** $x = 39$

3. $-72 = 3x$ **c.** $x = 18$

4. $x - 22 = 17$ **d.** $x = 16$

5. $\frac{x}{4} > 17$ **e.** $x = -24$

6. $x - 18 \leq 33$ **f.** $x \leq 51$

Multi-Step Problem Solving

7. Paul attended basketball camp for a week. He paid $36, which was $\frac{3}{8}$ the cost of the camp. Paul's parents paid the rest of the camp fee. How much did his parents pay? Show the steps you used and justify your solution. **EE** **MP**

1 Analyze

2 Plan

3 Solve

4 Justify and Evaluate

_____

_____

_____

_____

Got it?

8. Sophia charges $7 an hour to rake leaves plus a $5 fee to remove the leaves. Her neighbors hire her to rake and remove the leaves. How much will Sophia earn if she rakes the leaves for 4 hours and 15 minutes? Show the steps you used and justify your solution. **EE** **MP**

_____

_____

_____

_____

_____

EE = Expressions, Equations, and Relationships   **MP** = Mathematical Processes

Answering the Essential Question

Use what you learned about inequalities to complete the graphic organizer.

TEKS 6.1(D), 6.1(F), 6.1(G)

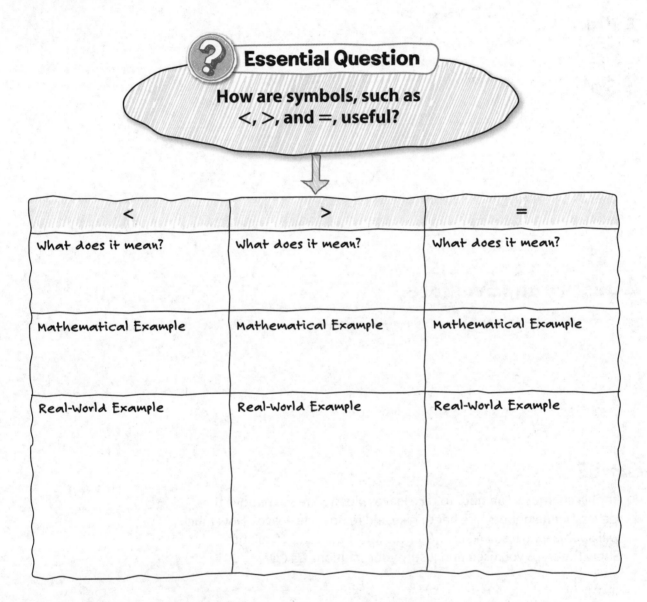

Essential Question

How are symbols, such as
<, >, and =, useful?

<	>	=
What does it mean?	What does it mean?	What does it mean?
Mathematical Example	Mathematical Example	Mathematical Example
Real-World Example	Real-World Example	Real-World Example

 Answer the Essential Question. HOW are symbols, such as <, >, and =, useful? Verbally share your response with a partner, seeking and providing clarification as needed.

Chapter 9

Represent Geometry with Algebra

Texas Essential Knowledge and Skills

Targeted TEKS
6.8 The student applies mathematical process standards to use geometry to represent relationships and solve problems. *Also addresses 6.10.*

Mathematical Processes
6.1, 6.1(A), 6.1(B), 6.1(C), 6.1(D), 6.1(E), 6.1(F), 6.1(G)

Essential Question

HOW does measurement help you solve problems in everyday life?

Math in the Real World

Gardens Each spring, blue bonnets can be spotted throughout the Texas Hill Country. The bluebonnet is the state flower of Texas.

A garden designer plants Texas Blue Bonnets in a 5 foot by 3 foot plot. What area of the garden do the blue bonnets cover? In the diagram below, shade the area covered by blue bonnets.

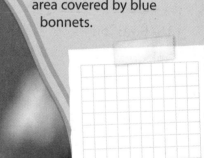

Area = _____

Go Online!
www.connectED.mcgraw-hill.com

Watch Worksheets Vocab Tutor Tools Check

What Tools Do You Need?

Vocab

Vocabulary

acute triangle	formula	scalene triangle
adjacent angles	height	square
area	isosceles triangle	straight angle
base	obtuse triangle	supplementary angles
complementary angles	parallelogram	three-dimensional figure
congruent angles	prism	trapezoid
congruent figures	rectangle	triangle
cubic units	rectangular prism	vertical angles
equiangular triangle	rhombus	volume
equilateral triangle	right triangle	

Review Vocabulary

Using a graphic organizer can help you to remember important vocabulary terms. Fill in the graphic organizer below for the word *area*.

Area

Definition

Units of Measure

Real-World Examples

Quick Review

Review 6.10(A)

Example 1

Solve x + 4 = 19.3.

$x + 4 = 19.3$
$\underline{-4 = -4}$ Subtract 4 from both sides.
$x = 15.3$ Simplify.

Example 2

Solve 2.5x = 15.25.

$2.5x = 15.25$
$\dfrac{2.5x}{2.5} = \dfrac{15.25}{2.5}$ Divide each side by 2.5.
$x = 6.1$ Simplify.

Quick Check

Check

Addition and Subtraction Equations **Solve each equation.**

1. $x - 9.2 = 13.8$

$x = $ _____

Show your work.

2. $w + 1.35 = 4.91$

$w = $ _____

3. $r - 7.8 = 12.7$

$r = $ _____

Multiplication and Division Equations **Solve each equation.**

4. $\dfrac{x}{8.1} = 5$

$x = $ _____

5. $17.2y = 61.92$

$y = $ _____

6. $\dfrac{m}{0.3} = 90$

$m = $ _____

7. The track team has 17 members. They stopped at a restaurant on the way home from a meet. If the total bill was $96.56, what equation can be used to find the average cost per member? Solve your equation.

_____

How Did You Do?

Which problems did you answer correctly in the Quick Check? Shade those exercise numbers below.

①   ②   ③   ④   ⑤   ⑥   ⑦

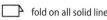 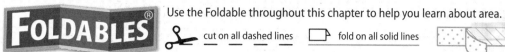
Area

rectangles
and
parallelograms

triangles

trapezoids

Use the Foldable throughout this chapter to help you learn about area.

✂ - - - - - - - - cut on all dashed lines   ◻ fold on all solid lines   tape to page 770

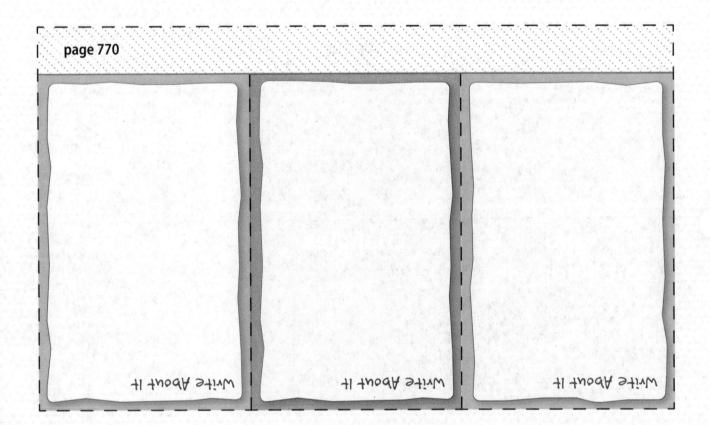

page 770

Write About It

Write About It

Write About It

Angle Relationships

 Launch the Lesson: Real World

Texas Essential Knowledge and Skills

Targeted TEKS
6.10(A) Model and solve one-variable, one-step equations and inequalities that represent problems, including geometric concepts.

Mathematical Processes
6.1(A), 6.1(B), 6.1(C), 6.1(D), 6.1(F)

Stephanie is making a quilt to donate for a charity auction. She uses geometric concepts to place designs in the quilt.

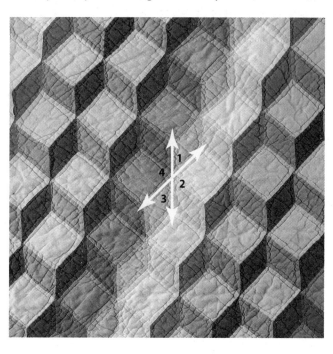

Vocabulary
straight angle
congruent angles
vertical angles
adjacent angles
supplementary angles
complementary angles

Essential Question
HOW does measurement help you solve problems in everyday life?

1. Which angles appear to be acute angles? _____

2. Which angles appear to be obtuse angles? _____

3. **MP** **Analyze Relationships** What do you notice about ∠1 and ∠3 and about ∠2 and ∠4?

_____

_____

Which **MP** **Mathematical Processes** did you use?
Shade the circle(s) that applies.

Ⓐ Apply Math to the Real World.   Ⓔ Organize Ideas.

Ⓑ Use a Problem-Solving Model.   Ⓕ Analyze Relationships.

Ⓒ Select Tools and Techniques.   Ⓖ Justify Arguments.

Ⓓ Use Multiple Representations.

Pairs of Angles

Words	**Adjacent angles** share a vertex and a side.
Model	
	∠1 and ∠2 are adjacent angles.
Words	**Vertical angles** are formed when two lines intersect. Vertical angles have the same measure.
Model	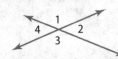
	∠1 and ∠3 are vertical angles. ∠2 and ∠4 are vertical angles.
Words	Two angles that have a sum of 180° are **supplementary angles**.
Model	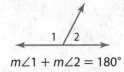
	$m\angle 1 + m\angle 2 = 180°$
Words	Two angles that have a sum of 90° are **complementary angles**.
Model	
	$m\angle 1 + m\angle 2 = 90°$

Straight angles are angles that measure 180°. Two angles that are supplementary form a straight angle. Two angles with the same degree measure are **congruent angles**. Vertical angles are congruent angles. You can classify pairs of angles based on their relationship.

Tutor

Examples

Classify each pair of angles as *adjacent, vertical, supplementary, complementary,* or *neither.*

1.

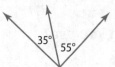

Since the angles share a vertex and a side, they are adjacent angles. Since 35° + 55° = 90°, they are also complementary angles.

2.

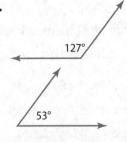

Since 127° + 53° = 180°, the angles are supplementary angles.

Got It? Do these problems to find out.

Classify each pair of angles as *adjacent, vertical, supplementary, complementary,* or *neither.*

a.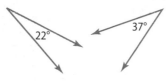

b.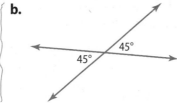

Show your work.

a. _____

b. _____

Determine Missing Measures

You can write and solve an equation to find a missing measure.

Tutor

Examples

Write and solve an equation to determine the value of *x* in each figure.

3.

118° x°

Since the angles form a straight line, they are supplementary.

$$118° + x° = 180°$$ Definition of supplementary angles

$$-118° \quad = -118°$$ Subtract 118 from each side.

$$x° = 62°$$ Simplify.

So, the value of *x* is 62.

4.

x°
36°

Since the angles form a right angle, they are complementary.

$$x° + 36° = 90°$$ Definition of complementary angles

$$-36° = -36°$$ Subtract 36 from each side.

$$x° = 54°$$ Simplify.

So, the value of *x* is 54.

Got It? Do these problems to find out.

c.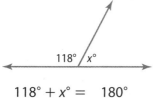

51° (3x)°

d.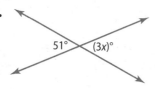

58° x°

c. _____

d. _____

Example

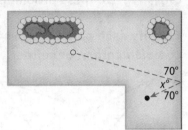

5. Neal is playing miniature golf and is trying to bounce the golf ball off the side and into the hole. Write and solve an equation to determine the value of *x*.

The three angles form a straight angle.

$$70° + x° + 70° = 180°$$ Definition of straight angle

$$x° + 140° = 180°$$ Add.

$$-140° = -140°$$ Subtract 140 from each side.

$$x° = 40°$$ Simplify.

So, *x* = 40.

Guided Practice

Classify each pair of angles as *adjacent, vertical, supplementary, complementary,* or *neither.* (Examples 1 and 2)

1. _____

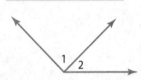

2. _____

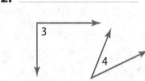

Write and solve an equation to determine the value of *x* in each figure.

(Examples 3 and 4)

3. _____

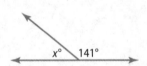

4. _____

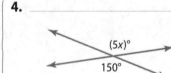

5. Lena is piecing together a rectangular picture frame. At each corner are two congruent angles. Write and solve an equation to determine the value of *x*. (Example 5)

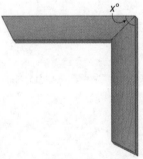

_____

_____

6. ⑦ **Building on the Essential Question** How can you use complementary angles to solve real-world problems?

_____

_____

_____

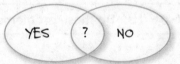

Independent Practice

6.10(A), 6.1(A), 6.1(D) TEKS

Classify each pair of angles as *adjacent, vertical, supplementary, complementary,* or *neither.* (Examples 1 and 2)

1. _____

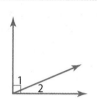

2. _____

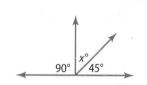

3. _____

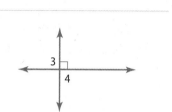

Write and solve an equation to determine the value of *x* in each figure.
(Examples 3 and 4)

4. _____

5. _____

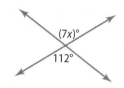

6. _____

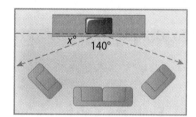

7. A video game console requires a 140° span in a room. The angles on each side are congruent. Write and solve an equation to determine the measure of each angle. (Example 5)

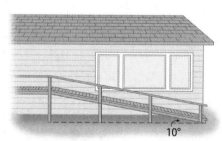

_____

8. The angle a wheelchair ramp makes with the ground can be no more than 10°. What is the degree measure of the supplement

of 10°? _____

Determine whether each statement is *sometimes, always,* or *never* true. Justify your response.

9. Two right angles are supplementary. _____

_____

10. Vertical angles are complementary. _____

_____

11. A pair of angles can be complementary and supplementary. _____

_____

Use the diagram at the right to determine each angle measure.

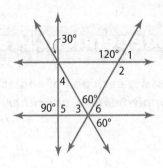

12. $m\angle 1 =$ _____

13. $m\angle 2 =$ _____

14. $m\angle 3 =$ _____

15. $m\angle 4 =$ _____

16. $m\angle 5 =$ _____

17. $m\angle 6 =$ _____

18. Angle M and angle N are complementary. Angle N and angle P are supplementary. Angle M measures 23°. Determine the measures

of angles N and P. _____

 H.O.T. Problems Higher-Order Thinking

19. **Evaluate** Two angles are complementary to the same angle. What can you conclude about the two angles? Justify your response.

_____

_____

_____

20. **Create** Draw a pair of congruent, adjacent, and supplementary angles.

_____

21. **Evaluate** Can two acute angles be supplementary? Justify your response.

_____

_____

_____

22. **Analyze** Angles R and S are supplementary. The measure of angle R is 36 more than angle S. Determine the measure of each angle. _____

23. **Evaluate** Explain why obtuse angles do not have complements. _____

_____

_____

24. **Analyze** In the diagram, $m\angle 1 = m\angle 3$. What can you conclude about the

relationship between $\angle 2$ and $\angle 4$? _____

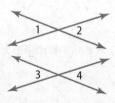

Multi-Step Problem Solving

25. The larger angle is 5 degrees greater than twice the size of the smaller angle. What relationship do the angles have? **EE** **MP**

Ⓐ vertical

Ⓑ complementary

Ⓒ supplementary

Ⓓ no relationship

Use a problem-solving model to solve this problem.

1 Analyze

**Read the problem. Circle the information you know.
Underline what the problem is asking you to find.**

2 Plan

What will you need to do to solve the problem? Write your plan in steps.

Step 1 Write an equation to represent the situation.

Step 2 Determine the degree measure of each angle and their relationship.

3 Solve

Use your plan to solve the problem. Show your steps.

Let x = the measure of the smaller angle. Five degrees greater than twice the size means the equation is $2x + 5 = 65$.

$2x + 5 = 65$ Write the equation.

$2x = 60$ Subtract 5.

$x = 30$ Divide by 2.

> **Read to Succeed!** 👀
> The phrase "greater than" means addition and "twice" means to multiply by 2.

The smaller angle is ⬚°. Since the two angles are ⬚° and ⬚°, there is no relationship. Choice ⬚ is correct. Fill in that answer choice.

4 Justify and Evaluate

How do you know your solution is accurate?

_____

_____

_____

EE = Expressions, Equations, and Relationships   **MP** = Mathematical Processes

More **Multi-Step** Problem Solving

Use a problem-solving model to solve each problem.

26. The lines represent two roads on a map. What relationship do angles 1 and 2 have, and what is the measure of angle 1?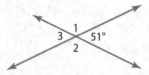

Ⓐ adjacent; 129°

Ⓑ adjacent; 51°

Ⓒ vertical; 129°

Ⓓ vertical; 51°

27. Blue River and Short River form angles. What is the value of $\frac{1}{2}x - \frac{1}{2}$?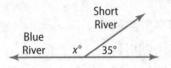

28. Two wooden beams cross to form four angles as shown. What is the value of $x - 6$? EE N MP

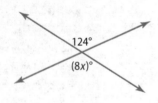

29. If the supplement of an angle is 159°, then what is 11° more than twice its complement? EE N MP

EE = Expressions, Equations, and Relationships   N = Number and Operations   MP = Mathematical Processes

Angles in a Triangle

INQUIRY HOW can I select tools and techniques to determine the sum of angle measures in a triangle?

Lamont has a metal bracket that is in the shape of an angle that attaches a bag to the frame of a bike. The angle of the bracket measures 35°. Lamont wonders if it will fit exactly into the frame of the bike by the handlebars.

Texas Essential Knowledge and Skills

Targeted TEKS
6.8(A) Extend previous knowledge of triangles and their properties to include the sum of angles of a triangle, the relationship between the lengths of sides and measures of angles in a triangle, and determining when three lengths form a triangle.

Mathematical Processes
6.1(C), 6.1(D), 6.1(E), 6.1(F), 6.1(G)

Hands-On Activity 1

Tools

Triangle means *three angles*. In this activity, you will use virtual manipulatives to explore how the three angles of a triangle are related.

Step 1 Select the straight line tool to draw any triangle.

Step 2 Select the protractor tool to measure each angle. Record the angle measures.

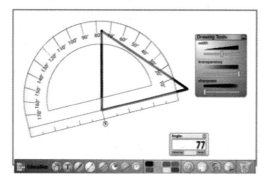

1. What is the sum of the angles in the triangle you drew?

Investigate

Collaborate

Work with a partner.

2. **MP Select Tools and Techniques** Select the Virtual Manipulatives straight line tool to draw three different triangles. Draw your triangles in the blank screen below.

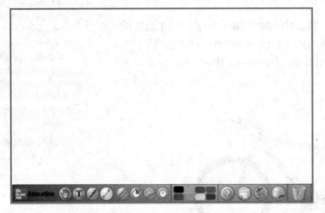

3. **MP Select Tools and Techniques** Select the protractor tool to measure and record each angle measure. Then complete the table below.

Triangle	Measure of Angle 1	Measure of Angle 2	Measure of Angle 3	Sum of Angle Measures
1				
2				
3				

4. **MP Analyze Relationships** Analyze the pattern shown in the table. Make a conjecture about the sum of angle measures in any triangle.

_____

5. **MP Justify Arguments** Explain how using a hand-held protractor can give different measurements than measuring angles using technology.

_____

_____

_____

6. **MP Justify Arguments** Refer to the real-world scenario presented at the beginning of this lab. Write and solve an equation that can be used to find the missing angle in the triangle represented by the bicycle diagram. Will Lamont's metal bracket fit in the frame? Justify your response.

_____

_____

_____

Hands-On Activity 2

You can also use paper and pencil to explore the sum of the angles in a triangle.

Step 1 | On a separate piece of paper, draw a triangle like the one shown below.

Step 2 | Label the corners 1, 2, and 3. Then tear off each corner.

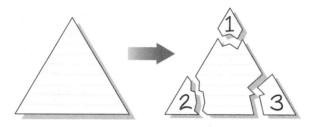

Step 3 | Rearrange the torn pieces so that the corners all meet at one point. Label the torn pieces with 1, 2, and 3.

7. What does each torn corner represent?

8. The point where these corners meet is the vertex of another angle. Classify this angle as *acute*, *right*, *obtuse*, or *straight*. Explain.

9. Without using a protractor, determine the measure of the angle you classified in Exercise 8. Explain.

10. **MP Justify Arguments** Make a conjecture about the sum of angle measures in any triangle. Justify your response.

Analyze and Reflect

Work with a partner to complete the table. The first one is done for you.

Angles in a Triangle		
Measure of Angle 1	**Measure of Angle 2**	**Measure of Angle 3**
62°	47°	71°
11. 38°		83°
12.	61.7°	100.9°
13. 141.8°	19.1°	

14. **MP Organize Ideas** A triangle has two congruent angles and one angle that is 117°. Write and solve an equation to find the two missing angle measures.

_____

15. **MP Organize Ideas** An *equiangular triangle* has three congruent angles. Write and solve an equation that can be used to find the measure of each angle.

_____

On Your Own

Create

16. **MP Justify Arguments** In the space below, draw several triangles, each with an obtuse angle. Based on what you learned in this Inquiry Lab, is it possible for a triangle to have two obtuse angles? Justify your response.

_____

_____

_____

17. **INQUIRY** HOW can I select tools and techniques to determine the sum of angle measures in a triangle?

_____

_____

_____

_____

Launch the Lesson: Vocabulary

A **triangle** is a figure with three sides and three angles.

Sort the figures below by writing the number of each figure in the table under either the "Triangle" column or "Not a Triangle" column.

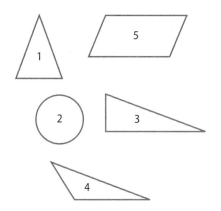

Triangle	Not a Triangle

Texas Essential Knowledge and Skills

Targeted TEKS
6.8(A) Extend previous knowledge of triangles and their properties to include the sum of angles of a triangle, the relationship between the lengths of sides and measures of angles in a triangle, and determining when three lengths form a triangle. *Also addresses 6.10(A).*

Mathematical Processes
6.1(A), 6.1(B), 6.1(C), 6.1(D), 6.1(F)

Vocab

Vocabulary
triangle
acute triangle
right triangle
obtuse triangle
scalene triangle
isosceles triangle
equilateral triangle

Real-World Investigation

1. What are the characteristics of those figures classified as triangles?

2. **MP Analyze Relationships** What do you notice about the lengths and angles of each of the triangles above?

Essential Question

HOW does measurement help you solve problems in everyday life?

Which MP **Mathematical Processes** did you use?
Shade the circle(s) that applies.

Ⓐ Apply Math to the Real World.
Ⓑ Use a Problem-Solving Model.
Ⓒ Select Tools and Techniques.
Ⓓ Use Multiple Representations.

Ⓔ Organize Ideas.
Ⓕ Analyze Relationships.
Ⓖ Justify Arguments.

Work Zone

Key Concept

Classify Triangles

Classify by Angles

Acute Triangle

all acute angles

Right Triangle

1 right angle

Obtuse Triangle

1 obtuse angle

Classify by Sides

Scalene Triangle

no congruent sides

Isosceles Triangle

at least 2 congruent sides

Equilateral Triangle

3 congruent sides

All triangles can be classified by their angles and by the lengths of their sides.

Tutor

Examples

Classify each triangle by its angles and its sides.

1.

58°
2.5 m
1.3 m
32°
2.1 m

There is 1 right angle. There are no congruent sides. The triangle is a right scalene triangle.

2.

60°
60°   60°

All three angles are acute. All three sides are congruent. The triangle is an acute equilateral triangle.

> Show your work.

Got It? Do these problems to find out.

a. _____

b. _____

Classify each triangle by its angles and its sides.

a.
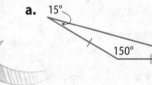
15°
150°   15°

b.
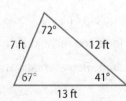
72°
7 ft   12 ft
67°   41°
13 ft

Sum of Angle Measures in a Triangle

Words   The sum of the measures of the angles in a triangle is 180°.

Model

Symbols $x + y + z = 180$

You can write and solve an equation to determine a missing angle measure of a triangle.

Tutor

Examples

Write and solve an equation to determine the value of x in each figure.

3.

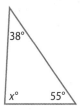

$$38° + 55° + x° = 180°$$ Write the equation.

$$93° + x° = 180°$$ Add.

$$\underline{-93° \qquad = -93°}$$ Subtract 93 from each side.

$$x = 87°$$ Simplify.

So, the value of x is 87.

4.

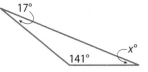

$$141° + 17° + x° = 180°$$ Write the equation.

$$158° + x° = 180°$$ Add.

$$\underline{-158° \qquad = -158°}$$ Subtract 158 from each side.

$$x = 22°$$ Simplify.

So, the value of x is 22.

Show your work.

Got It? Do these problems to find out.

c.

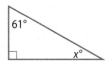

d.

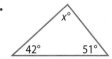

c. _____

d. _____

Example

5. The jungle gym shown is constructed using congruent triangles. Each side length of the triangle is 28 inches. Two of the angles in the triangles are 60° each. Classify the triangle and determine the measure of the third angle in the triangle.

Each side length of the triangles is 28 inches. So, it is an equilateral triangle.

$$60° + 60° + x° = 180°$$ Sum of Measures of a Triangle
$$120° + x° = 180°$$ Add.
$$\underline{-120° \qquad = -120°}$$ Subtract 120 from each side.
$$x° = 60°$$ Simplify.

So, $x = 60$. Since each angle measures 60°, the triangles are also acute triangles.

Guided Practice

Classify each triangle by its angles and its sides. (Examples 1 and 2)

1. _____

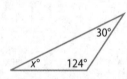

2. _____

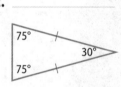

Write and solve an equation to determine the value of *x* in each figure.
(Examples 3 and 4)

3. _____

4. _____

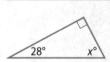

5. The pennant shown is in the shape of a triangle. Classify the triangle and determine the measure of the third angle in the triangle. (Example 5)

_____

_____

6. ❓ **Building on the Essential Question** How can you use equations and diagrams to solve problems in everyday life?

_____

_____

_____

Rate Yourself!

How well do you understand triangles? Circle the image that applies.

Clear   Somewhat   Not So
         Clear   Clear

Find out online. Use the Self-Check Quiz.

Check ✓

Independent Practice

6.8(A), 6.10(A), 6.1(A), 6.1(D)

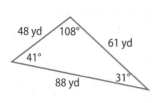

Classify each triangle by its angles and its sides. (Examples 1 and 2)

1. _____

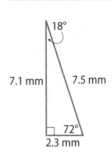

18°

7.1 mm   7.5 mm

72°
2.3 mm

2. _____

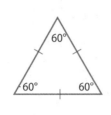

60°

60°   60°

3. _____

48 yd   108°
41°   61 yd
88 yd   31°

Determine the value of x in each figure. (Examples 3 and 4)

4. _____

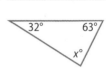

32°   63°

x°

5. _____

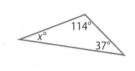

114°
x°
37°

6. _____

93°
46°
x°

7. The two sides of the caution sign form a triangle. Each of those side lengths measure 24 inches. Two of the angles in the triangle measure 70° each. Classify the triangle and determine the measure of the third angle in the triangle.

(Example 5) _____

8. Kitchens can be considered efficient when the triangle formed by the sink, stove, and refrigerator is close to an equilateral triangle. Can the kitchen floor plan in the diagram be considered an efficient plan? Explain.

_____

_____

_____

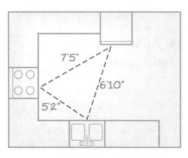

Write and solve an equation to determine the value of x in each figure.

9. _____

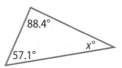

88.4°

57.1°   x°

10. _____

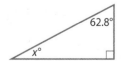

62.8°
x°

11. An acute equilateral triangle can be divided in half with a segment from a vertex to the middle of the opposite side. What type(s) of triangles are formed? What are the angle measures of the two new triangles?

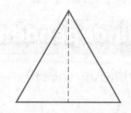

_____

12. Determine the values of x and y in the figure at the right.

_____

13. Determine the value of x in the figure at the right.

_____

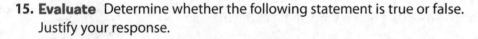

H.O.T. Problems Higher-Order Thinking

14. Analyze What can you conclude about the two acute angles in a right triangle? Justify your response.

_____

_____

_____

15. Evaluate Determine whether the following statement is true or false. Justify your response.

> *If the sum of two acute angles in a triangle is less than 90°, then the triangle is obtuse.*

_____

_____

_____

16. Analyze Determine the sum of the measures of ∠1, ∠2, and ∠3 in the diagram at the right.

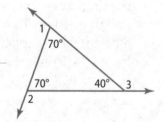

_____

17. Create Draw an example of an acute scalene triangle. Label your triangle with measurements to justify your response.

Multi-Step Problem Solving

18. The right triangle shown represents a tabletop. What is the value of *x*?

EE **MP**

Ⓐ 90

Ⓑ 15

Ⓒ 6

Ⓓ 1

Use a problem-solving model to solve this problem.

1 Analyze

Read the problem. Circle the information you know.
Underline what the problem is asking you to find.

2 Plan

What will you need to do to solve the problem? Write your plan in steps.

Step 1   Determine the relationship between the expressions in the triangle.

Step 2   Write and solve an equation to represent the relationship.

3 Solve

Use your plan to solve the problem. Show your steps.

In the right triangle, the two acute angles labeled 8*x* and 7*x* must have a sum of 90°.

$8x + 7x = 90$ Write the equation.

$\boxed{}\,x = 90$ Combine like terms.

$x = \boxed{}$ Divide.

So, $x = \boxed{}$. Choice $\boxed{}$ is correct. Fill in that answer choice.

Read to Succeed!

The angles of a triangle have a sum of 180°.

4 Justify and Evaluate

How do you know your solution is accurate?

_____

_____

_____

EE = Expressions, Equations, and Relationships   **MP** = Mathematical Processes

Use a problem-solving model to solve each problem.

19. A triangular sticker has side lengths of 5 centimeters, 4 centimeters, and 5 centimeters. How can the triangle be classified? **EE** **N** **MP**

   Ⓐ scalene triangle

   Ⓑ isosceles triangle

   Ⓒ equilateral triangle

   Ⓓ parallel triangle

20. A semi-truck is hauling a portion of a historic home to the town square. The truck cannot make a turn less than 45°. Can the truck make the turn from point A to point B? Explain your response. **EE** **N** **MP**

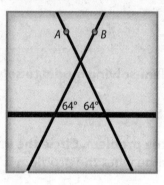

21. What is the value of *y* in the diagram below? **EE** **N** **MP**

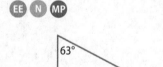

22. In a right triangle, one acute angle is 5 degrees smaller than the other acute angle. What are the angle measures of the triangle? Explain how you found your answer. **EE** **N** **MP**

Side and Angle Relationships of Triangles

 Launch the Lesson: Real World

Cedric wants to make a pennant like the one shown. The pennant is in the shape of an isosceles triangle. Let's investigate the relationship between the lengths of sides and measures of the angles in an isosceles triangle.

1. Draw the triangular outline of the pennant in the space below. Label the vertices *A, B,* and *C* so that the shortest side is *AB*. (Sides can be named by their endpoints, so side *AB* is the side with endpoints *A* and *B*.)

 Show your work.

2. What is true about sides *BC* and *AC*? _____

3. Select a tool to measure the angle opposite side *BC*. Then measure

   the angle opposite side *AC*. What do you notice? _____

   _____

 TEKS

Texas Essential Knowledge and Skills

Targeted TEKS
6.8(A) Extend previous knowledge of triangles and their properties to include the sum of angles of a triangle, the relationship between the lengths of sides and measures of angles in a triangle, and determining when three lengths form a triangle. *Also addresses 6.10(A).*

Mathematical Processes
6.1(A), 6.1(B), 6.1(C), 6.1(F), 6.1(G)

Vocab
 Vocabulary
equiangular triangle

 Essential Question
HOW does measurement help you solve problems in everyday life?

Which MP Mathematical Processes did you use?
Shade the circle(s) that applies.

Ⓐ Apply Math to the Real World.
Ⓑ Use a Problem-Solving Model.
Ⓒ Select Tools and Techniques.
Ⓓ Use Multiple Representations.
Ⓔ Organize Ideas.
Ⓕ Analyze Relationships.
Ⓖ Justify Arguments.

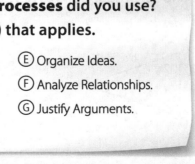

Relationships of Sides and Angles of Isosceles Triangles

Words In an isosceles triangle, the angles opposite the two congruent sides are congruent.

Model

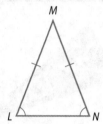

$LM \cong NM$

$\angle L \cong \angle N$

$m\angle L = m\angle N$

Example

Tutor

1. Write and solve equations to determine the values of *x* and *y* in the figure.

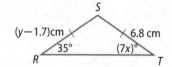

Determine the value of *x*.

Since $RS \cong TS$, the angles opposite these sides are also congruent. So, $\angle R \cong \angle T$, which means that $m\angle R = m\angle T$.

$35 = 7x$	Write the equation. $m\angle R = m\angle T$
$\dfrac{35}{7} = \dfrac{7x}{7}$	Divide each side by 7.
$5 = x$	Simplify.

Determine the value of *y*.

$y - 1.7 = 6.8$	Write the equation. $RS \cong TS$
$\underline{+1.7 = +1.7}$	Add 1.7 to each side.
$y = 8.5$	Simplify.

So, the values of *x* and *y* in the figure are $x = 5$ and $y = 8.5$.

Got It? Do this problem to find out.

Write and solve equations to determine the values of *x* and *y* in the figure.

Show your work.

a.

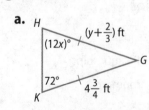

a. _____

Relationships of Sides and Angles of Equilateral Triangles

Key Concept

Words   In an equilateral triangle, all three angles are congruent and each measures 60°.

Model

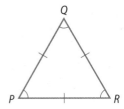

Symbols $PQ \cong RQ \cong PR$

$\angle P \cong \angle Q \cong \angle R$

$m\angle P = m\angle Q = m\angle R = 60°$

An equilateral triangle can also be called an **equiangular triangle**, since it has three congruent angles. Let x represent the measure, in degrees, of each angle of an equilateral triangle. So, $x + x + x = 180$ and $x = 60$.

Tutor

Example

2. **Write and solve equations to determine the values of x and y in the figure.**

Determine the value of x. Since $\triangle WVZ$ is equilateral, it is also equiangular.

So, $m\angle W = 60°$.

$4x = 60$ Write the equation.

$\dfrac{4x}{4} = \dfrac{60}{4}$ Divide each side by 4.

$x = 15$ Simplify.

Determine the value of y.

$6.1y = 25.62$ Write the equation. $WZ \cong VZ$

$\dfrac{6.1y}{6.1} = \dfrac{25.62}{6.1}$ Divide each side by 6.1.

$y = 4.2$ Simplify.

So, the values of x and y in the figure are $x = 15$ and $y = 4.2$.

Got It? Do this problem to find out.

Show your work.

b.

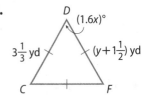

b. _____

Example

3. Some traffic signs, like the Yield sign shown, are in the shape of an equilateral triangle. Write and solve an equation to determine the value of x.

In an equilateral triangle, each angle measure is 60°.

$\frac{2}{3}x = 60$ Write the equation.

$\dfrac{\frac{2}{3}x}{\frac{2}{3}} = \dfrac{60}{\frac{2}{3}}$ Divide each side by $\frac{2}{3}$.

$x = 90$ Simplify.

So, $x = 90$.

Guided Practice

Write and solve equations to determine the values of x and y in each figure.
(Examples 1 and 2)

1.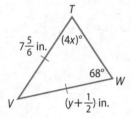

2.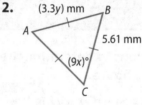

3. A Warren truss bridge design consists of structures composed of isosceles triangles as shown. Write and solve an equation to determine the value of y on the bridge design below. (Example 3)

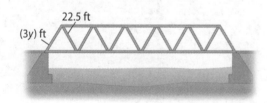
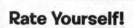

4. ? **Building on the Essential Question** How are the lengths of sides and measures of angles in an isosceles triangle related?

Rate Yourself!

Are you ready to move on?
Shade the section that applies.

I have a few questions.
I'm ready to move on.
I have a lot of questions.

Find out online. Use the Self-Check Quiz.

Check

Independent Practice

6.8(A), 6.10(A), 6.1(A), 6.1(C), 6.1(F), 6.1(G) TEKS

Write and solve equations to determine the values of *x* and *y* in each figure. (Examples 1 and 2)

1.

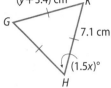

$(y+3.4)$ cm K
G
7.1 cm
$(1.5x)°$
H

2.

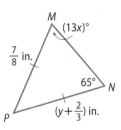

M $(13x)°$
$\frac{7}{8}$ in.
65° N
P $(y+\frac{2}{3})$ in.

3. A 20-sided number cube is made up of equilateral triangles. Write and solve an equation to determine the value of *x* on the number cube shown. (Example 3)

$(x+3.8)$ mm

13 mm

4. The flag of Jamaica consists of two green isosceles triangles and two black isosceles triangles. Determine the value of each variable.

$u°$
64°
136°
$z°$
$y°$
$w°$

5. A *regular hexagon* is a six-sided figure with congruent sides and congruent angles. A regular hexagon can be composed of six equilateral triangles. Write and solve an equation to determine the value of *x* on the regular hexagon shown. Then determine the sum of the six interior angles of a regular hexagon.

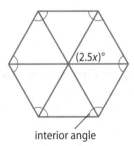

$(2.5x)°$

interior angle

6. In $\triangle PQR$, $m\angle P = 46x$ and $m\angle R = 7x$.

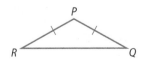

P
R   Q

a. Write and solve an equation to find the measure of each angle.

b. Classify the triangle based on its angles.

7. Find the Error Miguel is determining the measure of angle S in the figure shown. He says the measure of angle S is 70°, because $\triangle SQR$ is an isosceles triangle, so there are two congruent angles. Determine the error in Miguel's reasoning. Then determine the correct measure of angle S. Justify your response.

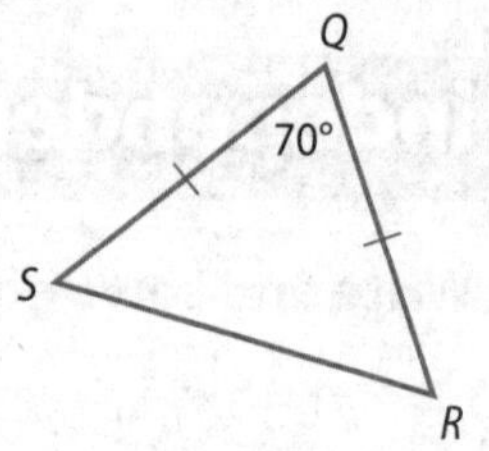

_____

_____

_____

H.O.T. Problems Higher-Order Thinking

8. Analyze In $\triangle ABC$, if side AB is congruent to side CB and $\angle A$ is congruent to $\angle B$, what must be true about $\triangle ABC$? Justify your response.

_____

_____

_____

9. Create Draw a scalene triangle at the right. Measure the sides and angles of your triangle to the nearest tenth of a centimeter. Make a conjecture about the relationship between the sides and angles of a scalene triangle.

Show your work.

_____

_____

_____

Evaluate Determine whether each statement below is *always*, *sometimes*, or *never* true. Justify your response.

10. An equilateral triangle is an acute triangle.

_____

_____

11. An isosceles triangle is an acute triangle.

_____

_____

_____

_____

Multi-Step Problem Solving

12. A rhombus can be formed using two equilateral triangles. Write and solve an equation to determine the value of z in the rhombus shown.
EE **MP**

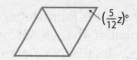

Use a problem-solving model to solve this problem.

1 Analyze

Read the problem. Circle the information you know.
Underline what the problem is asking you to find.

2 Plan

What will you need to do to solve the problem? Write your plan in steps.

Step 1   Determine the angle's measure.

Step 2   Write and solve an equation to determine the value of z.

Read to Succeed!

An equilateral triangle is also equiangular, meaning all three angles are congruent.

3 Solve

Use your plan to solve the problem. Show your steps.

Equilateral triangles have all three sides and all three angles congruent. So, each angle is $180° \div 3$ or ☐°.

$$\frac{5}{12}z = 60 \qquad \text{Write the equation.}$$

$$\left(\frac{\boxed{}}{\boxed{}}\right) \cdot \frac{5}{12}z = 60\left(\frac{\boxed{}}{\boxed{}}\right) \qquad \text{Multiply by the reciprocal.}$$

$$z = \boxed{} \qquad \text{Multiply.}$$

So, $z = \boxed{}$. Complete the grid.

4 Justify and Evaluate

How do you know your solution is accurate?

_____

_____

_____

EE = Expressions, Equations, and Relationships   **MP** = Mathematical Processes

More Multi-Step Problem Solving

Use a problem-solving model to solve each problem.

13. Delta is the fourth letter of the Greek alphabet. The symbol for this letter is an isosceles triangle. Determine the value of *y* in this triangle. **N EE MP**

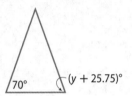

70°   (*y* + 25.75)°

14. Each of the students in the table was given a set of toothpicks to create a triangle. Only one of these students was able create an equilateral triangle using all of their toothpicks. Which student was able to make an equilateral triangle and how many toothpicks were used on each side of this triangle? **EE MP**

Student	Total Toothpicks
Charles	16
Victor	21
Kya	25
Sheela	28

15. In an isosceles triangle, the third angle is ten times the measure of each of the congruent angles. What is the measure, in degrees, of the largest angle? **EE MP**

16. The frame of a rooftop is an isosceles triangle. The base of the triangle is the horizontal beam that helps to support the roof. Write and solve an equation to determine the value of *x* and then find the amount of wood needed to build the frame. **N EE MP**

(*x* + 11.5) ft   20.5 ft

(4*x*) ft

N = Number and Operations   **EE** = Expressions, Equations, and Relationships   **MP** = Mathematical Processes

Model Triangle Inequalities

INQUIRY HOW can I select tools and techniques to determine when three lengths form a triangle?

Tad has different lengths of decorative cord to edge triangular pillows. He has cord in lengths of 3 inches, 4 inches, 5 inches, 8 inches, 13 inches, and 15 inches. Can he form triangles with these side lengths?

Hands-On Activity

Step 1 Measure and cut several plastic straws into lengths that equal 3, 4, 4, 5, 8, 8, 8, 13, 15, 15, and 15 centimeters.

Step 2 Arrange three of the pieces that equal 3 centimeters, 4 centimeters, and 8 centimeters to determine if they form a triangle.

Step 3 Since a triangle cannot be formed, side lengths of 3, 4, and 8 do not determine a triangle. We can show this using an inequality.

$$3 + 4 \overset{?}{>} 8$$
$$\underline{-4 \ -4}$$
$$3 \overset{?}{>} 4$$

Since 3 is not greater than 4, the inequality $3 + 4 > 8$ is not true and is shown by the model.

Step 4 Continue using pieces of straw to try to form triangles using the different combinations listed in the table. Determine if the lengths form a triangle. Complete the table.

Side 1	Side 2	Side 3	Do they form a triangle?
3 cm	4 cm	8 cm	no
4 cm	5 cm	8 cm	
4 cm	4 cm	8 cm	
8 cm	8 cm	13 cm	
8 cm	8 cm	8 cm	

Investigate

Collaborate

Work with a partner. Determine if a triangle can be made using the given side lengths. Circle *yes* if you can make a triangle or *no* if you cannot.

1. 5 cm, 8 cm, 15 cm
   Yes or No

2. 3 cm, 5 cm, 15 cm
   Yes or No

3. 15 cm, 15 cm, 15 cm
   Yes or No

Analyze and Reflect

Collaborate

4. **MP** **Analyze Relationships** Refer to the table in the Activity. Transfer your results into the fourth column and then complete the fifth column.

Side 1	Side 2	Side 3	Do they form a triangle?	Is Side 1 + Side 2 > Side 3?
3 cm	4 cm	8 cm	no	
4 cm	5 cm	8 cm		
4 cm	4 cm	8 cm		
8 cm	8 cm	13 cm		
8 cm	8 cm	8 cm		

5. **MP** **Analyze Relationships** What do you notice about the triangles that could not be made and the sum of the lengths of the first two sides compared to the

   third side? _____

   _____

6. **MP** **Justify Arguments** Refer to the second row of the table. Write inequalities to represent each combination of sides of the triangle. Solve each inequality to justify your answer.

   _____

Create

On Your Own

7. **MP** **Analyze Relationships** Two of the sides of a triangle are 3 inches and 6 inches. Determine the greatest whole number

   length of the third side. Draw and label the triangle. _____

8. **INQUIRY** HOW can I select tools and techniques to determine when three lengths form a triangle?

   _____

   _____

Triangle Inequalities

Launch the Lesson: Real World

Texas Essential Knowledge and Skills

Targeted TEKS
6.8(A) Extend previous knowledge of triangles and their properties to include the sum of angles of a triangle, the relationships between the lengths of sides and measures of angles in a triangle, and determining when three lengths form a triangle. *Also addresses 6.10(A).*

Mathematical Processes
6.1(A), 6.1(B), 6.1(C), 6.1(D), 6.1(F)

Caleb has three lengths of wood, 7 feet, 2 feet, and 10 feet. He would like to build a ramp using those three lengths. Can he create a triangular ramp?

1. Using a ruler, draw a line that is 10 centimeters long. Let each centimeter represent one foot of the lengths of wood. From one endpoint, draw a 7-centimeter line. From the other endpoint, draw a 2-centimeter line.

Essential Question

HOW does measurement help you solve problems in everyday life?

2. **MP Analyze Relationships** What do you notice about the two sides that are 7 centimeters and 2 centimeters in relation to the third side?

_____

3. **MP Analyze Relationships** Is Caleb able to build a ramp using boards that are 7 feet, 3 feet, and 10 feet? Explain.

_____

4. **MP Analyze Relationships** What is the shortest whole number length the 2-foot board should be in order to form a triangle with the 7-foot and 10-foot boards?

_____

Which MP **Mathematical Processes** did you use?
Shade the circle(s) that applies.

- (A) Apply Math to the Real World.
- (B) Use a Problem-Solving Model.
- (C) Select Tools and Techniques.
- (D) Use Multiple Representations.
- (E) Organize Ideas.
- (F) Analyze Relationships.
- (G) Justify Arguments.

Triangle Inequalities

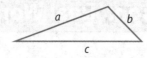

Words   The sum of the lengths of any two sides of a triangle must be greater than the length of the third side.

Model

a   *b*

c

Symbols $a + b > c$ $a + c > b$ $b + c > a$

When a triangle is formed, any two sides must have a sum greater than the third side. If any two sides do not have a sum greater than the third side, then the triangle cannot be formed.

Tutor

Examples

Determine if the side lengths given form a triangle. Justify your response.

1. 14 inches, 17 inches, 25 inches

Check each inequality.

$14 + 17 \overset{?}{>} 25$	$17 + 25 \overset{?}{>} 14$	$14 + 25 \overset{?}{>} 17$
$31 > 25$ ✓	$42 > 14$ ✓	$39 > 17$ ✓

Since each inequality is true, the triangle can be formed.

2. 4.1 centimeters, 2.2 centimeters, 8.3 centimeters

Check each inequality.

$4.1 + 2.2 \overset{?}{>} 8.3$	$2.2 + 8.3 \overset{?}{>} 4.1$	$4.1 + 8.3 \overset{?}{>} 2.2$
$6.3 > 8.3$ ✗	$10.5 > 4.1$ ✓	$12.4 > 2.2$ ✓

Since one inequality is false, the triangle cannot be formed.

Got It? Do these problems to find out.

Show your work.

Determine if the side lengths given form a triangle. Justify your response.

    a. 6 ft, 6 ft, 12 ft

    b. 7.2 m, 8.9 m, 11.3 m

a. _____

b. _____

Order Sides and Angles of Triangles

In the previous lesson, you learned that if a triangle is isosceles, then the angles opposite the congruent sides are congruent. In an equilateral triangle, since all three sides are congruent, all three angles are congruent. In a scalene triangle, there is a special relationship between the longest side and largest angle, and the shortest side and smallest angle.

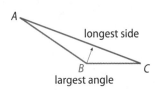

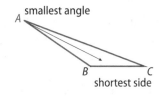

Notice the largest angle is opposite the longest side. Similarly, the smallest angle is opposite the shortest side. You can order the sides and angles based on these relationships.

Examples

Tutor

3. **Order the sides of the triangle from least to greatest side length.**

The smallest angle is ∠S. The side opposite ∠S is $\overline{RT}$. So, $\overline{RT}$ is the shortest side.

The largest angle is ∠R. The side opposite ∠R is $\overline{TS}$. So, $\overline{TS}$ is the longest side.

From least to greatest side length, the sides are $\overline{RT}$, $\overline{RS}$, and $\overline{TS}$.

> **Sides of Triangles**
> Sides can be named by their end points. The side of △RST that has end points R and S is side RS or $\overline{RS}$.

4. **Order the angles of the triangle from least to greatest angle measure.**

The shortest side, $\overline{ML}$, is opposite ∠N. The longest side, $\overline{MN}$, is opposite ∠L.

From least to greatest angle measure, the angles are ∠N, ∠M, ∠L.

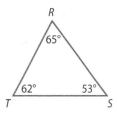

Got It? Do these problems to find out.

c.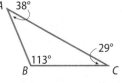

d.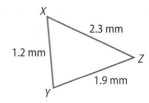

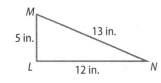

Show your work.

c. _____

d. _____

Example

5. Caroline, Leslie, and Pam are playing soccer. Caroline is trying to decide if she should pass the ball to Leslie or Pam. Which player should she pass the soccer ball to so that she has to kick the shorter distance? Justify your response.

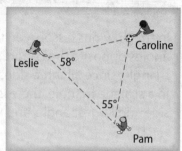

The angle near Pam is less than the angle near Leslie. So, the distance between Caroline and Leslie is less than the distance between Caroline and Pam. So, Caroline should pass the ball to Leslie.

Guided Practice

Determine if the side lengths given form a triangle. Justify your response. (Examples 1 and 2)

1. 7 ft, 9 ft, 18 ft _____

2. 9.1 mm, 10.6 mm, 19.5 mm

_____

Order the sides of the triangle from least to greatest. (Examples 3 and 4)

3. _____

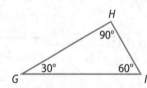

4. Amarillo, Lubbock, and Wichita Falls, Texas form a triangle. Between which two cities is the distance the greatest? (Example 5) _____

5. (?) **Building on the Essential Question** How can you use mental math to order the angles of a triangle from least to greatest angle measure? _____

_____

Rate Yourself!

How confident are you about triangle inequalities? Check the box that applies.

☹ ☹ ☺

□ □ □ □ □

Find out online. Use the Self-Check Quiz. **Check** ✓

Independent Practice

6.8(A), 6.10(A), 6.1(A), 6.1(D) TEKS

Determine if the side lengths given form a triangle. Justify your response. (Examples 1 and 2)

1. 2.1 in., 4 in., 7.9 in.

2. 4 ft, 8 ft, 12 ft

3. 6.4 mm, 12.9 mm, 14.2 mm

Order the sides or angles of each triangle from least to greatest. (Examples 3 and 4)

4.
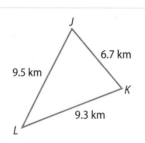

5.
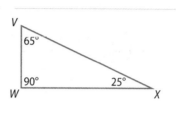

6.
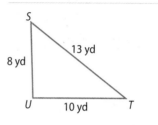

7. Anthony drew plans for a triangular porch. Determine if the triangle can be made. Justify your response. (Example 5)

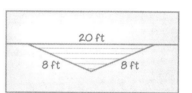

8. The triangle at the right has two of the three sides labeled. What are the possible whole number lengths of the third side?

9. The map at the right shows Ellie's locker, her English class, and the cafeteria. Is her locker closer to English class or the cafeteria? Justify your response.

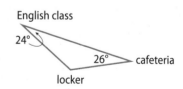

10. Determine if the following statement is *always*, *sometimes*, or *never* true. Justify your response.

> *If the sum of two congruent lengths equals the length of a third side, then the triangle created is isosceles.*

11. Patrick needs to walk from his cabin to the firepit. He can walk directly from his cabin to the firepit or walk to the dock then to the firepit. Which path is the shorter route? Justify your response.

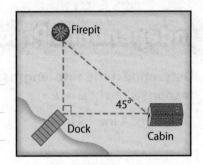

_____

_____

_____

12. The two congruent sides in an isosceles triangle each measure 4 inches. What are the possible whole number measures of the length of the third side?

_____

 H.O.T. Problems Higher-Order Thinking

13. Create Draw △ABC so that $\overline{AB}$ is the longest side and $\overline{BC}$ is the shortest side.

14. Analyze Explain why the side opposite the obtuse angle in an obtuse triangle will always be the longest side.

_____

_____

_____

15. Analyze The triangle at the right shows two of the three side lengths. Each side has a whole number length. What is the greatest perimeter it can have? Justify your response.

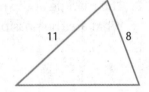

_____

_____

_____

16. Create The length of one side of a triangle is 5 inches. Draw a triangle in which the 5-inch side is the shortest side. Then draw a triangle in which the 5-inch side is the longest side. Label all three sides and angles to justify your response.

_____

Name _____

Multi-Step Problem Solving

17. Meg lives 1.5 miles from school and Joseph lives 3.5 miles from school. Meg rides her bike to school in 6 minutes. At that rate, what is the maximum amount of time it would take Meg to ride her bike from her house to Joseph's house? Assume the distance between the two houses is an integer. **P EE MP**

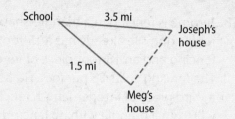

Ⓐ 8 minutes   Ⓒ 16 minutes

Ⓑ 12 minutes   Ⓓ 20 minutes

Use a problem-solving model to solve this problem.

1 Analyze

Read the problem. Circle the information you know. Underline what the problem is asking you to find.

2 Plan

What will you need to do to solve the problem? Write your plan in steps.

Step 1   Determine the greatest possible distance, as an integer, between the two houses.

Step 2   Use a proportion to determine the time it takes Meg to ride to Joseph's house.

Read to Succeed!

In any triangle, the sum of the lengths of any two sides must be greater than the length of the third side.

3 Solve

Use your plan to solve the problem. Show your steps.

The possible distances between Meg's house and Joseph's house are 3 miles and 4 miles. Set up two proportions to determine how long it takes Meg to ride her bike each distance.

$$\frac{1.5 \text{ miles}}{6 \text{ min}} = \frac{3 \text{ miles}}{x \text{ min}} \qquad\qquad \frac{1.5 \text{ miles}}{6 \text{ min}} = \frac{4 \text{ miles}}{x \text{ min}}$$

$x = $ _____ min $x = $ _____ min

The maximum time it takes Meg is _____ minutes, so choice _____ is correct. Fill in that answer choice.

4 Justify and Evaluate

How do you know your solution is accurate?

_____

_____

Use a problem-solving model to solve each problem.

18. Jerome is fencing in a triangle-shaped pen for his dog. He already has a 15-foot piece of fencing and an 18-foot piece of fencing. The fencing costs $3 per foot. He wants to buy a third piece of integer-length fencing that will form a triangle with no fencing left over. What is the difference between the maximum amount and minimum amount he would spend on the third piece to form the triangular pen? **EE** **N** **MP**

15 ft   18 ft

(A) $84   (C) $90

(B) $87   (D) $96

19. Determine which of these combinations will form a triangle. What is the perimeter(s) of the triangle(s) that can be formed? **EE** **N** **MP**

Combination	Side 1	Side 2	Side 3
A	15.6	2.1	10
B	13	26	13
C	8.2	7.1	16
D	$6\frac{1}{2}$	$4\frac{3}{4}$	$9\frac{1}{2}$

20. An isosceles triangle has congruent sides that each measure 3 feet and a base angle of measure of $x°$ as shown in the sketch. The third side has a whole number length. If $x < 60°$, what are the possibilities of the perimeter of the triangle? **EE** **N** **MP**

3 ft   3 ft

$x°$

21. Using the information given in the diagram, list all of the segments in order from longest to shortest. Explain how you arrived at your answer. **EE** **MP**

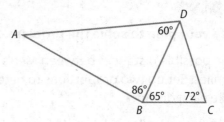

A   *D*   60°

86° 65° 72°

B   *C*

Mathematical Process
6.1(B) Use a problem-solving model that incorporates analyzing given information, formulating a plan or strategy, determining a solution, justifying the solution, and evaluating the problem-solving process and the reasonableness of the solution.
Targeted TEKS 6.8(D)

Amazing Array

A designer wants to arrange 12 mosaic tiles into a rectangular shape with the least perimeter possible.

What are the dimensions of the rectangle?

Analyze *What are the facts?*

Twelve tiles will be arranged with the least perimeter possible.

Plan *What is your strategy to solve this problem?*

Use graph paper. Make diagrams of 12 squares to represent 12 tiles.

Solve *How can you apply the strategy?*

A rectangle with dimensions of 12 and 1 has a perimeter of _____.

A rectangle with dimensions of 3 and 4 has a perimeter of _____.

A rectangle with dimensions of 2 and 6 has a perimeter of _____.

So, the least perimeter has dimensions of _____.

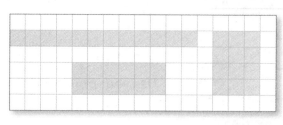

Justify and Evaluate *Does the answer make sense?*

Use addition to check your answer.

$3 + 4 + 3 + 4 = 14$ $2 + 6 + 2 + 6 = 16$ $12 + 1 + 12 + 1 = 26$

Dynamic Dimensions

For a school assignment, Santiago has to give three different possibilities for the dimensions of a rectangle that has a perimeter of 2.8 meters and an area less than 0.5 square meter. One of the diagrams he drew is shown at the right.

What are two other possibilities for the dimensions of the rectangle?

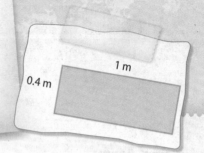

0.4 m

1 m

Analyze

Read the problem. What are you being asked to find?

I need to find _____ .

Underline key words and values in the problem. What information do you know?

The perimeter of the rectangle is [ ] meters, and the area

is less than _____ .

Plan

Choose a problem-solving strategy.

I will use the _____ strategy.

Solve

Use your problem-solving strategy to solve the problem.

So, the dimensions of two possible rectangles are

_____

Justify and Evaluate

Use information from the problem to check your answer.

Reread the problem. Check that both conditions have been met.

Perimeter: [ ] = 2.8   Area: [ ] < 0.5 and [ ] < 0.5

Multi-Step Problem Solving

Collaborate

Work with a small group to solve the following problems. Show your work on a separate piece of paper.

1. Decorations

A rectangular table that is placed lengthwise against a wall is 8 feet long and 4 feet wide. Balloons will be attached 8 inches apart along the three exposed sides, with one balloon at each of the four corners.

How many balloons are needed?

2. Geography

The mall is 15 miles from your home. Your school is one-half of the way from your home to the mall. The library is two-fifths of the way from your school to the mall.

How many miles is it from your home to the library?

3. Electronics

Music, Movies, and More was having a one-day sale on CDs and DVDs. There were 107 people who bought CDs and 132 people who bought DVDs. 92 customers bought only CDs. Some people bought both CDs and DVDs, and 48 customers did not buy CDs or DVDs.

How many customers were at the sale?

4. Geometry

Make a figure that contains three triangles, a parallelogram, and a trapezoid using 7 congruent line segments. Draw your figure below.

Use any strategy!

Vocabulary Check Vocab

1. Define *triangle*. Give an example of an obtuse isosceles triangle. **TEKS** 6.8(A), 6.1(D)

_____

Key Concept Check

2. Complete the graphic organizer by giving a definition for each classification of triangle. **TEKS** 6.8(A), 6.1(E)

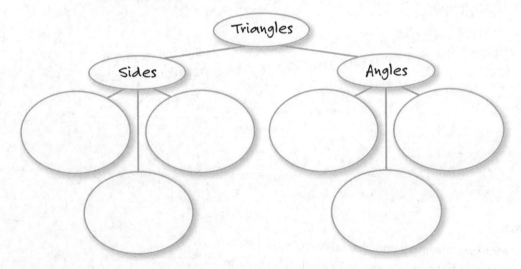

3. **MP** **Analyze Relationships** Paolo is enclosing an area on the side of his garage. He has two lengths of fencing, both 7 feet long. Can he build a triangular area if the whole 15-foot side of the garage is used? Explain. **TEKS** 6.8(D)

_____

Multi-Step **Problem Solving**

4. A truck is located at point A and traveling northeast. The truck cannot make a turn less than 90°. Which of the following is the least number of turns the truck needs to do to reach point B?

EE **MD** **MP**

Ⓐ 1

Ⓒ 4

Ⓑ 2

Ⓓ 5

EE = Expressions, Equations, and Relationships   **MD** = Measurement and Data   **MP** = Mathematical Processes

Area of Rectangles

Texas Essential
Knowledge and Skills

Targeted TEKS
6.8(D) Determine solutions for problems involving the area of rectangles, parallelograms, trapezoids, and triangles and volume of right rectangular prisms where dimensions are positive rational numbers. *Also addresses 6.8(C), 6.10(A).*

Mathematical Processes
6.1(A), 6.1(B), 6.1(C), 6.1(D), 6.1(F)

 ## Launch the Lesson: Vocabulary

A **rectangle** is a four-sided figure with opposite sides congruent and four right angles. Using right angle symbols to denote 90° angles and tick marks to denote congruent sides, label the rectangle below.

1. If one side of the rectangle is 15 inches, what is the length of the opposite side? _____

2. What is the sum of the four angles of the rectangle? _____

Vocabulary
rectangle
area
formula
square

Essential Question
HOW does measurement help you solve problems in everyday life?

 ## Real-World Link

3. The Texas state flag is in the shape of a rectangle and is comprised of three smaller rectangles. Label the flag with congruent tick marks and right angle symbols.

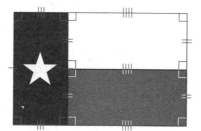

Which MP Mathematical Processes did you use?
Shade the circle(s) that applies.

Ⓐ Apply Math to the Real World.

Ⓔ Organize Ideas.

Ⓑ Use a Problem-Solving Model.

Ⓕ Analyze Relationships.

Ⓒ Select Tools and Techniques.

Ⓖ Justify Arguments.

Ⓓ Use Multiple Representations.

Area of a Rectangle

Words The area A of a rectangle is the product of the length ℓ and width w.

Model

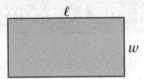

Formula $A = \ell w$

The **area** of a figure is the number of square units needed to cover a surface. You can use a formula to find the area of a rectangle. A **formula** is an equation that shows a relationship among certain quantities. You can write equations to determine solutions for problems involving area of rectangles.

Tutor

Examples

Write an equation to determine the area of each rectangle.

1.

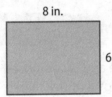

8 in.

6 in.

$A = \ell w$	Area of a rectangle
$A = 8 \cdot 6$	Replace ℓ with 8 and w with 6.
$A = 48$	Multiply.

The area is 48 square inches.

2.

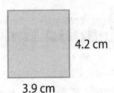

4.2 cm

3.9 cm

$A = \ell w$	Area of a rectangle
$A = 3.9 \cdot 4.2$	Replace ℓ with 3.9 and w with 4.2.
$A = 16.38$	Multiply.

The area is 16.38 square centimeters.

Got It? Do these problems to find out.

Write an equation to determine the area of each rectangle.

a.

16 m

3 m

b.

4 in.

$2\frac{2}{5}$ in.

Show your work.

a. _____

b. _____

Copyright © McGraw-Hill Education

A **square** is a rectangle with all sides congruent. Since the length and width are congruent, you can write the formula for the area of a square using an exponent.

Area of a Square

Key Concept

Words   The area A of a square is the length of a side s squared.

Model

s

s

Formula $A = s^2$

Examples

Tutor

Write an equation to determine the area of each square.

3. $A = s^2$ Area of a square

$A = 9^2$ Replace s with 9.

$A = 81$ Multiply.

So, the area is 81 square inches.

9 in.

9 in.

4. $A = s^2$ Area of a square

$A = \left(\boxed{}\right)^2$ Replace s with $\boxed{}$.

$A = \boxed{}$ Multiply.

So, the area is $\boxed{}$ square centimeters.

4.8 cm

4.8 cm

> **Got It?** Do these problems to find out.

c.   6.1 m

6.1 m

d. $\frac{5}{6}$ ft

$\frac{5}{6}$ ft

c. _____

d. _____

Tutor

Example

5. A regulation wrestling mat is a square with 38-foot sides. What is the area of a regulation wrestling mat?

$A = s^2$ Area of a square

$A = 38^2$ Replace s with 38.

$A = 1,444$ Multiply.

So, the area of a regulation wrestling mat is 1,444 square feet.

Guided Practice

Write an equation to determine the area of each rectangle. (Examples 1 and 2)

1. _____

12 yd

5 yd

2. _____

5.3 m

0.4 m

Write an equation to determine the area of each square. (Examples 3 and 4)

3. _____

13 in.

13 in.

4. _____

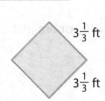

$3\frac{1}{3}$ ft

$3\frac{1}{3}$ ft

5. A glass baking dish measures 9 inches by 13 inches. What is the area of the baking dish? (Example 5)

_____

6. **Building on the Essential Question** How can you use the formula for area of a square to solve real-world problems?

_____

_____

_____

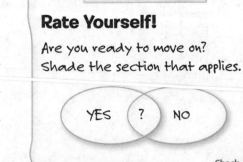

Rubberball/Getty Images   Copyright © McGraw-Hill Education

Independent Practice

6.8(D), 6.8(C), 6.10(A), 6.1(A), 6.1(D)

Write an equation to determine the area of each rectangle. (Examples 1 and 2)

1. _____

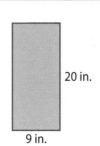

20 in.

9 in.

2. _____

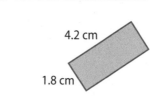

4.2 cm

1.8 cm

3. _____

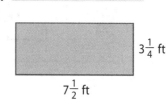

$3\frac{1}{4}$ ft

$7\frac{1}{2}$ ft

Write an equation to determine the area of each square. (Examples 3 and 4)

4. _____

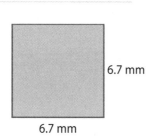

6.7 mm

6.7 mm

5. _____

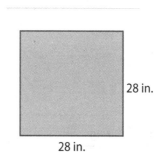

28 in.

28 in.

6. _____

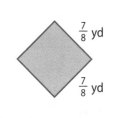

$\frac{7}{8}$ yd

$\frac{7}{8}$ yd

7. The floor of a domed camping tent measures 7 feet by 9 feet. What is the area of the floor of the tent? (Example 5) _____

8. Meagan and her friends are knitting small squares to join together to form a blanket. The side length of each square must be 7 inches. The blanket will be a square with 10 squares on each side. What is the total area of the blanket?

_____

9. The McCulloughs are replacing the flooring in their kitchen with ceramic tiles. They are deciding between 12-inch square tiles and 6-inch square tiles. What is the difference in the area of the two tiles they are considering?

_____

10. The floor spaces of two cages are shown. The square footage of Cage 1 is large enough for one guinea pig. For each additional guinea pig, the cage should be 1 square foot larger. How many guinea pigs should be kept in Cage 2? _____

Cage 1

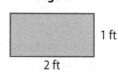

1 ft

2 ft

Cage 2

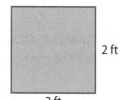

2 ft

2 ft

Determine the area of each shaded region.

11. _____

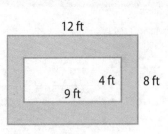

12 ft

4 ft
9 ft
8 ft

12. _____

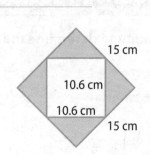

15 cm

10.6 cm

10.6 cm

15 cm

The area of each rectangle is 120 square meters. Write and solve an equation to determine the missing measure.

13. _____

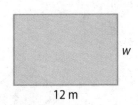

w

12 m

14. _____

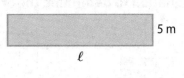

5 m

ℓ

 H.O.T. Problems Higher-Order Thinking

15. Create Give the dimensions of two different rectangles that have the same

area. _____

16. Create Draw and label a rectangle that has an area of 48 square units.

 Show your work.

17. Analyze What is the area of the rectangle in square feet? _____

12 in.

18 in.

18. Analyze Of all the possible rectangles with a perimeter of 36 feet, what are the dimensions with the greatest area? Justify your response.

_____

Multi-Step Problem Solving

19. Mitchell is building a rectangular deck. He ordered 15 deck boards that are each $5\frac{1}{2}$ inches wide and 16 feet long. He will place the deck boards as shown with a $\frac{1}{4}$-inch gap between each deck board. What will be the total area taken up by the deck?

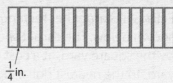

$\frac{1}{4}$ in.

Ⓐ $7\frac{1}{3}$ ft²   Ⓒ $114\frac{2}{3}$ ft²

Ⓑ 110 ft²   Ⓓ 1,376 ft²

Use a problem-solving model to solve this problem.

1 Analyze

Read the problem. Circle the information you know.
Underline what the problem is asking you to find.

2 Plan

What will you need to do to solve the problem? Write your plan in steps.

Step 1   Find the area of the 15 deck boards and the area of the gaps.

Step 2   Add to determine the total area.

3 Solve

Use your plan to solve the problem. Show your steps.

Convert $5\frac{1}{2}$ inches to feet. $5\frac{1}{2}$ in. = $\frac{11}{24}$ ft. The area of one deck board is $\frac{11}{24} \times 16 =$ _____ ft². The area of 15 deck boards is $15 \times 7\frac{1}{3} =$ _____ ft². The area of one gap is $\frac{1}{48} \times 16 =$ _____ ft².

There are 14 gaps, so the total area of the gaps is $\frac{1}{3} \times 14 =$ _____ ft².

The total area of the boards and gaps is _____ + _____ = _____ ft².

Choice _____ is correct. Fill in that answer choice.

Read to Succeed!

The width of the deck board is given in inches. The other dimensions are given in feet. You need to convert measurements to the same unit.

4 Justify and Evaluate

How do you know your solution is accurate?

_____

_____

_____

_____

Ⓝ = Number and Operations   ⒺⒺ = Expressions, Equations, and Relationships   ⓂⓅ = Mathematical Processes

More Multi-Step Problem Solving

Use a problem-solving model to solve each problem.

20. Felisa will carpet her rectangular living room shown below. The carpet she selected is sold by the square yard, at a cost of $32 per square yard. To the nearest dollar, how much will it cost to carpet the living room?

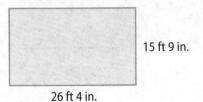

15 ft 9 in.

26 ft 4 in.

Ⓐ $1,386

Ⓑ $1,475

Ⓒ $4,424

Ⓓ $13,272

21. Daniel drew the following design using congruent blue and white rectangles. What is the total area of the blue regions? N EE MP

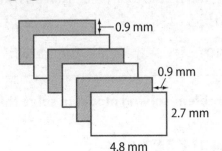

0.9 mm

0.9 mm

2.7 mm

4.8 mm

22. The table shows the dimensions of four rectangles. How many inches wider is the rectangle with the greatest area than the rectangle with the least area? N P EE MP

Rectangle	Width (ft)	Length (ft)
A	$2\frac{1}{2}$	3
B	4	$1\frac{1}{2}$
C	$3\frac{3}{4}$	$\frac{1}{2}$
D	$4\frac{1}{3}$	2

23. The golden rectangle is frequently used in art and architecture. The length of a golden rectangle is approximately 1.6 times its width. If the length of a golden rectangle is about 7.2 meters, what is the approximate area of the rectangle, in square centimeters? Explain how you solved the problem. N P EE MP

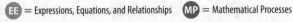

Ⓝ = Number and Operations   Ⓟ = Proportionality   EE = Expressions, Equations, and Relationships   MP = Mathematical Processes

722   Chapter 9 Represent Geometry with Algebra

Model Area of Parallelograms

INQUIRY HOW can I analyze relationships to model and connect the area of a parallelogram to the area of a rectangle?

Elise wants to make a banner in the shape of a parallelogram. Her parallelogram has a base of 2 feet and a height of 3 feet. What is the area of her parallelogram?

Texas Essential Knowledge and Skills

Targeted TEKS
6.8(B) Model area formulas for parallelograms, trapezoids, and triangles by decomposing and rearranging parts of these shapes.

Mathematical Processes
6.1(C), 6.1(D), 6.1(F), 6.1(G)

Hands-On Activity 1

Another type of two-dimensional figure is a *parallelogram*. A parallelogram has opposite sides parallel and congruent.

Parallelograms	Not Parallelograms

Make a parallelogram to represent Elise's banner.

Step 1 Start with a rectangle. Trace the rectangle shown at the right. We will decompose and rearrange the rectangle to form a parallelogram.

3 feet

2 feet

Step 2 Cut a triangle from one side of the rectangle you traced and move it to the other side to form a parallelogram. Tape the parallelogram to the right.

3 feet

2 feet

The rectangle was rearranged to form the parallelogram. Nothing was removed

or added, so the parallelogram has _____ area as the rectangle.

Step 3 Multiply the base and height of the parallelogram to find the area. The base of the parallelogram is 2 feet and the height is 3 feet.

☐ feet × ☐ feet = ☐ square feet

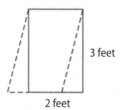

Hands-On Activity 2

Determine the area of the parallelogram below.

Step 1   Trace the parallelogram on grid paper and cut it out.

Step 2   Fold and cut along the dotted line.

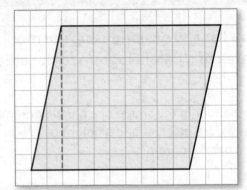

Step 3   Move the triangle to the right to make a rectangle. Tape the rectangle in the space provided.

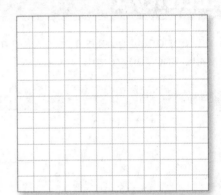

Step 4   Count the number of square units in the rectangle.

The area is ⬚ square units.

Hands-On Activity 3

Determine the area of the parallelogram below.

Step 1   Trace the parallelogram and cut it out.

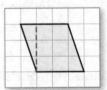

Step 2   Fold and cut along the dotted line. Then move the triangle to the right to make a rectangle. Tape it in the space provided.

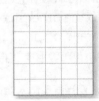

Step 3   Count the number of square units in the rectangle.

The area is ⬚ square units.

Investigate

Collaborate

MP **Select Tools and Techniques** Work with a partner. Determine the area of each parallelogram by decomposing and rearranging each rectangle.

1. $A =$ _____ square units

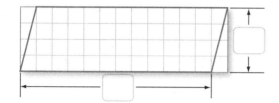

Show your work.

2. $A =$ _____ square units

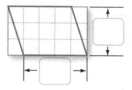

3. $A =$ _____ square units

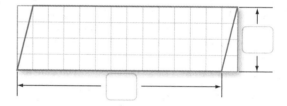

4. $A =$ _____ square units

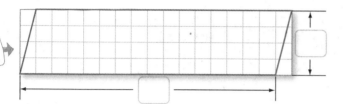

5. $A =$ _____ square units

6. $A =$ _____ square units

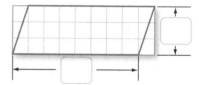

7. $A =$ _____ square units

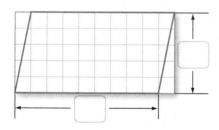

8. $A =$ _____ square units

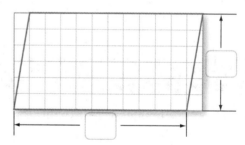

9. $A =$ _____ square units

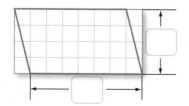

10. $A =$ _____ square units

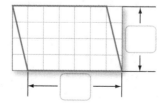

Analyze and Reflect

Collaborate

The table shows the dimensions of several rectangles and the corresponding dimensions of several parallelograms if each rectangle was decomposed and rearranged to form a parallelogram. Work with a partner to complete the table. The first one is done for you.

	Rectangle	Length (ℓ)	Width (w)	Parallelogram	Base (b)	Height (h)	Area (units^2)
	Rectangle 1	6	2	Parallelogram 1	6	2	12
11.	Rectangle 2	12	4	Parallelogram 2			
12.	Rectangle 3	7	3	Parallelogram 3			
13.	Rectangle 4	5	4	Parallelogram 4			
14.	Rectangle 5	10	6	Parallelogram 5			
15.	Rectangle 6	6	4	Parallelogram 6			
16.	Rectangle 7	15	9	Parallelogram 7			
17.	Rectangle 8	9	3	Parallelogram 8			

18. A rectangle was rearranged to form a parallelogram. How is the height of the parallelogram similar to and different from the width of the rectangle?

_____

_____

19. (MP) **Analyze Relationships** If you were to draw three different parallelograms, each with a base of 6 units and a height of 4 units, how would the areas

compare? _____

Create

On Your Own

20. (MP) **Analyze Relationships** Write a rule that gives the area of a parallelogram.

_____

21. **INQUIRY** HOW can I analyze relationships to model and connect the area of a parallelogram to the area of a rectangle?

_____

_____

_____

Area of Parallelograms

Targeted TEKS
6.8(D) Determine solutions for problems involving the area of rectangles, parallelograms, trapezoids, and triangles and volume of right rectangular prisms where dimensions are positive rational numbers. *Also addresses 6.8(B), 6.8(C), 6.10(A).*

 Launch the Lesson: Vocabulary

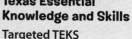 **Texas Essential Knowledge and Skills**

A **parallelogram** is a two-dimensional figure with opposite sides parallel and opposite sides the same length. A **rhombus** is a parallelogram with four equal sides. Fill in the lines in the diagram with *parallelogram*, *rhombus*, or *square* and draw an example of each.

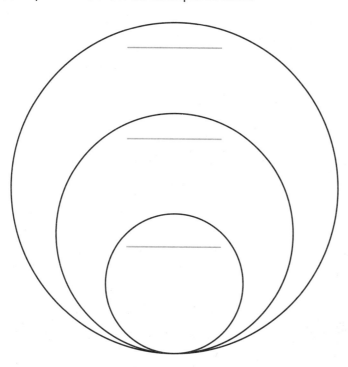

Mathematical Processes
6.1(A), 6.1(B), 6.1(D), 6.1(F)

Vocabulary
parallelogram
rhombus
base
height

 Essential Question

HOW does measurement help you solve problems in everyday life?

 Real-World Link

Expert skateboarders can slide down the railings of stairs safely. A parallelogram is used to build a staircase. How many sets of parallel lines are shown in the parallelogram to the right? _____

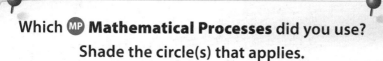

Which MP Mathematical Processes did you use?
Shade the circle(s) that applies.

Ⓐ Apply Math to the Real World.
Ⓑ Use a Problem-Solving Model.
Ⓒ Select Tools and Techniques.
Ⓓ Use Multiple Representations.
Ⓔ Organize Ideas.
Ⓕ Analyze Relationships.
Ⓖ Justify Arguments.

Key Concept > Area of a Parallelogram

Work Zone

Words   The area A of a parallelogram is the product of its base b and its height h.

The area formula of a parallelogram is developed from the area formula of a rectangle because a rectangle can be decomposed and rearranged to form a parallelogram.

Model

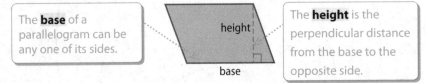

Rectangle   Parallelogram

Symbols $A = bh$

The area of a parallelogram is related to the area of a rectangle as you discovered in the previous Hands-On Lab.

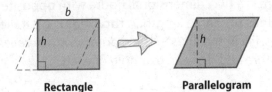

The **base** of a parallelogram can be any one of its sides.

The **height** is the perpendicular distance from the base to the opposite side.

Quadrilaterals

Quadrilaterals are two-dimensional figures with four sides and four angles.

Parallelograms include special quadrilaterals, such as rectangles, squares, and rhombi.

Tutor

Examples

1. **Determine the area of the parallelogram.**

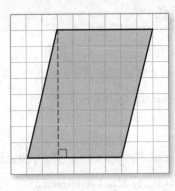

The base is 6 units, and the height is 8 units.

$A = bh$ Area of parallelogram

$A = 6 \cdot 8$ Replace b with 6 and h with 8.

$A = 48$ Multiply.

The area is 48 square units or 48 units^2.

2. Determine the area of the parallelogram.

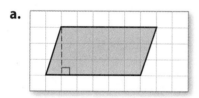

11.7 cm   13 cm

20.8 cm

Estimate A ≈ 20 • 12 or 240 cm²

$A = bh$ Area of a parallelogram

$A = 20.8 \cdot 11.7$ Replace *b* with 20.8 and *h* with 11.7.

$A = 243.36$ Check for Reasonableness 243.36 ≈ 240 ✓

The area is 243.36 square centimeters or 243.36 cm².

> **Height of Parallelograms**
> Be careful to use the correct measurement for the height. In the parallelogram in Example 2, the height is not 13 centimeters. It is 11.7 centimeters. The height of a parallelogram is perpendicular to the base.

Got It? Do these problems to find out.

a.

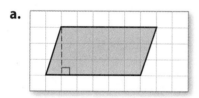

b.

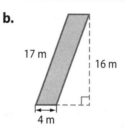

17 m   16 m

4 m

Show your work.

a. _____

b. _____

Find Missing Dimensions

To find missing dimensions, use the formula for the area of a parallelogram to write an equation. Replace the variables with the known measurements. Then solve the equation for the remaining variable.

Tutor

Example

3. Write and solve an equation to determine the missing dimension of the parallelogram.

$A = bh$ Area of a parallelogram

$45 = 9 \cdot h$ Replace *A* with 45 and *b* with 9.

$\dfrac{45}{9} = \dfrac{9 \cdot h}{9}$ Divide each side by 9.

$5 = h$ Simplify.

So, the height is 5 inches.

9 in.

h

$A = 45$ in²

> **Checking Your Work**
> To check your work, replace *b* and *h* in the formula with 9 and 5.
> $A = bh$
> $A = 9 \cdot 5$
> $A = 45$ ✓

Got It? Do these problems to find out.

c.

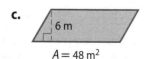

6 m

$A = 48$ m²

d.

$8\frac{1}{2}$ yd

$A = 108\frac{3}{8}$ yd²

c. _____

d. _____

Example

Height of
Parallelograms

For the parallelogram formed by the area shaded black in Example 4, its height, 12 inches, is labeled outside the parallelogram.

4. Romilla is painting a replica of the national flag of Trinidad and Tobago for a research project. Determine the area of the black stripe.

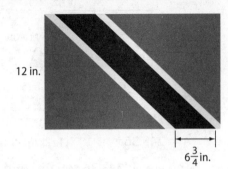

12 in.

$6\frac{3}{4}$ in.

The black stripe is shaped like a parallelogram. So, use the formula $A = bh$.

$A = bh$ Area of a parallelogram

$A = 6\frac{3}{4} \cdot 12$ Replace b with $6\frac{3}{4}$ and h with 12.

$A = 81$ $6\frac{3}{4} \cdot 12 = \frac{27}{4} \cdot 12$, or 81

The area of the flag that is black is 81 square inches.

Guided Practice

Determine the area of each parallelogram. (Examples 1 and 2)

1. _____

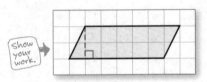

Show your work.

2. _____

$10\frac{1}{3}$ ft

$5\frac{2}{3}$ ft

3. _____

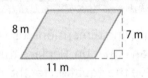

8 m   7 m

11 m

4. Write and solve an equation to determine the height of a parallelogram if its base is 35.8 centimeters and its area is 784.02 square centimeters. (Example 3)

_____

5. The size of the parallelogram piece in a set of tangrams is shown at the right. Determine the area of the piece. (Example 4)

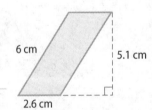

6 cm   5.1 cm

2.6 cm

_____

6. **?** **Building on the Essential Question** How is the area formula for a parallelogram connected to the area formula for a rectangle?

_____

_____

_____

Rate Yourself!

How confident are you about the area of parallelograms? Shade the ring on the target.

I'm on target.

I need help.

Find out online. Use the Self-Check Quiz.

Check

FOLDABLES Time to update your Foldable!

Independent Practice

6.8(B), 6.8(C), 6.8(D), 6.10(A), 6.1(A), 6.1(D), 6.1(F) **TEKS**

Determine the area of each parallelogram. (Examples 1 and 2)

1. _____

Show your work.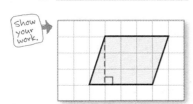

2. base, 6 millimeters; height, 4 millimeters

_____

3. _____

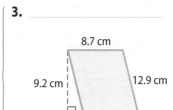

8.7 cm

9.2 cm | 12.9 cm

4. Write and solve an equation to determine the base of a parallelogram with an area of 24 square feet and height $3\frac{3}{4}$ feet. (Example 3) _____

_____

5. Determine the area of the parking space shown to the right.

(Example 4) _____

6. **STEM** An architect designed three different parallelogram-shaped brick patios. Determine the missing dimensions in the table.

Patio	Base (ft)	Height (ft)	Area (ft²)
1	$15\frac{3}{4}$		147
2		$11\frac{1}{4}$	$140\frac{5}{8}$
3	$10\frac{1}{4}$		$151\frac{3}{16}$

18 ft

$9\frac{1}{4}$ ft

7. The base of a building is shaped like a parallelogram. The first floor has an area of 20,000 square feet. If the base of this parallelogram is 250 feet, can its height be 70 feet? Explain.

_____

_____

8. **MP** **Analyze Relationships** Draw and label a parallelogram with a base twice as long as the height and an area less than 60 square inches. Determine the area.

_____

Show your work.

9. **MP Use Multiple Representations** Draw five parallelograms that each have a height of 4 centimeters and different base measurements on centimeter grid paper.

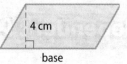

   a. **Table** Make a table with a column for base, height, and area.

Base (cm)	Height (cm)	Area (cm²)
	4	
	4	
	4	
	4	
	4	

   b. **Graph** Graph the ordered pairs (base, area).

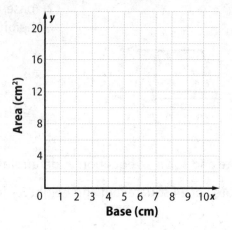

   c. **Words** Describe the graph. _____

   _____

   d. **Equation** Write the equation that represents the graph.

   _____

   e. **Analyze** What type of relationship is shown by the table and graph? Explain.

   _____

   _____

H.O.T. Problems Higher-Order Thinking

10. **Analyze** If $x = 5$ and $y < x$, which figure has the greater area? Explain your reasoning.

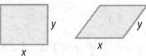

   _____

   _____

   _____

11. **Analyze** Explain how the formula for the area of a parallelogram is related

   to the formula for the area of a rectangle. _____

   _____

   _____

   _____

Multi-Step Problem Solving

12. Li is designing a flower bed for a school project. His design consists of a square inside a parallelogram. The shaded area will be planted with small shrubs. In order to get the correct number of shrubs, Li needs to determine the area of the shaded region once he has the dimensions. Which of the following formulas can be used to find the area of the shaded region? **EE** **MP**

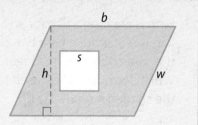

Ⓐ $A = b \cdot h - s^2$
Ⓒ $A = b \cdot w + s^2$
Ⓑ $A = b \cdot w - s^2$
Ⓓ $A = b \cdot h + s^2$

Use a problem-solving model to solve this problem.

1 Analyze

Read the problem. Circle the information you know. Underline what the problem is asking you to find.

2 Plan

What will you need to do to solve the problem? Write your plan in steps.

Read to Succeed!

Be careful when finding the area of a parallelogram that the slant height is not used. The height of the parallelogram is perpendicular to the base.

Step 1 Determine the formula for the area of the parallelogram and square.

Step 2 Subtract the area of the square from the area of the parallelogram.

3 Solve

Use your plan to solve the problem. Show your steps.

Area of Parallelogram − Area of Square = Area of Shaded Region
$$b \cdot h \qquad - \qquad s^2 \qquad = \qquad b \cdot h - s^2$$

The formula is $A = b \cdot h - s^2$, so choice _____ is correct. Fill in that answer choice.

4 Justify and Evaluate

How do you know your solution is accurate?

_____

_____

_____

EE = Expressions, Equations, and Relationships   **MP** = Mathematical Processes

More Multi-Step Problem Solving

Use a problem-solving model to solve each problem.

13. Beth is creating a flag for an art project. The flag is rectangular with two parallelograms of the same dimensions as seen in the diagram. Which formula can be used to find the area of the shaded region?

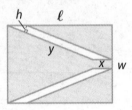

Ⓐ $A = l \cdot w - y \cdot h$

Ⓑ $A = l \cdot w - x \cdot h$

Ⓒ $A = l \cdot w - 2 \cdot x \cdot h$

Ⓓ $A = l \cdot w - 2 \cdot y \cdot h$

14. The side of an office building is made of mirrored glass panels in the shape of parallelograms. If one parallelogram-shaped piece of glass has a base of 8.5 feet and a height of 4 feet, determine how many windows there are in an 850 square foot area. **EE** **N** **MP**

_____

15. An area of 861 square feet is used for 4 identical parking spaces as seen in the diagram below. Use the information in the diagram to find the height of one parallelogram-shaped parking space, *h*. **EE** **N** **MP**

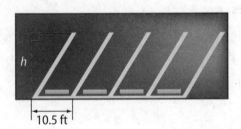

_____

16. A rectangle is drawn with dimensions 6 units long and 4 units wide. Then a triangle is cut from the rectangle with dimensions shown, and placed on the left side of the rectangle to form a parallelogram. **EE** **N** **MP**

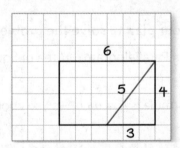

What are the area and perimeter of the original rectangle? What are the area and perimeter of the parallelogram formed by cutting and moving the triangle?

_____

_____

_____

Hands-On Lab 7-a
Model Area of Triangles

INQUIRY HOW can I analyze relationships to model and connect the area of a triangle to the area of a parallelogram?

Yurri is making a mosaic and is cutting rectangular tiles to make triangular tiles. He wants to find the area of the triangular tiles he is cutting.

What do you know? _____

_____

What do you need to know? _____

_____

Texas Essential Knowledge and Skills TEKS

Targeted TEKS
6.8(B) Model area formulas for parallelograms, trapezoids, and triangles by decomposing and rearranging parts of these shapes.

Mathematical Processes
6.1(C), 6.1(D), 6.1(F), 6.1(G)

Hands-On Activity 1

Watch ▶

Yurri starts with a rectangular piece that is 4 inches by 6 inches, similar to the size of an index card.

Step 1 Determine the area of an index card.

A = length × width

A = ☐ inches × ☐ inches

A = ☐ square inches

4 in.

6 in.

Step 2 Use an index card. Draw a diagonal line across your index card from one corner to another. Then cut across the line. Draw the resulting figures in the space below.

 Show your work. ➡

Step 3 Determine the area of one of the remaining triangles. The triangle is exactly half the size of the related rectangle.

The rectangle is decomposed into two congruent triangles.

So, the area of the rectangle can be divided by 2 to determine the area of one triangle.

The area is ☐ ÷ 2, or ☐ square inches.

Hands-On Activity 2

You can also determine the area of a triangle from the area of a related parallelogram.

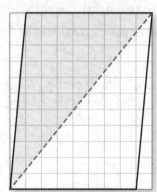

Step 1 Copy the parallelogram shown on grid paper.

Step 2 Draw a diagonal as shown by the dashed line. Cut out the parallelogram. The area of the parallelogram is ☐ square units.

Step 3 Cut along the diagonal to form two triangles. Then find the area of one triangle. The triangle is half the size of the parallelogram. So, the area of the parallelogram can be divided by 2 to determine the area of one triangle.

The parallelogram is decomposed into 2 congruent triangles.

So, the area of one triangle is ☐ ÷ 2 or ☐ square units.

Investigate

On Your Own

Work with a partner to determine the area of each shaded triangle by first determining the area of the parallelogram.

1.

length: _____
width: _____

area: _____ × _____ = _____
area of triangle = _____ square units

2.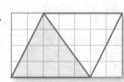

base: _____
height: _____

area: _____ × _____ = _____
area of triangle = _____ square units

3.

length: _____
width: _____

area: _____ × _____ = _____
area of triangle = _____ square units

4.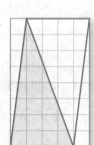

base: _____
height: _____

area: _____ × _____ = _____
area of triangle = _____ square units

Investigate

Work with a partner to determine the area of each shaded triangle by first determining the area of each parallelogram.

5. A = _____ square feet

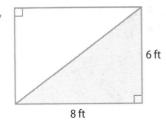

6 ft

8 ft

6. A = _____ square meters

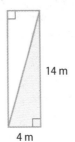

14 m

4 m

7. A = _____ square centimeters

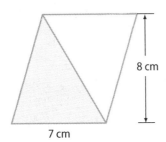

8 cm

7 cm

8. A = _____ square feet

2 ft

6 ft

MP Analyze Relationships Draw dotted lines to show the parallelogram or rectangle that can be used to determine the area of each triangle. Then determine the area of each triangle.

9. A = _____ square inches

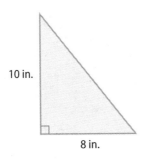

10 in.

8 in.

10. A = _____ square yards

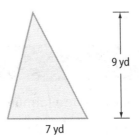

9 yd

7 yd

11. A = _____ square centimeters

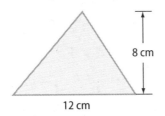

8 cm

12 cm

12. A = _____ square feet

16 ft

3 ft

Analyze and Reflect

The table shows the dimensions of several parallelograms. Use the area of each parallelogram to determine the missing information for each triangle. Work with a partner to complete the table. The first one is already done for you.

	Parallelogram	Base, b	Height, h	Area of Parallelogram (units squared)	Triangle created with diagonal	Base, b	Height, h	Area of Each Triangle (units squared)
	A	4	5	20	A	4	5	10
13.	B	4	6		B	4		12
14.	C	2	5		C	2	5	
15.	D	3	4		D	3	4	
16.	E	6	3		E		3	9
17.	F	8	5		F	8	5	
18.	G	5	7		G	5		17.5
19.	H	9	7		H	9	7	
20.	I	11	5		I	11	5	

21. **MP Analyze Relationships** How is the area of the parallelogram related to the area of a triangle with the same base and height?

_____

_____

_____

Create

22. **MP Analyze Relationships** Write a formula that relates the area A of a triangle to the lengths of its base b and height h.

_____

23. **INQUIRY** HOW can I analyze relationships to model and connect the area of a triangle to the area of a parallelogram?

_____

_____

Area of Triangles

 Launch the Lesson: Real World

The Biosphere 2 complex in Tucson, Arizona, researches Earth and its living systems. Sections of the building are interlocking triangles of the same size.

1. There are two triangles that are outlined in the photo.

   They have the _____ size and the _____ shape.

2. Draw the figure formed by the two triangles.

3. How many small triangles make up the outlined parallelogram? _____

   How many small triangles make up each outlined triangle? _____

4. Describe the relationship between the area of one outlined triangle and the area of the outlined parallelogram.

   _____

   _____

5. Draw another parallelogram like the one in the photo. Separate it into two triangles. Describe the relationship between the area of one triangle and the parallelogram.

   _____

   _____

Texas Essential Knowledge and Skills

Targeted TEKS
6.8(D) Determine solutions for problems involving the area of rectangles, parallelograms, trapezoids, and triangles and volume of right rectangular prisms where dimensions are positive rational numbers. *Also addresses 6.8(B), 6.8(C), 6.10(A).*

Mathematical Processes
6.1(A), 6.1(B), 6.1(D), 6.1(F)

Vocabulary
congruent figures

Essential Question
HOW does measurement help you solve problems in everyday life?

Which MP Mathematical Processes did you use?
Shade the circle(s) that applies.

Ⓐ Apply Math to the Real World.
Ⓑ Use a Problem-Solving Model.
Ⓒ Select Tools and Techniques.
Ⓓ Use Multiple Representations.
Ⓔ Organize Ideas.
Ⓕ Analyze Relationships.
Ⓖ Justify Arguments.

Area of a Triangle

Words		Model	Parallelogram

Words A parallelogram can be decomposed into two congruent triangles. So, the area *A* of a triangle is one half the product of the base *b* and its height *h*.

Symbols $A = \frac{1}{2}bh$ or $A = \frac{bh}{2}$

Model Parallelogram

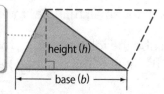

Triangle

Congruent figures are figures that are the same shape and size.

A parallelogram can be formed by two congruent triangles. Since congruent triangles have the same area, the area of a triangle is one half the area of the parallelogram.

The base of a triangle can be any one of its sides. The height is the perpendicular distance from that base to the opposite vertex.

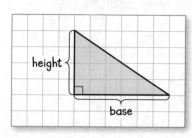

height (*h*)

base (*b*)

Watch Tutor

Examples

1. Determine the area of the triangle.

height

base

By counting, you find that the measure of the base is 6 units and the height is 4 units.

$A = \frac{1}{2}bh$ Area of a triangle

$A = \frac{1}{2}(6)(4)$ Replace *b* with 6 and *h* with 4.

$A = \frac{1}{2}(24)$ Multiply.

$A = 12$ Multiply.

The area of the triangle is 12 square units.

Mental Math

You can use mental math to multiply $\frac{1}{2}(6)(4)$. Think: Half of 6 is 3, and 3 × 4 is 12.

2. **Determine the area of the triangle.**

12.1 m

6.4 m

$A = \dfrac{1}{2}bh$ Area of a triangle

$A = \dfrac{1}{2}(12.1)(6.4)$ Replace b with 12.1 and h with 6.4.

$A = \dfrac{1}{2}(77.44)$ Multiply.

$A = 38.72$ Divide. $\dfrac{1}{2}(77.44) = 77.44 \div 2$, or 38.72

The area of the triangle is 38.72 square meters.

Got It? Do these problems to find out.

a.

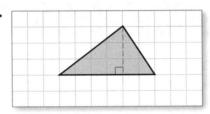

b.

$9\frac{3}{4}$ ft

7 ft

Show your work.

a. _____

b. _____

Determine Missing Dimensions

You can write and solve equations to determine missing dimensions.

Tutor

Example

3. **Write and solve an equation to determine the missing dimension of the triangle.**

6 cm

b

$A = 24.9$ cm²

$A = \dfrac{bh}{2}$ Area of a triangle

$24.9 = \dfrac{b \cdot 6}{2}$ Replace A with 24.9 and h with 6.

$24.9(2) = \dfrac{b \cdot 6}{2}(2)$ Multiply each side by 2.

$49.8 = b \cdot 6$ Simplify.

$\dfrac{49.8}{6} = \dfrac{b \cdot 6}{6}$ Divide each side by 6.

$8.3 = b$ Simplify.

So, the base is 8.3 centimeters.

Check for Reasonableness
To check your work, replace b and h with the measurements and solve to find the area.

Got It? Do these problems to find out.

c.

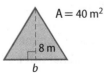
$A = 40$ m²

8 m

b

d.

$A = 78\frac{1}{8}$ yd²

h

$12\frac{1}{2}$ yd

c. _____

d. _____

Example

The front of a camping tent has the dimensions shown. How much material was used to make the front of the tent?

$A = \frac{1}{2}bh$ Area of a triangle

$A = \frac{1}{2}(5)(3)$ Replace b with 5 and h with 3.

$A = \frac{1}{2}(15)$ or 7.5   Multiply.

The front of the tent has an area of 7.5 square feet.

Guided Practice

Determine the area of each triangle. (Examples 1 and 2)

1.

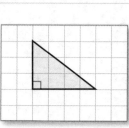

2.

$8\frac{1}{4}$ ft

12 ft

3.

11.25 m

15.6 m

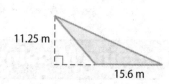

4. Tayshan designs uniquely-shaped ceramic floor tiles. Write and solve an equation to determine the base of the tile shown. (Example 3)

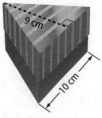

b

6 in.

$A = 21$ in^2

5. Consuela made a triangular paper box as shown. What is the area of the top of the box? (Example 4)

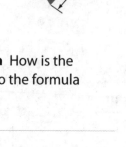

9 cm

10 cm

Rate Yourself!

☐ I understand how to determine the area of a triangle.

▷▷ Great! You're ready to move on!

☐ I still have questions about the area of a triangle.

 No problem! Go online to access a Personal Tutor. Check ✓

6. (?) **Building on the Essential Question** How is the formula for the area of a triangle related to the formula for the area of a parallelogram?

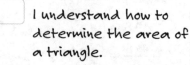 Time to update your Foldable!

Photodisc/Getty Images   Copyright © McGraw-Hill Education

Chapter 9 Represent Geometry with Algebra

Independent Practice

6.8(B), 6.8(C), 6.8(D), 6.10(A), 6.1(A), 6.1(D), 6.1(F)

Determine the area of each triangle. (Examples 1 and 2)

1. _____

Show your work.

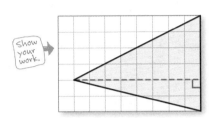

2. _____

16 cm

24.8 cm

3. _____

36 ft $41\frac{1}{2}$ ft

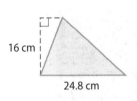

Write and solve an equation to determine the missing dimension of each triangle described. (Examples 3)

4. height: $14\frac{1}{2}$ in.

area: $253\frac{3}{4}$ in^2

5. base: 27 cm

area: 256.5 cm^2

6. Ansley is going to help his father shingle the roof of their house. What is the area of the triangular portion of one end of the roof? (Example 4)

4 yd

7 yd

7. **MP Use Multiple Representations** The table shows the areas of a triangle where the base of the triangle stays the same but the height changes.

a. **Algebra** Write an algebraic expression that can be used to find the area of a triangle that has a base of 5 units and a height of n units. _____

b. **Graph** Graph the ordered pairs (height, area).

Area of Triangles		
Base (units)	Height (units)	Area (units^2)
5	2	5
5	4	10
5	6	15
5	8	20
5	n	?

(graph with y-axis labeled 3, 6, 9, 12, 15, 18, 21, 24, 27, 30 and x-axis labeled 1 2 3 4 5 6 7 8 9 10)

c. **Words** Describe the graph. _____

8. What is the area of the triangle on the flag of the Philippines, in inches?

Explain your reasoning. _____

_____

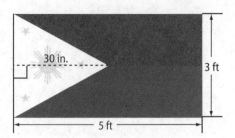

30 in.

3 ft

5 ft

9. Find the Error Dwayne is finding the base of the triangle shown. Its area is 100 square meters. Determine his mistake and correct it.

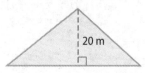

20 m

$$100 = (b)20$$
$$100 = 20b$$
$$5 = b$$

H.O.T. Problems Higher-Order Thinking

10. Analyze How can you use triangles to find the area of the hexagon shown? Draw a diagram to support your answer.

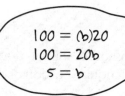

_____

_____

11. Create Draw a triangle and label its base and height. Draw another triangle that has the same base, but a height twice that of the first triangle. Determine the area of each triangle. Then write a ratio that expresses the area of the first triangle to the area of the second triangle.

_____

_____

_____

12. Analyze The triangle shown has an area of $8\frac{15}{16}$ square feet. What is the height, in inches?

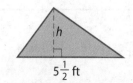

h

$5\frac{1}{2}$ ft

_____

Name _____

Multi-Step Problem Solving

13. The triangle on the grid represents a triangular-shaped pillow. What is the area of the triangle?

Ⓐ 270 in²

Ⓑ 135 in²

Ⓒ 45 in²

Ⓓ 15 in²

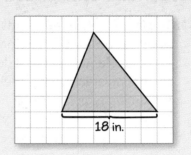

18 in.

Use a problem-solving model to solve this problem.

1 Analyze

Read the problem. Circle the information you know.
Underline what the problem is asking you to find.

2 Plan

What will you need to do to solve the problem? Write your plan in steps.

| Step 1 | Determine the height of the triangle. |

| Step 2 | Use the formula $A = \frac{1}{2} bh$ to find the area of the triangle. |

Read to Succeed!
Remember to determine the scale of the grid.

3 Solve

Use your plan to solve the problem. Show your steps.

Each square on the grid represents $18 \div \boxed{}$ or $\boxed{}$ inches.

The height of the triangle is $\boxed{} \times \boxed{}$ or $\boxed{}$ inches.

The area of the triangle is $\frac{1}{2} bh$ or $\frac{1}{2} \cdot \boxed{} \cdot \boxed{}$.

The area is $\boxed{}$ square inches.

Choice $\boxed{}$ is correct. Fill in that answer choice.

4 Justify and Evaluate

How do you know your solution is accurate?

_____

_____

_____

EE = Expressions, Equations, and Relationships   MP = Mathematical Processes

More Multi-Step Problem Solving

Use a problem-solving model to solve each problem.

14. The figure below represents a swimming pool. A rope is attached from point A to C, and triangle ABC will be a designated adult swimming area. What is the area of the adult swimming region? **EE** **MP**

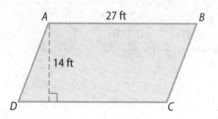

A ⃝ 41 ft²

B ⃝ 82 ft²

C ⃝ 189 ft²

D ⃝ 378 ft²

15. The triangle on the grid outlines the border of a town. Each square on the grid represents a side length of 1.5 miles. What is the area of the town in square miles? **EE** **MP**

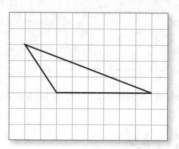

16. The table shows the dimensions of three triangles. How much greater is the area of triangle C than triangle A, in square centimeters? **EE** **MP**

Triangle	Base	Height
A	8.5 cm	6 cm
B	7 cm	7 cm
C	9 cm	6.5 cm

17. Marco is going to paint 30% of the triangle. How many square inches will he paint? **EE** **P** **MP**

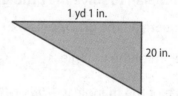

EE = Expressions, Equations, and Relationships   **P** = Proportionality   **MP** = Mathematical Processes

Model Area of Trapezoids

INQUIRY HOW can I analyze relationships to model and connect the area of a trapezoid to the area of a parallelogram?

Lizette is building a garden in the shape of a trapezoid. The garden is 6 feet wide in the back, 10 feet wide in the front, and 5 feet from back to front. She wants to find the area of the garden.

Texas Essential Knowledge and Skills

Targeted TEKS
6.8(B) Model area formulas for parallelograms, trapezoids, and triangles by decomposing and rearranging parts of these shapes.

Mathematical Processes
6.1(C), 6.1(D), 6.1(F), 6.1(G)

Hands-On Activity 1

You can model the area of a trapezoid by composing a parallelogram.

Step 1 Trace the trapezoid below on grid paper. Label the height h and label the bases b_1 and b_2.

A trapezoid has two bases, b_1 and b_2. The height h of a trapezoid is the perpendicular distance between the bases.

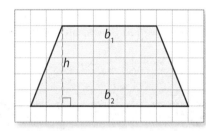

The shorter base b_1 represents the garden width of _____.

The longer base b_2 represents the garden width of _____.

The height h represents the garden dimension of _____.

Step 2 Cut out another trapezoid that is identical to the one in Step 1.

Step 3 Tape the trapezoids together as shown. A parallelogram can be decomposed into two congruent trapezoids.

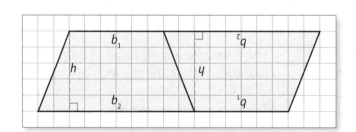

Step 4 Determine the area of the parallelogram. Then divide by 2 to determine the area of each trapezoid.

$$\boxed{} \times \boxed{} = \boxed{} \qquad \boxed{} \div 2 = \boxed{}$$

So, the area of the garden is $\boxed{}$ square feet.

Hands-On Activity 2

Discover the formula for the area of a trapezoid by decomposing a parallelogram.

Step 1 What figure is formed by the two trapezoids in Activity 1?

_____

Write an addition expression to represent the length of the base

of the entire figure. _____

Step 2 Write a formula for the area A of the parallelogram using b_1, b_2, and h.

_____

Step 3 How does the area of each trapezoid compare to the area of the

parallelogram? _____

_____

Step 4 Write a formula for the area A of each trapezoid using b_1, b_2, and h.

_____

Hands-On Activity 3

Another way to determine the area of a trapezoid is to decompose it to determine which figures form the trapezoid. Determine the area of the trapezoid shown below.

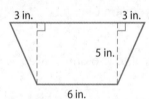

Step 1 The trapezoid is composed of one rectangle and two congruent triangles. Determine the area of the three shapes.

The area of the rectangle is ☐ × ☐ = ☐ square inches.

The area of each triangle is $\dfrac{☐ \times ☐}{☐}$ = ☐ square inches.

Step 2 Add the areas.

☐ + ☐ + ☐ = ☐ square inches

Investigate

MP **Select Tools and Techniques** Work with a partner. Determine the area of each trapezoid by drawing and decomposing the related parallelogram.

1. $A =$ _____ square units

2. $A =$ _____ square units

Show your work.

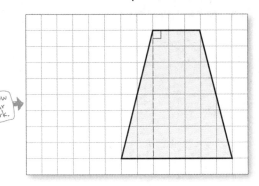

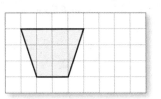

Work with a partner. Determine the area of each trapezoid by using the formula.

3. $A = \dfrac{\left(\boxed{} + \boxed{}\right)\boxed{}}{\boxed{}}$

$A =$ _____ square units

4. $A = \dfrac{\left(\boxed{} + \boxed{}\right)\boxed{}}{\boxed{}}$

$A =$ _____ square units

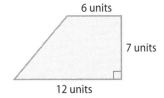

6 units

7 units

12 units

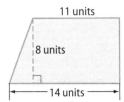

11 units

8 units

14 units

Work with a partner. Decompose each trapezoid to determine the area.

5. $A =$ _____ square units

6. $A =$ _____ square units

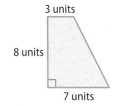

3 units

8 units

7 units

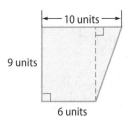

10 units

9 units

6 units

Analyze and Reflect

The table shows the dimensions of several parallelograms and corresponding trapezoids. Complete the table. The first one is done for you.

Dimensions of Parallelogram	Area of Parallelogram	Length of Trapezoid b_1	Length of Trapezoid b_2	Trapezoid Height	Area of Trapezoid
4, 7	28	2	5	4	14
7. (6, 11)		5	6	6	
8. (5, 12)		8	4	5	
9. $b = 11$ $h = 3$		7	4	3	

10. **MP Analyze Relationships** Compare the dimensions of the parallelogram to the dimensions of the corresponding trapezoid. What pattern do you see?

_____

_____

_____

11. **MP Analyze Relationships** Compare the area of the parallelogram to the area of the corresponding trapezoid. What pattern do you see in the table?

_____

_____

Create

12. **MP Analyze Relationships** Write the formula for the area A of a trapezoid with bases b_1 and b_2 and height h. _____

13. **INQUIRY** HOW can I analyze relationships to model and connect the area of a trapezoid to the area of a parallelogram?

_____

_____

Lesson 8
Area of Trapezoids

Launch the Lesson: Real World

Kiana has a bay window in her room. The window seat is in the shape of a trapezoid. She needs to measure the seat in order to sew a cushion for the seat. The blue trapezoid in the diagram below represents the dimensions of the window seat. Use the diagram below to describe the relationship between trapezoids and rectangles.

1. Find the dimensions of each figure.

Trapezoid	Rectangle
base 1: ☐ units	length: ☐ units
base 2: ☐ units	height: ☐ units
height: ☐ units	

2. What is the relationship between the measures of the rectangle and the measures of the trapezoid?

_____

_____

_____

3. **MP Analyze Relationships** How is the area of a trapezoid related to the area of a rectangle?

_____

_____

Which **MP Mathematical Processes** did you use?
Shade the circle(s) that applies.

Ⓐ Apply Math to the Real World.
Ⓑ Use a Problem-Solving Model.
Ⓒ Select Tools and Techniques.
Ⓓ Use Multiple Representations.
Ⓔ Organize Ideas.
Ⓕ Analyze Relationships.
Ⓖ Justify Arguments.

Texas Essential Knowledge and Skills

Targeted TEKS
6.8(D) Determine solutions for problems involving the area of rectangles, parallelograms, trapezoids, and triangles and volume of right rectangular prisms where dimensions are positive rational numbers. *Also addresses 6.8(B), 6.8(C), 6.10(A).*

Mathematical Processes
6.1(A), 6.1(B), 6.1(D), 6.1(F)

Vocabulary
trapezoid

Essential Question
HOW does measurement help you solve problems in everyday life?

Key Concept **Area of a Trapezoid**

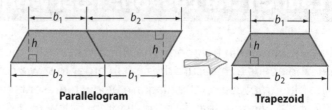

Words A parallelogram can be decomposed into two congruent trapezoids. So, the area *A* of a trapezoid is one-half the product of the height *h* and the sum of the bases b_1 and b_2.

Model

Parallelogram

Trapezoid

Symbols $A = \frac{1}{2}h(b_1 + b_2)$

A **trapezoid** has two parallel bases, b_1 and b_2. The height of a trapezoid is the distance between the bases.

The height is the perpendicular distance between the bases.

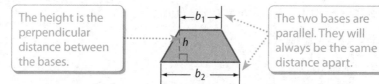

The two bases are parallel. They will always be the same distance apart.

When finding the area of a trapezoid, it is important to follow the order of operations. In the formula, the bases are to be added before multiplying by $\frac{1}{2}$ of the height *h*.

Tutor

Examples

1. **Determine the area of the trapezoid.**

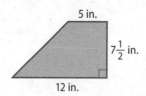

5 in.

$7\frac{1}{2}$ in.

12 in.

The bases are 5 inches and 12 inches.

The height is $7\frac{1}{2}$ inches.

$A = \frac{1}{2}h(b_1 + b_2)$ Area of a trapezoid

$A = \frac{1}{2}\left(7\frac{1}{2}\right)(5 + 12)$ Replace *h* with $7\frac{1}{2}$, b_1 with 5, and b_2 with 12.

$A = \frac{1}{2}\left(7\frac{1}{2}\right)(17)$ Add 5 and 12.

$A = 63\frac{3}{4}$ Multiply.

The area of the trapezoid is $63\frac{3}{4}$ square inches.

2. Determine the area of the trapezoid.

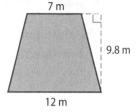

7 m

9.8 m

12 m

$A = \frac{1}{2}h(b_1 + b_2)$ — Area of a trapezoid

$A = \frac{1}{2}(9.8)(7 + 12)$ — Replace h with 9.8, b_1 with 7, and b_2 with 12.

$A = \frac{1}{2}(9.8)(19)$ — Add 7 and 12.

$A = 93.1$ — Multiply.

So, the area of the trapezoid is 93.1 square meters.

Got It? Do these problems to find out.

a.

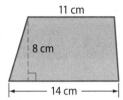

11 cm

8 cm

14 cm

b.

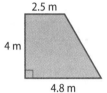

2.5 m

4 m

4.8 m

c.

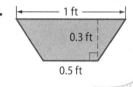

1 ft

0.3 ft

0.5 ft

a. _____

b. _____

c. _____

Determine the Missing Height

You can use the related equation, $h = \dfrac{2A}{b_1 + b_2}$, to determine the height of a trapezoid given the area and the lengths of the two bases.

Tutor

Example

3. The trapezoid has an area of 108 square feet. Write the equation to determine the height.

12 ft

h

15 ft

$h = \dfrac{2A}{b_1 + b_2}$ — Height of a trapezoid

$h = \dfrac{2(108)}{12 + 15}$ — Replace A with 108, b_1 with 12, and b_2 with 15.

$h = \dfrac{216}{27}$ — Multiply 2 and 108. Add 12 and 15.

$h = 8$ — Divide.

So, the height of the trapezoid is 8 feet.

Be Precise

Check your answer by using the formula for the area of a trapezoid.

Got It? Do these problems to find out.

d. $A = 24 \text{ cm}^2$

   $b_1 = 4 \text{ cm}$

   $b_2 = 12 \text{ cm}$

   $h = ?$

e. $A = 21 \text{ yd}^2$

   $b_1 = 2\frac{1}{3} \text{ yd}$

   $b_2 = 4\frac{2}{3} \text{ yd}$

   $h = ?$

d. _____

e. _____

Example

4. The shape of Hudspeth County, Texas, resembles a trapezoid. Determine the approximate area of this county.

$A = \frac{1}{2}h(b_1 + b_2)$ Area of a trapezoid

$A = \frac{1}{2}(65)(45 + 96)$ Replace h with 65, b_1 with 45, and b_2 with 96.

$A = \frac{1}{2}(65)(141)$ Add 45 and 96.

$A = 4{,}582.5$ Multiply.

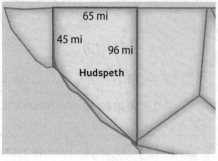

So, the approximate area of the county is 4,582.5 square miles.

Guided Practice

Determine the area of each trapezoid. Round to the nearest tenth if necessary. (Examples 1 and 2)

1. _____

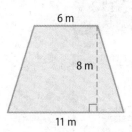

6 m

8 m

11 m

Show your work.

2. _____

7 ft

8 ft

15.6 ft

3. A trapezoid has an area of 15 square feet. If the bases are 4 feet and 6 feet, write an equation to determine the height of the trapezoid. (Example 3) _____

4. In the National Hockey League, goaltenders can play the puck behind the goal line only in a trapezoid-shaped area, as shown at the right. Determine the area of the trapezoid. (Example 4) _____

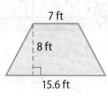

18 ft

11 ft

28 ft

5. ❓ **Building on the Essential Question** How is the formula for the area of a trapezoid related to the formula for the area of a parallelogram? _____

_____

_____

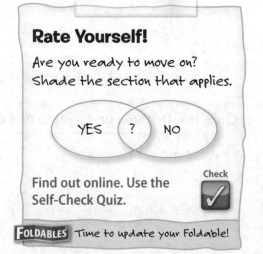

Rate Yourself!

Are you ready to move on?
Shade the section that applies.

YES   ?   NO

Find out online. Use the Self-Check Quiz.

Check ✓

FOLDABLES Time to update your Foldable!

Independent Practice

6.8(B), 6.8(C), 6.8(D), 6.10(A), 6.1(A), 6.1(D)

Determine the area of each trapezoid. Round to the nearest tenth if necessary. (Examples 1 and 2)

1. _____

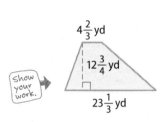

$4\frac{2}{3}$ yd

$12\frac{3}{4}$ yd

Show your work.

$23\frac{1}{3}$ yd

2. _____

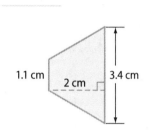

1.1 cm   2 cm   3.4 cm

3. _____

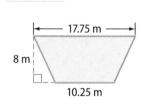

17.75 m

8 m

10.25 m

4. A trapezoid has an area of 150 square feet. The bases are 14 feet and 16 feet. Write an equation to determine the height of the trapezoid. (Example 3)

5. A trapezoid has an area of 402.8 square meters. The bases are 14.6 meters and 35.4 meters. Write an equation to determine the height of the trapezoid. (Example 3)

6. Determine the area of the patio shown. (Example 4)

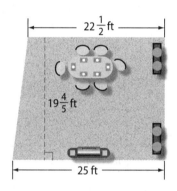

$22\frac{1}{2}$ ft

$19\frac{4}{5}$ ft

25 ft

7. Use the diagram that shows the lawn that surrounds an office building.

a. What is the area of the lawn? _____

b. If one bag of grass seed covers 2,000 square feet, how many bags are needed to seed the lawn?

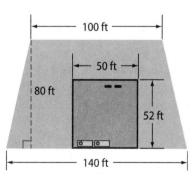

100 ft

50 ft

80 ft   52 ft

140 ft

8. **MP Analyze Relationships** Tiles are being placed in front of a fireplace to create a trapezoidal hearth. The hearth will have a height of 24 inches and bases that are 48 inches and 60 inches. If the tiles cover 16 square inches, how many tiles will be needed?

H.O.T. Problems Higher-Order Thinking

Create Draw and label each figure. Then determine the area.

9. a trapezoid with no right angles and an area less than 12 square centimeters

10. a trapezoid with a right angle and an area greater than 40 square inches

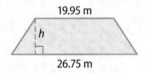

11. Analyze Apply what you know about rounding to explain how to estimate the height h of the trapezoid shown if the area is 235.5 m^2.

19.95 m

h

26.75 m

12. Analyze Find two possible lengths of the bases of a trapezoid with a height of 1 foot and an area of 9 square feet. Explain how you found your answer.

13. Analyze The area of a trapezoid is 36 square inches. The height is 4 inches and one base is twice the length of the other base. What are the lengths of the bases?

14. Analyze How can you use the formula for area of a parallelogram to determine the area of a trapezoid if you forgot the formula for area of a trapezoid?

Multi-Step Problem Solving

15. The figure on the grid represents a parking lot. Asphalt for the parking lot costs $8.95 per square foot. How much will it cost to asphalt the parking lot, to the nearest cent? **EE** **MP**

Ⓐ $290.88

Ⓒ $18,616.00

Ⓑ $805.50

Ⓓ $37,232.00

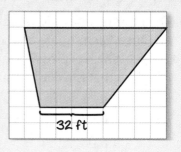

Use a problem-solving model to solve this problem.

1 Analyze

Read the problem. Circle the information you know.
Underline what the problem is asking you to find.

2 Plan

What will you need to do to solve the problem? Write your plan in steps.

Step 1 Determine the area of the trapezoid.

Step 2 Multiply to determine the cost of the asphalt.

3 Solve

Use your plan to solve the problem. Show your steps.

Each square on the grid represents a length of $32 \div 4$ or 8 feet. The two bases are 32 feet and 72 feet. The height is 40 feet.

$A = \frac{1}{2}h(b_1 + b_2)$ Area of a trapezoid

$A = \frac{1}{2}(40)(72 + 32)$ Replace h with 40, b_1 with 72, and b_2 with 32.

$A = 2,080$ Multiply.

So, the cost of the asphalt is $8.95 × 2,080 or $18,616. Choice _____ is correct. Fill in that answer choice.

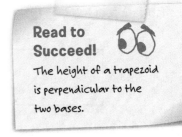

Read to Succeed!

The height of a trapezoid is perpendicular to the two bases.

4 Justify and Evaluate

How do you know your solution is reasonable?

_____

_____

_____

More Multi-Step Problem Solving

Use a problem-solving model to solve each problem.

16. The figure on the grid represents the floor of an office. Each square on the grid represents 2 units. Which expression represents an area of a floor that is twice this size? **EE** **N** **MP**

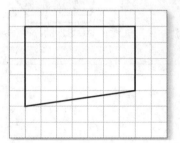

Ⓐ $\frac{1}{2}(7)(4 + 5)$

Ⓑ $7(4 + 5)$

Ⓒ $\frac{1}{2}(14)(8 + 10)$

Ⓓ $(14)(8 + 10)$

17. A farmer spread fertilizer onto the plot of land shown below. He uses 4 scoops of fertilizer per square meter. If he used 312 scoops, what is the height of the trapezoid in meters? **EE** **P** **MP**

8 m   4 m

18. In the figure below, the area inside ABEF will be colored red. What will be the red area, in square feet? **EE** **P** **MP**

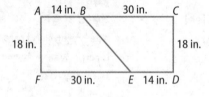

A 14 in. B   30 in.   C

18 in.   18 in.

F   30 in.   E 14 in. D

19. Suppose the bases and height of a trapezoid are all multiplied by 3. How will the area change? **EE** **P** **MP**

Volume of Rectangular Prisms

Launch the Lesson: Vocabulary

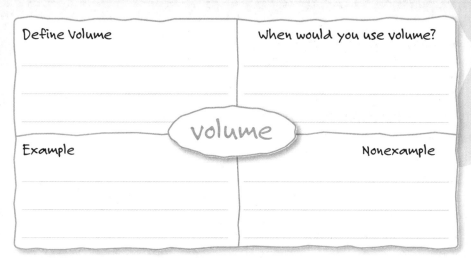

Define Volume

When would you use volume?

Example

volume

Nonexample

Texas Essential Knowledge and Skills

Targeted TEKS
6.8(D) Determine solutions for problems involving the area of rectangles, parallelograms, trapezoids, and triangles and volume of right rectangular prisms where dimensions are positive rational numbers. *Also addresses 6.8(C), 6.10(A).*

Mathematical Processes
6.1(A), 6.1(B), 6.1(D), 6.1(F)

Vocabulary
three-dimensional figure
prism
rectangular prism
volume
cubic units

Essential Question
HOW does measurement help you solve problems in everyday life?

Real-World Investigation

Watch ▶

The dimensions of an aquarium are shown. What is the volume of the aquarium?

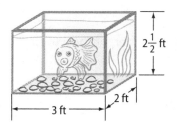
$2\frac{1}{2}$ ft
3 ft
2 ft

1. What is the area of the base of the aquarium? _____

2. What is the height of the aquarium?

   _____

3. Fill in the blanks to find the volume.

   _____ × _____ × _____ = _____
   length   width   height

Which MP Mathematical Processes did you use?
Shade the circle(s) that applies.

Ⓐ Apply Math to the Real World.

Ⓑ Use a Problem-Solving Model.

Ⓒ Select Tools and Techniques.

Ⓓ Use Multiple Representations.

Ⓔ Organize Ideas.

Ⓕ Analyze Relationships.

Ⓖ Justify Arguments.

Volume of a Rectangular Prism

Words The volume *V* of a rectangular prism is the product of its length ℓ, width *w*, and height *h*.

Model

Symbols $V = \ell wh$ or $V = Bh$

Work Zone

Cubes

Cubes are special rectangular prisms. All three dimensions are equal. So, the volume of a cube can be written using the formula $v = s^3$.

A **three-dimensional figure** has length, width, and height. A **prism** is a three-dimensional figure with two parallel bases that are congruent figures. In a **rectangular prism**, the bases are congruent rectangles.

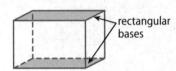

rectangular bases

Volume is the amount of space inside a three-dimensional figure. It is measured in **cubic units**, which can be written using abbreviations and an exponent of 3, such as units³ or in³.

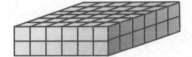

Decomposing the prism tells you the number of cubes of a given size it will take to fill the prism. The volume of a rectangular prism is related to its dimensions, length, width, and height.

Another method to decompose a rectangular prism is to determine the area of the base (*B*) and multiply it by the height (*h*).

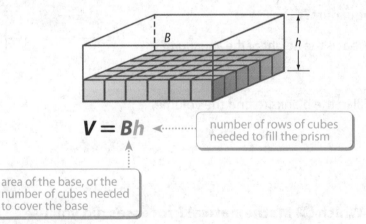

$$V = Bh$$

number of rows of cubes needed to fill the prism

area of the base, or the number of cubes needed to cover the base

Example

Tutor

1. **Determine the volume of the rectangular prism.**

B, or the area of the base, is 10.1 × 12.3 or 124.23 square centimeters. The height of the prism is 6 centimeters.

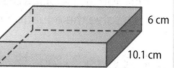

6 cm
10.1 cm
12.3 cm

$V = Bh$ Volume of rectangular prism

$V = 124.23 \times 6$ Replace *B* with 124.23 and *h* with 6.

$V = 745.38$ Multiply.

The volume is 745.38 cubic centimeters.

Got It? Do these problems to find out.

a.

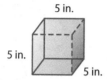

5 in.
5 in.
5 in.

b.

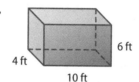

6 ft
4 ft
10 ft

> **Decomposing Figures**
>
> You can think of the volume of the prism as consisting of six congruent slices. Each slice contains the area of the base, 124.23 cm², multiplied by a height of 1 cm.

Show your work.

a. _____

Example

 Real World

Tutor

b. _____

2. **A cereal box has the dimensions shown. What is the volume of the cereal box?**

Estimate 10 × 3 × 10 = 300

8 in.
$12\frac{1}{2}$ in.
$3\frac{1}{4}$ in.

$V = \ell wh$ Volume of a rectangular prism

$V = 8 \times 3\frac{1}{4} \times 12\frac{1}{2}$ Replace ℓ with 8, *w* with $3\frac{1}{4}$, and *h* with $12\frac{1}{2}$.

$V = \dfrac{\overset{1}{\cancel{8}}}{1} \times \dfrac{13}{\underset{1}{\cancel{4}}} \times \dfrac{25}{\underset{1}{\cancel{2}}}$ Write as improper fractions. Then divide out common factors.

$V = \dfrac{325}{1}$ or 325   Multiply.

The volume of the cereal box is 325 cubic inches.

Check for Reasonableness 325 ≈ 300 ✓

Got It? Do this problem to find out.

c. Determine the volume of a container that measures 4 inches long, 5 inches high, and $8\frac{1}{2}$ inches wide.

c. _____

Determine Missing Dimensions

To determine missing dimensions of a rectangular prism, write an equation and replace the variables with known measurements. Then solve the equation for the unknown measurement.

Tutor

Example

3. Write and solve an equation to determine the missing dimension of the prism.

$V = \ell wh$	Volume of rectangular prism
$102.9 = 6 \times 4.9 \times h$	Replace V with 102.9, ℓ with 6, and w with 4.9.
$102.9 = 29.4h$	Multiply.
$\dfrac{102.9}{29.4} = \dfrac{29.4h}{29.4}$	Divide each side by 29.4.
$3.5 = h$	Simplify.

4.9 m
6 m
$V = 102.9 \text{ m}^3$
h

The height of the prism is 3.5 meters.

Check $6 \times 4.9 \times 3.5 = 102.9$ ✓

Guided Practice

Show your work.

1. A rectangular kitchen sink is 25.25 inches long, 19.75 inches wide, and 10 inches deep. Determine the amount of water that can be contained in the sink. (Examples 1 and 2) _____

2. Write and solve an equation to determine the missing dimension of a rectangular prism with a volume of 126 cubic centimeters, a width of 7.875 centimeters, and a height of 2 centimeters. (Example 3) _____

3. (?) **Building on the Essential Question** Why can you use either the formula $V = \ell wh$ or $V = Bh$ to find the volume of a rectangular prism?

_____

_____

_____

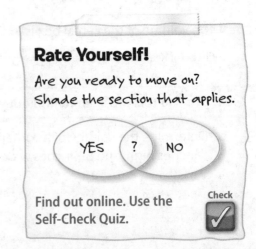

Rate Yourself!

Are you ready to move on?
Shade the section that applies.

YES   ?   NO

Find out online. Use the Self-Check Quiz.

Check ✓

Independent Practice

6.8(C), 6.8(D), 6.10(A), 6.1(A) TEKS

Determine the volume of each prism. (Example 1)

1.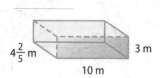

$4\frac{2}{5}$ m   3 m
10 m

Show your work.

2.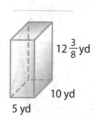

$12\frac{3}{8}$ yd
10 yd
5 yd

3.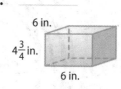

6 in.
$4\frac{3}{4}$ in.
6 in.

4. A fishing tackle box is 13 inches long, 6 inches wide, and $2\frac{1}{2}$ inches high. What is the volume of the tackle box? (Example 2)

5. Determine the length of a rectangular prism having a volume of 2,830.5 cubic meters, width of 18.5 meters, and height of 9 meters.
(Example 3)

Write and solve an equation to determine the missing dimension of each prism. (Example 3)

6.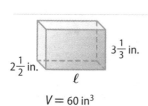

$3\frac{1}{3}$ in.
$2\frac{1}{2}$ in.
ℓ
$V = 60 \text{ in}^3$

7.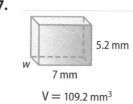

5.2 mm
w
7 mm
$V = 109.2 \text{ mm}^3$

8. **MP Analyze Relationships** In Japan, farmers have created watermelons in the shape of rectangular prisms. Determine the volume of a prism-shaped watermelon in cubic inches if its length is 10 inches, its width is $\frac{2}{3}$ foot, and its height is 9 inches.

9. The glass container shown is filled to a height of 2.25 inches.

a. How much sand is currently in the container? _____

b. How much more sand could the container hold before it overflows? _____

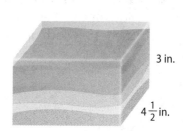

3 in.
$4\frac{1}{2}$ in.
5 in.

c. What percent of the container is filled with sand? _____

10. **MP** **Apply Math to the Real World** Refer to the graphic novel frame below
   for Exercises a–c.

a. The shorter container has a length, width, and height of 8 inches each.

   What is its volume? _____

b. The taller container has a length of 6 inches, a width of 8 inches, and

   a height of 10 inches. What is its volume? _____

c. How much more is the volume of the shorter container than the volume of

   the taller container? _____

H.O.T. Problems Higher-Order Thinking

11. **Analyze** Refer to the prism at the right. If all the dimensions of the prism
    doubled, would the volume double? Explain your reasoning.

_____

_____

12. **Evaluate** Which has the greater volume: a prism with a length of 5 inches,
    a width of 4 inches, and a height of 10 inches, or a prism with a length of
    10 inches, a width of 5 inches, and a height of 4 inches? Justify your selection.

_____

_____

13. **Create** Write a real-world problem in which you need to find the volume of
    a right rectangular prism. Solve your problem.

_____

_____

Multi-Step Problem Solving

14. If the fish tank shown is 80% filled with water, how much water is in the tank? Ⓟ ⒠⒠ ⓂⓅ

Ⓐ 5,772 cubic inches

Ⓑ 4,617.6 cubic inches

Ⓒ 1,154.4 cubic inches

Ⓓ 384.8 cubic inches

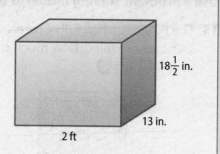

$18\frac{1}{2}$ in.

13 in.

2 ft

Use a problem-solving model to solve this problem.

1 Analyze

Read the problem. Circle the information you know. Underline what the problem is asking you to find.

2 Plan

What will you need to do to solve the problem? Write your plan in steps.

Step 1   Determine the volume of the tank.

Step 2   Multiply to determine the volume of water in the tank.

Read to Succeed!

The dimensions of the fish tank are given in feet and inches. Convert 2 feet to inches before finding the volume.

3 Solve

Use your plan to solve the problem. Show your steps.

$V = \ell \cdot w \cdot h$ Volume of a rectangular prism

$V = 24 \cdot 13 \cdot 18.5$ $\ell = 24$ in., $w = 13$ in., $h = 18.5$ in.

$V = $ _____   Multiply.

To find 80% of the volume, multiply by 0.80. The volume of water is _____ × 0.80

or _____ cubic inches. Choice _____ is correct. Fill in that answer choice.

4 Justify and Evaluate

How do you know your solution is reasonable?

_____

_____

_____

Ⓟ = Proportionality   ⒠⒠ = Expressions, Equations, and Relationships   ⓂⓅ = Mathematical Processes

More Multi-Step Problem Solving

Use a problem-solving model to solve each problem.

15. The figure is a box full of cereal. If a case of 24 boxes are filled, how much cereal is there in all?

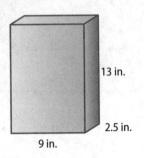

13 in.

2.5 in.

9 in.

Ⓐ 292.5 cubic inches

Ⓑ 588 cubic inches

Ⓒ 1,176 cubic inches

Ⓓ 7,020 cubic inches

16. A storage cube that has an edge length of 16 centimeters is being packed in a cardboard box with a length of 28 centimeters, a width of 18 centimeters, and a height of 22 centimeters. The extra space is being filled with packing peanuts. How many cubic centimeters of peanuts are needed to fill the space? Ⓝ Ⓔ Ⓜ

_____

_____

17. What is the volume of the statue in cubic feet? Round to the nearest hundredth. Ⓔ Ⓜ

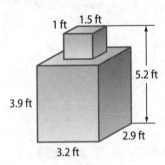

1 ft 1.5 ft

5.2 ft

3.9 ft

2.9 ft

3.2 ft

_____

18. One cube has a side length of 1 millimeter, and another cube has a side length of 1 centimeter. What is the ratio of the smaller volume to the greater volume? Express the numerator and denominator using the same units. Explain how you found your answer. Ⓔ Ⓟ Ⓜ

_____

_____

_____

_____

_____

21ST CENTURY CAREER

Parks and Recreation Planner

Do you enjoy thinking about how your community might look 10 years in the future? If so, a career in parks and recreation planning might be a perfect fit for you. Most planners are employed by local governments. They assess the best use for the land and create short and long term plans for various parks and recreation areas. They make recommendations based on the location of roads, schools, and residential areas. A parks and recreation planner uses mathematics, science, and computer software to complete their work.

Mathematical Process
6.1(A) Apply mathematics to problems arising in everyday life, society, and the workplace.
Targeted TEKS 6.8(D)

TEKS

Is This the Career for You?

Are you interested in a career as a parks and recreation planner? Take some of the following courses in high school.

◆ **Economics**
◆ **Environmental Design**
◆ **Geometry**

Turn the page to find out how math relates to a career in Community Planning.

College & Career
READINESS

Explore college and careers at ccr.mcgraw-hill.com

767

You be the Parks and Recreation Planner!

For each problem, use the information in the designs.

1. What is the area of the playground in Design 2? _____

2. In Design 2, how much larger is the area of the soccer field than the area of the playground? _____

3. In Design 1, the amphitheater has a stage. What is the area of the amphitheater without the stage? _____

4. The cost of building the amphitheater including the stage is $225 a square yard. The budget provided to build the amphitheater is $65,000. Are they within budget? Explain.

_____

_____

_____

_____

Design 1

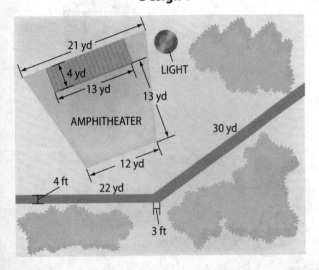

Design 2

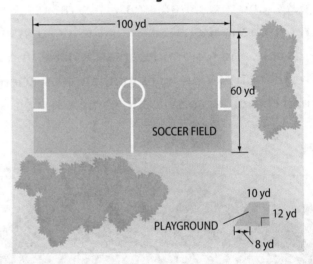

It's time to update your career portfolio! The New York City Department of Parks and Recreation has a free "Park Planner Game" online. Go to the Website to create your own park with trees, sports fields, and paths, while trying to stay under budget. Prepare a brief oral presentation and present it to your classmates. As others are presenting, listen carefully to their presentations. At the end, ask any clarifying questions.

_____

What is something you really want to do in the next ten years?

· _____

· _____

· _____

· _____

· _____

Chapter Review TEKS

Vocabulary Check

Work with a partner to unscramble each of the clue words.

SEBA ☐☐☐☐

HGEHTI ☐☐☐☐☐☐

LAEGARLAPLORM ☐☐☐☐☐☐☐☐☐☐☐☐☐

MHOBRUS ☐☐☐☐☐☐☐

NETRUGNOC ☐☐☐☐☐☐☐☐☐

AROMLUF ☐☐☐☐☐☐☐

Complete each sentence using one of the unscrambled words above.

1. The shortest distance from the base of a parallelogram to its opposite side

   is the _____ .

2. A _____ is a quadrilateral with opposite sides parallel and
   opposite sides congruent.

3. Any side of a parallelogram is a _____ .

4. A parallelogram with four congruent sides is a _____ .

5. If two shapes have the same measure they are _____ .

6. A _____ is an equation that shows a relationship among
   certain quantities.

Use Your **FOLDABLES**

Collaborate

Use your Foldable to help review the chapter. Share your Foldable with a partner and take turns summarizing what you learned in this chapter, while the other partner listens carefully. Seek clarification of any concepts, as needed. **TEKS** 6.1(E)

Tape here

Area

| Real-World Examples | Real-World Examples | Real-World Examples |

Got it?

Match each expression with correct steps used to find the area of the trapezoid. **TEKS** 6.8(C), 6.8(D)

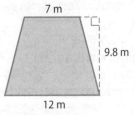

7 m

9.8 m

12 m

1. Write the correct area formula.

2. Replace h with 9.8.

3. Replace b_1 with 7 and replace b_2 with 12.

4. Add.

5. Multiply.

a. $A = \frac{1}{2}(9.8)(b_1 + b_2)$

b. $A = \frac{1}{2}bh$

c. $A = \frac{1}{2}(9.8)(19)$

d. $A = \frac{1}{2}h(b_1 + b_2)$

e. $A = 93.1$

f. $A = \frac{1}{2}(9.8)(7 + 12)$

6. Jean was flying a kite like the one shown. If the height of the yellow triangle is 60% the length of its base, what is the area of the yellow triangle? Show the steps you used and justify your solution. (EE) (MP)

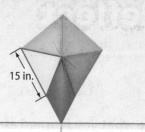

15 in.

1 Analyze

2 Plan

3 Solve

4 Justify and Evaluate

_____

_____

_____

_____

Got it?

7. The area of a rectangular photograph is 24 square inches. If the perimeter of the photograph is 20 inches, what are the dimensions of the photograph? Show the steps you used and justify your solution. (EE) (MP)

_____

_____

(EE) = Expressions, Equations, and Relationships   (MP) = Mathematical Processes

Reflect

 Answering the Essential Question

Use what you learned about area to complete the graphic organizer.
List several real-world examples for each figure.

 Essential Question

How does measurement help you
solve problems in everyday life?

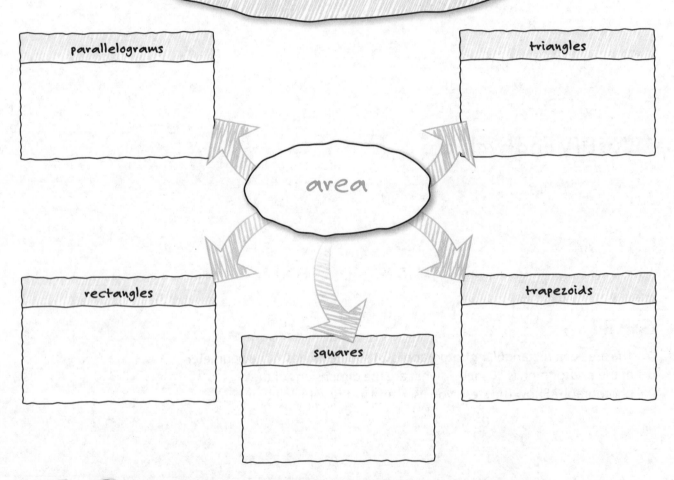

parallelograms

triangles

area

rectangles

trapezoids

squares

 Answer the Essential Question. How does measurement help
you solve problems in everyday life? Verbally share your response with
a partner, seeking and providing clarification as needed.

Chapter 10

Statistical Measures and Displays

Texas Essential Knowledge and Skills

Targeted TEKS

6.12 The student applies mathematical process standards to use numerical and graphical representations to analyze problems. *Also addresses 6.13.*

Mathematical Processes
6.1, 6.1(A), 6.1(B), 6.1(C), 6.1(D), 6.1(E), 6.1(F), 6.1(G)

Essential Question

HOW are the mean, median, and mode helpful in describing data?

Math in the Real World

Roller Coaster The table shows the top speeds of several roller coasters at Six Flags Over Texas.

Roller Coaster	Speed (mph)
Mr. Freeze: Reverse Blast	70
Shockwave	55
Texas Giant	64
Titan	85

Draw bars to represent the speed of each roller coaster.

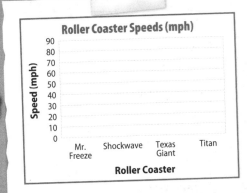

Roller Coaster Speeds (mph)

Vocab

Vocabulary

average	measure of center
box plot	measures of spread
categorical data	median
cluster	mode
distribution	outliers
dot plot	peak
first quartile	percent bar graph
frequency distribution	quartiles
gap	range
histogram	relative frequency
interquartile range	stem-and-leaf plot
key	stems
leaves	symmetric distribution
mean	third quartile

Review Vocabulary

Graphic Organizer One way to remember vocabulary terms is to connect them to an opposite term or example. Use this information to complete the graphic organizer.

> quotient

⬇

Definition	
Opposite	
Example	

6.12(C), 6.1(A)

Quick Review

Example 1

Determine $12.53 + 9.87 + 16.24 + 22.12$.

```
  2 1 1
 12.53
  9.87     Add.
 16.24
+ 22.12
 60.76
```

Example 2

Michelle read 56.5 pages of her book on Monday and Tuesday. If she read the same number of pages each day, how many pages did she average each day?

$56.5 \div 2 = 28.25$ Divide the total number of pages by the number of days.

Michelle averaged 28.25 pages per day.

Quick Check

 Check

Add Decimals Determine each sum.

1. $6.20 + 31.59 + 11.11 + 19.85 =$ _____

2. $22.69 + 15.45 + 9.87 + 26.79 =$ _____

 Show your work.

3. Sonya went to the baseball game. She paid $10.50 for admission. She bought a drink for $2.75, a bag of popcorn for $4.60, and a hot dog for $3.75. How much did she spend in total?

_____

Divide Decimals Determine each quotient.

4. $79.2 \div 6 =$ _____

5. $72.60 \div 3 =$ _____

6. $240.5 \div 13 =$ _____

7. The Chen family drove 345.6 miles on their vacation. They drove the same amount each of the 3 days. How many miles did they drive each day?

_____

How Did You Do?

Which problems did you answer correctly in the Quick Check? Shade those exercise numbers below.

      7

FOLDABLES® Use the Foldable throughout this chapter to help you learn about statistical measures.

✂ ── ── ── cut on all dashed lines   ⬜ fold on all solid lines   ▨ tape to page 874

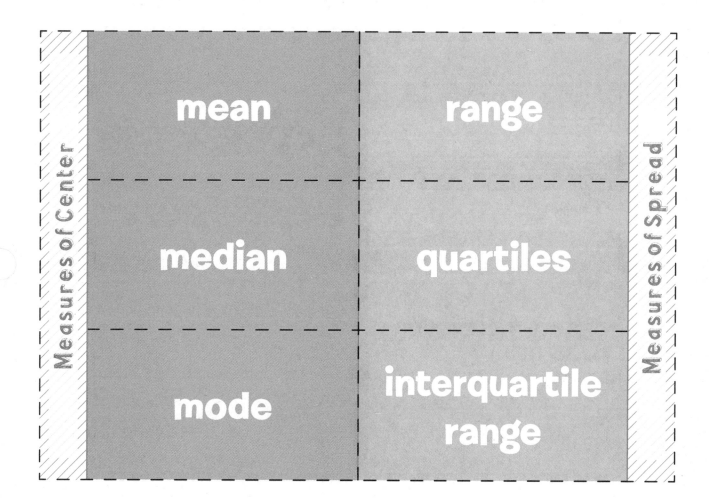

FOLDABLES®

Use the Foldable throughout this chapter to help you learn about statistical measures.

✂ cut on all dashed lines   ⬚ fold on all solid lines   tape to page 874

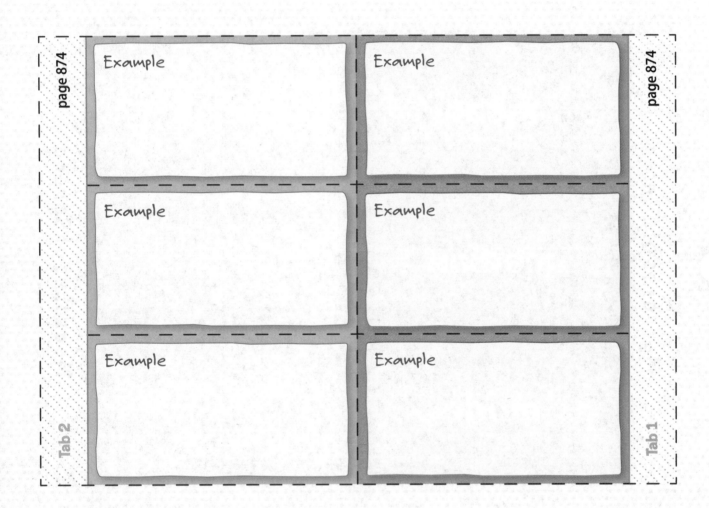

page 874

Example

Example

Example

Example

Example

Example

page 874

Tab 2

Tab 1

Statistical Variability

INQUIRY HOW can I analyze relationships to distinguish between situations that yield data with and without variability?

Anderson Advertising is collecting information for a pizza shop. They want to know the number of toppings most customers prefer on their pizza. They will use this information to determine the weekly special.

Texas Essential Knowledge and Skills

Targeted TEKS
6.13(B) Distinguish between situations that yield data with and without variability.

Mathematical Processes
6.1(C), 6.1(D), 6.1(E), 6.1(F), 6.1(G)

Hands-On Activity 1

Statistics deals with collecting, organizing, and interpreting pieces of information, or *data*. One way to collect data is by asking statistical questions. A statistical question is a question that yields data with variability.

The table below gives some examples of questions that yield data with variability and questions that yield data without variability.

Results with variability	Results without variability
How many text messages do you send each day?	What is the height in feet of the tallest mountain in Colorado?
What is the minimum driving age for each state in the United States?	How many people attended last night's jazz concert?

Create a survey similar to the one Anderson Advertising would use to survey your classmates. Consider a cheese pizza with no additional toppings as a pizza with one topping.

Step 1 Write a survey question. *How many toppings do you like on your pizza?*

Step 2 Survey your classmates.

Step 3 Record the results in the table to the right. Add additional numbers of toppings to the table as necessary.

How Many Toppings Do Your Like on Your Pizza?	
Number of Toppings	**Number of Responses**

Why is *How many toppings do you like on your pizza?* a question that results in data with variability?

_____

_____

Hands-On Activity 2

Sometimes a set of data can be organized into intervals to more easily organize it. This often happens when the set of data has a wide range of values.

Suppose you want to determine the number of video games each of your math classmates has at home.

Step 1 Write the survey question. *How many different video games do you own?*

Step 2 Survey your classmates.

Step 3 Record the results in the table to the right.

How Many Different Video Games Do You Own?	
Number of Video Games	**Number of Responses**
less than 5	
5–9	
10–14	
15 or more	

Hands-On Activity 3

Tools

You can use surveys to provide information about patterns in the responses.

Suppose you surveyed five students using the survey question, *How many Web sites did you visit before school this morning?* The students said 4, 3, 5, 1, and 2 Web sites. If the total amount was equally distributed among all five students, how many Web sites did each student visit?

Step 1 Make a stack of centimeter cubes to represent the number of Web sites visited by each student as shown.

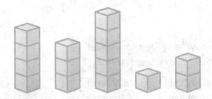

Step 2 Move the cubes so that each stack has the same number of cubes. Draw your models in the space below.

There are five stacks with ☐ cubes in each stack. So, if the responses were

equally distributed, each student visited ☐ Web sites before school.

Investigate

Collaborate

Work with a partner. State whether each question results in data with variability. Explain your reasoning.

1. Who was the first president of the United States?

_____

_____

2. How much time do the students in my school spend on the Internet each night?

_____

_____

3. What is the height of the tallest waterslide at Wild Rides Water Park?

_____

_____

4. What are the cabin rental prices for each of the state parks in Kentucky?

_____

_____

Work with a partner. Determine the equal share if the total number of centimeter cubes were equally distributed among the groups. Draw your models in the space provided.

5.

 Show your work.

6.

7.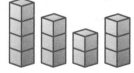

8.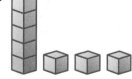

Analyze and Reflect

Collaborate

Work with a partner to determine the equal share for each exercise. Use concrete models if needed. The first one is done for you.

	Scenario	Responses	Response Total	Number of Responses	Equal Share
	Rainfall (in.)	7, 5, 2, 6	$7 + 5 + 2 + 6 = 20$	4	5
9.	Books Read	8, 7, 3			
10.	Eggs Hatched	5, 2, 3, 6			
11.	States Visited	1, 4, 2, 5, 3			
12.	Photos Taken	5, 3, 7, 2, 4, 3			

13. **MP Analyze Relationships** Compare the answers you provided in the table above. How does the response total and the number of responses relate to the equal share? Write a rule you can use to evenly distribute a data set without using centimeter cubes. _____

Create

On Your Own

14. **MP Apply Math to the Real World** Write a survey question that yields data without variability. Rewrite the question so that it yields data with variability.

_____

_____

15. **MP Apply Math to the Real World** Write a real-world problem that involves equal shares. Find the equal share of your data set.

_____

_____

_____

16. **INQUIRY** HOW can I analyze relationships to distinguish between situations that yield data with and without variability?

_____

_____

Launch the Lesson: Real World

Texas Essential Knowledge and Skills

Targeted TEKS
6.12(C) Summarize numeric data with numerical summaries, including the mean and median (measures of center) and the range and interquartile range (IQR) (measures of spread), and use these summaries to describe the center, spread, and shape of the data distribution. *Also addresses 6.12(A), 6.12(B), 6.13(A).*

Mathematical Processes
6.1(A), 6.1(B), 6.1(D), 6.1(F)

Tina and her friends downloaded songs for 6 weeks, as shown in the table at the right.

Number of Songs Downloaded Each Week					
12	6	10	9	4	1

1. How many total songs were downloaded? _____

2. On average, how many songs did they download each week?

☐	÷	☐	=	☐
total		number of weeks		average per week

Vocabulary
mean
average
distribution

3. On the number line below, draw an arrow that points to the average. Plot the number of songs downloaded on the number line.

0 1 2 3 4 5 6 7 8 9 10 11 12

Essential Question
HOW are the mean, median, and mode helpful in describing data?

4. How far below the average is 1? 4? 6? How far above the average is 9? 10? 12? _____

5. What is the sum of the distances between the average and the points below the average? above the average? _____

6. Explain why the average is the balance point of the data.

_____

_____

_____

Which MP Mathematical Processes did you use?
Shade the circle(s) that applies.

Ⓐ Apply Math to the Real World.
Ⓑ Use a Problem-Solving Model.
Ⓒ Select Tools and Techniques.
Ⓓ Use Multiple Representations.

Ⓔ Organize Ideas.
Ⓕ Analyze Relationships.
Ⓖ Justify Arguments.

Summarize Data Using the Mean

The **mean** of a data set is the sum of the data divided by the number of pieces of data. It is the balance point for the data set.

On the previous page, you found a single number to describe the number of songs downloaded each week. The **average**, or mean, summarizes the data using a single number.

You can summarize data by determining the mean of a set of data shown in graphical displays such as pictographs and dot plots. The mean describes the center of a data distribution. The **distribution** of a set of data shows the arrangement of data values.

 Real World

Watch Tutor

Example

> **Including Data**
> Even if a data value is 0, it still should be counted in the total number of pieces of data.

1. Determine the mean cost of a children's ticket for the five different museums shown in the pictograph. Use the mean to summarize the center of the distribution.

Cost per Children's Ticket ($ = $1)

Austin's Children's Museum	$ $ $ $ $ $ $
Children's Museum of Houston	$ $ $ $ $ $ $ $
Johnson Space Center	$ $ $ $ $ $ $ $ $ $ $ $ $ $
Museum of Nature and Science	$ $ $ $ $ $ $
San Antonio Children's Museum	$ $ $ $ $ $ $ $

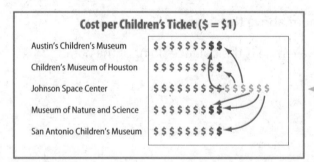

Cost per Children's Ticket ($ = $1)

Austin's Children's Museum	$ $ $ $ $ $ $ $ $
Children's Museum of Houston	$ $ $ $ $ $ $ $ $
Johnson Space Center	$ $ $ $ $ $ $ $ $ $ $ $ $ $
Museum of Nature and Science	$ $ $ $ $ $ $ $ $
San Antonio Children's Museum	$ $ $ $ $ $ $ $ $

Rearrange the symbols so that each museum has an equal number.

Each museum costs an average of $9. The data are centered around $9 per ticket.

 Show your work.

Got It? Do this problem to find out.

a. _____

a. The table shows the number of CDs a group of friends bought. Determine the mean number of CDs the group bought. Use the mean to summarize the center of the distribution.

Number of CDs Purchased

3	4	6
0	2	

Examples

Tutor

2. The dot plot shows the recorded high temperatures for six days in Little Rock, Arkansas. Determine the mean temperature. Use the mean to summarize the center of the distribution.

High Temperatures

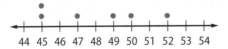

44 45 46 47 48 49 50 51 52 53 54

$$\text{mean} = \frac{45 + 45 + 47 + 49 + 50 + 52}{6}$$ ◂······ sum of the data

◂······ number of data items

$$= \frac{288}{6} \text{ or } 48$$ Simplify.

The mean is 48 degrees. The data are centered around 48 degrees.

3. The dot plot shows the number of runs a baseball team had for each game of a 4-game series. Determine the mean number of runs for the series. Use the mean to summarize the center of the distribution.

Number of Runs

0 1 2 3 4 5 6 7 8 9 10

$$\text{mean} = \frac{\boxed{}}{\boxed{}}$$ ◂······ sum of the data

◂······ number of data items

$$= \frac{\boxed{\ }}{\boxed{\ }} \text{ or } \boxed{\ }$$ Simplify.

The mean number of runs for the series is $\boxed{\ }$. The data are centered around $\boxed{\ }$ runs.

Got It? Do this problem to find out.

b. The dot plot shows the number of books Deanna read each week of a reading challenge. Determine the mean number of books she read. Use the mean to summarize the center of the distribution.

Books Read

0 1 2 3 4 5 6

Dot Plots

In a dot plot, individual data values are represented as dots above a number line.

Show your work.

b. _____

Example

4. The number of minutes Mary Anne spent talking on her cell phone each month for the past five months were 494, 502, 486, 690, and 478. Suppose the mean for six months was 532 minutes. How many minutes did she talk on her cell phone during the sixth month?

If the mean is 532, the sum of the six pieces of data must be 532 × 6 or 3,192. You can create a bar diagram.

494	502	486	690	478	?

← ---------- 3,192 ---------- →

$$3{,}192 - (494 + 502 + 486 + 690 + 478) = 3{,}192 - 2{,}650$$
$$= 542$$

Mary Anne talked 542 minutes during the sixth month.

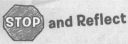

STOP and Reflect

The mean is sometimes described as the balance point. Explain below what this means using the data set {2, 2, 3, 8, 10}.

Guided Practice

1. The dot plot shows the number of beads sold. Determine the mean number of beads. Use the mean to summarize the center of the distribution (Examples 1–3)

Number of Beads

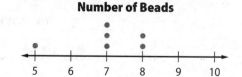

2. The table shows the area of various lakes in Texas, rounded to the nearest tenth. If the average area is 45.97 square miles, what is the approximate area of Lake Palestine?

(Example 4)

Lake	Area (sq mi)
Lake Fork	43.3
Lake Bridgeport	18.7
Richland Chambers Lake	70.3
Lake Amistad	101.4
Lake Nasworthy	2.2
Lake Palestine	

3. **?** **Building on the Essential Question** Why is it helpful to determine the mean of a data set?

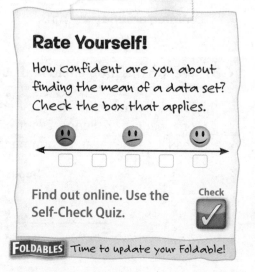

Rate Yourself!

How confident are you about finding the mean of a data set? Check the box that applies.

☐ ☐ ☐ ☐ ☐

Find out online. Use the Self-Check Quiz.

Check ✓

FOLDABLES Time to update your Foldable!

Independent Practice

6.12(B), 6.12(C), 6.1(A), 6.1(D)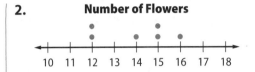

Determine the mean for each data set. Use the mean to summarize the center of the distribution. (Examples 1–3)

1.

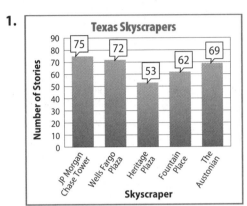

Texas Skyscrapers

2.   Number of Flowers

3. Financial Literacy Jamila babysat nine times. She earned $15, $20, $10, $12, $20, $16, $80, and $18 for eight babysitting jobs. How much did she earn the ninth time if the mean of the data set is $24? (Example 4) _____

4. **MP** **Apply Math to the Real World** Refer to the graphic novel frame below for Exercises a–b.

a. What is the mean number of wins for the Cranes? for the Panthers?

_____

b. Based on your answer for part a, is the mean a good measure for determining which team has the better record? Explain.

_____

5. A *stem-and-leaf plot* is a display that organizes data from least to greatest. The digits of the least place value form the leaves, and the next place-value digits form the stems. The stem-and-leaf plot shows Marcia's scores on several tests. Determine the mean test score.

Stem	Leaf
7	8
8	5 8 9
9	2 6

7|8 = 78

6. **MP Use Multiple Representations** The table shows the 5-day forecast.

a. **Numbers** What is the difference between the mean high and mean low temperature for this 5-day period? Justify your answer.

_____

_____

b. **Graph** Make a double-line graph of the high and low temperatures for the 5-day period.

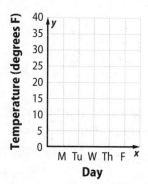

Day	High Temperature (°F)	Low Temperature (°F)
Monday	32	25
Tuesday	31	24
Wednesday	29	21
Thursday	33	23
Friday	35	23

 H.O.T. Problems Higher-Order Thinking

7. **Create** Create a data set that has five values. The mean of the data set should be 34. _____

8. **Analyze** The mean of a set of data is 45 years. Find the missing numbers in the data set {40, 45, 48, ?, 54, ?, 45}. Explain the method or strategy you used.

_____

_____

9. **Analyze** The mean weight of the seven linemen on a football team is 215 pounds. The mean weight of the four backfield players is 184 pounds. What is the mean weight of the 11-member team? Round to the nearest tenth.

_____

_____

10. **Analyze** If 99 students had a mean quiz score of 82, how much is the mean score increased by the addition of a single score of 99? Explain.

_____

_____

_____

_____

Multi-Step Problem Solving

11. Edward's family owns a tree farm, which is open every day of the week except Monday. Edward kept track of how many trees were sold each day for two weeks. How much greater was the mean number of trees for Week 2 than for Week 1? **MD** **MP**

Week 1		Week 2	
Day	Trees	Day	Trees
Tuesday	7	Tuesday	10
Wednesday	12	Wednesday	8
Thursday	6	Thursday	12
Friday	14	Friday	17
Saturday	22	Saturday	31
Sunday	17	Sunday	18

Use a problem-solving model to solve this problem.

1 Analyze

Read the problem. Circle the information you know. Underline what the problem is asking you to find.

2 Plan

What will you need to do to solve the problem? Write your plan in steps.

Step 1 Determine the mean for each week.

Step 2 Subtract to find how much greater the mean for Week 2 is than Week 1.

> **Read to Succeed!**
> To determine the mean, add each value in the set and divide by the number of values in the set.

3 Solve

Use your plan to solve the problem. Show your steps.

Week 1: $\dfrac{7 + 12 + 6 + 14 + 22 + 17}{6} =$ _____

Week 2: $\dfrac{10 + 8 + 12 + 17 + 31 + 18}{6} =$ _____

So, Week 2's mean is $16 - 13$ or _____ trees greater. Complete the grid.

4 Justify and Evaluate

How do you know your solution is reasonable?

_____

_____

_____

MD = Measurement and Data   **MP** = Mathematical Processes

More Multi-Step Problem Solving

Use a problem-solving model to solve each problem.

12. The dot plot shows how many minutes Mr. Elliot's piano students said they practiced on the day before their lessons. Imala practiced 31 minutes but forgot to tell Mr. Elliot. If Imala's time were included, by how much time (in minutes) would the mean increase? **MD** **N** **MP**

Minutes of Practice

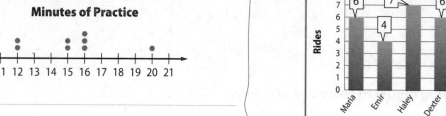

13. The graph shows how many rides a group of friends went on at the fair. Each ride cost $2.75. What was the mean amount of money, in dollars, spent per person to go on the rides? **MD** **N** **MP**

14. For Quon's first six quizzes, he had a mean score of 33 points. After the seventh quiz, his mean score was 32 points. After the eighth quiz, the mean was 34. What was the difference in scores between his seventh and eighth quizzes? **MD** **N** **MP**

15. Create a list of 8 values with a mean of 26. Justify your response. **MD** **N** **MP**

MD = Measurement and Data   **N** = Number and Operations   **MP** = Mathematical Processes

Median and Mode

Launch the Lesson: Vocabulary

You can also summarize a data set using the median or mode. The mean, median, and mode are called **measures of center** because they describe the center of a set of data.

Find the definition of each term in the glossary. Then complete the graphic organizer.

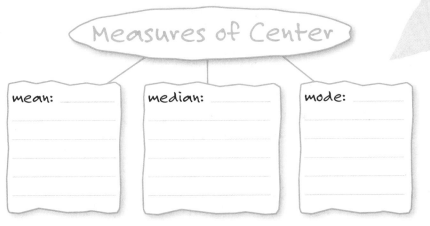

Measures of Center

mean: _____

median: _____

mode: _____

Texas Essential Knowledge and Skills

Targeted TEKS

6.12(C) Summarize numeric data with numerical summaries, including the mean and median (measures of center) and the range and interquartile range (IQR) (measures of spread), and use these summaries to describe the center, spread, and shape of the data distribution. *Also addresses 6.12(A), 6.12(B), 6.13(A).*

Mathematical Processes
6.1(A), 6.1(B), 6.1(D), 6.1(F)

Vocabulary
measures of center
median
mode

Essential Question
HOW are the mean, median, and mode helpful in describing data?

Real-World Investigation

The table shows the number of Atlantic hurricanes in different years.

Atlantic Hurricanes						
5	15	9	7	4	9	8

1. Order the data from least to greatest. Circle the number in the middle of your list. _____

2. Determine the mean. Compare the middle number to the mean of the data. Round to the nearest hundredth if necessary.

_____

Which MP **Mathematical Processes** did you use?
Shade the circle(s) that applies.

Ⓐ Apply Math to the Real World.

Ⓑ Use a Problem-Solving Model.

Ⓒ Select Tools and Techniques.

Ⓓ Use Multiple Representations.

Ⓔ Organize Ideas.

Ⓕ Analyze Relationships.

Ⓖ Justify Arguments.

Summarize Data Using the Median and Mode

Work Zone

The **median** of a list of values is the value appearing at the center of a sorted version of the list, or the mean of the two central values, if the list contains an even number of values.

The **mode** is the number or numbers that occur most often.

Just as mean is one value used to summarize a data set, the median and mode also summarize the center of a data distribution with a single number. If there is more than one number that occurs with the same frequency, a data set may have more than one mode.

Watch Tutor

Examples

1. The table shows the number of monkeys at eleven different zoos. Determine the median and mode to summarize the center

Number of Monkeys					
28	36	18	25	12	44
	18	42	34	16	30

Order the data from least to greatest.

Median   12, 16, 18, 18, 25, (28,) 30, 34, 36, 42, 44   28 is in the center.

Mode   12, 16, ⌈18, 18,⌉ 25, 28, 30, 34, 36, 42, 44   18 occurs most often.

The median is 28 monkeys. The mode is 18 monkeys.

- -

2. Dina recorded her scores on 7 tests in the table. Determine the median and mode to summarize the center of the data.

Test Scores			
93	88	94	93
	85	97	90

Circle the number in the center. This is the median.

Circle the most frequently occurring numbers. This is the mode.

The median is a score of ☐ . The mode is a score of ☐ .

Got It? Do this problem to find out.

 Show your work.

a. The list shows the number of stories in the 11 tallest buildings in Springfield. Determine the median and mode to summarize the center of the data.

40, 38, 40, 37, 33, 30, 20, 24, 21, 17, 19

a. _____

Tutor

Examples

3. Determine the median and mode of the cost of sweaters to summarize the center of the data.

Median 16.95, <u>18.99, 19.90,</u> 21.50

$$\frac{18.99 + 19.90}{2} = \frac{38.89}{2}$$

$$= 19.445$$

$$\approx \$19.45$$

> There are an even number of data values. So, to find the median, find the mean of the two central values.

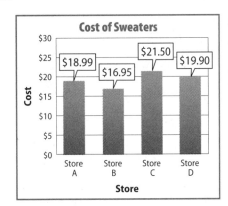

Cost of Sweaters

| | $18.99 | $16.95 | $21.50 | $19.90 |

Mode There is no mode.

- -

4. Miguel researched the average precipitation in several states. Determine and compare the median and mode of the average precipitation.

State	Precipitation (in.)	State	Precipitation (in.)
Alabama	58.3	Louisiana	60.1
Florida	54.5	Maine	42.2
Georgia	50.7	Michigan	32.8
Kentucky	48.9	Missouri	42.2

Median 32.8, 42.2, 42.2, <u>48.9, 50.7,</u> 54.5, 58.3, 60.1

$$\frac{48.9 + 50.7}{2} = \frac{99.6}{2}$$

$$= 49.8$$

Mode 32.8, 42.2, 42.2, 48.9, 50.7, 54.5, 58.3, 60.1

The median is 49.8 inches and the mode is 42.2 inches. The median is 7.6 inches greater than the mode.

Got It? Do these problems to find out.

Show your work.

b. Determine the median and mode of the costs in the table to summarize the center of the data.

Cost of Backpacks ($)			
16.78	48.75	31.42	18.38
22.89	51.25	28.54	26.79

b. _____

c. Determine and compare the median and mode of the costs in the table to summarize the center of the data.

Cost of Juice ($)			
1.65	1.97	2.45	2.87
2.35	3.75	2.49	2.87

c. _____

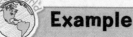

Example

5. Summarize the daily high temperatures using the measures of center.

Daily High Temperature (°F)			
72	73	67	65
	71	64	71

Mean $\dfrac{72 + 73 + 67 + 65 + 71 + 64 + 71}{7} = \dfrac{483}{7}$ or 69°

Median 64, 65, 67, (71,) 71, 72, 73

Mode 64, 65, 67, (71, 71), 72, 73

The median and mode are both 71 degrees. They are both 2 degrees greater than the mean. The data follows the measures of center in that the temperatures are close to the measures of center.

Show your work.

d. _____

Got It? Do this problem to find out.

d. Summarize the cost of CDs using the measures of center.

Cost of CDs ($)		
11.95	12.89	19.99
19.99	12.59	18.49

Guided Practice

1. Determine and compare the median and mode for the following set of data. Monthly spending: $46, $62, $62, $57, $50, $42, $56, $40 (Examples 1–4)

_____

2. Summarize the daily high temperatures using the measures of center. (Example 5)

Daily High Temperature (°F)			
34	35	31	36
	31	24	33

_____
_____
_____
_____

3. (?) **Building on the Essential Question** How are mean and median similar? _____

_____

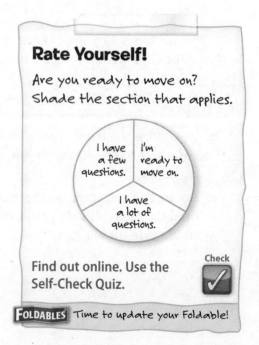

Rate Yourself!

Are you ready to move on? Shade the section that applies.

I have a few questions. | I'm ready to move on.

I have a lot of questions.

Find out online. Use the Self-Check Quiz.

Check ✓

FOLDABLES Time to update your Foldable!

Independent Practice

6.12(B), 6.12(C), 6.13(A), 6.1(F) **TEKS**

Determine and compare the median and mode for each set of data. (Examples 1–4)

1. math test scores: 97, 85, 92, 86 _____

2.

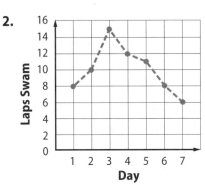

3. Summarize the average speeds using the measures of center. (Example 5)

_____

_____

_____

Average Speeds (mph)			
40	52	44	46
52	40	44	50
41	44	44	50

4. **MP** **Apply Math to the Real World** Refer to the graphic novel frame below for Exercises a–b.

a. Determine the median and mode for each team's wins.

_____

_____

b. Which team had the better record? Justify your response.

_____

_____

5. A Louisville newspaper claims that during seven days, the high temperature in Lexington was typically 6° warmer than the high temperature in Louisville. What measure was used to make this claim?

Justify your answer. _____

Daily High Temperatures (°F)							
Louisville				Lexington			
75	50	80	72	80	73	75	74
	70	84	70		71	76	76

_____

_____

6. **Select Tools and Techniques** Use the Internet to find the high temperatures for each of the last seven days in a city near you. Then find the median high temperature.

_____

_____

H.O.T. Problems Higher-Order Thinking

7. Analyze The ticket prices for a concert series were $12, $37, $45, $18, $8, $25, and $18. What was the ticket price of the eighth and final concert in this series if the set of 8 prices had a mean of $23, a mode of $18, a median of $19.50?

_____

8. Evaluate One evening at a local pizzeria, the following number of toppings were ordered on each large pizza.

3, 0, 1, 1, 2, 5, 4, 3, 1, 0, 0, 1, 1, 2, 2, 3, 6, 4, 3, 2, 0, 2, 1, 3

Determine whether each statement is *true* or *false*. Explain your reasoning.

a. The greatest number of people ordered a pizza with 1 topping.

_____

b. Half the customers ordered pizzas with 3 or more toppings, and half the customers ordered pizzas with less than 3 toppings.

_____

_____

9. Evaluate In the data set {3, 7, 4, 2, 31, 5, 4}, which measure best describes the set of data: mean, median, or mode? Explain your reasoning.

_____

_____

10. Create Create a list of six values where the mean, median, and mode are 45, and only two of the values are the same.

_____

Multi-Step Problem Solving

11. Four students kept track of how long they did homework for five nights. For which student do the mean, median, and mode all have the same value?

Day	Emma	Rosario	Peter	Su
1	1.25	1.25	1	0.75
2	0.75	2.25	1.75	2.5
3	1	1.5	1	1.5
4	1.25	2	0.5	0.75
5	2	0.75	1.5	2

Ⓐ Emma   Ⓒ Peter

Ⓑ Rosario   Ⓓ Su

Use a problem-solving model to solve this problem.

1 Analyze

Read the problem. Circle the information you know. Underline what the problem is asking you to find.

2 Plan

What will you need to do to solve the problem? Write your plan in steps.

Step 1   Determine the mean, median, and mode for each student.

Step 2   Compare the measures.

Read to Succeed!

Mean – divide the sum of the values by the number of values

Median – the middle value when the data are ordered

Mode – most occurring number

3 Solve

Use your plan to solve the problem. Show your steps.

	Mean	Median	Mode
Emma			
Rosario			
Peter			
Su			

Since _____ has all three measures the same, choice ____ is correct. Fill in that answer choice.

4 Justify and Evaluate

How do you know your solution is reasonable?

_____

_____

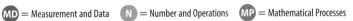

MD = Measurement and Data   **N** = Number and Operations   **MP** = Mathematical Processes

More Multi-Step Problem Solving

Use a problem-solving model to solve each problem.

12. Four drivers recorded the distance they drove each day for a week. Which driver's data set has a mode that is greater than the mean or median AND a median with the lowest value of the three measures?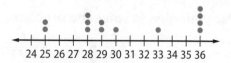

- Ⓐ Kadisha: 8, 17, 23, 16, 17, 18, 125
- Ⓑ Cole: 14, 26, 34, 22, 47, 22, 45
- Ⓒ Fabian: 7, 12, 11, 23, 13, 23, 30
- Ⓓ Ling: 52, 36, 41, 31, 31, 37, 59

13. The graph shows the number of cell phones per 100 people in certain countries. How much would the difference between the median and the mode change if Finland were not included in the data?

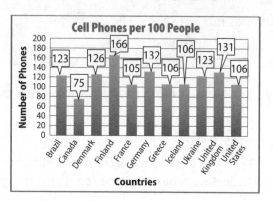

14. What is the difference between the medians of Kendra's sprint times and Hakim's sprint times?

Kendra's Sprint Times (seconds)			
12	14	11	13
15	13	15	14
11	14	17	12

Hakim's Sprint Times (seconds)			
11	11	15	13
14	16	15	14
13	15	12	16

15. For which data set is the median a better predictor of the rest of the data than the mode? Explain your answer.

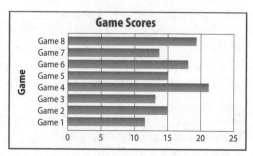

MD = Measurement and Data   N = Number and Operations   MP = Mathematical Processes

Measures of Spread

 ## Launch the Lesson: Vocabulary

Texas Essential Knowledge and Skills

Targeted TEKS
6.12(C) Summarize numeric data with numerical summaries, including the mean and median (measures of center) and the range and interquartile range (IQR) (measures of spread), and use these summaries to describe the center, spread, and shape of the data distribution. *Also addresses 6.12(A), 6.12(B), 6.13(A).*

Mathematical Processes
6.1(A), 6.1(B), 6.1(D), 6.1(F)

Measures of spread are used to describe the distribution, or spread, of the data. They describe how the values of a data set vary with a single number. A *quartile* is one measure of variation.

Look in a dictionary and find words that begin with *quar-*. Write two of the words and their definitions.

Word beginning with quar-	Definition

Vocab

Vocabulary
measures of spread
quartiles
first quartile
third quartile
interquartile range
range
outliers

Based on the definitions you found, fill in the blank below.

Quartiles are values that divide a set of data into _____ equal parts.

 ## Real-World Investigation

Essential Question
HOW are the mean, median, and mode helpful in describing data?

James asked his classmates how many hours of TV they watch on a typical day.

1. Divide the data into 4 equal parts. Draw a circle around each part.

2. How many data values are in each group? _____

Hours of TV Watched

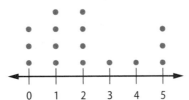

0   1   2   3   4   5

Which MP Mathematical Processes did you use?
Shade the circle(s) that applies.

(A) Apply Math to the Real World.
(B) Use a Problem-Solving Model.
(C) Select Tools and Techniques.
(D) Use Multiple Representations.
(E) Organize Ideas.
(F) Analyze Relationships.
(G) Justify Arguments.

Summarize Data Using Measures of Spread

Quartiles are values that divide the data set into four equal parts.

First and Third Quartiles

The first and third quartiles are the medians of the data values less than the median and the data values greater than the median, respectively.

Interquartile Range (IQR)

The difference between the first and third quartiles of the data set.

Range

The difference between the greatest and least data values.

Measures of variation of a data set are shown below.

$$Q_1 \qquad \text{median} \qquad Q_3$$

$$0,\ 0,\ 1,\ 1,\ 2,\ 2,\ 2,\ 3,\ \ 4,\ 5,\ 6,\ 6,\ 7,\ 7,\ 7,\ 8$$

The median of the data values less than the median is the first quartile or Q_1; in this case, 1.5.

The median of the data values greater than the median is the third quartile or Q_3; in this case, 6.5.

One-fourth of the data lie below the first quartile and one-fourth of the data lie above the third quartile. So, one-half of the data lie between the first quartile and third quartile.

Tutor

Example

1. **Determine the measures of spread to summarize the data.**

   Range $70 - 1$ or 69 mph

   Quartiles Order the numbers.

Animal	Speed (mph)
cheetah	70
lion	50
cat	30
elephant	25
mouse	8
spider	1

   $$Q_1 \qquad \text{median} = 27.5 \qquad Q_3$$

   $$1 \quad 8 \quad 25 \quad 30 \quad 50 \quad 70$$

   Interquartile Range $50 - 8$ or 42 $\quad Q_3 - Q_1$

   The range is 69, the median is 27.5, the first quartile is 8, the third quartile is 50, and the IQR is 42.

Interquartile Range

If the interquartile range is low, the middle data are grouped closely together.

Show your work.

Got It? Do this problem to find out.

a. _____

a. Determine the measures of spread to summarize the data 64, 61, 67, 59, 60, 58, 57, 71, 56, and 62.

Determine Outliers and Interpret Data

An **outlier** is a data value that is either much *greater* or much *less* than the median. If a data value is more than 1.5 times the value of the interquartile range beyond the quartiles, it is an outlier.

Tutor

Example

2. **The ages of candidates in an election are 23, 48, 49, 55, 57, 63, and 72. Determine any outliers in the data.**

Determine the interquartile range: $63 - 48 = 15$

Multiply the interquartile range by 1.5: $15 \times 1.5 = 22.5$

Subtract 22.5 from the first quartile and add 22.5 to the third quartile to find the limits for the outliers.

$$48 - 22.5 = 25.5 \qquad\qquad 63 + 22.5 = 85.5$$

The only age beyond the limits is 23. So, it is the only outlier.

Got It? Do this problem to find out.

Show your work.

b. The lengths, in feet, of various bridges are 88, 251, 275, 354, and 1,121. Determine any outliers in the data set.

b. _____

Tutor

Example

3. **The table shows a set of scores on a science test in two different classrooms. Compare and contrast their measures of spread.**

Determine the measures of spread for both rooms.

Room A	Room B
72	63
100	93
67	79
84	83
65	98
78	87
92	73
87	81
80	65

	Room A	**Room B**
Range	$100 - 65 = 35$	$98 - 63 = 35$
Median	80	81
Q_3	$\dfrac{87 + 92}{2} = 89.5$	$\dfrac{87 + 93}{2} = 90$
Q_1	$\dfrac{67 + 72}{2} = 69.5$	$\dfrac{65 + 73}{2} = 69$
IQR	$89.5 - 69.5 = 20$	$90 - 69 = 21$

Both classrooms have a range of 35 points, but Room B has an interquartile range of 21 points while Room A's interquartile range is 20 points. There are slight differences in the medians as well as the third and first quartiles.

Got It? Do this problem to find out.

c. _____

c. Temperatures for the first half of the year are given for Antelope, Montana, and Augusta, Maine. Compare and contrast the measures of spread of the two cities.

Month	Antelope, MT	Augusta, ME
January	21	28
February	30	32
March	42	41
April	58	53
May	70	66
June	79	75

Guided Practice

1. The average wind speeds for several cities in Pennsylvania are given in the table. (Examples 1 and 2)

   a. Determine the range of the data. _____

   b. Determine the median and the first and third quartiles.

   _____

   c. Determine the interquartile range. _____

   d. Determine any outliers in the data. _____

Wind Speed	
Pennsylvania City	Speed (mph)
Allentown	8.9
Erie	11.0
Harrisburg	7.5
Middletown	7.7
Philadelphia	9.5
Pittsburgh	9.0
Williamsport	7.6

2. The heights of several types of palm trees, in feet, are 40, 25, 15, 22, 50, and 30. The heights of several types of pine trees, in feet, are 60, 75, 45, 80, 75, and 70. Compare and contrast the measures of spread of both kinds of trees. (Example 3)

_____

_____

_____

_____

3. ② **Building on the Essential Question** Describe the difference between measure of center and measure

   of spread. _____

_____

_____

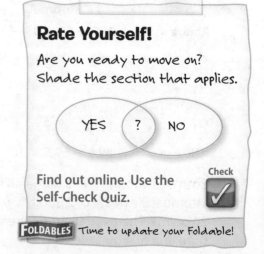

Rate Yourself!

Are you ready to move on?
Shade the section that applies.

YES   ?   NO

Find out online. Use the Self-Check Quiz.

Check ✓

FOLDABLES Time to update your Foldable!

Independent Practice

1. The table shows the number of golf courses in various states. (Examples 1 and 2)

   a. Determine the range of the data. _____

   b. Determine the median and the first and third quartiles.

   _____

   c. Determine the interquartile range. _____

   d. Determine any outliers in the data. _____

Number of Golf Courses			
California	1,117	New York	954
Florida	1,465	North Carolina	650
Georgia	513	Ohio	893
Iowa	437	South Carolina	456
Michigan	1,038	Texas	1,018

For each data set, determine the median, the first and third quartiles, and the interquartile range. (Example 1)

2. texts per day: 24, 53, 38, 12, 31, 19, 26

3. daily attendance at the water park: 346, 250, 433, 369, 422, 298

4. The table shows the number of minutes of exercise for each person. Compare and contrast the measures of spread for both weeks. (Example 3)

Minutes of Exercise		
	Week 1	Week 2
Tanika	45	30
Tasha	40	55
Tyrone	45	35
Uniqua	55	60
Videl	60	45
Wesley	90	75

5. **STEM** The table shows the number of known moons for each planet in our solar system. Use the measures of spread to describe the data.

Known Moons of Planets			
Mercury	0	Jupiter	63
Venus	0	Saturn	34
Earth	1	Uranus	27
Mars	2	Neptune	13

6. MP Select Tools and Techniques The *double stem-and-leaf plot*, where the stem is in the middle and the leaves are on either side, shows the high temperatures for two cities in the same week. Use the measures of spread to describe the data in the stem-and-leaf plot.

Minneapolis		Columbus
5 3 1 0	2	5 7 9 9
6 4	3	7
3	4	8
	5	
	6	2

6|3 = 36°   2|5 = 25°

_____

_____

_____

7. Find the Error Hiroshi was finding the measures of spread of the following set of data: 89, 93, 99, 110, 128, 135, 144, 152, and 159. Determine his mistake and correct it.

median = 128
first quartile = 99
third quartile = 144
interquartile range = 45
range = 70

_____

_____

_____

_____

 H.O.T. Problems Higher-Order Thinking

8. Create Create a list of data with at least six numbers that has an interquartile range of 15 and two outliers. _____

9. Evaluate How is finding the first and third quartiles similar to finding the median? _____

_____

10. Analyze Explain why the median is not affected by very high or very low values in the data. _____

_____

_____

11. Analyze Determine the range and IQR of each data set. Which measure of spread tells you more about the distribution of the data values? Justify your response.

Data Set A	Data Set B
1, 2, 2, 2, 3, 3, 4, 5, 5, 5, 6, 6, 17, 19, 21	1, 2, 9, 17, 17, 17, 17, 17, 17, 18, 18, 18, 19, 20, 21

_____

_____

_____

_____

Multi-Step Problem Solving

12. Carmen and Noah are running for president of the middle school student government. Votes are counted by classroom. What is the difference between the interquartile ranges for the two candidates? **MD** **N** **MP**

Voting Results					
Room Number	Number of Votes		Room Number	Number of Votes	
	Carmen	Noah		Carmen	Noah
1	12	9	5	8	17
2	6	18	6	2	13
3	14	8	7	18	7
4	20	6	8	12	12

Use a problem-solving model to solve this problem.

1 Analyze

**Read the problem. Circle the information you know.
Underline what the problem is asking you to find.**

2 Plan

**What will you need to do to solve the problem?
Write your plan in steps.**

Step 1   Order the values for each person from least to greatest.

Step 2   Determine the IQR for each data set.

Step 3   Subtract to find the difference.

Read to Succeed!

Interquartile range is the difference between the third quartile and the first quartile.

3 Solve

Use your plan to solve the problem. Show your steps.

Carmen: 2, 6, 8, 12, 12, 14, 18, 20   IQR: 16 − 7 or 9

Noah: 6, 7, 8, 9, 12, 13, 17, 18   IQR: 15 − 7.5 or 7.5

The difference between the interquartile ranges is 9 − 7.5 or 1.5.

Complete the grid.

4 Justify and Evaluate

How do you know your solution is reasonable?

_____

_____

_____

MD = Measurement and Data   **N** = Number and Operations   **MP** = Mathematical Processes

More Multi-Step Problem Solving

Use a problem-solving model to solve each problem.

13. Melissa is keeping track of the temperature in her town at noon each day. She has recorded the temperature for six days so far. How much greater will the interquartile range be if Saturday's temperature is 70°F than if it is 58°F? **MD** **N** **MP**

Temperature at Noon	
Day	Temperature (°F)
Sunday	64
Monday	72
Tuesday	58
Wednesday	54
Thursday	60
Friday	62
Saturday	?

14. Jamal cut out these shapes from construction paper. What is the interquartile range for the areas of the shapes? **MD** **EE** **N** **MP**

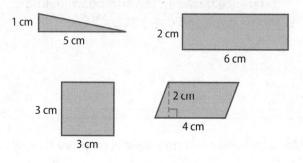

15. Tamiko is training for a bicycle race. She made a graph of the number of miles she rode each week for 6 weeks. If the median at Week 7 increases by 1.5, how many miles did she ride in Week 7? **MD** **N** **MP**

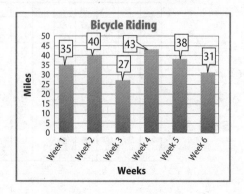

16. Describe the measures of spread for the data set. Change the data set by adding an outlier. Describe the new measures of spread. **MD** **N** **MP**

1,124	465
650	976
840	711
712	925

N = Number and Operations   **EE** = Expressions, Equations, and Relationships   **MD** = Measurement and Data   **MP** = Mathematical Processes

Lesson 4
Dot Plots

Texas Essential Knowledge and Skills

Targeted TEKS
6.12(A) Represent numeric data graphically, including dot plots, stem-and-leaf plots, histograms, and box plots. *Also addresses 6.12(B), 6.13(A).*

Mathematical Processes
6.1(A), 6.1(B), 6.1(D), 6.1(F)

Students in Mr. Cotter's class were asked how many after-school activities they have. Their responses are shown in the table.

Step 1 Use the data to fill in the frequency table.

Number of Activities			
0	2	1	3
1	1	3	4
2	1	0	1
2	3	2	1

→

Number of Activities	
Number	**Tally**
0	
1	
2	
3	
4	

Vocabulary

dot plot

Essential Question

HOW are the mean, median, and mode helpful in describing data?

Step 2 Turn the table so the number of activities is along the bottom on a number line. Instead of tally marks, place dots above the number line. The dots for 0 activities have been placed for you.

The data is now represented in a *dot plot*.

Which MP Mathematical Processes did you use?
Shade the circle(s) that applies.

Ⓐ Apply Math to the Real World.

Ⓔ Organize Ideas.

Ⓑ Use a Problem-Solving Model.

Ⓕ Analyze Relationships.

Ⓒ Select Tools and Techniques.

Ⓖ Justify Arguments.

Ⓓ Use Multiple Representations.

Represent and Interpret Data in Dot Plots

One way to give a picture of data is to make a dot plot. A **dot plot** is a visual display of a distribution of data values where each data value is shown as a dot or other mark, sometimes an X, above a number line. A dot plot is also known as a line plot.

Example

Tutor

1. Jasmine asked her class how many pets they had. The results are shown in the table. Represent the data in a dot plot. Then interpret the data presented in the graph.

Number of Pets					
3	2	2	1	3	1
0	1	0	2	3	4
0	1	1	4	2	2
1	2	2	3	0	2

Step 1 Draw and label a number line.

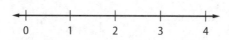

Step 2 Place as many dots above each number as there are responses for that number. Include a title.

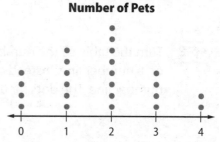

Number of Pets

Step 3 Interpret the data. 24 students responded to the question. No one has more than 4 pets. Four students have no pets. The response given most is 2 pets. This represents the mode.

Got It? Do this problem to find out.

Show your work.

a. _____

a. Javier asked the members of his 4-H club how many projects they were taking. The results are shown in the table. Represent the data in a dot plot. Then interpret the data in the graph.

Number of Projects				
2	4	3	3	1
0	5	4	2	2
1	3	2	1	2

Describe the Center and Spread of Dot Plots

You can describe a set of data using measures of center as well as measures of spread. The range of the data and any outliers are also useful in describing the data.

Examples

Tutor

The dot plot shows the prices of cowboy hats.

Prices of Cowboy Hats

Price ($)

2. Determine the median and mode of the data. Then describe the center of the data distribution using them.

There are 16 hat prices, in dollars, represented in the dot plot. The median is between the 8th and 9th pieces of data.

The two middle numbers, shown on the dot plot, are 40 and 45. So, the median is $42.50. This means that half of the cowboy hats cost more than $42.50 and half cost less than $42.50.

The number that appears most often is 50. So, the mode of the data is 50. This means that more cowboy hats cost $50 than any other price.

Show your work.

3. Determine the range and any outliers of the data. Then describe the spread of the data distribution using them.

The range of the prices is $75 — $30 or $45. The limits for the outlier are $12.50 and $72.50. So, $75 is an outlier. This tells us that most of the prices are much less than $75, but no less than $30.

Got It? Do this problem to find out.

b. The dot plot shows the number of magazines sold. Determine the median, mode, range, and any outliers of the data. Then describe the center and spread of the data distribution using them.

Number of Magazines Sold

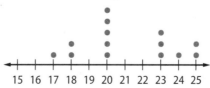

b. _____

Example

Tutor

4. The dot plot shows the amount James deposited in his savings account each month. Describe the center and spread of the data.

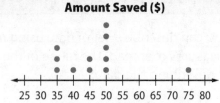
Amount Saved ($)

25 30 35 40 45 50 55 60 65 70 75 80

The mean is $46.67. The median is $47.50, and the mode is $50. So, the majority of the data are close to the measures of center.

The range of the data is $75 − $35 or $40. The interquartile range is $Q_3 − Q_1$, or $50 − $37.50 = $12.50. So, half of the amounts are between $37.50 and $50. There is one outlier at $75.

Got It? Do this problem to find out.

c. The dot plot shows the prices of sweaters in a store. Describe the center and spread of the data.

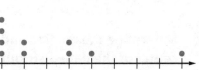
Sweater Prices ($)

25 30 35 40 45 50 55 60 65

Guided Practice

1. Represent the data in a dot plot. Interpret the data by describing the center and spread. (Examples 1–4)

Calories in Serving of Peanut Butter			
190	160	210	210
200	185	190	190
185	200	190	210
190	185	200	200

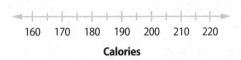

160 170 180 190 200 210 220

Calories

---

2. **?** **Building on the Essential Question** How is using a dot plot useful to interpret data?

Rate Yourself!

How confident are you about line plots? Check the box that applies.

Find out online. Use the Self-Check Quiz.

Check

Copyright © McGraw-Hill Education

Name _____ My Homework _____

Independent Practice

6.12(A), 6.12(B), 6.13(A), 6.1(F) **TEKS**

Represent each set of data in a dot plot. Determine the median, mode, range, and any outliers. Then interpret the data by describing the center and spread. (Examples 1–3)

1. Length of summer camps in days:

7, 7, 12, 10, 5, 10, 5, 7, 10, 9, 7, 9, 6, 10, 5, 8, 7, and 8

_____

_____

_____

_____

Number of Days

2.

Students' Estimates of Room Length (m)				
10	11	12	12	13
13	13	14	14	14
15	15	15	15	15
16	16	16	17	17
17	17	18	18	25

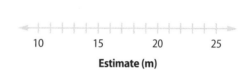

Estimate (m)

_____

_____

_____

3. The dot plot shows the number of songs in play lists. Describe the center and spread of data. (Example 4)

Number of Songs in Play Lists

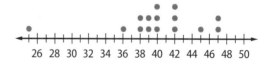

_____

_____

_____

MP **Analyze Relationships** The number of runs a softball team scored in their last five games is shown in the dot plot. How many runs would the team need to score in the next game so that each statement is true?

4. The range is 10. _____

5. Another mode is 11. _____

6. The median is 9.5. _____

Runs Scored

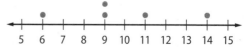

7. Find the Error Dwayne is describing the data in the dot plot. Determine his mistake and correct it.

High Temperature (°F)

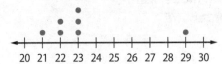

20 21 22 23 24 25 26 27 28 29 30

The median and the mode are 23°F. The outlier of the data set is 20°F.

 H.O.T. Problems Higher-Order Thinking

8. Create Write a survey question that has a numerical answer. Some examples are "How many CDs do you have?" or "How many feet long is your bedroom?" Ask your friends and family the question. Record the results and organize the data in a dot plot. Use the dot plot to make conclusions about your data. For example, interpret the data using the measures of center and spread.

9. Analyze There are several sizes of flying disks in a collection. The range is 8 centimeters. The median is 22 centimeters. The smallest size is 16 centimeters. What is the largest disk in the collection?

10. Evaluate Determine whether the statement is *true* or *false*. Explain.

Dot plots display individual data.

11. Analyze The dot plot shows the number of visitors to the National Wildlife Refuge each day for two weeks. If the four dots at 56 were not included in the data set, which measure of center would be most affected? Justify your response.

Number of Visitors

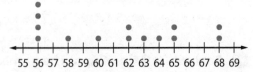

55 56 57 58 59 60 61 62 63 64 65 66 67 68 69

Multi-Step Problem Solving

12. Which description matches the data in the dot plot of U.S. presidents' years in office? (Round decimals to the nearest whole number.) Ⓝ MD MP

Ⓐ mean: 5, mode: 8, median: 7, range: 10, interquartile range: 4, outlier: 12

Ⓑ mean: 6, mode: 8, median: 6, range: 8, interquartile range: 6, outlier: 12

Ⓒ mean: 6, mode: 8, median: 6, range: 10, interquartile range: 4, no outlier

Ⓓ mean: 7, mode: 8, median: 5, range: 12, interquartile range: 4, no outlier

Presidents' Years in Office 1901–2009

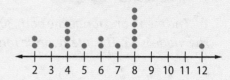

Use a problem-solving model to solve this problem.

1 Analyze

Read the problem. Circle the information you know. Underline what the problem is asking you to find.

2 Plan

What will you need to do to solve the problem? Write your plan in steps.

Step 1 Determine the measures of center.

Step 2 Determine the measures of spread.

Read to Succeed!

Determine the measures of center and spread and compare your answers to the answer choices, making sure to account for each measure.

3 Solve

Use your plan to solve the problem. Show your steps.

mean: about [ ]   range: 12 − 2 or [ ]   mode: [ ]

IQR: 8 − 4 or [ ]   median: [ ]   outlier: [ ]

Choice [ ] lists the correct measures. Fill in that answer choice.

4 Justify and Evaluate

How do you know your solution is reasonable?

_____

_____

Ⓝ = Number and Operations   MD = Measurement and Data   MP = Mathematical Processes

More Multi-Step Problem Solving

Use a problem-solving model to solve each problem.

13. Which dot plot matches Noshi's description of his quiz scores?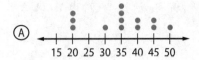

The mean and range are both 30.
The mode is 35. The interquartile range is 15.

Ⓐ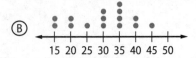

Ⓑ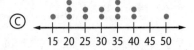

Ⓒ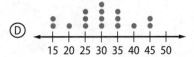

Ⓓ

14. Liliana is shopping for pencils that are sold by the dozen (12). She finds out how much one pencil costs at each price and makes a dot plot. What price should have three marks above it?

Pencil Prices (per dozen)				
4 for $4.80	4 for $9.60	1 for $2.40	4 for $14.40	2 for $6.00
2 for $3.60	12 for $14.40	4 for $7.20	1 for $3.60	6 for $14.40

Price for One Pencil ($)

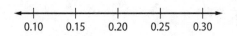

15. Joseph asked his friends how many pages of their history book they had read. He made a dot plot to show his data and he said that the mean was 6. Then he noticed that he'd forgotten to include one number on the dot plot. What number did he forget?

Number of Pages Read

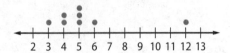

16. The Math Club has been selling cookies during lunch. Make a dot plot to show the number of cookies sold each day. Describe the data's measures of spread and center.

Number of Cookies Sold

12, 16, 10, 12, 15, 13, 14, 20, 15, 15,
13, 11, 13, 14, 15, 14, 11, 12, 13, 15

Stem-and-Leaf Plots

Launch the Lesson: Real World ▶

Amelia recorded the number of instant messages she sent during a 3-week period. How could she represent and describe the data?

Number of Instant Messages Sent Each Day for Three Weeks						
35	21	14	32	25	10	5
27	12	33	20	45	21	31
17	24	21	27	2	3	7

1. What are the measures of center for the data? Round to the nearest tenth if necessary.

2. Would a dot plot be an appropriate display for the data? Explain.

3. What place values are represented in the data values?

4. What is the range of the data?

Texas Essential Knowledge and Skills

Targeted TEKS
6.12(A) Represent numeric data graphically, including dot plots, stem-and-leaf plots, histograms, and box plots. *Also addresses 6.12(B), 6.13(A).*

Mathematical Processes
6.1(A), 6.1(B), 6.1(C), 6.1(D), 6.1(F)

Vocab

Vocabulary
stem-and-leaf plot
stems
leaves
key

Essential Question

HOW are the mean, median, and mode helpful in describing data?

Which ⓂⓅ Mathematical Processes did you use?
Shade the circle(s) that applies.

Ⓐ Apply Math to the Real World.

Ⓔ Organize Ideas.

Ⓑ Use a Problem-Solving Model.

Ⓕ Analyze Relationships.

Ⓒ Select Tools and Techniques.

Ⓖ Justify Arguments.

Ⓓ Use Multiple Representations.

Represent Data in a Stem-and-Leaf Plot

You can use a stem-and-leaf plot to organize large data sets so that they are easier to interpret. In a **stem-and-leaf plot**, the data are ordered from least to greatest and organized by place value.

Tutor

Example

1. Represent the data from the table in a stem-and-leaf plot.

Number of Instant Messages Sent Each Day for Three Weeks						
35	21	14	32	25	10	5
27	12	33	20	45	21	31
17	24	21	27	2	3	7

Step 1 Draw a vertical line and write the tens digits from least to greatest to the left of the line. These digits form the **stems**. Since the least value is 2 and the greatest value is 45, the stems are 0, 1, 2, 3, and 4.

Step 2 Write the ones digits in order to the right of the line with the corresponding stem. The ones digits form the **leaves**. Each leaf represents one data value, so repeating values are each represented.

Number of Instant Messages
Sent Each Day for Three Weeks

Stem	Leaf
0	2 3 5 7
1	0 2 4 7
2	0 1 1 1 4 5 7 7
3	1 2 3 5
4	5

Step 3 Include a **key** that explains the stems and leaves.

2 | 7 = 27 messages

Show your work.

Got It? Do this problem to find out.

a. Represent the data given in a stem-and-leaf plot.

Calcium per serving in selected vegetables (mg): 14, 19, 10, 38, 32, 33, 40, 61, 34, 38, 55, 27, 14, 48

a. _____

Interpret Stem-and-Leaf Plots

Stem-and-leaf plots are useful in interpreting data because you can see all of the data values, including the greatest and least.

Examples

Tutor

2. **The stem-and-leaf plot shows the approximate height of the twenty tallest waterfalls in the world. Interpret the data.**

The tallest waterfall in the world is about 980 meters.

The median is 610 meters, so half of the waterfalls in the list are at least 610 meters tall.

The range of values is 980 − 460 or 520 meters.

Most values occur in the 600 − 690 interval.

Approximate Height of the 20 Tallest World Waterfalls

Stem	Leaf
4	6 7 9 9
5	0 3 6 8
6	0 1 1 5 6
7	0 4 6 7
8	0
9	5 8

4 | 6 = 460 meters

3. **The stem-and-leaf plot shows the number of miles driven by families on vacation. Interpret the data.**

The longest distance driven was 367 miles.

The median is 358 miles, so half of the families drove less than that and half drove more.

The range of miles driven is 367 − 340 or 27 miles.

The modes are 340, 358, and 361 miles.

Miles Driven on Vacation

Stem	Leaf
34	0 0 1 5 8
35	8 8 9
36	1 1 2 6 7

35 | 6 = 356 miles

Got It? Do this problem to find out.

b. Mrs. Hudson made the stem-and-leaf plot shown to represent the results of the math test scores for her students. Interpret the data.

Math Test Scores

Stem	Leaf
8	0 3 5 5 5 5 5 8 9
9	1 1 3 3 5 5 8 8
10	0 0

9 | 1 = 91%

b. _____

Example

4. The stem-and-leaf plot shows the time, in seconds, that each member of the track team ran a 100-meter sprint. Interpret the data.

The range of times is 13.3 − 11.6 or 1.7 seconds.

The mode is 12.2 seconds and the median is 12.2 seconds.

Most of the times were in the 12.0 − 12.9 interval.

100-meter Times (s)

Stem	Leaf
11	6 6 7 8 9 9
12	1 2 2 2 5 8 8
13	0 0 1 1 3

12 | 5 = 12.5 seconds

Guided Practice

1. Represent the data set in a stem-and-leaf plot. (Example 1)
Minutes spent on homework:
37, 28, 25, 29, 31, 45, 32, 31, 46, 39

2. The stem-and-leaf plot shows the number of Calories in various snack foods. Interpret the data. (Examples 2–4)

Number of Calories in Selected Snack Foods

Stem	Leaf
24	0 4 4 8
25	0 0 5 7 8
26	4 5
27	5
28	4

24 | 4 = 244 Calories

3. **Building on the Essential Question** Which measure(s) of center are easier to determine in a stem-and-leaf plot? Explain.

Rate Yourself!

Are you ready to move on?
Shade the section that applies.

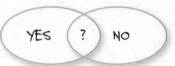

YES   ?   NO

Find out online. Use the Self-Check Quiz.

Check ✓

Independent Practice

Represent each data set in a stem-and-leaf plot. (Example 1)

1. Wait time for amusement park rides (min): 81, 76, 55, 90, 71, 80, 83, 85, 79, 99, 70, 75, 70, 92

2. Weight of potatoes (oz): 10.5, 11.7, 12 14.4, 12.3, 10.8, 11.6, 12.0, 11.9, 11.0

Interpret the data shown in each stem-and-leaf plot (Examples 2–4)

3. **Points Scored by the Tigers**

Stem	Leaf
5	2 4 8
6	5 6
7	0 4 7 8
8	0 6 8 9

5 | 2 = 52 points

_____

_____

_____

4. **Concerts Performed**

Stem	Leaf
11	6 6 7 8 9 9
12	1 2 2 2 5 8 8
13	0 0 1 1 3

11 | 6 = 116 concerts

_____

_____

_____

5. A *back-to-back stem-and-leaf plot* can be used to compare two sets of data. The leaves for one set of data are on one side of the stem and the leaves for the other set of data are on the other side of the stem. Compare the wind speeds for both cities.

Wind Speeds (mph)

Eaton	Stem	Strayer
9 8 3 1	1	1 4 8 8 9
3 2 0 0	2	6 7 9
1	3	4

3 | 4 = 34 mph

_____

_____

_____

writing the stems for the data
d 20, which represent the
t went on vacation
d correct it.

🚂 Problems Higher-Order Thinking

eate Represent the height, in inches, of your classmates in a stem-and-leaf plot. Then describe the center and spread of the data.

8. **Analyze** Explain the benefits of including a key in a stem-and-leaf plot.

9. **Analyze** A stem-and-leaf plot has a leaf of 0 for the stem 5. It has no leaves for the stem 6. Explain the difference between having a leaf of 0 and no leaves for a stem.

10. **Evaluate** Give an example of a set of data where a stem-and-leaf plot may not be the most appropriate representation for the data.

11. **Evaluate** Explain the benefits of using a stem-and-leaf plot over a dot plot.

Multi-Step Problem Solving

12. The stem-and-leaf plot shows the average number of minutes students spent on math homework over one week. What is the difference between the median and the mode of the data?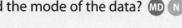

Ⓐ 0   Ⓒ 2

Ⓑ 1   Ⓓ 3

Time Spent Studying (min)

Stem	Leaf
1	6 8
2	0 1 3 6 6 7 9
3	0 2 3 4 5 8
4	0

2 | 1 = 21 minutes

Use a problem-solving model to solve this problem.

1 Analyze

Read the problem. Circle the information you know. Underline what the problem is asking you to find.

2 Plan

What will you need to do to solve the problem? Write your plan in steps.

Step 1   Determine the median and mode of the data.

Step 2   Subtract to find the difference.

Read to Succeed!

The median is the middle number when the data are arranged from least to greatest. The mode is the value that occurs the most.

3 Solve

Use your plan to solve the problem. Show your steps.

median: ☐

mode: ☐

The difference between the median and mode is ☐ — ☐

or ☐. Choice ☐ is correct. Fill in that answer choice.

4 Justify and Evaluate

How do you know your solution is reasonable?

_____

_____

_____

MD = Measurement and Data   N = Number and Operations   MP = Mathematical Processes

More Multi-Step Problem Solving

Use a problem-solving model to solve each problem.

13. Maria made a stem-and-leaf plot of her weekly quiz scores for 10 weeks.

Test Scores

Stem	Leaf
7	6
8	0 4 8 8
9	2 2 2 6
10	0

$8 \mid 4 = 84\%$

What is the difference between the mean and the median of the data? **MD** **N** **MP**

Ⓐ 0.8

Ⓑ 1.2

Ⓒ 2.0

Ⓓ 3.2

14. Tomas works part time on the weekends. He made a stem-and-leaf plot of the amount he earned over 10 weekends.

Amount Earned ($)

Stem	Leaf
2	5
3	0 5 5
4	0 0 5 5
5	0 5

$5 \mid 0 = \$50$

Which measure of center is most affected by including the data value $35? **MD** **N** **MP**

_____

15. The double stem-and-leaf plot shows the number of minutes Ciana and Liam exercised over 10 days.

Minutes Exercising

Ciana	Stem	Liam
9 8	1	7 9
8 8 5	2	6 7 7
6 0 0	3	0 5 5
2 1	4	0 3

$5 \mid 2 = 25$ minutes $2 \mid 5 = 25$ minutes

What is the difference between the interquartile ranges of the two data sets?

_____

16. Create a data set with 10 data entries that has a range of 20 and a median of 24. Make a stem-and-leaf plot of the data. **MD** **N** **MP**

_____

_____

MD = Measurement and Data   **N** = Number and Operations   **MP** = Mathematical Processes

Mathematical Process
6.1(B) Use a problem-solving model that incorporates analyzing given information, formulating a plan or strategy, determining a solution, justifying the solution, and evaluating the problem-solving process and the reasonableness of the solution.

Targeted TEKS 6.12(A)

Speak to Me

Amy surveyed 112 students with the statistical question, "Do you speak Spanish, French, both languages, or neither language?" 42 students speak French, 38 students speak Spanish, and 11 students speak both languages.

Use a Venn diagram to find how many students speak neither Spanish nor French.

 Analyze *What are the facts?*

- You know [ ] classmates speak Spanish and [ ] classmates speak French.

- You know that [ ] students speak both languages.

 Plan *What is your strategy to solve this problem?*

Make a Venn diagram to organize the information. Use logical reasoning to find the answer.

 Solve *How can you apply the strategy?*

Draw and label two overlapping circles to represent the two languages. Since 11 students speak both languages, place an 11 in the section that is part of both circles. Use subtraction to determine the number for each of the other sections.

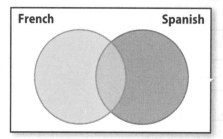

only French: 42 − [ ] = [ ]

only Spanish: 38 − [ ] = [ ]

neither: 112 − [ ] − [ ] − [ ] = [ ]

So, [ ] students speak neither French nor Spanish.

 Justify and Evaluate *Does the answer make sense?*

Check each circle to see if the appropriate number of students is represented.

Battle of the Mascots

Nick conducted a survey of 103 students about a new school mascot. The results showed that 52 students liked Cubs, 36 students liked Bears, and 28 students liked Lions. There were 12 students that liked both Cubs and Lions, 15 students liked both Cubs and Bears, and 5 students liked Bears and Lions. There were 3 students that liked all three mascots.

How many students did not like any of the mascots?

 Analyze

Read the problem. What are you being asked to find?

I need to _____

 Plan

Choose a problem-solving strategy.

I will use the _____ strategy.

 Solve

Use your problem-solving strategy to solve the problem.

 Justify and Evaluate

Use information from the problem to check your answer.

_____

_____

Multi-Step Problem Solving

Work with a small group to solve the following problems. Show your work on a separate piece of paper.

1. Marketing

A survey showed that 70 customers bought white bread, 63 bought wheat bread, and 35 bought rye bread. Of those who bought exactly two types of bread, 12 bought wheat and white, 5 bought white and rye, and 7 bought wheat and rye. Two customers bought all three.

How many customers bought only wheat bread?

2. Pets

Dr. Poston is a veterinarian. One week she treated 20 dogs, 16 cats, and 11 birds. Some owners had more than one pet, as shown in the table.

How many owners had only a dog as a pet?

Pet	Number of Owners
dog and cat	7
dog and bird	5
cat and bird	3
dog, cat, and bird	2

3. Sports

The Student Council surveyed a group of 24 students by asking, "Do you like softball, basketball, both, or neither?" The results showed that 14 students liked softball, and 18 liked basketball. Of these, 8 liked both.

How many students liked just softball and how many liked just basketball?

Use any strategy!

4. Money

Jorge has $138.22 in his savings account. He deposits $10.75 every week and withdraws $31.68 every four weeks.

What will his balance be in 8 weeks?

Vocabulary Check

1. Define *interquartile range.* Then determine the interquartile range of the following data set {22, 18, 38, 6, 24, 18}. **TEKS** 6.12(C), 6.1(D)

Key Concept Check

2. Complete the graphic organizer by providing a definition for each measure of center. **TEKS** 6.12(C), 6.1(E)

Mean	Median	Mode

3. **MP** **Select Tools and Techniques** Use the table that shows the lengths of different lizards. Determine and compare the median and mode of the data. **TEKS** 6.12(B), 6.1(C)

Lizard Length (cm)			
14	12	14	14
19	18	11	14
30	12	19	15

Multi-Step Problem Solving

4. The table shows the number of minutes spent doing different exercises. The mean time spent doing exercises is 18.2 minutes. How many minutes were spent doing sit-ups? **MD MP**

   Ⓐ 12.5   Ⓒ 29

   Ⓑ 15   Ⓓ 38

Daily Exercises	
Exercise	**Time (min)**
Pull-ups	8
Push-ups	10
Running	38
Sit-ups	■
Weight lifting	20

MD = Measurement and Data   **MP** = Mathematical Processes

Histograms

 ## Launch the Lesson: Real World

Alicia researched the average price of concert tickets. The table shows the results. Let's investigate another way to display this data.

Average Ticket Prices of Top 10 Money-Earning Concerts				
$83.87	$68.54	$51.53	$62.10	$59.58
$47.22	$66.58	$88.49	$50.63	$68.98

1. Fill in the tally column and frequency column on the frequency table.

Average Ticket Prices of Top 10 Money-Earning Concerts		
Price	**Tally**	**Frequency**
$25.00–$49.99		
$50.00–$74.99		
$75.00–$99.99		

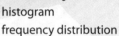

2. What does each tally mark represent? _____

3. What is one advantage of using the frequency table?

_____

_____

4. What is one advantage of using the first table?

_____

_____

Which **MP** Mathematical Processes did you use?
Shade the circle(s) that applies.

Ⓐ Apply Math to the Real World.

Ⓑ Use a Problem-Solving Model.

Ⓒ Select Tools and Techniques.

Ⓓ Use Multiple Representations.

Ⓔ Organize Ideas.

Ⓕ Analyze Relationships.

Ⓖ Justify Arguments.

Texas Essential Knowledge and Skills

Targeted TEKS
6.12(A) Represent numeric data graphically, including dot plots, stem-and-leaf plots, histograms, and box plots. *Also addresses 6.12(B), 6.13(A).*

Mathematical Processes
6.1(A), 6.1(B), 6.1(D), 6.1(F)

Vocabulary

histogram

frequency distribution

Essential Question

HOW are the mean, median, and mode helpful in describing data?

Interpret Data in a Histogram

Data from a frequency table can be represented as a histogram.
A **histogram** is a type of bar graph used to represent numerical data that have been organized into equal intervals. These intervals allow you to see the **frequency distribution** of the data, or how many pieces of data are in each interval.

There is no space between bars.

Because all of the intervals are equal, all of the bars have the same width.

Intervals with a frequency of 0 have a bar height of 0.

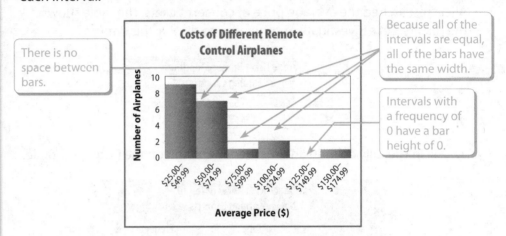

Costs of Different Remote Control Airplanes

The scale of a histogram includes all numbers in the data set.
The intervals should organize the data to make it easy to interpret.

Tutor

Example

1. **Refer to the histogram above. Interpret the histogram. How many remote control airplanes cost at least $100?**

There are $9 + 7 + 1 + 2 + 1$ or 20 prices, in dollars, recorded. More remote control airplanes had prices between $25.00 and $49.99 than any other range. There were no airplanes recorded with a price between $125.00 and $149.99.

Two remote control airplanes had prices between $100.00–$124.99 and one remote control airplane had a price between $150.00–$174.99. So, $2 + 1$, or 3, remote control airplanes had prices that were at least $100.

Show your work.

Got It? Do this problem to find out.

a. _____

a. Refer to the histogram above. How many remote control airplanes cost less than $75?

Represent Data in a Histogram

You can use a histogram to represent data from a table.

Example

Watch Tutor

2. The table shows the number of daily visitors to selected state parks. Draw a histogram to represent the data.

Daily Visitors to Selected State Parks				
108	209	171	152	236
165	244	263	212	161
327	185	192	226	137
193	235	207	382	241

Step 1 Make a frequency table to organize the data. Use a scale from 100 through 399 with an interval of 50.

Daily Visitors to Selected State Parks		
Visitors	**Tally**	**Frequency**
100–149	||	2
150–199	⨼⨼ ||	7
200–249	⨼⨼ |||	8
250–299	|	1
300–349	|	1
350–399	|	1

Step 2 Draw and label a horizontal and vertical axis. Include a title. Show the intervals from the frequency table on the horizontal axis. Label the vertical axis to show the frequencies.

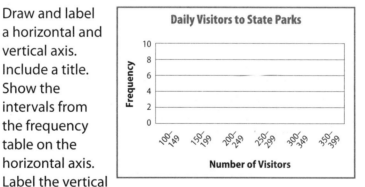

Step 3 For each interval, draw a bar whose height is given by the frequencies.

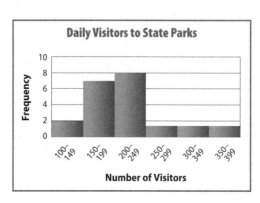

STOP and Reflect

When is a histogram more useful than a table with individual data? Explain below.

Copyright © McGraw-Hill Education

Got It? Do this problem to find out.

b. The list at the right shows a set of test scores. Choose intervals, make a frequency table, and construct a histogram to represent the data.

Test Scores						
72	97	80	86	92	98	88
76	79	82	91	83	90	76
81	94	96	92	72	83	85
65	91	92	68	86	89	97

Test Scores		
Score	Tally	Frequency

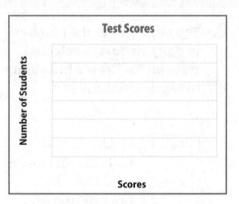

Test Scores

Number of Students

Scores

Guided Practice

1. The frequency table below shows the number of books read on vacation by the students in Mrs. Angello's class. (Examples 1 and 2)

a. Draw a histogram to represent the data.

b. Interpret the data in the histogram. _____

_____

_____

c. How many students read six or more books? _____

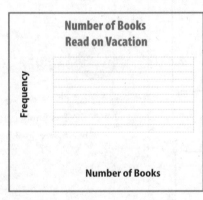

Number of Books Read on Vacation

Frequency

Number of Books

Number of Books Read		
Books	Tally	Frequency
0–2	卌 I	6
3–5	卌 卌	10
6–8	卌 II	7
9–11	III	3
12–14	IIII	4

2. **?** **Building on the Essential Question** Why would you create a frequency table before creating a histogram?

_____

_____

_____

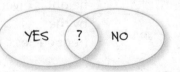

Rate Yourself!

Are you ready to move on? Shade the section that applies.

YES   ?   NO

Find out online. Use the Self-Check Quiz.

Check

Independent Practice

6.12(A), 6.12(B), 6.13(A), 6.1(D), 6.1(F)

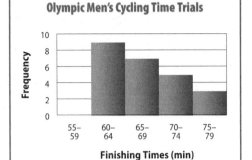

For Exercises 1–4, use the histogram at the right. (Example 1)

1. Interpret the histogram. _____

   _____

   _____

2. Which interval has 7 cyclists? _____

3. Which interval represents the greatest number of cyclists?

   _____

4. How many cyclists had a time less than 70 minutes?

   _____

5. Draw a histogram to represent the set of data. (Example 2)

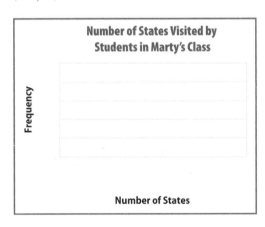

Number of States Visited by Students in Marty's Class		
Number of States	**Tally**	**Frequency**
0–4 |卌||||	9
5–9	|||	3
10–14	卌	5
15–19	|||	3
20–24	卌|	6
25–29			1

Number of States Visited by Students in Marty's Class

Frequency

Number of States

MP Select Tools and Techinques For Exercises 6 and 7, refer to the histograms below.

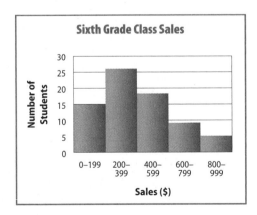

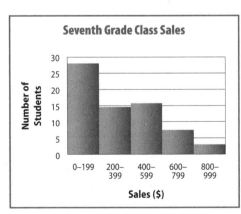

6. About how many students from both grades earned $600 or more?

   _____

7. Which grade had more students earn between $400 and $599?

   _____

8. **MP Analyze Relationships** The following data provides the number of Calories of various types of frozen bars.
{25, 35, 200, 280, 80, 80, 90, 40, 45, 50, 50, 60, 90, 100, 120, 40, 45, 60, 70, 350}

   a. Draw a histogram to represent the data.

   b. Determine the measures of center.

   Calories of Various Types of Frozen Bars

   Number of Bars

   Calories

   _____

   c. Can you determine the measures of center only from the histogram? Explain.

   _____

   _____

🔥 H.O.T. Problems Higher-Order Thinking

9. **Create** Give a set of data that could be represented by both histograms below.

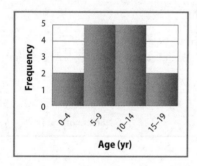
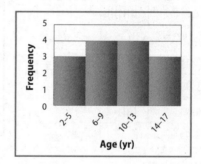

_____

10. **Evaluate** Identify the interval that is not equal to the other three. Explain your reasoning.

   | 15–19 | | 30–34 | | 40–45 | | 45–49 |

_____

11. **Analyze** The table shows a set of plant heights. Describe two different sets of intervals that can be used in representing the set in a histogram. Compare and contrast the two sets of intervals.

Plant Heights (in.)		
12	7	15
8	24	41
16	18	27
43	33	11
24	10	22

   _____

   _____

   _____

Multi-Step Problem Solving

12. The histogram shows the distances a volleyball team travels to their games. What percentage of the games did they travel more than 24 miles? Round to the nearest tenth.

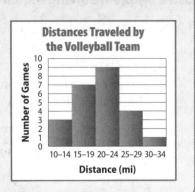

Distances Traveled by the Volleyball Team

Use a problem-solving model to solve this problem.

1 Analyze

Read the problem. Circle the information you know.
Underline what the problem is asking you to find.

2 Plan

What will you need to do to solve the problem?
Write your plan in steps.

> **Step 1**   Determine how many games were more than 24 miles away. Determine the total number of games.

> **Step 2**   Express as a percent.

Read to Succeed!

The percentage is the number of games greater than 24 miles divided by the total number of games. The decimal is then expressed as a percent.

3 Solve

Use your plan to solve the problem. Show your steps.

Number of games greater than 24 miles away: ☐

Total number of games: ☐

So, ☐ out of ☐ games were played greater than 24 miles away.

This is ☐ ÷ ☐ or ☐ or ☐ % of the games.

Complete the grid.

4 Justify and Evaluate

How do you know your solution is reasonable?

_____

_____

More Multi-Step Problem Solving

Use a problem-solving model to solve each problem.

13. The histogram shows the average monthly temperature for cities in the United States for the month of August. What percent of cities have a monthly temperature of less than 80°F? Round to the nearest tenth. (N) (MD) (MP)

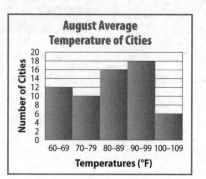

August Average Temperature of Cities

14. The students in Mrs. Sanchez's class recorded their heights. The histogram shows the heights of the students. What fraction of the students are taller than 55 inches? Simplify your answer. (MD) (N) (P) (MP)

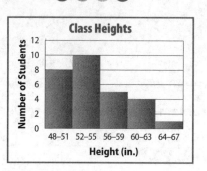

Class Heights

15. A government program plants small trees in parks. The histogram shows the number of trees planted in 48 different parks. What is the difference in the number of parks that had the most trees planted and the least trees planted? (MD) (MP)

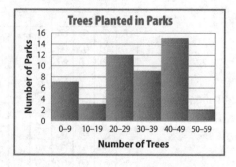

Trees Planted in Parks

16. Valley View Middle School is holding a fundraiser for a local charity. The table shows the number of classes that raised money. Create a histogram for the data. Then find the percent of classes that raised $75 or more. (N) (P) (MD) (MP)

Amount ($)	Number of Classes
25–49	|||
50–74	⊮|||||
75–99	⊮ ⊮
100–124	⊮|||

Launch the Lesson: Real World

The table shows the number of touchdowns scored by each of the 16 teams in the National Football Conference in a recent year. What percent of the teams scored more than 37.5 touchdowns?

47	41	35	38	28	54	49	24
49	44	27	34	37	44	26	36

1. Plot the scores on a dot plot.

24 26 28 30 32 34 36 38 40 42 44 46 48 50 52 54

2. Determine the median, lower extreme, upper extreme, first quartile and third quartile of the data. Place a star on the number line above for each value.

median: _____   first quartile: _____

lower extreme: _____   third quartile: _____

upper extreme: _____

3. What percent of the teams scored less than 31 touchdowns?

_____

4. What percent of the teams scored more than 37.5 touchdowns?

_____

Texas Essential Knowledge and Skills

Targeted TEKS
6.12(A) Represent numeric data graphically, including dot plots, stem-and-leaf plots, histograms, and box plots. *Also addresses 6.13(A).*

Mathematical Processes
6.1(A), 6.1(B), 6.1(D), 6.1(F)

Vocab
Vocabulary
box plot

Essential Question
HOW are the mean, median, and mode helpful in describing data?

Which MP Mathematical Processes did you use?
Shade the circle(s) that applies.

(A) Apply Math to the Real World.   (E) Organize Ideas.

(B) Use a Problem-Solving Model.   (F) Analyze Relationships.

(C) Select Tools and Techniques.   (G) Justify Arguments.

(D) Use Multiple Representations.

Represent Data in a Box Plot

A **box plot**, or box-and-whisker plot, uses a number line to show the distribution of a set of data by using the median, quartiles, and extreme values. A *box* is drawn around the quartile values, and the *whiskers* extend from each quartile to the extreme data points that are not outliers. The median is marked with a vertical line. The figure below is a box plot.

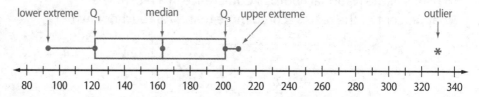

Box plots separate data into four parts. Even though the parts may differ in length, each contains 25% of the data. The box shows the middle 50% of the data.

Watch Tutor

Example

1. **Represent the car speed data in a box plot.**

25 35 27 22 34 40 20 19 23 25 30

Step 1 Order the numbers from least to greatest. Then draw a number line that covers the range of the data.

Step 2 Find the median, the extremes, and the first and third quartiles. Mark these points above the number line.

Q_1: 22   median: 25 Q_3: 34

lower extreme: 19   upper extreme: 40

10 15 20 25 30 35 40 45 50

Step 3 Draw the box so that it includes the quartile values. Draw a vertical line through the box at the median value. Extend the whiskers from each quartile to the extreme data points. Include a title.

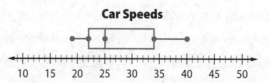

Car Speeds

10 15 20 25 30 35 40 45 50

Got It? Do this problem to find out.

a. Represent the data in a box plot.

{$20, $25, $22, $30, $15, $18, $20, $17, $30, $27, $15}

a. _____

Interpret Data in a Box Plot

Though a box plot does not show individual data, you can use it to interpret data.

Examples
Tutor

Refer to the box plot in Example 1.

2. Half of the drivers were driving faster than what speed?

Half of the 11 drivers were driving faster than 25 miles per hour.

3. What does the box plot's length tell about the data?

The length of the left half of the box plot is short. This means that the speeds of the slowest half of the cars are concentrated. The speeds of the fastest half of the cars are spread out.

Got It? Do this problem to find out.

b. What percent were driving faster than 34 miles per hour?

b. _____

Example
Tutor

4. The box plot below shows the daily attendance at a fitness club. Determine the median and the measures of spread. Then interpret the data.

Fitness Club Attendance

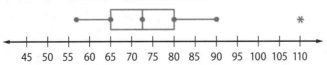

45 50 55 60 65 70 75 80 85 90 95 100 105 110

The median is 72.5. The first quartile is 65 and the third quartile is 80. The range is 54 and the interquartile range is 15. There is an outlier at 110. Both whiskers are approximately the same size so the data, without the outlier, is spread evenly below and above the quartiles.

> **Box Plots**
> • If the length of a whisker or box is short, the values of the data in that part are concentrated.
> • If the length of a whisker or box is long, the values of the data in that part are spread out.

> **Outliers**
> If the data set includes outliers, then the whiskers will not extend to the outliers, just to the previous data point. Outliers are represented with an asterisk (*) on the box plot.

Got It? Do this problem to find out.

c. _____

c. The number of games won in the American Football Conference in a recent year is displayed below. Determine the median and the measures of spread. Then interpret the data.

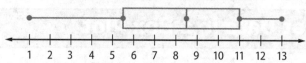

American Football Conference Wins

1 2 3 4 5 6 7 8 9 10 11 12 13

Guided Practice

1. Use the table. (Examples 1–3)

   a. Represent the data in a box plot.

Depth of Recent Earthquakes (km)						
5	15	1	11	2	7	3
9	5	4	9	10	5	7

   2   4   6   8   10   12   14   16

   b. What percent of the earthquakes were between 4 and 9 kilometers deep?

   _____

   c. Write a sentence explaining what the length of the box plot means.

   _____

   _____

2. Determine the median and the measures of spread for the box plot shown. Then interpret the data. (Example 4)

   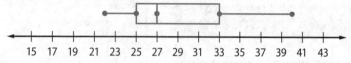

   Average Gas Mileage for Various Sedans

   15 17 19 21 23 25 27 29 31 33 35 37 39 41 43

   _____

   _____

   _____

3. (?) **Building on the Essential Question** How is the information you can learn from a box plot different from what you can learn from the same set of data shown in a dot plot?

   _____

   _____

Independent Practice

6.12(A), 6.12(B), 6.13(A), 6.1(A)

Represent each set of data in a box plot. (Example 1)

1. {65, 92, 74, 61, 55, 35, 88, 99, 97, 100, 96}

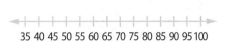

35 40 45 50 55 60 65 70 75 80 85 90 95 100

2.

Cost of MP3 Players ($)	
95	55
105	100
85	158
122	174
165	162

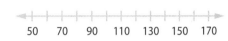

50   70   90   110   130   150   170

3. The table shows the length of coastline for the 13 states along the Atlantic Coast. (Examples 1–3)

Length of Coastline (mi)	
28	130
580	127
100	301
228	40
31	187
192	112
13	

a. Represent the data in a box plot.

0   100   200   300   400   500   600

b. Half of the states have a coastline less than how many miles?

_____

c. Write a sentence describing what the length of the box plot tells about the number of miles of coastline for states along the Atlantic coast.

_____

_____

_____

4. The amount of Calories for a serving of certain fruits is displayed. Determine the median and the measures of spread. Then interpret the data. (Example 4)

Number of Calories

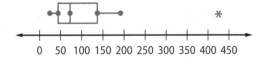

0   50   100   150   200   250   300   350   400   450

_____

_____

_____

5. **MP Use Multiple Representations** A *double box plot* can be used to compare two sets of data. The box plots are graphed on the same number line. The double box plot below shows the number of students in homerooms in each grade.

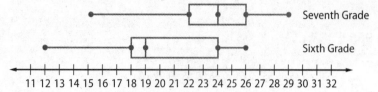

Number of Students in Homerooms

a. Compare the median number of students in a homeroom for each grade.

_____

b. Compare the range of students in a homeroom for each grade.

_____

c. Compare the middle 50% of homerooms for each grade.

_____

_____

d. Interpret the double box plot.

_____

_____

_____

_____

 H.O.T. Problems Higher-Order Thinking

6. **Create** Write a set of data that contains 12 values for which the box plot has no whiskers. State the median, first and third quartiles, and lower and upper extremes.

_____

_____

7. **Create** Write a set of data that, when displayed in a box plot, will result in a long box and short whiskers. Draw the box plot.

_____

8. **Evaluate** Explain a disadvantage of using a box plot over using a dot plot.

_____

_____

9. **Analyze** What can you conclude from a box plot where the length of the left box and whisker is the same as the length of the right box and whisker?

_____

Multi-Step Problem Solving

10. The box plot shows the range of prices of 50 board games available at a local toy store. About how many of the available board games cost less than $10? **MD** **P** **MP**

Prices of Board Games ($)

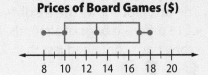

Ⓐ 2 games

Ⓑ 6 games

Ⓒ 13 games

Ⓓ 38 games

Use a problem-solving model to solve this problem.

1 Analyze

Read the problem. Circle the information you know. Underline what the problem is asking you to find.

Read to Succeed!

A box plot shows the data divided into quartiles, or four sections.

2 Plan

What will you need to do to solve the problem? Write your plan in steps.

| Step 1 | Determine the section of the box plot representing less than $10. |

| Step 2 | Determine the approximate number of board games that cost less than $10. |

3 Solve

Use your plan to solve the problem. Show your steps.

The section of the box plot that represents less than $10 is the _____.

The left whisker represents one-_____ of the data.

Since one-fourth of the board games cost less than $10, about ____ ÷ ____ or about ____

games cost less than $10. Choice ____ is correct. Fill in that answer choice.

4 Justify and Evaluate

How do you know your solution is reasonable?

_____

_____

_____

P = Proportionality   **MD** = Measurement and Data   **MP** = Mathematical Processes

More **Multi-Step** Problem Solving

Use a problem-solving model to solve each problem.

11. The box plot shows the weights, in ounces, of 15 different bags of almonds. About how many bags contained less than 27 ounces?

Weights of Bags of Almonds (oz)

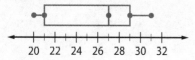

Ⓐ 11 bags

Ⓑ 8 bags

Ⓒ 4 bags

Ⓓ 0 bags

12. The data shows the amounts of flour used in different cookie recipes. What is the third quartile of the data? MD MP

Cups of Flour Used for Cookies						
0.5	1	0.75	1	1.5	1.25	0.75
1.5	0.75	1.75	0.5	0.5	1.5	1

13. The dot plot shows the ages of dogs at a dog park. What is the first quartile of the data? MD MP

Ages of Dogs at a Dog Park

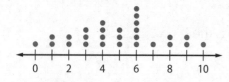

14. Mr. Jensen assigned a quiz to his math students. The data shows all his students' grades. Create a box plot for the data. Then find the percent of students that scored 82 or higher. N P MD MP

Math Quiz Grades						
75	81	80	94	77	78	80
74	96	87	84	91	90	83
79	87	100	97	78	76	82

Math Quiz Grades

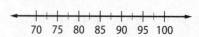

Shape of Data Distributions

Texas Essential Knowledge and Skills

Targeted TEKS
6.12(B) Use the graphical representation of numeric data to describe the center, spread, and shape of the data distribution. *Also addresses 6.12(C), 6.13(A).*

Mathematical Processes
6.1(A), 6.1(B), 6.1(D), 6.1(F)

 Launch the Lesson: Vocabulary

Recall that the distribution of a set of data shows the arrangement of data values. The words below show some of the ways the distribution of data can be described. Match the words below to their definitions.

cluster	The left side of the distribution looks like the right side.
gap	The numbers that have no data value.
peak	The most frequently occurring values, or mode.
symmetry	Data that are grouped closely together.

Vocabulary

symmetric distribution
cluster
gap
peak

Essential Question

HOW are the mean, median, and mode helpful in describing data?

 ## Real-World Investigation

The dot plot shows the costs, in dollars, for parasailing for different companies on a certain beach.

1. Draw a vertical line through the middle of the data. What do you notice?

_____

2. Use one of the words shown above to write a sentence about

   the data. _____

Parasailing Costs ($)

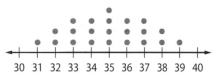

30 31 32 33 34 35 36 37 38 39 40

 Which MP Mathematical Processes did you use?
Shade the circle(s) that applies.

Ⓐ Apply Math to the Real World.

Ⓑ Use a Problem-Solving Model.

Ⓒ Select Tools and Techniques.

Ⓓ Use Multiple Representations.

Ⓔ Organize Ideas.

Ⓕ Analyze Relationships.

Ⓖ Justify Arguments.

Describe the Shape of a Distribution

Data that are evenly distributed between the left side and the right side have a **symmetric distribution**. The distribution shown has a **cluster** of several data values within the interval 10–12. The **gaps** 9 and 13 have no data values. The value 10 is a **peak** because it is the most frequently occurring value.

Examples

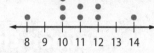

Tutor

Describe the shape of each distribution.

1. The dot plot shows the temperature in degrees Fahrenheit in a city over several days.

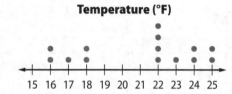

Temperature (°F)

You can use clusters, gaps, peaks, outliers and symmetry to describe the shape. The shape of the distribution is not symmetric because the left side of the data does not look like the right side of the data. There is a gap from 19–21. There are clusters from 16–18 and 22–25. The distribution has a peak at 22. There are no outliers.

2. The box plot shows the number of visitors to a gift shop in one month.

Number of Visitors to a Gift Shop

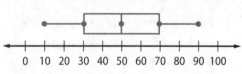

You cannot identify gaps, peaks, and clusters.
Each box and whisker has the same length. So, the data is evenly distributed. The distribution is symmetric since the left side of the data looks like the right side. There are no outliers.

Show your work.

Got It? Do this problem to find out.

a. _____

a. Use clusters, gaps, peaks, outliers, and symmetry to describe the shape of the distribution at the right.

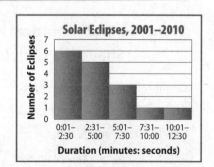

Solar Eclipses, 2001–2010

Number of Eclipses

Duration (minutes: seconds)

Describe the Center and Spread

Key Concept

Use the following flow chart to decide which measures of center and spread are most appropriate to describe a data distribution.

Is the data distribution symmetric?

Yes

No

Use the **mean** to describe the center. Use the **interquartile range** to describe the spread.

Use the **median** to describe the center. Use the **interquartile range** to describe the spread.

STOP and Reflect

Explain below which measures are most appropriate to describe the center and spread of a symmetric distribution.

If there is an outlier, the distribution is not usually symmetric.

 Example

Tutor

3. The dot plot shows the number of states visited by students in a class.

Number of States Visited

10 11 12 13 14 15 16 17 18 19 20

a. **Choose the appropriate measures to describe the center and spread of the distribution. Justify your response based on the shape of the distribution.**

The data are not symmetric and there is an outlier, 19. The median and interquartile range are appropriate measures to use.

b. **Write a few sentences describing the center and spread of the distribution using the appropriate measures.**

The median is 12 states. The first quartile is 11. The third quartile is 13. The interquartile range is 13−11, or 2 states.

Show your work.

The data are centered around 12 states. The spread of the data around the center is about 2 states.

Got It? Do this problem to find out.

b. Describe the center and spread of the distribution. Justify your response based on the shape of the distribution. Then describe the center and spread.

Ages of Tennis Players (yr)

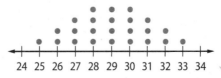

24 25 26 27 28 29 30 31 32 33 34

b. _____

1. The histogram shows the wait times in minutes for entering a concert. Describe the shape of the distribution. (Example 1)

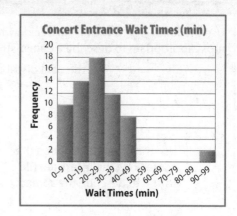

Concert Entrance Wait Times (min)

Wait Times (min)

_____

_____

_____

_____

_____

2. The dot plot shows the weights in pounds of several dogs. Describe the shape of the distribution. (Example 2)

Weights of Dogs (lb)

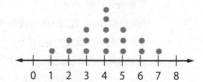

_____

_____

_____

3. The dot plot shows the number of hours several students spent on the Internet during the week. (Example 3)

   a. Choose the appropriate measures to describe the center and spread of the distribution. Justify your response based on the shape of the distribution. _____

Number of Hours Spent on the Internet

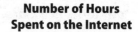

_____

_____

   b. Write a few sentences describing the center and spread of the distribution using the appropriate measures. Round to the nearest tenth if necessary.

_____

_____

_____

4. **?** **Building on the Essential Question** Why does the choice of measure of center and spread vary based on the type of data display? _____

_____

_____

_____

_____

Rate Yourself!

How well do you understand how to describe the shape of a distribution? Circle the image that applies.

Clear

Somewhat Clear

Not So Clear

Find out online. Use the Self-Check Quiz.

Check

Independent Practice

1. The histogram shows the average animal speeds in miles per hour of several animals. Describe the shape of the distribution. (Example 1)

_____

_____

_____

_____

_____

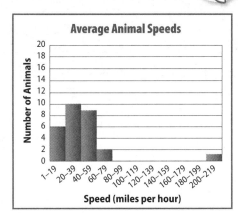

2. The box plot shows the science test scores for Mrs. Everly's students. Describe the shape of

the distribution. (Example 2) _____

_____

_____

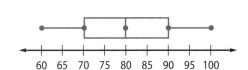

3. The dot plot shows the number of text messages sent by different students in one day. (Example 3)

   a. Choose the appropriate measures to describe the center and spread of the distribution. Justify your response based on the shape of the distribution.

   _____

   _____

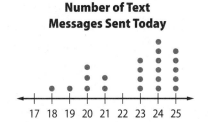

   b. Write a few sentences describing the center and spread of the distribution using the appropriate measures.

   _____

   _____

4. **MP** **Analyze Relationships** Fill in the graphic organizer to show when to use each measure regarding the shape of the distribution.

Measure	Symmetric or Not Symmetric
mean	
median	
interquartile range	

5. A distribution that is not symmetric is called *skewed*. A distribution that is *skewed left* shows data that is more spread out on the left side than on the right side. A distribution that is *skewed right* shows data that is more spread out on the right side than on the left side. The box plot shows the heights in feet of several trees.

Height of Trees (ft)

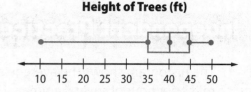

a. Explain how you know the distribution is not symmetric.

_____

b. Is the distribution skewed left or skewed right? Explain.

_____

_____

_____

c. Use appropriate measures to describe the center and spread of the distribution. Justify your choice of measure based on the shape of the distribution. _____

_____

_____

 H.O.T. Problems Higher-Order Thinking

6. Create Draw a dot plot for which the median is the most appropriate measure to describe the center of the distribution.

_____

7. Analyze Explain why you cannot describe the specific location of the center of the box plot shown using the most appropriate measures. _____

Calories in Servings of Fruits

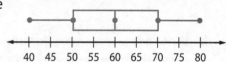

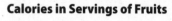

_____

_____

_____

8. Evaluate Tyra created the dot plot shown to represent the ages of the staff at the community pool. She concludes that since there is a peak at 19, the median is 19. She also concludes the two data values that are 25 to be outliers, so there are no gaps. Evaluate her conclusions.

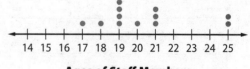

Ages of Staff Members

_____

_____

_____

Multi-Step Problem Solving

9. The dot plot shows the ages of the students in Session 1 of Mr. Garcia's martial arts class. For Session 2, the students were the same except that a 12-year old dropped out and a 9-year old enrolled. Which shows the best measures of center and spread for the **Session 2** data distribution?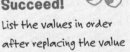

Ages in Martial Arts Class— Session 1

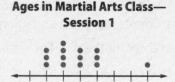

Ⓐ mean ≈ 11.6, range = 7

Ⓑ mean ≈ 11.8, range = 6

Ⓒ median = 11, interquartile range = 3

Ⓓ median = 11.5, interquartile range = 2

Use a problem-solving model to solve this problem.

1 Analyze

**Read the problem. Circle the information you know.
Underline what the problem is asking you to find.**

2 Plan

**What will you need to do to solve the problem?
Write your plan in steps.**

Read to Succeed!
List the values in order after replacing the value of 12 with the value of 9.

| **Step 1** | Determine the data set with the values adjusted. |

| **Step 2** | Determine the mean, median, range, and interquartile range of the new data set. |

3 Solve

Use your plan to solve the problem. Show your steps.
The new data set is 9, 10, 10, 10, 11, 11, 11, 11, 12, 12, 13, 13, 13, 16.

The mean is ⬚, range is ⬚, median is ⬚, and interquartile

range is ⬚. Choice ⬚ is correct. Fill in that answer choice.

4 Justify and Evaluate

How do you know your solution is reasonable?

_____

_____

_____

Ⓝ = Number and Operations   ᴹᴰ = Measurement and Data   ᴹᴾ = Mathematical Processes

More Multi-Step Problem Solving

Use a problem-solving model to solve each problem.

10. The dot plot shows the amount of time students recorded engaging in physical activity for Week 1. For Week 2, $\frac{2}{3}$ as many students recorded 5 hours, $\frac{2}{3}$ as many students recorded 6 hours, and twice as many students recorded 10 hours.

**Hours of Physical Activity—
Week 1**

Which option shows the best measures of center and spread for the Week 2 data distribution? **MD** **N** **MP**

- Ⓐ mean ≈ 5.9, range = 6
- Ⓑ mean ≈ 6.6, range = 6
- Ⓒ median = 5, interquartile range = 3
- Ⓓ median = 6, interquartile range = 6

11. The stem-and-leaf plot shows students' quiz scores in Ms. Warren's math class.

Quiz Scores

Stem	Leaf
7	5 5 5
8	0 0 0 5 5 5 5
9	0 0 0 0 5 5 5
10	0 0 0

$7 \mid 5 = 75\%$

Lola found the range and the best measure of center for the data distribution. What two measures did Lola find? What is the sum of the two numbers Lola found? **MD** **N** **MP**

_____

12. Donte's bicycle repair shop was open 20 days last month. He recorded the number of repairs the shop completed each day. The box plot shows a summary of the data.

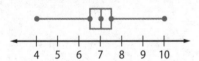

What is the greatest possible number of repairs Donte's shop could have completed last month? **MD** **MP**

_____

13. The histogram summarizes the players' heights on Rachel's volleyball team.

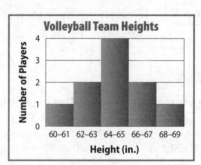

a. What are the range and best measure of center if all the heights are even integers?

b. What are the range and best measure of center if all the heights are odd integers? **MD** **N** **MP**

_____

_____

Hands-On Lab 9-a
Collect Data

Texas Essential Knowledge and Skills

Targeted TEKS
6.12(C) Summarize numeric data with numerical summaries, including the mean and median (measures of center) and the range and interquartile range (IQR) (measures of spread), and use these summaries to describe the center, spread, and shape of the data distribution. *Also addresses 6.12(B), 6.13(A), 6.13(B).*

Mathematical Processes
6.1(C), 6.1(D), 6.1(E), 6.1(F), 6.1(G)

INQUIRY HOW can I select techniques to answer a survey question and summarize the results?

Aribelle surveyed students in the cafeteria lunch line. She asked the statistical question, *How many photos are currently stored in your cell phone?* She wants to organize the data and choose an appropriate way to display the results of her survey.

Hands-On Activity

You can collect, organize, display, and interpret data in order to answer a survey question.

Step 1 Make a data collection plan. Aribelle chose to survey students in the cafeteria.

Step 2 Collect the data. The results of the survey are provided below.

55, 47, 58, 50, 66, 47, 54, 64, 47, 65,
43, 44, 51, 81, 54, 45, 57, 52, 58, 60

Step 3 Organize the data. Place the values in order from least to greatest.

_____

_____

Step 4 Describe the data. There were a total of ☐ responses. The

responses measure the number of _____ . The data was

collected using a _____ . One attribute of the data is the

median, which is ☐ photos. Another attribute is the interquartile

range, which is ☐ photos. There is an outlier at ☐ photos.

Step 5 Create a display of the data. Explain why a box plot would be an appropriate display of Aribelle's data. _____

_____

_____

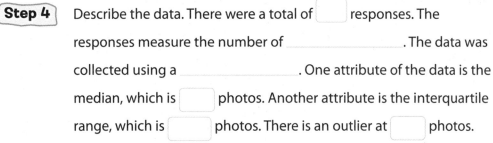

Investigate

Work with a partner. Collect data in order to answer a survey question.

1. Write a survey question. _____

2. Collect the data and record the results in a table.

3. Create a display of the data.

Analyze and Reflect

4. **MP Analyze Relationships** Write a few sentences describing your results. Include the number of responses you recorded, how the responses were measured and/or gathered, and their overall pattern. _____

_____

_____

5. **MP Analyze Relationships** Write a few sentences describing the center and spread of the distribution. _____

_____

_____

Create

6. **INQUIRY** HOW can I select techniques to answer a survey question and summarize the results? _____

_____

_____

Summarize Categorical Data

 Launch the Lesson: Real World

A fruit juice manufacturer is researching which of its flavors the public favors most. It surveyed 100 people and those surveyed were able to choose more than one juice type. The table shows the number of favorable responses by fruit juice type. How can we summarize this data?

Number of Favorable Responses by Juice Type			
Type	Responses	Type	Responses
Apple	35	Kiwi-strawberry	39
Cranberry	18	Orange	44
Grape	22	Pomegranate	16
Grapefruit	29	Strawberry-banana	27

1. What percent of people like apple juice? _____

2. What percent of people like pomegranate juice? _____

3. Which type of fruit juice is favored by the most people?

_____

4. Which type of fruit juice is favored by the least number of people?

_____

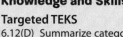

Texas Essential Knowledge and Skills

Targeted TEKS
6.12(D) Summarize categorical data with numerical and graphical summaries, including the mode, the percent of values in each category (relative frequency table), and the percent bar graph, and use these summaries to describe the data distribution.

Mathematical Processes
6.1(A), 6.1(B), 6.1(C), 6.1(D), 6.1(F)

 Vocab

Vocabulary
categorical data
relative frequency
percent bar graph

Essential Question
HOW are the mean, median, and mode helpful in describing data?

Which MP Mathematical Processes did you use?
Shade the circle(s) that applies.

Ⓐ Apply Math to the Real World.
Ⓑ Use a Problem-Solving Model.
Ⓒ Select Tools and Techniques.
Ⓓ Use Multiple Representations.
Ⓔ Organize Ideas.
Ⓕ Analyze Relationships.
Ⓖ Justify Arguments.

Summarize Categorical Data Using the Mode

Categorical data is data that can be divided into categories based on the attributes of the data. You can summarize categorical data using the mode.

Examples

Tutor

The table shows the number of students that play each instrument.

Number of Students per Instrument			
Instrument	Number of Students	Instrument	Number of Students
Bass	3	Drums	16
Cello	4	Flute	6
Clarinet	3	Violin	8

1. Summarize the data using the mode.

More students play the drums, so drums is the mode. The number of students that chose drums is twice that of the next popular instrument, the violin.

2. Represent the data in a bar graph. Summarize and describe the data distribution.

Draw a bar graph with each category (instrument) along the horizontal axis and the number of students along the vertical axis.

Show your work.

The bar for drums is the tallest, so it is the mode. The same number of students play the bass and clarinet.

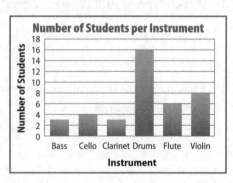

Got It? Do this problem to find out.

a. The table shows the flavors of gum that are most popular. Summarize the data using the mode. Interpret its meaning.

a. _____

Flavor	Number of People	Flavor	Number of People
Cherry	5	Peppermint	9
Cinnamon	8	Spearmint	7
Grape	3	Watermelon	5

Summarize Categorical Data Using Relative Frequency

You can summarize categorical data using a relative frequency table. **Relative frequency** is the ratio of the number of times a category is represented to the total number of pieces of data. A relative frequency table shows the percent of values in each category.

Example

Tutor

3. The table shows the number of students that have visited various states. Determine the relative frequency for each state. Summarize and describe the data using the relative frequency.

State	Number of Students	Relative Frequency
California	12	12 ÷ 40 = 0.3 or 30%
Florida	15	
Georgia	3	
Maine	7	
North Carolina	3	

The total number of students that were surveyed is ☐.

Divide the value for each category by the total number of students to find the relative frequency. Complete the table.

Most students have visited California, Florida, and Maine. More than a third of the students have visited Florida.

Got It? Do this problem to find out.

Show your work.

b. The table shows the number of students that speak various languages. Determine the relative frequency for each language. Summarize and describe the data using the relative frequency.

Language	Number of Students	Relative Frequency
Arabic	2	
French	15	
German	6	
Spanish	27	

b. _____

Summarize Categorical Data Using a Percent Bar Graph

You can use a percent bar graph to summarize categorical data. A **percent bar graph** shows the relative frequency of each category in a single bar.

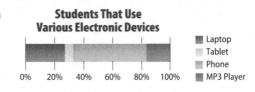

Students That Use Various Electronic Devices

0% 20% 40% 60% 80% 100%

■ Laptop
□ Tablet
■ Phone
■ MP3 Player

Example

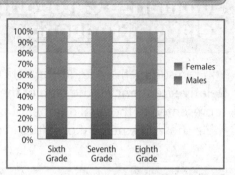

Tutor

4. The percent bar graph shows the percent of each grade level that is male or female. Summarize and describe the data shown in the graph.

There are more males in sixth and seventh grade than females. The number of males and females in eighth grade is about the same.

Guided Practice

1. The table shows the number of vehicles of each type at a dealership. Summarize the data using the mode. (Examples 1 and 2)

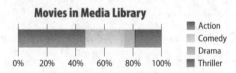

Type of Vehicle	Number of Vehicles
4-door	58
Truck	29
Hybrid	13
Van	37

2. The table shows the number of each type of animal at a refuge. Determine the relative frequency for each animal. Summarize the data using the relative frequency. (Example 3)

Animal	Frequency	Relative Frequency
Cheetah	6	
Leopard	9	
Lion	5	

3. The percent bar graph shows the percent of each genre of movie that is in Kevin's media library. Summarize and describe the data distribution. (Example 4)

Movies in Media Library

■ Action
■ Comedy
■ Drama
■ Thriller

0%   20%   40%   60%   80%   100%

4. ? **Building on the Essential Question** How can you use measures of center to summarize categorical data?

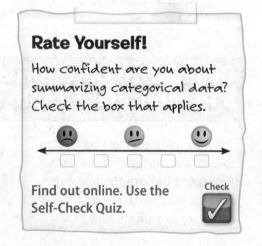

Rate Yourself!

How confident are you about summarizing categorical data? Check the box that applies.

Find out online. Use the Self-Check Quiz.

Check ✓

Independent Practice

6.12(D), 6.1(A), 6.1(D) · TEKS

The table shows the number of people that chose specific places they like to jog. (Examples 1–3)

Place	Number of People
Track	16
Path	22
Treadmill	9
Gravel	2
Sidewalk	15

1. Summarize the data using the mode.

_____

2. Represent the data in a bar graph. Summarize and describe the data distribution.

_____

_____

3. Determine the relative frequency for each place. Round to the nearest tenth if necessary.

_____

_____

Summarize the data in each percent bar graph. (Example 4)

4.

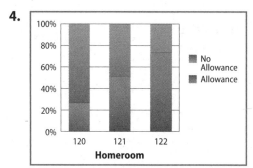

5. **Time Spent After School**

■ Chores
■ Homework
■ Practice

0% 20% 40% 60% 80% 100%

_____

_____

_____

_____

_____

_____

_____

6. **MP Use Multiple Representations** The table shows the results of a survey about favorite types of stores.

Type of Store	Number of Students
Clothing	19
Electronics	11
Thrift	5
Toy	15

a. What is the mode of the data?

b. Determine the relative frequency of each type of store.

c. Represent the relative frequencies of the data in a percent bar graph.

H.O.T. Problems Higher-Order Thinking

7. **Evaluate** Explain the benefits of determining the relative frequency of categories in a data set.

8. **Analyze** How can a percent bar graph be used to describe the data distribution of a set?

9. **Create** Write a real-world problem in which you would find the relative frequency of each category and then represent the data in a percent bar graph.

Multi-Step Problem Solving

10. In voting for a sixth-grade field trip, 120 students chose the zoo, $\frac{1}{4}$ as many chose the museum, and $\frac{5}{12}$ as many chose the aquarium. What is the relative frequency of the students that chose museum?

MD **P** **MP**

ⓐ 15% ⓒ 30%

ⓑ 25% ⓓ 60%

Sixth Grade Field Trip	
Field Trip Choice	Relative Frequency
Zoo	
Museum	?
Aquarium	

Use a problem-solving model to solve this problem.

1 Analyze

Read the problem. Circle the information you know. Underline what the problem is asking you to find.

2 Plan

What will you need to do to solve the problem? Write your plan in steps.

Step 1 Determine the number of students that chose each field trip location.

Step 2 Determine the relative frequency of the students that chose museum.

Read to Succeed!

The relative frequency of a category is the ratio of that category to the total number of values.

3 Solve

Use your plan to solve the problem. Show your steps.

The number of students that chose zoo: ☐

The number of students that chose museum: $\frac{1}{4}$ of 120 or ☐

The number of students that chose aquarium: $\frac{5}{12}$ of 120 or ☐

The total number of students is ☐ + ☐ + ☐ or ☐ .

Since 30 students chose museum, the relative frequency is $\frac{30}{200}$ or ☐ %.

Choice ☐ is correct. Fill in that answer choice.

4 Justify and Evaluate

How do you know your solution is accurate?

_____

_____

MD = Measurement and Data   **P** = Proportionality   **MP** = Mathematical Processes

More Multi-Step Problem Solving

Use a problem-solving model to solve each problem.

11. The sixth-graders at High Point Middle School voted for a class mascot. Sixty voted for tiger, $\frac{9}{10}$ as many voted for ram, and $\frac{3}{5}$ as many voted for bulldog.

Sixth Grade Mascot	
Mascot Choice	**Relative Frequency**
Tiger	
Ram	
Bulldog	?

What was the relative frequency of bulldog in the voting? (MD) (N) (P) (MP)

(A) 24%

(B) 36%

(C) 54%

(D) 60%

12. Mr. Rosario has 120 students in his physical education classes. He made the percent bar graph shown to represent the activities his students chose for the week.

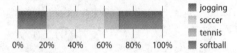

How many students chose the mode? (MD) (N) (P) (MP)

13. The table shows data about lunch choices a cafeteria staff has prepared.

Entree	Number	Relative Frequency
Salad	24	30%
Burger		37.5%
Pizza		20%
Fish		12.5%

The cafeteria manager asks the staff to prepare 15 taco entrees. After those 15 entrees are added to the data, what is the relative frequency of the mode? Round to the nearest tenth. (MD) (N) (P) (MP)

14. The table shows the results of a survey about ice cream.

Favorite Flavor	Votes
Chocolate Chip	4
Vanilla	8
Fudge Riot	12
Chocolate	8
Strawberry	4

Tobias made a bar graph of the data and concluded that the distribution is symmetric and the mode has a relative frequency of 33.3%. Is Tobias's statement correct? Explain. (MD) (P) (MP)

(MD) = Measurement and Data   (N) = Number and Operations   (P) = Proportionality   (MP) = Mathematical Processes

Select an Appropriate Representation

Launch the Lesson: Real World

Texas Essential Knowledge and Skills

Targeted TEKS
6.12(A) Represent numeric data graphically, including dot plots, stem-and-leaf plots, histograms, and box plots. *Also addresses 6.12(B), 6.12(D).*

Mathematical Processes
6.1(A), 6.1(B), 6.1(D), 6.1(F)

The displays show the length of various rivers in Texas.

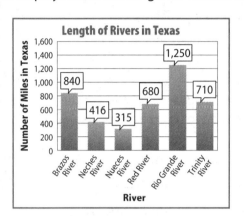

Length of Rivers in Texas

Number of Miles in Texas

840, 416, 315, 680, 1,250, 710

Brazos River, Neches River, Nueces River, Red River, Rio Grande River, Trinity River

River

Length of Rivers in Texas	
Length (mi)	Number of Rivers
201–400	
401–600	
601–800	
801–1,000	
1,001–1,200	
1,201–1,400	

Essential Question

HOW are the mean, median, and mode helpful in describing data?

1. Use the bar graph to fill in the "Number of Rivers" column in the table.

2. Which display allows you to find the number of miles the Rio Grande River is in Texas?

_____

3. In which display is it easier to find the number of rivers that have 801 or more miles in Texas? Explain.

_____

_____

Which **MP** Mathematical Processes did you use?
Shade the circle(s) that applies.

Ⓐ Apply Math to the Real World.   Ⓔ Organize Ideas.

Ⓑ Use a Problem-Solving Model.   Ⓕ Analyze Relationships.

Ⓒ Select Tools and Techniques.   Ⓖ Justify Arguments.

Ⓓ Use Multiple Representations.

Statistical Representations

Type of Display	Best used to
Bar Graph	show the number of items in specific categories
Box Plot	show measures of variation for a set of data, also useful for very large sets of data
Histogram	show frequency of data divided into equal intervals
Line Graph	show change over a period of time
Dot Plot	show how many times each number occurs

Data can often be represented in several different ways. The representation you choose depends on your data and what you want to show.

Tutor

Example

1. **Which display allows you to tell the mode of the data?**

Lasagna Orders Each Night

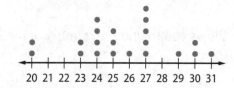

Lasagna Orders Each Night

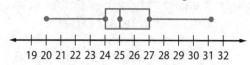

The dot plot shows each night's data. The number of orders that occurs most frequently is 27. The box plot shows the spread of the data, but does not show individual data so it does not show the mode.

Got It? Do this problem to find out.

Show your work.

a. Which of the above displays allows you to easily find the median of the data?

a. _____

Examples

Tutor

2. A survey compared different brands of sunscreen. The table shows the number of first-choice responses for each brand. Select an appropriate type of display to compare the number of responses. Justify your response.

Brand	Number of Responses
A	13
B	4
C	9
D	19
E	3

These data show the number of responses for each brand. A bar graph would be the best display to compare the responses.

 STOP and Reflect

What type of data are best represented in a bar graph? Explain below.

3. Represent the data in an appropriate display.

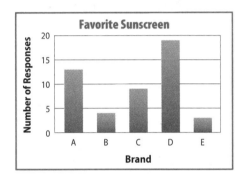

Favorite Sunscreen

Got It? Do these problems to find out.

The table shows the score of each game the Bears softball team played in one season.

Softball Game Scores				
5	7	2	1	2
3	1	2	2	4

 Show your work.

b. Select an appropriate type of display to allow you to find the mode. Explain your choice.

b. _____

c. Represent the data in an appropriate display.

Guided Practice

1. Which display makes it easier to determine the greatest number of calendars sold? Justify your reasoning. (Example 1)

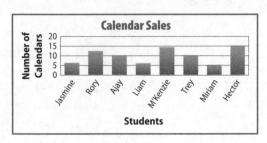

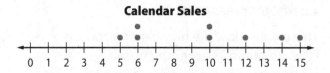

_____

_____

Select an appropriate type of display for data gathered about each situation. Justify your reasoning. (Example 2)

2. the favorite cafeteria lunch item of the sixth-grade students

_____

_____

3. the temperature from 6 A.M. to 12:00 P.M.

_____

_____

4. Select and make an appropriate display for the following data. (Example 3)

Number of Minutes Run Each Day									
30	40	25	30	35	35	40	15	20	25
25	35	35	30	45	15	20	25	30	30

_____

5. (?) **Building on the Essential Question** Why is it important to choose the appropriate display for a set of data?

_____

_____

_____

Rate Yourself!

How confident are you about selecting an appropriate display? Shade the ring on the target.

I'm on target.

I need help.

Find out online. Use the Self-Check Quiz.

Check ✓

Independent Practice

6.12(A), 6.12(B), 6.12(D), 6.1(C) TEKS

1. Which display makes it easier to determine the number of counties with 3 or less trails? Justify your reasoning. (Example 1)

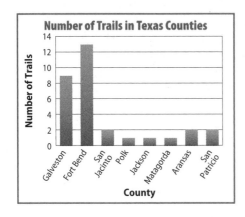

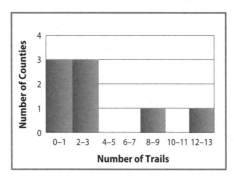

_____

_____

_____

Select an appropriate type of display for data gathered about each situation. Justify your reasoning. (Example 2)

2. the test scores each student had on a language arts test

_____

3. the median age of people who voted in an election

_____

4. **MP Select Tools and Techniques** Select and make an appropriate type of display for the situation. (Example 3)

Show your work.

South American Country	Water Area (km²)	South American Country	Water Area (km²)
Argentina	47,710	Guyana	18,120
Bolivia	15,280	Paraguay	9,450
Chile	12,290	Peru	5,220
Ecuador	6,720	Venezuela	30,000

_____

5. **MP Apply Math to the Real World** Use the Internet or another source to find a set of data that is displayed in a bar graph, line graph, frequency table, or circle graph. Was the most appropriate type of display used? What other ways

might these same data be displayed? _____

6. **MP** **Analyze Relationships** Fill in the graphic organizer below.

Display	What it shows
dot plot	
histogram	
box plot	
bar graph	

7. Display the data in the bar graph using another type of display. Compare the advantages of each display.

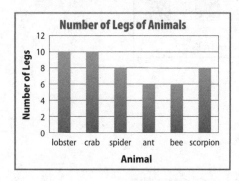

_____

_____

_____

H.O.T. Problems Higher-Order Thinking

8. **Evaluate** Determine whether the following statement is *true* or *false*. If true, explain your reasoning. If false, give a counterexample.

   Any set of data can be displayed using a line graph.

_____

_____

_____

9. **Evaluate** Which type of display allows you to easily find the mode of the data?

   Explain your reasoning. _____

_____

10. **Analyze** The table shows the number of each type of plant at a botanical garden. The director of the garden would like to add cacti so that the relative frequency of the plant is 50%.

    How many cactus plants should the director add? _____

Type of Plant	Frequency
Rose	13
Cactus	18
Palm	4
Ferns	15

Multi-Step Problem Solving

11. The table shows the distance 12 students on the track team ran one week. The next week, each student ran exactly twice as far as they did Week 1. Which statement is true about finding the mode of the data for Week 2? MD MP

Number of Miles Run Week 1			
5	7	4	9
10	4	7	4
8	4	6	4

Ⓐ A dot plot will best show that the mode is 8.

Ⓑ A box plot will best show that the mode is 8.

Ⓒ A dot plot will best show that the mode is 11.

Ⓓ A box plot will best show that the mode is 11.

Use a problem-solving model to solve this problem.

1 Analyze

Read the problem. Circle the information you know.
Underline what the problem is asking you to find.

2 Plan

What will you need to do to solve the problem? Write your plan in steps.

Step 1   Determine the values for Week 2.

Step 2   Determine the mode of the Week 2.

3 Solve

Use your plan to solve the problem. Show your steps.

The values for Week 2 are 10, 20, 16, 14, 8, 8, 8, 14, 12, 18, 8, 8.

The mode is ⬚.

Since a box plot does not show the mode, a dot plot is the best representation to show the mode. Choice ⬚ is correct. Fill in that answer choice.

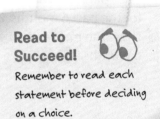

Read to Succeed! Remember to read each statement before deciding on a choice.

4 Justify and Evaluate

How do you know your solution is accurate?

_____

_____

_____

MD = Measurement and Data   MP = Mathematical Processes

More Multi-Step Problem Solving

Use a problem-solving model to solve each problem.

12. The table shows the number of books each student in an afterschool club read in January. In February, each student met the goal of reading one more book than they did in January. Which statement is true about the mode of the data for February? **MD MP**

Number of Books Read in January			
7	1	4	4
5	6	8	9
4	5	7	3

Ⓐ A box plot will best show that the number of books read most is 6 books.

Ⓑ A box plot will best show that the number of books read most is between 5 and 8.

Ⓒ A histogram will best show that the number of books read most is between 4 and 7.

Ⓓ A dot plot will best show that the number of books read most is 5.

13. Dana created a histogram and a box plot using the data showing the number of minutes she exercised each day for 10 days.

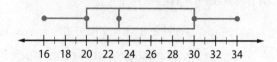

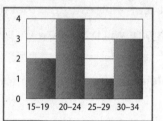

Which representation can she use to determine how many days she exercised 25 minutes or more? How many days did she exercise for 25 minutes or more? **MD MP**

_____

14. A real estate agent wants to create a display to show the trend in the median sales of houses over the past 6 months. He has 50 data entries for each month for the past 6 months. Explain what two types of displays he can use, one to show the median and one to show the trend in the median over the past 6 months. **MD MP**

_____

_____

_____

Select Appropriate Units and Tools

INQUIRY HOW can I select tools to determine a measureable attribute?

Each item in a backpack has different attributes, such as color, size, and weight. Some of the attributes of the objects can be measured.

Hands-On Activity

You can choose the appropriate unit and tool to measure an object.

Step 1 Select an object in your classroom such as a desk, book, backpack, or trash can.

Step 2 List all of the measureable attributes of your object in the Step 3 table. Choose from among length, weight or mass, or capacity.

Step 3 Select an appropriate tool and measure each attribute. Record each measure using appropriate units in the table below.

Object	Attribute	Tool	Measurement

Step 4 Choose a different object with at least one attribute that requires the use of a different tool to measure. Then repeat steps 1–3.

Object	Attribute	Tool	Measurement

Step 5 Write and solve a real-world problem in which one of your measurements is needed to solve the problem.

_____

Texas Essential Knowledge and Skills

Targeted TEKS
6.12(C) Summarize numeric data with numerical summaries, including the mean and median (measures of center) and the range and interquartile range (IQR) (measures of spread), and use these summaries to describe the center, spread, and shape of the data distribution.

Mathematical Processes
6.1(C), 6.1(D), 6.1(E), 6.1(F), 6.1(G)

Investigate

Work with a partner. Choose an attribute common to several similar objects and use the appropriate unit and tool to measure.

1. Choose a set of objects and a measurable attribute.

    _____

2. Measure the attribute and record the results in a table.

3. Create a display of the data.

Analyze and Reflect

4. **MP Analyze Relationships** Write a few sentences describing your data. Include the number of observations, how the data was measured, and the overall pattern of the data. _____

    _____

    _____

    _____

5. **MP Analyze Relationships** Explain how the way you measured the objects influenced the shape of the display. _____

    _____

    _____

Create

6. **INQUIRY** HOW can I select tools to determine a measureable attribute?

    _____

    _____

21ST CENTURY CAREER

Environmental Engineer

Are you concerned about protecting the environment? If so, you should think about a career in environmental science. Environmental engineers apply engineering principles along with biology and chemistry to develop solutions for improving the air, water, and land. They are involved in pollution control, recycling, and waste disposal. Environmental engineers also determine methods for conserving resources and for reducing environmental damage caused by construction and industry.

Mathematical Process
6.1(A) Apply mathematics to problems arising in everyday life, society, and the workplace.
Targeted TEKS 6.12(B)

Is This the Career for You?

Are you interested in a career as an environmental engineer? Take some of the following courses in high school.
◆ Algebra
◆ Biology
◆ Environmental Science
◆ Environmental History

College & Career
READINESS

Explore college and careers at **ccr.mcgraw-hill.com**

Thinking Green!

Use the information in the table to solve each problem. Round to the nearest tenth if necessary.

1. Determine the mean, median, and mode of the percent of recycled glass data.

2. If County E is removed from the recycled aluminum cans data, which changes the most: the mean, median, or mode? Does this make sense? Explain your reasoning.

3. Find the range, quartiles, and interquartile range of the percent of recycled newspapers data. _____

4. Find any outliers in the percent of recycled plastic bottles data. _____

5. Make a box plot of the percent of recycled glass data.

6. Refer to the box plot you made in Exercise 5. Compare the parts of the box and the *lengths of the whiskers*. What does this tell you about the data? _____

Percent of Materials That Are Recycled				
County	Aluminum Cans (%)	Glass (%)	Newspapers (%)	Plastic Bottles (%)
A	15	13	41	7
B	4	17	28	15
C	31	17	81	7
D	14	21	38	23
E	48	16	66	53
F	12	29	33	16
G	6	26	22	8

TEKS Career Project

It's time to update your career portfolio! Describe an environmental issue that concerns you. Explain how you, as an environmental engineer, would work to resolve this issue. Then research how the issue is being addressed by environmental scientists today. Prepare a brief oral presentation and present it to your classmates. As others are presenting, listen carefully to their presentations. At the end, ask any clarifying questions.

Choose your favorite school activity or volunteer job. Could it lead to a possible career? If so, what is it?

-
-
-
-

Chapter Review

Vocabulary Check

 Work with a partner to reconstruct the vocabulary word and definition from the letters under the grid. The letters for each column are scrambled directly under that column. Seek clarification of the term as needed.

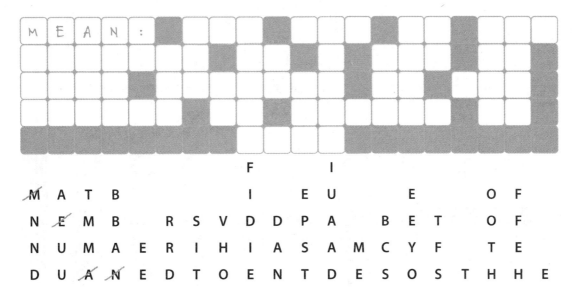

M E A N :

F   I

M A T B   I   E U   E   O F
N E M B   R S V D D P A   B E T   O F
N U M A E R I H I A S A M C Y F   T E
D U A N E D T O E N T D E S O S T H H E

Complete each sentence using the vocabulary list at the beginning of the chapter.

1. The _____ is the number(s) or item(s) that appear most often in a set of data.

2. Numbers that are used to describe the center of a set of data are _____.

3. The difference between the greatest number and the least number in a set of data is the _____.

4. The _____ of a list of values is the value appearing at the center of a sorted version of the list, or the mean of the two central values, if the list contains an even number of values.

5. The _____ is the distance between the first and third quartiles of a data set.

6. A value that is much higher or much lower than the other values of a data set is a(n) _____.

Use Your FOLDABLES

Use your Foldable to help review the chapter. Share your Foldable with a partner and take turns summarizing what you learned in this chapter, while the other partner listens carefully. Seek clarification of any concepts, as needed. **TEKS** 6.1(E)

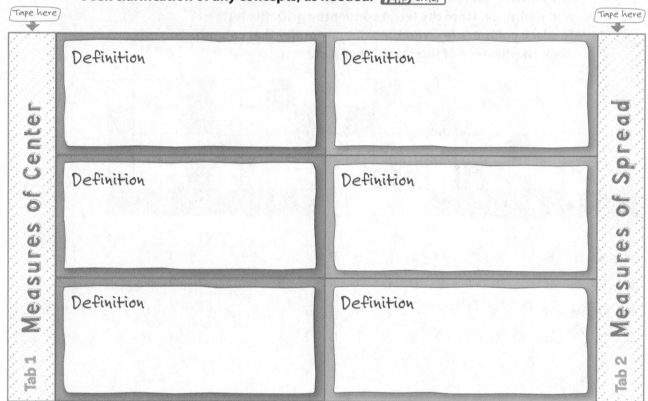

Got it?

Complete the cross number puzzle by finding the mean of each data set.

TEKS 6.12(C)

Across

1. {563, 462, 490}

3. {260, 231, 248, 257}

5. {140, 163, 133, 116}

6. {21, 9, 18}

8. {145, 158, 182, 171}

9. {113, 82, 98, 91}

11. {7960, 8624, 8298, 8366}

12. {4625, 3989, 5465}

Down

1. {62, 58, 51, 41}

2. {5326, 5048, 4968}

3. {269, 293, 281}

4. {103, 89, 98, 98}

7. {720, 597, 756}

8. {142, 169, 150, 155}

10. {588, 615, 652, 653}

11. {70, 89, 90}

13. The table shows the number of cans a homeroom collected for the canned-food drive. How many cans does the homeroom need to bring in on Friday to have an average of 55 cans a day? Show the steps you used and justify your solution.

Day	Cans Collected
Monday	45
Tuesday	50
Wednesday	48
Thursday	60

1 Analyze

2 Plan

3 Solve

4 Justify and Evaluate

_____

_____

_____

Got it?

14. The number of points Erica scored in each round of a game are shown in the table. She scored the lowest amount of points in Round 3. If the range of her scores was 18, how many points did Erica score in round 3? Show the steps you used and justify your solution.

Round	Points Earned
1	89
2	76
3	?
4	84
5	73

N = Number and Operations   **MD** = Measurement and Data   **MP** = Mathematical Processes

Reflect

 Answering the Essential Question

Use what you learned about mean, median, and mode to complete the
graphic organizer. **TEKS** 6.1(D), 6.1(F), 6.1(G)

? Essential Question

HOW are the mean, median,
and mode helpful in
describing data?

	mean	median	mode
definition			
When is it appropriate to use?			
How does an outlier affect it?			

? Answer the Essential Question. HOW are the mean, median,
and mode helpful in describing data? Verbally share your response with
a partner, seeking and providing clarification as needed.

_____

_____

Chapter 11

Personal Financial Literacy

Copyright © McGraw-Hill Education, Photos by Casagrande/Getty Images

Texas Essential Knowledge and Skills

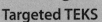

Targeted TEKS

6.14 The student applies mathematical process standards to develop an economic way of thinking and problem solving useful in one's life as a knowledgeable consumer and investor.

Mathematical Processes

6.1, 6.1(A), 6.1(B), 6.1(C), 6.1(D), 6.1(E), 6.1(F), 6.1(G)

Essential Question

HOW can I become a knowledgeable consumer and investor?

Math in the Real World

Paying for College Celia has been accepted to two colleges. One is a private university with out-of-state tuition of $20,000 a year. The other is a nearby public university with tuition of $16,000. Determine which option is more affordable.

Private University	
Out-of-state Tuition	
Housing (per year)	$4,000
Meal Plan (per year)	$3,000
Books (per year)	$1,700
Total Yearly Cost	

Public University	
In-state Tuition	
Housing (per year)	$3,000
Meal Plan (per year)	$3,800
Books (per year)	$2,500
Total Yearly Cost	

Vocabulary

balance a check register	debit card	savings
borrower	deposit	scholarships
checking account	grants	student loans
check register	interest	transaction
credit card	lender	transfer
credit history	lifetime income	withdrawal
credit report	salary	work-study

Review Vocabulary

Deposits and Withdrawals A financial account often consists of money that someone, the *account holder*, has put into a bank or other financial institution. Money that is put into an account is called a *deposit*. The account holder can then take the money out of the account, usually according to certain rules. Money that is taken out of the account is called a *withdrawal*. There are different kinds of banking and investment accounts, which you will learn about in more detail in this chapter. Complete the graphic organizers below to show how the process of depositing money and withdrawing money works. Use the terms *deposit*, *withdrawal*, and *bank account*.

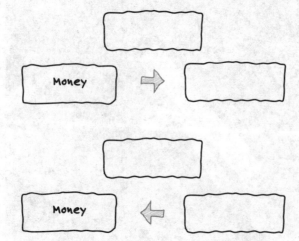

Your Turn! You will solve this problem in the chapter.

Review 6.3(C), 6.3(E) TEKS

Example 1

Tom owes his uncle $37. Write an integer that can represent this situation.

Owing money can be expressed as a negative integer.

So, the integer −$37 represents this situation.

Example 2

Marjorie earns $800 per week. There are 52 weeks in one year. What is her annual salary?

Determine $800 × 52.

```
    800
  ×  52
   1600
+ 40000
 41,600
```

Marjorie's annual salary is $41,600.

Quick Check

Check

Integers **Write an integer to represent each situation.**

1. Jacinta deposited $48 into her checking account. _____

2. Charlotte owes her sister $51. _____

3. Felisa withdrew $19 from her checking account. _____

Multiply Rational Numbers **Determine each annual salary.**

4. Javier earns $1,100 per week. There are 52 weeks in one year.

   What is his annual salary? _____

5. Sara earns $2,350 every two weeks. There are 52 weeks in

   one year. What is her annual salary? _____

6. Gena earns $4,500 every month. What is her annual salary?

How Did You Do?

**Which problems did you answer correctly in the Quick Check?
Shade those exercise numbers below.**

  ① ② ③ ④ ⑤ ⑥

Checking Accounts

Launch the Lesson: Real World

Taylor earned her first paycheck from her after-school job working at a grocery store. But before she spends it, she will put the money in her checking account. A **checking account** is a type of bank account in which users **deposit**, or add, money into the account from which they can make purchases and pay bills. Account holders can also make a **withdrawal**, or take out money from their accounts.

1. Is Taylor's paycheck a deposit or a withdrawal? Explain.

   _____

   _____

2. Taylor wants to take $15 out of her account for bus fare. Will this be a deposit or a withdrawal? Explain.

   _____

   _____

3. Complete the graphic organizer by listing some other examples of deposits and withdrawals.

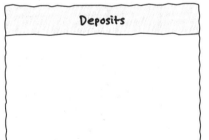

Deposits	Withdrawals

Texas Essential Knowledge and Skills

Targeted TEKS
6.14(A) Compare the features and costs of a checking account and a debit card offered by different local financial institutions. *Also addresses 6.14(C).*

Mathematical Processes
6.1(A), 6.1(B), 6.1(E), 6.1(F), 6.1(G)

Vocab

Vocabulary

balance a check register
checking account
check register
deposit
transaction
transfer
withdrawal

Essential Question

HOW can I become a knowledgeable consumer and investor?

Which MP **Mathematical Processes** did you use?
Shade the circle(s) that applies.

Ⓐ Apply Math to the Real World.
Ⓑ Use a Problem-Solving Model.
Ⓒ Select Tools and Techniques.
Ⓓ Use Multiple Representations.
Ⓔ Organize Ideas.
Ⓕ Analyze Relationships.
Ⓖ Justify Arguments.

Compassionate Eye Foundation/Robert Kent/Getty Images

Copyright © McGraw-Hill Education

Checking Accounts and Debit Cards

A **transaction** is the movement or exchange of money. Deposits and withdrawals are two types of transactions. A **transfer** occurs when money is moved between accounts, such as from a checking into a savings account. A **check register** is a written record of all transactions. To **balance a check register** is to keep an account of all transactions and the final balance in the account.

Examples

Tutor

1. **Meredith's initial balance in her checking account was $117.82 on November 1. Balance the check register to determine the final balance in her checking account on November 30.**

Start with $117.82.
Add each deposit.
Subtract each
withdrawal.

So, Meredith's final

balance is $ _____ .

Check No.	Date	Transaction	Withdrawal	Deposit	Balance
1476	11/03	groceries	$95.38		$
	11/11	transfer from savings		$25.00	$
	11/15	paycheck		$800.00	$
1477	11/15	utility bill	$75.56		$
1478	11/24	rent	$675.00		$
	11/30	paycheck		$800.00	$

- -

2. **Lee is comparing the features and costs of a checking account and debit card offered by the financial institutions shown. If Lee uses online banking and averages 25 transactions a month, which bank should he choose?**

The monthly cost to use Washington Bank is $20.

The monthly cost to use First Savings Bank is $5 + (20 − 10)($0.50) or $10.

Since $10 < $20, Lee should choose First Savings Bank.

> **Washington Bank**
> Checking Accounts
> and Debit Cards
>
> $20 monthly fee for
> unlimited transactions
>
> **FREE** online banking!

> ***First Savings Bank***
>
> **Free checking
> and debit card!***
>
> *up to 15 transactions;
> Each additional transaction costs $0.50.
>
> **$5 monthly fee
> for online banking**

 Show your work.

Got It? Do this problem to find out.

a. Refer to Example 1. On December 1, Meredith wrote a check for $46.75 to pay her cell phone bill. What is her balance after this transaction?

a. _____

Independent Practice

6.14(A), 6.14(D), 6.1(A), 6.1(E), 6.1(F), 6.1(G)

1. Robert's initial balance in his checking account was $89.25 on January 1. Balance the check register to determine the final balance in his checking account on January 31. (Example 1)

So, Robert's final balance is $ _____ .

Check No.	Date	Transaction	Withdrawal	Deposit	Balance
	1/02	paycheck		$460.00	$
880	1/08	cell phone bill	$65.00		$
881	1/11	groceries	$134.05		$
	1/17	paycheck		$460.00	$
	1/29	transfer from savings		$75.00	$
882	1/31	rent	$700.00		$

2. Yolanda's initial balance in her checking account was $234.45 on May 1. Balance the check register to determine the final balance in her checking account on May 30. (Example 1)

So, Yolanda's final balance is $ _____ .

Check No.	Date	Transaction	Withdrawal	Deposit	Balance
1012	5/04	groceries	$102.78		$
	5/12	paycheck		$917.00	$
1013	5/19	credit card bill	$322.00		$
1014	5/21	utility bill	$129.29		$
1015	5/27	rent	$510.00		$
	5/30	paycheck		$917.00	$

For Exercises 3–6, refer to the checking account features shown. (Example 2)

3. If Parker uses online banking and averages 20 transactions a month, which bank should he choose? Justify your response.

_____

_____

_____

FIRST CITY BANK
Checking Accounts
and Debit Cards

$9.99 monthly fee
for unlimited transactions
Free online banking!

4. If Parker doesn't use online banking and averages 20 transactions a month, which bank should he choose? Justify your response.

_____

_____

MAIN STREET BANK
CHECKING ACCOUNTS
AND DEBIT CARDS

Free Checking!*
*up to 10 transactions;
Each additional transaction costs $0.15

$4.99 monthly fee for online banking

5. If Parker uses online banking and averages 45 transactions a month, which bank should he choose? Justify your response.

_____

_____

6. If Parker doesn't use online banking and averages 45 transactions a month, which bank should he choose? Justify your response.

_____

_____

Multi-Step Problem Solving

Use a problem-solving model to solve each problem.

7. The activity of an account with a beginning balance of $300 is shown below. A transaction on November 4th brings the balance to $600. What was the transaction?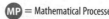

Date	Transaction	Amount
10/28	deposit	$452
11/2	withdrawal	$50
11/3	transfer from Savings	$200

- Ⓐ a withdrawal of $342
- Ⓑ a deposit of $158
- Ⓒ a deposit of $58
- Ⓓ a withdrawal of $302

8. A local bank offers a checking account that charges an annual fee of $50, but waives that fee if you sign up for online banking. The bank charges an ATM fee of $2.50 per transaction. If you opened that checking account, signed up for online banking and made 5 ATM transactions each month, what would the account cost per year, rounded to the nearest dollar?

- Ⓐ $50
- Ⓑ $150
- Ⓒ $120
- Ⓓ $200

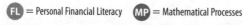

FL = Personal Financial Literacy   **MP** = Mathematical Processes

FL Personal Financial Literacy Project

Compare Checking Accounts Use the Internet or another source to look up several checking accounts offered by several local banks or financial institutions. Identify at least two different kinds of checking accounts from at least three banks, and compare and contrast the features and fees for each. Make sure you note whether they require minimum balances or direct deposit from an employer. Also make note of any fees associated with the accounts, including how often they are charged and for what reasons they might be waived. Determine the overall cost of each account and identify the most and least expensive options. **TEKS** 6.14(A), 6.14(C), 6.1(A), 6.1(E), 6.1(F), 6.1(G)

Debit and Credit Cards

Launch the Lesson: Vocabulary

A **debit card** is a card that allows a buyer to make purchases while immediately removing money from a linked account. A purchase made with a **credit card** allows a buyer to put off paying for a purchase , but the buyer may have to pay interest. **Interest** is a charge for the use of credit or borrowed money, if the balance is not paid off in a set amount of time. Use the terms *debit card* and *credit card* to label the Venn diagram.

1. Add the letters of the following statements to their correct locations in the Venn diagram.

    A. immediately removes money from a linked account

    B. allows a buyer to make purchases

    C. allows the buyer to put off payment

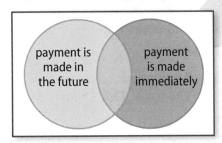

payment is made in the future   payment is made immediately

Real-World Link

2. Jared's uncle used a credit card to purchase a lawnmower that cost $225. The store will offer him no interest charges for six months if he uses the store credit card. The minimum monthly payment is $25. If he only pays the minimum payment each month, will he pay off the debt in six months? Justify your response.

Which **MP** Mathematical Processes did you use?
Shade the circle(s) that applies.

Ⓐ Apply Math to the Real World.

Ⓑ Use a Problem-Solving Model.

Ⓒ Select Tools and Techniques.

Ⓓ Use Multiple Representations.

Ⓔ Organize Ideas.

Ⓕ Analyze Relationships.

Ⓖ Justify Arguments.

Distinguish between Debit Cards and Credit Cards

Debit Card Features	Credit Card Features
• The purchase amount is immediately removed from a linked account, such as a checking account. • Many debit cards also work in ATMs. • Penalties are charged if the buyer spends more than the money in the linked account. • Debit cards allow the user to withdraw cash.	• Allow payments to be made in the future. • Credit cards have an assigned spending limit, and affect the user's credit rating. • Interest might be charged on the borrowed amount if the amount is not fully repaid. • Some credit cards allow the user to withdraw cash.

Examples

Tutor

Determine the effects of using a debit card or credit card for the purchase.

1. **Anna needs to pay a fee to participate in a soccer league. The fee is $25. She has $122.50 in her checking account.**

If Anna uses her debit card, the amount will immediately be removed from her checking account, but she will not have to pay an interest fee. If she uses a credit card, she may have to pay interest, but her checking account is not immediately affected.

2. **Eileen needs to purchase a new refrigerator that costs $1,100. The store offers no interest if she uses the store credit card and the balance is paid in full within six months. She has $1,200 in her checking account. Compare the advantages and disadvantages to using either a debit card or a credit card.**

Special Deal!
Refrigerators on Sale!

No interest for six months when you use your credit card!

If Eileen uses her debit card, she will not have to pay interest. However, she will only have $100 in her checking account after the purchase. If Eileen uses her credit card, she can defer the payments into the future, but she will have to pay interest after six months.

Show your work.

Got It? Do this problem to find out.

a. Seth will purchase a video game that costs $49.99. He has $235.00 in his checking account. Compare the advantages and disadvantages to using either a debit card or credit card.

a. _____

Independent Practice

Determine the effects of using a debit card or credit card for the purchase.
(Example 1)

1. Shannon will pay for an annual gym membership that costs $420. She has
$152.62 in her checking account.

_____

_____

_____

_____

2. Mr. Jenkins will purchase a riding lawnmower that costs $1,350. The store
offers no interest if he uses the store credit card and the balance is paid in
full within one year. He has $1,500 in his checking account. Compare the
advantages and disadvantages to using either a debit card or a credit card.
(Example 2)

Special Deal!
Riding Lawnmowers on sale!

No interest for one year
when you use your
credit card!

_____

_____

_____

3. **MP** **Apply Math to the Real World** Refer to the graphic novel frame below.
If a consumer pays only the minimum payment due, will they owe interest
fees on their next statement? Explain.

_____

_____

Multi-Step Problem Solving

Use a problem-solving model to solve each problem.

4. Cameron will spend $285.00 for a car repair. He has $277.00 in the account linked to his debit card. The bank charges a $7 penalty fee, per day, for using his debit card to make a purchase if he doesn't have enough funds in his account. What will he pay altogether if he chooses to use his debit card and doesn't put any more money in his account for 6 days? **FL MP**

Ⓐ $243.00

Ⓑ $285.00

Ⓒ $292.00

Ⓓ $327.00

5. Joan will spend $498.00 on a new washing machine. She will use her credit card to withdraw $500 cash to pay for the machine. The credit card company charges a $5.00 cash-withdrawal fee and 2% interest on the borrowed amount, but not including the cash-withdrawal fee. How much will Joan owe after one month? **FL P MP**

Ⓐ $515.00

Ⓑ $510.00

Ⓒ $505.00

Ⓓ $500.00

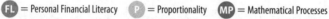 **FL** = Personal Financial Literacy   **P** = Proportionality   **MP** = Mathematical Processes

FL Personal Financial Literacy Project

Credit Cards and Debit Cards Many college students receive numerous offers for credit cards and debit cards when they enroll at a university. Visit the Web sites of a few public and private universities. Locate banks that sponsor these schools or that advertise on their Web sites. Research the charges associated with the credit cards and debit cards offered to students by at least three of these banks. Then compare these rates to the median credit card rates. The median rates can often be found in the financial section of a newspaper or on a news Web site.

TEKS 6.14(B), 6.1A, 6.1(B), 6.1(E), 6.1(F)

Credit Reports

Launch the Lesson: Real World

Michaela wants to obtain a loan to buy a car, but cannot because she hasn't established a **credit history**, or record of financial performance. Her credit history is reflected in her **credit report**, which is a summary of her financial history, including whether payments are made on time, how much debt a person has, and whether or not they have a history of repaying their debt. This report was requested by a **lender**, or someone who loans money, of a **borrower**, or someone who borrows money.

Michaela needs to prove she can successfully repay a loan to establish a positive credit history. A positive credit history is reflected in a high credit score.

Draw lines to match each action with whether that action will help build a positive credit history or a negative credit history.

1. Pay bills on time.

2. Borrow money that you can repay.

   • positive credit history

3. Acquire some debt, such as a loan.

   • negative credit history

4. Borrow more than you can repay.

5. Make late payments that will be reported to a credit reporting agency.

Texas Essential Knowledge and Skills

Targeted TEKS
6.14(E) Describe the information in a credit report and how long it is retained. *Also addresses 6.14(D), 6.14(F).*

Mathematical Processes
6.1(A), 6.1(B), 6.1(E), 6.1(F), 6.1(G)

Vocabulary
borrower
credit history
credit report
lender

Essential Question
HOW can I become a knowledgeable consumer and investor?

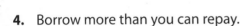

Which MP Mathematical Processes did you use? Shade the circle(s) that applies.

(A) Apply Math to the Real World.

(E) Organize Ideas.

(B) Use a Problem-Solving Model.

(F) Analyze Relationships.

(C) Select Tools and Techniques.

(G) Justify Arguments.

(D) Use Multiple Representations.

The Value of Credit Reports

Credit reports and scores are important because showing a positive credit history allows consumers to borrow money at lower interest rates.

Credit reports and credit scores are important to lenders because lenders might choose not to extend credit to a consumer with a negative credit history. Credit scores typically have a range from 300 to 850, with a higher value indicating a positive credit history. Negative credit actions are usually reflected on a credit report for at least seven years.

Examples

Tutor

1. **Identify the two borrowers most likely to be offered a loan, if the decision was solely based on their credit scores. Justify your response.**

Name	Credit Score	Name	Credit Score
J. Byrnes	660	F. Rodriguez	785
P. McMahon	750	K. Simmons	810

The individuals with the two highest credit scores are F. Rodriguez and K. Simmons. Those borrowers would most likely be offered a loan.

2. **The table shows some of the actions taken by two different borrowers. Explain the effect of these actions on each credit score. How long will any negative credit actions be reflected in the credit report?**

Name	Action
M. Gibson	Paid credit card bill late three months in a row.
T. Wilson	Repaid entire car loan early.

Making late payments on a credit card bill will lower M. Gibson's credit score. Repaying a loan early, or on time, will raise T. Wilson's credit score. The negative credit actions will usually remain in each individual's credit report for 7 years.

Show your work.

Got It? Do these problems to find out.

a. Identify the borrowers least likely to be offered a loan, if the decision was solely based on their credit scores. Justify your response.

Name	Credit Score	Name	Credit Score
M. Anderson	620	P. Pinckney	580
Y. Ling	495	R. Zengler	725

b. Mr. Watson paid his mortgage payment late four months in a row. Explain the effect of this action on his credit score.

a. _____

b. _____

Independent Practice

6.14(D), 6.14(E), 6.1(A), 6.1(E), 6.1(F), 6.1(G) TEKS

Complete each exercise using what you learned about credit reports.

1. Identify the two borrowers most likely to be offered a loan, if the decision was solely based on their credit scores. Justify your response. (Example 1)

Name	Credit Score	Name	Credit Score
A. Bailey	665	J. Moore	710
M. Caprette	770	H. Bixler	825

2. Identify the two borrowers least likely to be offered a loan, if the decision was solely based on their credit scores. Justify your response. (Example 1)

Name	Credit Score	Name	Credit Score
T. Evans	480	R. Alvarez	774
H. Sanchez	815	W. Burton	570

3. The table shows some of the actions taken by three different borrowers. Explain the effect of these actions on the credit scores for each borrower. How long will any negative credit actions be reflected in the credit report? (Example 2) _____

Name	Action
M. Lombardo	Made all of her student loan payments on time.
F. Johnson	Borrowed more than he could repay.
R. Garrett	Made 6 late car payments in one year.

4. Explain why it is important to establish a positive credit history.

5. Explain the value of credit reports to borrowers and to lenders.

Identify each statement as *true* or *false*. If the statement is false, correct it by writing a true statement.

6. Paying my bills late will most likely cause my credit score to go down.

7. My credit report cannot affect my future ability to obtain a loan.

8. A credit report is always correct and does not contain any errors.

9. Negative actions on a credit report usually remain for 7 years.

Use a problem-solving model to solve each problem.

10. Sarita has a credit score of 825. Jordan has a credit score that is $\frac{2}{3}$ that of Sarita's score. Jordan increased his credit score by 100 points when he fully repaid his student loan. Then his credit score decreased by 27 points when he made two late payments on his credit card. What is his credit score? (FL) (N) (MP)

    (A) 550

    (B) 650

    (C) 623

    (D) 677

11. Pedro has a credit score of 895 and Bettina has a credit score of 768. A banker has determined that both will receive a credit card, however, the borrower with the lowest credit score will be charged a $50.00 fee. If both receive a credit card with $1,500.00 available credit, what will Pedro's remaining available credit be after he buys a $425.00 bicycle? (FL) (MP)

    (A) $1,450.00

    (B) $1,075.00

    (C) $1,025.00

    (D) $475.00

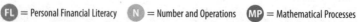

(FL) = Personal Financial Literacy   (N) = Number and Operations   (MP) = Mathematical Processes

(FL) Personal Financial Literacy Project

Credit Reports Use the internet to identify the three major credit reporting companies. Compare and contrast the type of information each reporting company collects about a consumer and how that information is used. Determine how each of the three companies determines a credit score, including the criteria and variables each uses.   **TEKS** 6.14(E), 6.1(A), 6.1(B), 6.1(E)

Paying for College

There are many ways to pay for school. Juan already has some money set aside, his **savings**, to pay for college, but he needs to find additional funds to pay the cost of tuition at the school he wishes to attend.

He might choose to apply for **student loans**, borrowed amounts that he will have to repay, usually with interest.

1. The college of his choice has an annual tuition of $13,000. If Juan attends college for four years, how much will he need to pay altogether for tuition?

2. Juan has $15,000 in his savings account to help pay for college. If he uses the entire amount, how much more will he need to pay for four years of college?

3. Juan borrows $11,000 to help pay for the second year of college. If the loan has an annual interest rate of 6.5%, how much interest would he owe at the end of one year, if he does not make any payments? (*Hint:* Determine 6.5% of $11,000.)

4. How much will Juan owe altogether on the loan at the end of his second year of college?

Which MP **Mathematical Processes** did you use?
Shade the circle(s) that applies.

Ⓐ Apply Math to the Real World.

Ⓑ Use a Problem-Solving Model.

Ⓒ Select Tools and Techniques.

Ⓓ Use Multiple Representations.

Ⓔ Organize Ideas.

Ⓕ Analyze Relationships.

Ⓖ Justify Arguments.

Texas Essential Knowledge and Skills

Targeted TEKS
6.14(G) Explain various methods to pay for college, including through savings, grants, scholarships, student loans, and work-study.

Mathematical Processes
6.1(A), 6.1(B), 6.1(E), 6.1(F), 6.1(G)

Vocabulary Vocab

savings

grants

scholarships

student loans

work-study

Essential Question
HOW can I become a knowledgeable consumer and investor?

Explain Methods to Pay for College

Student loans require repayment. There are other options that can help pay for college, that do not require repayment. **Grants** are awards from non-profit organizations, and **scholarships** are awards for good performance. Neither grants nor scholarships require repayment. **Work-study** is a program providing financial aid in return for student labor.

Examples

Tutor

Victor wants to attend a four-year university with an annual tuition of $14,850. He has $17,000 in savings and earned a scholarship for $4,000 for each year of college.

1. **How much more does Victor need to pay for the tuition for all four years?**

> **Step 1** Determine the total amount of the tuition for four years.
>
> $14,850 × 4 = $59,400

> **Step 2** Subtract the amount of savings.
>
> $59,400 − $17,000 = $42,400

> **Step 3** Subtract the amount of the scholarship.
>
> $4,000 × 4 = $16,000 The scholarships pays $4,000 each year for 4 years.
>
> $42,400 − $16,000 = $26,400

So, Victor will need an additional $26,400 to pay the tuition for all four years.

- - - - - - - - - - - - - - - - -

2. **Explain the advantages and disadvantages of Victor using a student loan, grant, or work-study for the remaining $26,400.**

A student loan requires repayment, usually with interest.

A grant does not require repayment, but Victor would have to apply for a grant. It is often easier to obtain a student loan than a grant.

Work-study does not require repayment, but Victor would have to work while he went to school, which could interfere with his studies.

Got It? Do this problem to find out.

Show your work.

a. Melanie wants to attend a two-year technical college. The annual tuition is $4,720. She has $3,800 saved and earned a grant for $1,900 each year. How much more does she need to pay the tuition for both years?

a. _____

Scholarships

Scholarships are usually rewards for performance, whether academic, athletic, or cross-curricular. They are usually competitive. If you are interested in pursuing a scholarship, you should talk to your school guidance counselor.

Independent Practice

Samuel wants to attend a four-year university with an annual tuition of $16,700. He has $21,000 in savings and earned a grant for $6,000 for each year of college.

1. How much more does Samuel need to pay for the tuition for all four years? (Example 1) _____

2. Explain the advantages and disadvantages of Samuel using a student loan or a scholarship to pay for the remaining amount. (Example 2)

_____

_____

_____

_____

Mei-Ling wants to attend a two-year university with an annual tuition of $8,250. She has $5,000 in savings and earned a work-study for $3,500 per year.

3. How much more does Mei-Ling need to pay for the tuition for both years? (Example 1) _____

4. Mei-Ling will take out a student loan to pay the additional cost. The annual interest rate is 6.25%. How much will Mei-Ling owe, in interest, at the end of one year if she does not repay the loan? _____

5. Explain the advantages and disadvantages of Mei-Ling using a student loan or a grant to pay for the remaining amount. (Example 2)

_____

_____

_____

6. Luis will attend a four-year university. The annual tuition is $13,875. The table shows the methods of payment that Luis is considering to help pay for the tuition. Describe one possible combination of methods that Luis could use to pay for college. Justify your response.

_____

_____

Method of Payment	Amount ($)
grant	$4,500 per year
savings	$19,700
scholarship	$5,400 per year
work-study	$7,000 per year
student loan	any amount with an interest rate of 7.5%

Multi-Step Problem Solving

Use a problem-solving model to solve each problem.

7. Katarina has a college savings account worth $8,000, which is $\frac{2}{3}$ the amount of one year's tuition at a four-year institution. She receives a scholarship for $16,000 and a grant for half of her first year of tuition, which only applies to the first year. She will take out a student loan on the remaining amount. How much will she need to borrow? **FL** **MP**

Ⓐ $32,000.00

Ⓑ $28,000.00

Ⓒ $18,000.00

Ⓓ $4,000.00

8. James has a college savings account worth $14,000. Tuition at his two-year technical college is $12,000 per year. He receives a scholarship for $\frac{1}{4}$ the amount of one year's tuition, renewable each year. He decides to participate in a work-study that pays him the remaining amount he needs. How much will the work-study pay him? **FL** **MP**

Ⓐ $ 4,000.00

Ⓑ $ 7,000.00

Ⓒ $10,000.00

Ⓓ $14,000.00

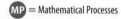 **FL** = Personal Financial Literacy   **MP** = Mathematical Processes

FL Personal Financial Literacy Project

Saving for College Determine the annual cost of tuition for a college of your choice. Assume you receive a grant for two-thirds of this tuition cost. Assuming you have no money already saved, how much would you need to borrow to have enough money available for the other third of your college tuition? Research student loan rates online. How much interest would you be charged if you had to borrow the entire cost of tuition for your final year of college? **TEKS** 6.14(H), 6.1(A), 6.1(B), 6.1(E), 6.1(F), 6.1(G)

Compare Annual Salaries

Launch the Lesson: Real World

A **salary** is a payment for work. **Lifetime income** is the total amount a worker is paid during his working career.

Lucinda is thinking about becoming a veterinarian or a veterinary technician. The table gives the average annual salary and number of years of *post-secondary*, or post high-school training required for each career.

Career	Average Annual Salary ($)	Number of Years of Education
Veterinarian	82,000	8
Veterinary Technician	30,000	2

1. If Lucinda started working as a veterinarian at age 26, and worked for 39 years, what will her lifetime income be? Assume the annual salary remained the same each year.

2. If Lucinda started working as a veterinary technician at age 20, and worked until age 65, for how many years will she work?

3. If Lucinda started working as a veterinary technician at age 20, and worked until age 65, what will her lifetime income be? Assume the annual salary remained the same each year.

4. Compare the lifetime incomes Lucinda could earn as a veterinarian or a veterinary technician.

Which MP **Mathematical Processes** did you use? Shade the circle(s) that applies.

(A) Apply Math to the Real World.

(B) Use a Problem-Solving Model.

(C) Select Tools and Techniques.

(D) Use Multiple Representations.

(E) Organize Ideas.

(F) Analyze Relationships.

(G) Justify Arguments.

Texas Essential Knowledge and Skills TEKS

Targeted TEKS
6.14(H) Compare the annual salary of several occupations requiring various levels of post-secondary education or vocational training and calculate the effects of the different annual salaries on lifetime income.

Mathematical Processes
6.1(A), 6.1(B), 6.1(E), 6.1(F), 6.1(G)

Vocab

Vocabulary

salary

lifetime income

Essential Question

HOW can I become a knowledgeable consumer and investor?

Compare Annual Salaries of Occupations

Although not always true, the annual salary of an occupation typically increases as the number of years of post-secondary training increases.

Examples

Tutor

1. **Calculate and compare the lifetime incomes for a programmer analyst and a medical transcriptionist. Assume a career of 30 years.**

Career	Average Annual Salary ($)	Number of Years of Education
Programmer analyst	74,960	4
Computer support specialist	46,260	2

Determine the lifetime income for a programmer analyst.

$74,960 \times 30 = \$2,248,800$

Determine the lifetime income for a computer support specialist.

$46,260 \times 30 = \$1,387,800$

A programmer analyst earns $2,248,800 − $1,387,800, or $861,000, more in lifetime income than a computer support specialist.

2. **Calculate and compare the lifetime incomes for a physical therapist's assistant and a physical therapist. Assume a career of 35 years.**

Career	Average Annual Salary ($)	Number of Years of Education
Physical therapist's assistant	37,710	2
Physical therapist	75,000	6

Determine the lifetime income for a physical therapist's assistant.

$37,710 \times 35 = \$1,319,850$

Determine the lifetime income for a physical therapist.

$75,000 \times 35 = \$2,625,000$

A physical therapist earns $2,625,000 − $1,319,850, or $1,305,150, more in lifetime income than a physical therapist's assistant.

Show your work.

Got It? Do this problem to find out.

a. Calculate and compare the lifetime income for an auto mechanic and an insurance agent. Assume a career of 40 years.

Career	Average Annual Salary ($)	Number of Years of Education
Auto mechanic	35,790	0
Insurance agent	46,770	0

a. _____

Independent Practice

1. Felipe is considering becoming a travel agent or a real estate agent. Calculate and compare the lifetime incomes for a travel agent and a real estate agent. Assume a career of 40 years. (Examples 1 and 2)

Career	Average Annual Salary ($)	Number of Years of Education
Travel agent	31,870	0
Real estate agent	42,600	0

_____

_____

_____

2. Lisa is considering becoming a pharmacist or a registered nurse. Calculate and compare the lifetime incomes for a pharmacist and a registered nurse. Assume a career of 30 years. (Examples 1 and 2)

Career	Average Annual Salary ($)	Number of Years of Education
Pharmacist	111,570	8
Registered nurse	64,960	2

_____

_____

_____

3. Daniela is considering becoming a high school teacher or a librarian. Calculate and compare the lifetime incomes for a high school teacher and a librarian. Assume a career of 35 years. (Examples 1 and 2)

Career	Average Annual Salary ($)	Number of Years of Education
High school teacher	53,230	4
Librarian	54,500	6

_____

_____

_____

4. Matthew is considering becoming a social worker or a delivery truck driver. Calculate and compare the lifetime incomes for a social worker and a delivery truck driver. Assume a career of 40 years. (Examples 1 and 2)

Career	Average Annual Salary ($)	Number of Years of Education
Social worker	42,480	4
Delivery truck driver	27,050	0

_____

_____

_____

Multi-Step Problem Solving

Use a problem-solving model to solve each problem.

5. Brian wants to become a sales manager. The number of years of college needed to become a sales manager is 4 years. The average annual income is $60,000. If Brian starts college at age 18, gets a job immediately out of college, and works until age 65, what will his lifetime income be? **FL** **MP**

- Ⓐ $1,800,000
- Ⓑ $1,980,000
- Ⓒ $2,580,000
- Ⓓ $2,820,000

6. Justine earned a total lifetime income of $1,050,000 as a flight attendant. Her sister Abigail earned a total lifetime income of $4,800,000 as an attorney. If each sister worked for 30 years, how much greater was Abigail's annual salary than Justine's? **FL** **MP**

- Ⓐ $3,750,000
- Ⓑ $125,000
- Ⓒ $160,000
- Ⓓ $35,000

 **FL** = Personal Financial Literacy **MP** = Mathematical Processes

FL Personal Financial Literacy Project

Lifetime Income Identify four different careers that interest you. Research each career to determine the following.

- a description of the tasks performed or job responsibilities
- years of secondary education required to train for the career
- the median annual income
- the lifetime income, if you worked until age 65
- the job outlook

Select the career in which you are the most interested and make a list of steps that you could start now, both educationally and financially, to ensure your success in this career in the future. **TEKS** TEKS 6.14(H), 6.1(B)

Chapter Review

Vocabulary Check

Work with a partner to complete the crossword puzzle using the vocabulary list at the beginning of the chapter.

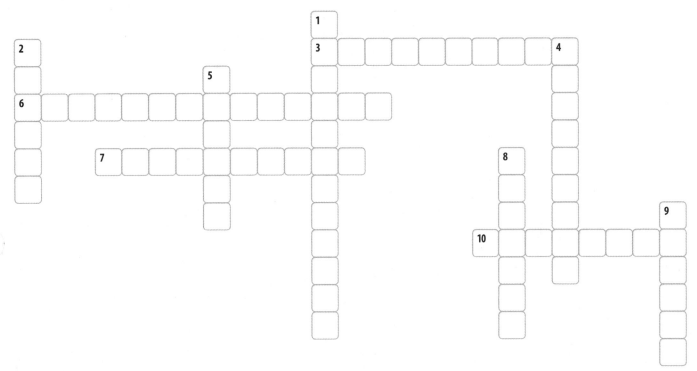

Down

1. awards for good performance
2. payment for work
4. a form of immediate payment
5. one who loans money
8. to put money in an account
9. awards from non-profit organizations

Across

3. a form of payment that allows a consumer to pay later
6. the amount a worker is paid in his entire career
7. the money taken from an account
10. one who takes money that must be repaid

Key Concept Check

1. Complete the graphic organizer to compare and contrast credit cards and debit cards. TEKS 6.14(G), 6.1(E)

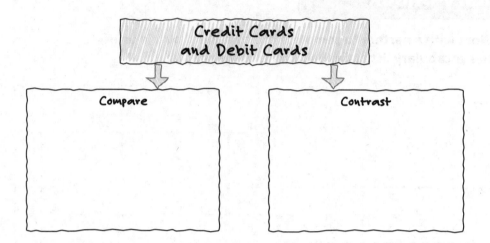

Credit Cards and Debit Cards

Compare

Contrast

2. Complete the graphic organizer to explain some of the various ways to pay for college. TEKS 6.14 (G), 6.1(E)

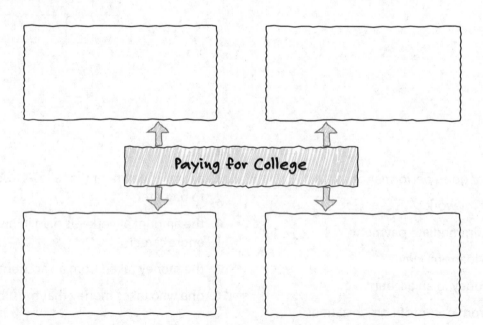

Paying for College

Multi-Step Problem Solving

3. The table shows the amount of funding Joanna will receive to attend a 2-year technical school. Tuition will cost $12,000 each year. She will take out a student loan on the remaining amount. If Joanna earns an average income of $32,000 per year after she graduates and pays back $2,000 of her student loan each year, how many years will it take her to repay her student loan, not including interest? **FL MP**

Method of Payment for College	Amount
Savings	$3,500.00
Scholarships	$4,000.00
Grants	$1,800.00

1 Analyze

2 Plan

3 Solve

4 Justify and Evaluate

_____

_____

_____

_____

Got it?

4. The table shows the amount of funding Hugo will receive to attend a 4-year college. Tuition will cost $8,000 each year. He will take out a student loan on the remaining amount. If Hugo pays back $250 of his student loan each month, how many years will it take him to repay his student loan, not including interest? **FL MP**

Method of Payment for College	Amount
Savings	$11,500.00
Scholarships	$6,000.00

_____

_____

_____

FL = Personal Financial Literacy   **MP** = Mathematical Processes

Reflect

 ## Answering the Essential Question

Use what you learned about financial literacy to complete the graphic organizer.

Checking Accounts and Debit and Credit Cards

Credit Reports

? Essential Question

HOW can I become a knowledgeable consumer and investor?

Paying for College

Compare Annual Salaries

Collaborate

? Answer the Essential Question. HOW can I become a knowledgeable consumer and investor? Verbally share your response with a partner, asking for and giving help, as needed.

Copyright © McGraw-Hill Education   (l to r)Antonio M. Rosario/Photographer's Choice/Getty Images, LatinStock Collection/Alamy, Corbis/PunchStock, L. Mouton/PhotoAlto, Mitch Reardon/Stone/Getty Images

Problem-Solving Projects

Real World

In the Problem-Solving Projects, you will apply the math you have learned so far to everyday life, society, and the workplace. Try them!

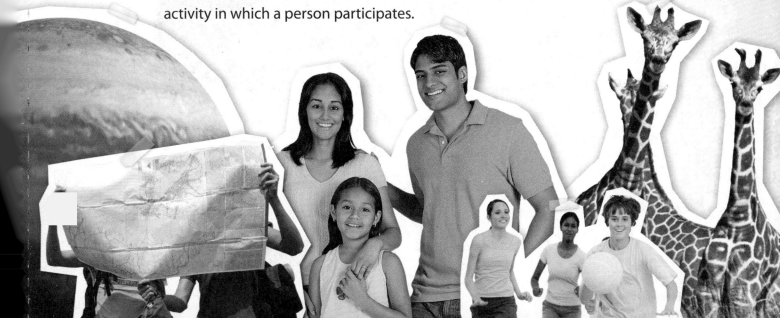

How will I get started?

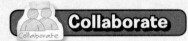**Collaborate**

⏻ **Go Online** You will work with a partner, or in a small group, to explore, research, and investigate a particular aspect of how mathematics is used in the real world. Each project will provide you with suggested activities in which to start your investigation.

▷ You can go online to watch a video about the description of your project.

Use the guiding questions in the Analyze section to help narrow your focus in your project and to help you think critically about how specific math topics you have learned are applied in the real world.

What will I do once the project is completed?

**Share**

Your group will prepare a presentation to share your results with your classmates.

Some ways in which you can demonstrate what you learned are to…

- create a powerpoint presentation.
- create a presentation, using an online presentation tool.
- create a video.
- create a music video.
- create a Web page or blog.
- create an advertisement.
- create a poster.
- create a brochure.
- write a letter.

PROJECT 1

Targeted TEKS
6.4(B), 6.4(C), 6.4(G),
6.12(A), 6.12(C), 6.13(A)

Watch ▶ **People Everywhere** Federal, state, and local governments use population data that are gathered from the U.S. Census to help them plan what services communities need. In this project you will:

- **Collaborate** with your classmates to collect data and to compare populations within Texas, your county, or city.

- **Share** the results of your research in a creative way.

- **? Reflect** on how you use mathematics to describe change and model real-world situations.

By the end of this project, you will have a better understanding of the population of people that live around you!

Collaborate

Go Online Work with your group to research and complete each activity. You will use your results in the Share section on the following page.

1. Use the U.S. Census Web site to find the total population for Texas. Then compare the following:
   - the ratio of males to females
   - the ratio of people in your age group to those in any other age group

2. Research the population density of Texas. Compare the results with all of the surrounding states. Plot your results on a number line. How does your state compare to others?

3. Research the growth rate of the population of Texas over the past ten U.S. Census reports. Display your results in a table and a line graph. Describe any patterns in the line graph.

4. Explain in a journal entry or blog how you could use population data to predict the population of Texas in 2020.

5. One way federal funds are distributed to states and counties is based on their population. Research the population of your county, as well as the surrounding counties. If $1,000,000 is to be divided among the counties, about what fraction of the money do you think your county would receive? Why?

Share

With your group, decide on a way to present what you have learned from each of the activities about the population of your state according to the U.S. Census. Some suggestions are listed below, but you can also think of other creative ways to present your information. Remember to show how you used math to complete each of the activities in this project!

- Create a presentation using the data you collected. Your presentation should include a spreadsheet, graph, and one other visual display.

- Write a persuasive letter to a local government official. In the letter, explain what you have learned in this project. Then lobby to have a new service provided for your community. This could be a new park, school, hospital, or whatever you think your community needs.

Check out the note on the right to connect this project with other subjects.

connect with **Science**

Environmental Literacy Select two states, other than Texas, and research the types of landforms found in these states. Some questions to consider are:

- What different types of landforms are found in these states?

- How do the landforms found in these states compare with those found in Texas?

Reflect

On Your Own

6. **Answer the Essential Question** How can you use mathematics to describe change and model real-world situations?

a. How did you use what you learned about ratios and rates to describe change and model the real-world situations in this project?

_____

_____

_____

b. How did you use what you learned about fractions, decimals, and percents to describe change and model the real-world situations in this project?

_____

_____

_____

PROJECT 2

Targeted TEKS
6.3(E), 6.11, 6.12(A),
6.1(A), 6.1(C), 6.1(D), 6.1(E)

Watch ▶ **Get Out the Map!** If you could go anywhere in the world, where would you go? This is your chance to explore someplace new. In this project you will:

- **Collaborate** with your classmates as you investigate a new place you would like to travel.
- **Share** the results of your research in a creative way.
- **?** **Reflect** on how mathematical ideas can be represented.

By the end of this project, you will have a better understanding of how to use a map to plan the perfect adventure!

Collaborate

⏻ Go Online Work with your group to research and complete each activity. You will use your results in the Share section on the following page.

1. Think of someplace new that you would like to travel. Investigate the population of the area you choose as well as any interesting geographical features. Make a list of area attractions that you'd like to visit, such as museums, amusement parks, historical sites, national parks, and so on.

2. Research information about the climate for the area of your location in the time of year you are planning to travel. Important information could include the monthly rainfall, the average daily high and low temperatures, humidity levels, and wind speeds. Create a visual display to share your results.

3. Find lodging in the location you chose. Then, using maps and descriptions available on the Internet, plot three or four area attractions on a coordinate plane. Label each point.

4. Create a budget for each day of the trip showing the cost of the travel, lodging, daily activities, and food. Calculate the cost for your entire family, not just yourself.

5. Use an online map or GPS device to determine the actual distances you will need to travel to get from where you are staying to any attraction you plan to visit. Then find the total distance you will travel during the entire trip.

Share

With your group, decide on a way to present what you have learned from each of the activities about the planning the perfect adventure. Some suggestions are listed below, but you can also think of other creative ways to present your information. Remember to show how you used math to complete each of the activities in this project!

- Create a travel brochure for your current location. Your objective is to increase the tourists for your town. The brochure should include each of the following: a detailed map, recommended restaurants, area attractions, and fun facts.

- Write a journal entry from the perspective of an early explorer who, 1,000 years ago, traveled to the location you chose. Then describe how technology makes planning, budgeting, and navigating at the same location much easier today.

connect with Science

Use the Internet to research what technology was used by early explorers to navigate through unknown territories. Some questions to consider are:

- What tools were used to help explorers travel in the right direction?

- What constellations were used by the explorers and how were they used?

Check out the note on the right to connect this project with other subjects.

Reflect

6. **?** **Answer the Essential Question** How can mathematical ideas be represented?

   a. How did you use what you learned about computing with multi-digit numbers, and multiplying and dividing fractions to represent mathematical ideas in this project?

   _____

   _____

   _____

   b. How did you use what you learned about integers and the coordinate plane to represent mathematical ideas in this project?

   _____

   _____

   _____

PROJECT 3

Targeted TEKS
6.4(C), 6.4(D), 6.5(A), 6.11,
6.12(C), 6.1(A), 6.1(C),
6.1(D), 6.1(E)

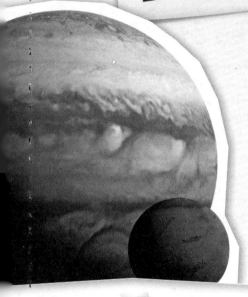

Watch ▷ **It's Out of This World** How fast do objects in our solar system travel through space? Let's explore the orbital speed of different planets and satellites! In this project you will:

- **Collaborate** with your classmates as you investigate the orbital speed of three planets.
- **Share** the results of your research in a creative way.
- ❓ **Reflect** on how you communicate mathematical ideas effectively.

Collaborate

⏻ **Go Online** Work with your group to research and complete each activity. You will use your results in the Share section on the following page.

1. Choose three planets in our solar system. Use the Internet to research each planet and find its average orbital speed in miles per second or kilometers per second. Organize the information in a table.

2. Find and record the orbital distance traveled in 1, 2, and 3 seconds for each planet you chose in Exercise 1. Then describe how the orbital distance of each planet changes with time.

3. For your three planets, list the ordered pairs representing (time, distance). Graph each set of ordered pairs on a coordinate plane and connect each set of points with a line. Compare the graphs. Then write equations to represent each relationship.

4. Research artificial satellites, such as the Hubble Space Telescope, that are orbiting Earth. Use the Internet to research three different satellites and determine the purpose of those satellites. Write a summary of your findings.

5. For each satellite you found in Exercise 4, find and record its average orbital speed in miles per second or kilometers per second. Organize the information in a table. Compare the orbital speeds.

With your group, decide on a way to present what you have learned from each of the activities. Some suggestions are listed below, but you can also think of other creative ways to present your information. Remember to show how you used math to complete each of the activities of this project!

- Create a presentation using the data you collected. Your presentation should include a spreadsheet, graph, and one other visual display.

- Write an article that would be published in a magazine from the perspective of a scientist. Include any important information that you found while researching the orbital speed of each planet.

Check out the note on the right to connect this project with other subjects.

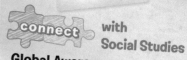

connect with **Social Studies**

Global Awareness Research the history of space exploration and write a summary of your findings. Some questions to consider are:

- What have scientists in the U.S. and other countries discovered recently about the solar system?

- Which countries have contributed the most to space exploration?

 **Reflect**

On Your Own

6. ❓ **Answer the Essential Question** How can you communicate mathematical ideas effectively?

a. How did you use what you learned about expressions and equations to communicate mathematical ideas effectively in this project?

_____

_____

_____

b. How did you use what you learned about functions and inequalities to communicate mathematical ideas effectively in this project?

_____

_____

_____

PROJECT 4

Targeted TEKS
6.8(D), 6.12(A), 6.12(C),
6.13(A), 6.1(A), 6.1(C),
6.1(D), 6.1(E), 6.1(F)

Watch ▶ **A New Zoo** A zoo is a great place to explore wild animals and learn about their habitats. In this project you will:

- **Collaborate** with your classmates as you explore some animals at the zoo and design your own zoo.

- **Share** the results of your research in a creative way.

- ② **Reflect** on how you use different measurements to solve real-life problems.

By the end of this Project, you may be interested in working at the zoo or even working as a designer to help create new living areas for the animals.

Collaborate

⏻ **Go Online** Work with your group to research and complete each activity. You will use your results in the Share section on the following page.

1. Choose 10 zoo animals. Research various characteristics of each animal, such as average weight, lifespan, incubation period, and the temperature of its natural habitat. Write a brief summary for each animal that you choose.

2. Create a bar graph that shows the average weight, the average lifespan, and the average incubation period for the 10 animals you chose.

3. Organize the characteristics found in Exercise 1 for each animal in a table or spreadsheet. Then describe how you could use these characteristics to help you design the animals' living spaces.

4. Research the amount of living space needed for each animal. Use this information to design and draw your own zoo. Be sure to include the dimensions and area. Which animals have the largest living areas? Explain why.

5. Find the area of each animal's enclosure that you designed in Exercise 4. Also, find the volume and surface area of any buildings at the zoo you designed.

Share

Collaborate

With your group, decide on a way to present what you have learned about designing a zoo. Some suggestions are listed below, but you can also think of other creative ways to present your information. Remember to show how you used mathematics to complete this project!

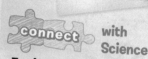 **with Science**

Environmental Literacy

Research the living conditions for animals in zoos today compared to the living conditions of the past. How has it changed over time? Things to consider:

- size of living space
- average lifespan difference
- behavior changes

- Design a web page that can be used to describe the zoo. Some questions to consider are:
  - Which zoo attractions should be promoted to get more tourists to visit your zoo?
  - Include a map of your zoo.
- Design a living area for a giant panda exhibit. Be sure to include drawings and explanations of why you designed the exhibit the way you did.

Check out the note on the right to connect this project with other subjects.

Reflect

On Your Own

6. **? Answer the Essential Question** How can you use different measurements to solve real-life problems?

   a. How did you use what you learned about area to solve real-life problems?

   _____

   _____

   _____

   b. How did you use what you learned about volume to solve real-life problems?

   _____

   _____

   _____

PROJECT 5

Watch

Let's Exercise Regular physical activity not only keeps you fit, but helps you think clearly and improve your mood. In this project you will:

- **Collaborate** with your classmates as you research physical fitness.
- **Share** the results of your research in a creative way.
- **(?) Reflect** on why learning mathematics is important.

By the end of this project, you just might be your family's personal trainer!

Collaborate

Collaborate

(U) Go Online Work with your group to research and complete each activity. You will use your results in the Share section on the following page.

1. Survey at least ten students about the number of times they participate in sports or other physical activities each week. Determine the mean. Then make a dot plot of the data.

2. Research 15 physical activities and the number of Calories burned per hour for each activity. Record the information and draw a box plot to represent the data.

3. Create a jogging schedule to train for a 5K run. Include the number of weeks needed to train and the increments of miles you would need to run. Calculate the number of Calories burned per run. Draw a line graph to represent the data.

4. Look up a fast food restaurant's menu that includes the number of Calories for each item. Record the number of Calories a person would consume if they ate at that restaurant for each meal in one day. Construct an appropriate graph to display your results.

5. Look at what the USDA considers a healthy diet. Based on what you learn, plan one day's worth of meals. Use a statistical display to compare this day's diet with the day's diet in Exercise 4.

Share

With your group, decide on a way to share what you have learned about physical fitness. Some suggestions are listed below, but you can also think other creative ways to present your information. Remember to show how you used mathematics to complete each of the activities of this project!

- Write an article for the food or health section of an online magazine.

- Act as a pediatrician and create a digital presentation that promotes physical fitness.

Check out the note on the right to connect this project with other subjects.

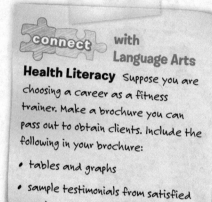

connect with **Language Arts**

Health Literacy Suppose you are choosing a career as a fitness trainer. Make a brochure you can pass out to obtain clients. Include the following in your brochure:

- tables and graphs
- sample testimonials from satisfied customers.

Reflect

On Your Own

6. **? Answer the Essential Question** Why is learning mathematics important?

a. How did you use what you learned about statistical measures to help you to understand why learning mathematics is important?

_____

_____

_____

b. How did you use what you learned about statistical displays to help you to understand why learning mathematics is important?

_____

_____

_____

Glossary/Glosario

The eGlossary contains words and definitions in the following 13 languages:

Arabic	Cantonese	Hmong	Spanish	Urdu
Bengali	English	Korean	Tagalog	Vietnamese
Brazilian Portuguese	Haitian Creole	Russian		

English	**Español**

absolute value   The distance between a number and zero on a number line.

acute angle   An angle with a measure greater than 0° and less than 90°.

acute triangle   A triangle having three acute angles.

Addition Property of Equality   If you add the same number to each side of an equation, the two sides remain equal.

additive inverse   Two integers that are opposites. The sum of an integer and its additive inverse is zero.

additive relationship   An algebraic relationship that compares the independent and dependent quantities of a relationship using addition. Written in the form $y = x + a$, where a is any rational number.

adjacent angles   Angles that have the same vertex, share a common side, and do not overlap.

algebra   A mathematical language of symbols, including variables.

algebraic expression   A combination of variables, numbers, and at least one operation.

analyze   To use observations to describe and compare data.

valor absoluto   Distancia entre un número y cero en la recta numérica.

ángulo agudo   Ángulo que mide más de 0° y menos de 90°.

triángulo acutángulo   Triángulo con tres ángulos agudos.

propiedad de adición de la igualdad   Si sumas el mismo número a ambos lados de una ecuación, los dos lados permanecen iguales.

inverso aditivo   Dos enteros opuestos.

relación aditiva   Una relación algebraica que compara las cantidades independientes y dependientes en una relación usando la adición. Está escrito en la forma $y = x + a$, cuando a es cualquier número racional.

ángulos adyacentes   Ángulos que comparten el mismo vértice y un común lado, pero no se sobreponen.

álgebra   Lenguaje matemático que usa símbolos, incluyendo variables.

expresión algebraica   Combinación de variables, números y, por lo menos, una operación.

analizar   Usar observaciones para describir y comparar datos.

angle   Two rays with a common endpoint form an angle. The rays and vertex are used to name the angle.

∠ABC, ∠CBA, or ∠B

ángulo   Dos rayos con un extremo común forman un ángulo. Los rayos y el vértice se usan para nombrar el ángulo.

∠ABC, ∠CBA o ∠B

area   The number of square units needed to cover the surface of a closed figure.

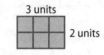

3 units

2 units

area = 6 square units

área   Número de unidades cuadradas necesarias para cubrir la superficie de una figura cerrada.

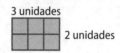

3 unidades

2 unidades

área = 6 unidades cuadradas

arithmetic sequence   A sequence in which the difference between any two consecutive terms is the same.

sucesión aritmética   Sucesión en la cual la diferencia entre dos términos consecutivos es constante.

Associative Property   The way in which numbers are grouped does not change the sum or product.

propiedad asociativa   La forma en que se agrupan tres números al sumarlos o multiplicarlos no altera su suma o producto.

average   The sum of two or more quantities divided by the number of quantities; the mean.

promedio   La suma de dos o más cantidades dividida entre el número de cantidades; la media.

Bb

balance a check register   To keep an account of all transactions and the final balance in the account.

hacer el balance del registro de cheques   Llevar la cuenta de todas las transacciones y el saldo final en la cuenta.

bar notation   A bar placed over digits that repeat to indicate a number pattern that repeats indefinitely.

notación de barra   Barra que se coloca sobre los dígitos que se repiten para indicar el número de patrones que se repiten indefinidamente.

base   Any side of a parallelogram.

base   Cualquier lado de un paralelogramo.

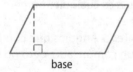

base

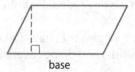

base

base   In a power, the number used as a factor. In 10^3, the base is 10. That is, $10^3 = 10 \times 10 \times 10$.

base   En una potencia, el número usado como factor. En 10^3, la base es 10. Es decir, $10^3 = 10 \times 10 \times 10$.

benchmark fractions   Fractions that are used when estimating part of a whole. For example, $\frac{1}{100}, \frac{1}{10}, \frac{1}{4}, \frac{1}{3}$ and their multiples.

fracciónes de referencia   Los fracciónes se utilizan para calcular una parte de un todo. Por ejemplo, $\frac{1}{100}, \frac{1}{10}, \frac{1}{4}, \frac{1}{3}$ y sus múltiplos.

benchmark percents Percents that are used when estimating part of a whole. For example, 1%, 10%, 25%, $33\frac{1}{3}$% and their multiples.

borrower Someone who borrowers money from a lender.

box plot A diagram that is constructed using five values.

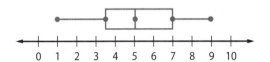

porcentajes de referencia Los porcentajes se utilizan para calcular una parte de un todo. Por ejemplo, 1%, 10%, 25%, $33\frac{1}{3}$% y sus múltiplos.

prestatario Alguien que toma dinero a préstamo de un prestamista.

diagrama de caja Diagrama que se construye usando cinco valores.

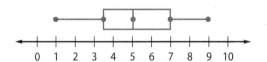

Cc

categorical data Data that can be divided into categories based on attributes of the data.

checking account A type of bank account in which users deposit money and from which they can withdraw money to make purchases or pay bills.

check register A written record of all transactions.

circle graph A graph that shows data as parts of a whole. In a circle graph, the percents add up to 100.

Area of Oceans

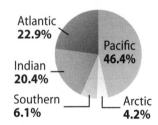

cluster Data that are grouped closely together.

coefficient The numerical factor of a term that contains a variable.

Commutative Property The order in which numbers are added or multiplied does not change the sum or product.

compatible numbers Numbers that are easy to use to perform computations mentally.

datos categóricos Datos que se pueden dividir en categorías basado en atributos de los datos.

cuenta de cheques Tipo de cuenta bancaria en la cual los usuarios depositan dinero y de la cual pueden retirar dinero para hacer compras o pagar cuentas.

registro de cheques Registro escrito de todas las transacciones.

gráfica circular Gráfica que muestra los datos como partes de un todo. En una gráfica circular los porcentajes suman 100.

Área de superficie de los océanos

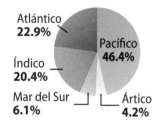

agrupamiento Conjunto de datos que se agrupan.

coeficiente El factor numérico de un término que contiene una variable.

propiedad conmutativa La forma en que se suman o multiplican dos números no altera su suma o producto.

números compatibles Números que son fáciles de usar para realizar computaciones mentales.

complementary angles   Two angles are complementary if the sum of their measures is 90°.

∠1 and ∠2 are complementary angles.

ángulos complementarios   Dos ángulos son complementarios si la suma de sus medidas es 90°.

∠1 y ∠2 son complementarios.

composite number   A whole number that has more than two factors.

número compuesto   Número entero que tiene más de dos factores.

congruent   Having the same measure.

congruente   Ques tienen la misma medida.

congruent angles   Angles that have the same measure.

ángulos congruentes   Ángulos que tienen la misma medida.

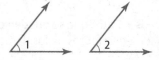

1 and ∠2 are congruent angles.

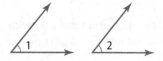

∠1 y ∠2 son congruentes.

congruent figures   Figures that have the same size and same shape; corresponding sides and angles have equal measures.

figuras congruentes   Figuras que tienen el mismo tamaño y la misma forma; los lados y los ángulos correspondientes con igual medida.

constant   A term without a variable.

constante   Un término sin una variable.

coordinate plane   A plane in which a horizontal number line and a vertical number line intersect at their zero points.

plano de coordenadas   Plano en que una recta numérica horizontal y una recta numérica vertical se intersecan en sus puntos cero.

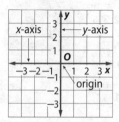

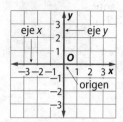

credit card   A card that allows a buyer to put off paying for a purchase until a time in the future.

tarjeta de crédito   Tarjeta que permite a un comprador postergar el pago de una compra hasta algún momento en el futuro.

credit history   A record of financial performance.

historial de crédito   Registro del desempeño financiero.

credit report   A summary of an individual's financial history.

informe crediticio   Resumen del historial financiero de una persona.

cubic units Used to measure volume. Tells the number of cubes of a given size it will take to fill a three-dimensional figure.

unidades cúbicas Se usan para medir el volumen. Indican el número de cubos de cierto tamaño que se necesitan para llenar una figura tridimensional.

3 cubic units

3 unidades cúbicas

Dd

data Information, often numerical, which is gathered for statistical purposes.

datos Información, con frecuencia numérica, que se recoge con fines estadísticos.

debit card A card that allows a buyer to make purchases while immediately removing money from a linked account.

tarjeta de débito Tarjeta que permite a un comprador hacer compras extrayendo de inmediato dinero de una cuenta asociada.

decimal A number that has a digit in the tenths place, hundredths place, and beyond.

decimal Número que tiene un dígito en el lugar de las décimas, centésimas y más allá.

defining the variable Choosing a variable and deciding what the variable represents.

definir la variable Elegir una variable y decidir lo que representa.

dependent quantity The variable in a relation with a value that depends on the value of the independent quantity.

la cantidad dependiente La variable en una relación cuyo valor depende del valor de la cantidad independiente.

deposit Add money to an account.

depositar Agregar dinero a una cuenta.

dimensional analysis The process of including units of measurement when you compute.

análisis dimensional Proceso que incluye las unidades de medida al hacer cálculos.

distribution The arrangement of data values.

distributión El arreglo de valores de datos.

Distributive Property To multiply a sum by a number, multiply each addend by the number outside the parentheses.

propiedad distributiva Para multiplicar una suma por un número, multiplica cada sumando por el número fuera de los paréntesis.

Division Property of Equality If you divide each side of an equation by the same nonzero number, the two sides remain equal.

propiedad de igualdad de la división Si divides ambos lados de una ecuación entre el mismo número no nulo, los lados permanecen iguales.

dot plot A diagram that shows the frequency of data on a number line. Also known as a line plot.

diagrama de puntos Diagrama que muestra la frecuencia de los datos sobre una recta numérica.

Ee

equals sign A symbol of equality, =.

signo de igualdad Símbolo que indica igualdad, =.

equation A mathematical sentence showing two expressions are equal. An equation contains an equals sign, =.

ecuación Enunciado matemático que muestra que dos expresiones son iguales. Una ecuación contiene el signo de igualdad, =.

equiangular triangle A triangle having three congruent angles.

triángulo equiangular Triángulo con tres ángulos congruentes.

equilateral triangle A triangle having three congruent sides.

triángulo equilátero Triángulo con tres lados congruentes.

equivalent expressions Expressions that have the same value.

expresiones equivalentes Expresiones que poseen el mismo valor, sin importer los valores de la(s) variable(s).

equivalent ratios Ratios that express the same relationship between two quantities.

razones equivalentes Razones que expresan la misma relación entre dos cantidades.

evaluate To find the value of an algebraic expression by replacing variables with numbers.

evaluar Calcular el valor de una expresión sustituyendo las variables por número.

exponent In a power, the number that tells how many times the base is used as a factor. In 5^3, the exponent is 3. That is, $5^3 = 5 \times 5 \times 5$.

exponente En una potencia, el número que indica las veces que la base se usa como factor. En 5^3, el exponente es 3. Es decir, $5^3 = 5 \times 5 \times 5$.

Ff

factor the expression The process of writing numeric or algebraic expressions as a product of their factors.

factorizar la expresión El proceso de escribir expresiones numéricas o algebraicas como el producto de sus factores.

factor tree Diagram that can be used to find the prime factorization of a number.

árbol de factores Una diagrama que se puede utiliza hallar la factorización prima de un número.

first quartile For a data set with median M, the first quartile is the median of the data values less than M.

primer cuartil Para un conjunto de datos con la mediana M, el primer cuartil es la mediana de los valores menores que M.

formula An equation that shows the relationship among certain quantities.

fórmula Ecuación que muestra la relación entre ciertas cantidades.

fraction A number that represents part of a whole or part of a set.

fracción Número que representa parte de un todo o parte de un conjunto.

$$\frac{1}{2}, \frac{1}{3}, \frac{1}{4}, \frac{3}{4}$$

$$\frac{1}{2}, \frac{1}{3}, \frac{1}{4}, \frac{3}{4}$$

frequency distribution How many pieces of data are in each interval.

distribución de frecuencias Cantidad de datos asociada con cada intervalo.

frequency table A table that shows the number of pieces of data that fall within the given intervals.

tabla de frecuencias Tabla que muestra el número de datos en cada intervalo.

gap An empty space or interval in a set of data.

laguna Espacio o intervalo vacío en un conjunto de datos.

geometric sequence A sequence in which each term is found by multiplying the previous term by the same number.

sucesión geométrica Sucesión en la cual cada término después del primero se determina multiplicando el término anterior por el mismo número.

grants Awards from non-profit organizations.

subvenciones Concesiones de organizaciones sin fines de lucro.

graph To place a dot at a point named by an ordered pair.

gráfica Colocar una marca puntual en el punto que corresponde a un par ordenado.

Greatest Common Factor (GCF) The greatest of the common factors of two or more numbers.

The greatest common factor of 12, 18, and 30 is 6.

máximo común divisor (MCD) El mayor de los factores comunes de dos o más números.

El máximo común divisor de 12, 18 y 30 es 6.

 Hh

height The shortest distance from the base of a parallelogram to its opposite side.

altura La distancia más corta desde la base de un paralelogramo hasta su lado opuesto.

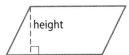
height

altura

histogram A type of bar graph used to display numerical data that have been organized into equal intervals.

histograma Tipo de gráfica de barras que se usa para exhibir datos que se han organizado en intervalos iguales.

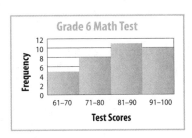

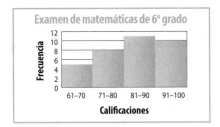

 Ii

Identity Properties Properties that state that the sum of any number and 0 equals the number and that the product of any number and 1 equals the number.

propiedades de identidad Propiedades que establecen que la suma de cualquier número y 0 es igual al número y que el producto de cualquier número y 1 es igual al número.

independent quantity The quantity in a relationship with a value that is subject to choice.

la cantidad independiente Cantidad en una relación cuyo valor está sujeto a elección.

inequality A mathematical sentence indicating that two quantities are not equal.

desigualdad Enunciado matemático que indica que dos cantidades no son iguales.

integer Any number from the set {... −4, −3, −2, −1, 0, 1, 2, 3, 4 ...} where ... means *continues without end*.

entero Cualquier número del conjunto {... −4, −3, −2, −1, 0, 1, 2, 3, 4 ...} donde ... significa que *continúa sin fin*.

interest A charge for the use of credit or borrowed money if the balance is not paid off in a set amount of time.

interés Cantidad que se cobra o se paga por el uso del dinero

interquartile range A measure of variation in a set of numerical data, the interquartile range is the distance between the first and third quartiles of the data set.

rango intercuartil El rango intercuartil, una medida de la variación en un conjunto de datos numéricos, es la distancia entre el primer y el tercer cuartil del conjunto de datos.

intersecting lines *Lines* that meet or cross at a common *point*.

rectas secantes *Rectas* que se intersectan o se cruzan en un *punto* común.

interval The difference between successive values on a scale.

intervalo La diferencia entre valores sucesivos de una escala.

inverse operations Operations which *undo* each other. For example, addition and subtraction are inverse operations.

operaciones inversas Operaciones que se *anulan* mutuamente. La adición y la sustracción son operaciones inversas.

isosceles triangle A triangle having at least two congruent sides.

triángulo isósceles Triángulo que tiene por lo menos dos lados congruentes.

Kk

---

key In a stem-and-leaf plot, it explains the stems and leaves.

leyenda En una diagrama de tallo y hojas, explica los tallos y las hojas.

Ll

---

least common denominator (LCD) The least common multiple of the denominators of two or more fractions.

mínimo común denominador (mcd) El menor múltiplo común de los denominadores de dos o más fracciones.

least common multiple (LCM) The smallest whole number greater than 0 that is a common multiple of each of two or more numbers.

The LCM of 2 and 3 is 6.

mínimo común múltiplo (mcm) El menor número entero, mayor que 0, múltiplo común de dos o más números.

El mcm de 2 y 3 es 6.

leaves The digits of the least place value of data in a stem-and-leaf plot.

hoja En un diagrama de tallo y hojas, los dígitos del menor valor de posición.

lender   Someone who loans money to a borrower.

prestamista   Alguien que presta dinero a un prestatario.

lifetime income   The total amount a worker is paid during their working career.

ingresos de toda la vida   Cantidad total que cobra un trabajador durante su vida laboral.

like terms   Terms that contain the same variable(s) to the same power.

términos semejantes   Términos que contienen la misma variable o variables elevadas a la misma potencia.

linear relationship   A relationship that forms a line when graphed.

relación lineal   Relación cuya gráfica es una recta.

line graph   A graph used to show how a set of data changes over a period of time.

gráfica lineal   Gráfica que se use para mostrar cómo cambian los valores durange un período de tiempo.

line plot   A diagram that shows the frequency of data on a number line. Also known as a dot plot.

esquema lineal   Diagrama que muestra la frecuencia de los datos sobre una recta numérica.

Mm

mean   The sum of the numbers in a set of data divided by the number of pieces of data.

media   La suma de los números en un conjunto de datos dividida entre el número total de datos.

measures of center   Numbers that are used to describe the center of a set of data. These measures include the mean, median, and mode.

medidas del centro   Numéros que se usan para describir el centro de un conjunto de datos. Estas medidas incluyen la media, la mediana y la moda.

measures of spread   A measure used to describe the distribution of data.

medidas de dispersión   Medida usada para describir la distribución de los datos.

median   A measure of center in a set of numerical data. The median of a list of values is the value appearing at the center of a sorted version of the list— or the mean of the two central values, if the list contains an even number of values.

mediana   Una medida del centro en un conjunto de datos numéricos. La mediana de una lista de valores es el valor que aparece en el centro de una versión ordenada de la lista, o la media de los dos valores centrales si la lista contiene un número par de valores.

mode   The number(s) or item(s) that appear most often in a set of data.

moda   Número(s) de un conjunto de datos que aparece(n) más frecuentemente.

Multiplication Property of Equality   If you multiply each side of an equation by the same nonzero number, the two sides remain equal.

propiedad de multiplicación de la igualdad   Si multiplicas ambos lados de una ecuación por el mismo número no nulo, lo lados permanecen iguales.

multiplicative relationship   An algebraic relationship that compares the independent and dependent quantities of a relationship using multiplication. Written in the form $y = ax$, where a is any rational number.

relación multiplicativa   Una relación algebraica que compara las cantidades independientes y dependientes en una relación usando la multiplicación. Está escrito en la forma $y = ax$, cuando a es cualquier número racional.

Nn

negative integer   A number that is less than zero. It is written with a − sign.

entero negativo   Número que es menor que cero y se escribe con el signo −.

numerical expression   A combination of numbers and operations.

expresión numérica   Una combinación de números y operaciones.

Oo

obtuse angle   Any angle that measures greater than 90° but less than 180°.

ángulo obtuso   Cualquier ángulo que mide más de 90° pero menos de 180°.

obtuse triangle   A triangle having one obtuse angle.

triángulo obtusángulo   Triángulo que tiene un ángulo obtuso.

opposites   Two integers are opposites if they are represented on the number line by points that are the same distance from zero, but on opposite sides of zero. The sum of two opposites is zero.

opuestos   Dos enteros son opuestos si, en la recta numérica, están representados por puntos que equidistan de cero, pero en direcciones opuestas. La suma de dos opuestos es cero.

ordered pair   A pair of numbers used to locate a point on the coordinate plane. The ordered pair is written in the form (x-coordinate, y-coordinate).

par ordenado   Par de números que se utiliza para ubicar un punto en un plano de coordenadas. Se escribe de la forma (coordenada x, coordenada y).

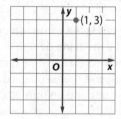

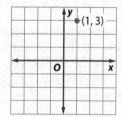

order of operations   The rules that tell which operation to perform first when more than one operation is used.

1. Simplify the expressions inside grouping symbols, like parentheses.

2. Find the value of all powers.

3. Multiply and divide in order from left to right.

4. Add and subtract in order from left to right.

orden de las operaciones   Reglas que establecen cuál operación debes realizar primero, cuando hay más de una operación involucrada.

1. Primero ejecuta todas las operaciones dentro de los símbolos de agrupamiento.

2. Evalúa todas las potencias.

3. Multiplica y divide en orden de izquierda a derecha.

4. Suma y resta en orden de izquierda a derecha.

origin The point of intersection of the *x*-axis and *y*-axis on a coordinate plane.

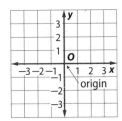

origen Punto de intersección de los ejes axiales en un plano de coordenadas.

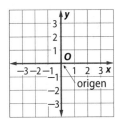

outlier A value that is much higher or much lower than the other values in a set of data.

valor atípico Dato que se encuentra muy separado de los otros valores en un conjunto de datos.

Pp

parallelogram A quadrilateral with opposite sides parallel and opposite sides congruent.

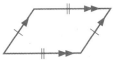

paralelogramo Cuadrilátero cuyos lados opuestos son paralelos y congruentes.

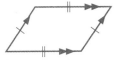

peak The most frequently occurring value in a line plot.

pico El valor que ocurre con más frecuencia en un diagrama de puntos.

percent A ratio that compares a number to 100.

por ciento Razón en que se compara un número a 100.

percent bar graph A graph that shows the relative frequency of each category in a single bar.

gráfica de barras de porcentaje Una gráfica que muestra la frecuencia relativa de cada categoría en una sola barra.

percent proportion One ratio or fraction that compares part of a quantity to the whole quantity. The other ratio is the equivalent percent written as a fraction with a denominator of 100.

$$\frac{part}{whole} = \frac{percent}{100}$$

proporción porcentual Razón o fracción que compara parte de una cantidad a toda la cantidad. La otra razón es el porcentaje equivalente escrito como fracción con 100 de denominador.

$$\frac{parte}{todo} = \frac{porcentaje}{100}$$

perfect square Numbers with square roots that are whole numbers. 25 is a perfect square because the square root of 25 is 5.

cuadrados perfectos Números cuya raíz cuadrada es un número entero. 25 es un cuadrado perfecto porque la raíz cuadrada de 25 es 5.

perimeter The distance around a figure.

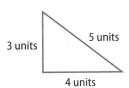

$P = 3 + 4 + 5 = 12$ units

perímetro La distancia alrededor de una figura.

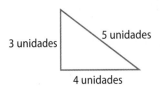

$P = 3 + 4 + 5 = 12$ unidades

population The entire group of items or individuals from which the samples under consideration are taken.

positive integer A number that is greater than zero. It can be written with or without a + sign.

powers Numbers expressed using exponents. The power 3^2 is read *three to the second power*, or *three squared*.

prime factorization A way of expressing a composite number as a product of its prime factors.

prime number A whole number with exactly two factors, 1 and itself.

prism A three-dimensional figure with at least three rectangular lateral faces and top and bottom faces parallel.

properties Statements that are true for any number.

proportion An equation stating that two ratios or rates are equivalent.

población El grupo total de individuos o de artículos del cual se toman las muestras bajo estudio.

entero positivo Número que es mayor que cero y se puede escribir con o sin el signo +.

potencias Números que se expresan usando exponentes. La potencia 3^2 se lee *tres a la segunda potencia* o *tres al cuadrado*.

factorización prima Una manera de escribir un número compuesto como el producto de sus factores primos.

número primo Número entero que tiene exactamente dos factores, 1 y sí mismo.

prisma Figura tridimensional que tiene por lo menos tres caras laterales rectangulares y caras paralelas superior e inferior.

propiedades Enunciados que son verdaderos para cualquier número.

proporción Ecuación que indica que dos razones o tasas son equivalentes.

Qq

quadrants The four regions in a coordinate plane separated by the x-axis and y-axis.

quadrilateral A closed figure having four sides and four angles.

quartiles Values that divide a data set into four equal parts.

cuadrantes Las cuatro regiones de un plano de coordenadas separadas por el eje x y el eje y.

cuadrilátero Figura cerrada que tiene cuatro lados y cuatro ángulos.

cuartiles Valores que dividen un conjunto de datos en cuatro partes iguales.

Rr

radical sign The symbol used to indicate a nonnegative square root, $\sqrt{}$.

range The difference between the greatest number and the least number in a set of data.

rate A ratio comparing two quantities with different kinds of units.

rate of change A rate that describes how one quantity changes in relation to another. A rate of change is usually expressed as a unit rate.

signo radical Símbolo que se usa para indicar una raíz cuadrada no negativa, $\sqrt{}$.

rango La diferencia entre el número mayor y el número menor en un conjunto de datos.

tasa Razón que compara dos cantidades que tienen diferentes tipos de unidades.

tasa de cambio Tasa que describe cómo cambia una cantidad con respecto a otra. Por lo general, se expresa como tasa unitaria.

ratio   A comparison of two quantities by division. The ratio of 2 to 3 can be stated as 2 out of 3, 2 to 3, 2 : 3, or $\frac{2}{3}$.

razón   Comparación de dos cantidades mediante división. La razón de 2 a 3 puede escribirse como 2 de cada 3, 2 a 3, 2 : 3 ó $\frac{2}{3}$.

rational number   A number that can be written as a fraction.

número racional   Número que se puede expresar como fracción.

ratio table   A table with columns filled with pairs of numbers that have the same ratio.

tabla de razones   Tabla cuyas columnas contienen pares de números que tienen una misma razón.

reciprocals   Any two numbers that have a product of 1. Since $\frac{5}{6} \times \frac{6}{5} = 1$, $\frac{5}{6}$ and $\frac{6}{5}$ are reciprocals.

recíproco   Cualquier par de números cuyo producto es 1. Como $\frac{5}{6} \times \frac{6}{5} = 1$, $\frac{5}{6}$ y $\frac{6}{5}$ son recíprocos.

rectangle   A parallelogram having four right angles.

rectángulo   Paralelogramo con cuatro ángulos rectos.

rectangular prism   A prism that has rectangular bases.

prisma rectangular   Una prisma que tiene bases rectangulares.

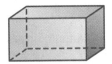

relative frequency   A ratio that compares the frequency of each category to the total.

frecuencia relativa   Razón que compara la frecuencia de cada categoría al total.

repeating decimal   The decimal form of a rational number.

decimal periódico   La forma decimal de un número racional.

rhombus   A parallelogram having four congruent sides.

rombo   Paralelogramo que tiene cuatro lados.

right angle   An angle that measures exactly 90°.

ángulo recto   Ángulo que mide exactamente 90°.

right triangle   A triangle having one right angle.

triángulo rectángulo   Triángulo que tiene un ángulo recto.

Ss

salary   Payment for work.

salario   Pago por el trabajo.

sample   A randomly selected group chosen for the purpose of collecting data.

savings   Money that is set aside for the future.

scale   The set of all possible values of a given measurement, including the least and greatest numbers in the set, separated by the intervals used.

scale   The scale gives the ratio that compares the measurements of a drawing or model to the measurements of the real object.

scale drawing   A drawing that is used to represent objects that are too large or too small to be drawn at actual size.

scale factor   A scale written as a ratio without units in simplest form.

scalene triangle   A triangle having no congruent sides.

scaling   To multiply or divide two related quantities by the same number.

scholarships   Awards for good performance.

sequence   A list of numbers in a specific order, such as 0, 1, 2, 3, or 2, 4, 6, 8.

solution   The value of a variable that makes an equation true. The solution of $12 = x + 7$ is 5.

solve   To replace a variable with a value that results in a true sentence.

square   A rectangle having four right angles and four congruent sides.

square root   The factors multiplied to form perfect squares.

statistical question   A question that anticipates and accounts for a variety of answers.

statistics   Collecting, organizing, and interpreting data.

muestra   Grupo escogido al azar o aleatoriamente que se usa con el propósito de recoger datos.

ahorros   Dinero que se guarda para el futuro.

escala   Conjunto de todos los valores posibles de una medida dada, incluyendo el número menor y el mayor del conjunto, separados por los intervalos usados.

escala   Razón que compara las medidas de un dibujo o modelo a las medidas del objeto real.

dibujo a escala   Dibujo que se usa para representar objetos que son demasiado grandes o demasiado pequeños como para dibujarlos de tamaño natural.

factor de escala   Escala escrita como una razón sin unidades en forma simplificada.

triángulo escaleno   Triángulo sin lados congruentes.

homotecia   Multiplicar o dividir dos cantidades relacionadas entre un mismo número.

becas   Concesiones por el buen desempeño.

sucesión   Lista de números en un orden específico como, por ejemplo, 0, 1, 2, 3 ó 2, 4, 6, 8.

solución   Valor de la variable de una ecuación que hace verdadera la ecuación. La solución de $12 = x + 7$ es 5.

resolver   Reemplazar una variable con un valor que resulte en un enunciado verdadero.

cuadrado   Rectángulo con cuatro ángulos rectos y cuatro lados congruentes.

raíz cuadrada   Factores multiplicados para formar cuadrados perfectos.

cuestión estadística   Una pregunta que se anticipa y da cuenta de una variedad de respuestas.

estadística   Recopilar, ordenar e interpretar datos.

stem-and-leaf plot   A system where data are organized from least to greatest. The digits of the least place value usually form the leaves, and the next place-value digits form the stems.

Stem	Leaf
1	2 4 5
2	
3	1 2 3 3 9
4	0 4 6 7

4 | 7 = 47

diagrama de tallo y hojas   Sistema donde los datos se organizan de menor a mayor. Por lo general, los dígitos de los valores de posición menores forman las hojas y los valores de posición más altos forman los tallos.

Tallo	Hojas
1	2 4 5
2	
3	1 2 3 3 9
4	0 4 6 7

4 | 7 = 47

stems   The digits of the greatest place value of data in a stem-and-leaf plot.

tallo   Los dígitos del mayor valor de posición de los datos en un diagrama de tallo y hojas.

straight angle   An angle that measures exactly 180°.

ángulo llano   Ángulo que mide exactamente 180°.

student loans   Borrowed amounts of money to pay for education.

préstamos estudiantiles   Cantidades de dinero que se toman prestadas para el pago de la educación.

Subtraction Property of Equality   If you subtract the same number from each side of an equation, the two sides remain equal.

propiedad de sustracción de la igualdad   Si sustraes el mismo número de ambos lados de una ecuación, los dos lados permanecen iguales.

supplementary angles   Two angles are supplementary if the sum of their measures is 180°.

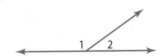

∠1 and ∠2 are supplementary angles.

ángulos suplementarios   Dos ángulos son suplementarios si la suma de sus medidas es 180°.

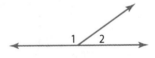

∠1 y ∠2 son suplementarios.

survey   A question or set of questions designed to collect data about a specific group of people, or population.

encuesta   Pregunta o conjunto de preguntas diseñadas para recoger datos sobre un grupo específico de personas o población.

symmetric distribution   Data that are evenly distributed.

distribución simétrica   Datos que están distribuidos.

Tt

term   Each number in a sequence.

término   Cada uno de los números de una sucesión.

term   Each part of an algebraic expression separated by a plus or minus sign.

término   Cada parte de un expresión algebraica separada por un signo más o un signo menos.

terminating decimal   A decimal is called terminating if its repeating digit is 0.

decimal finito   Un decimal se llama finito si el dígito que se repite es 0.

third quartile   For a data set with median M, the third quartile is the median of the data values greater than M.

tercer cuartil   Para un conjunto de datos con la mediana M, el tercer cuartil es la mediana de los valores mayores que M.

three-dimensional figure   A figure with length, width, and height.

figura tridimensional   Una figura que tiene largo, ancho y alto.

transaction   The movement or exchange of money.

transacción   Movimiento o intercambio de dinero.

transfer   A type of transaction that occurs when money is moved between accounts.

transferencia   Tipo de transacción que ocurre cuando se mueve dinero entre cuentas.

trapezoid   A quadrilateral with one pair of parallel sides.

trapecio   Cuadrilátero con un único par de lados paralelos.

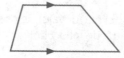

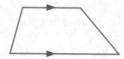

triangle   A figure with three sides and three angles.

triángulo   Figura con tres lados y tres ángulos.

Uu

unit price   The cost per unit.

precio unitario   El costo por cada unidad.

unit rate   A rate that is simplified so that it has a denominator of 1.

tasa unitaria   Tasa simplificada para que tenga un denominador igual a 1.

unit ratio   A unit rate where the denominator is one unit.

razón unitaria   Tasa unitaria en que el denominador es la unidad.

Vv

variable   A symbol, usually a letter, used to represent a number.

variable   Un símbolo, por lo general, una letra, que se usa para representar un número.

vertical angles   Opposite angles formed by the intersection of two lines. Vertical angles are congruent.

ángulos opuestos por el vértice   Ángulos opuestos formados por la intersección de dos rectas. Los ángulos opuestos por el vértice son congruentes.

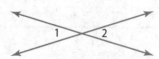

∠1 and ∠2 are vertical angles.

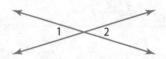

∠1 y ∠2 son ángulos opuestos por el vértice.

volume   The amount of space inside a three-dimensional figure. Volume is measured in cubic units.

volumen   Cantidad de espacio dentro de una figura tridimensional. El volumen se mide en unidades cúbicas.

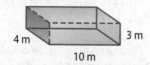

$V = 10 \times 4 \times 3 = 120$ cubic meters

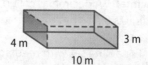

$V = 10 \times 4 \times 3 = 120$ metros cúbicos

Ww

withdrawal   Take out money from an account.

retiro   Extracción de dinero de una cuenta.

work-study   A program providing financial aid in return for student labor.

empleo y estudio   Programa que proporciona asistencia financiera a cambio del trabajo del estudiante.

Xx

x-axis   The horizontal line of the two perpendicular number lines in a coordinate plane.

eje *x*   La recta horizontal de las dos rectas numéricas perpendiculares en un plano de coordenadas.

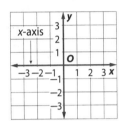

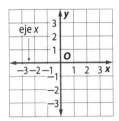

x-coordinate   The first number of an ordered pair. The *x*-coordinate corresponds to a number on the *x*-axis.

coordenada *x*   El primer número de un par ordenado, el cual corresponde a un número en el eje *x*.

Yy

y-axis   The vertical line of the two perpendicular number lines in a coordinate plane.

eje *y*   La recta vertical de las dos rectas numéricas perpendiculares en un plano de coordenadas.

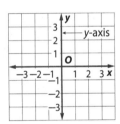

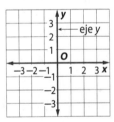

y-coordinate   The second number of an ordered pair. The *y*-coordinate corresponds to a number on the *y*-axis.

coordenada *y*   El segundo número de un par ordenado, el cual corresponde a un número en el eje *y*.

Zz

zero pair   The result when one positive counter is paired with one negative counter. The value of a zero pair is 0.

par nulo   Resultado de hacer coordinar una ficha positiva con una negativa. El valor de un par nulo es 0.

Chapter 6 Multiple Representations

Page 428 Chapter 6 Are You Ready?

1. > **3.** < **5.** 16 **7.** 115

Pages 435–436 Lesson 6-1 Independent Practice

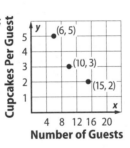

1.

Input (x)	3(x)	Output
0	3(0)	0
3	3(3)	9
9	3(9)	27

3.

Input (x)	$x + 2$	Output
0	0 + 2	2
1	1 + 2	3
6	6 + 2	8

5.

Number of Guests (x)	30 ÷ x	Cupcakes per Guest (y)
6	30 ÷ 6	5
10	30 ÷ 10	3
15	30 ÷ 15	2

7. She divided the independent quantity by 10 instead of dividing 10 by the independent quantity. 10 ÷ 2 = 5
9. Sample answer: To identify the independent quantity, work backward by performing the rule using the order of operations in reverse.   **11.** Sample answer: When the rule is multiplication or division, the inputs and outputs form equivalent ratios. When the rule is addition or subtraction, the inputs and outputs do not form equivalent ratios.

Pages 437–438 Lesson 6-1 Multi-Step Problem Solving

13. D **15.** 5

17.

Side Length (x)	4(x)	Perimeter (y)
$\frac{1}{3}$	$4\left(\frac{1}{3}\right)$	$1\frac{1}{3}$
$\frac{1}{2}$	$4\left(\frac{1}{2}\right)$	2
$1\frac{1}{2}$	$4\left(1\frac{1}{2}\right)$	6

Sample answer: As the side lengths increase, the perimeters increase. Each dependent quantity is 4 times the independent quantity.

Pages 443–444 Lesson 6-2 Independent Practice

1. add 9 to the position number; $n + 9$; 21   **3.** Sample answer: This is a geometric sequence. Each term is found by multiplying the previous term by 3; 486, 1,458, 4,374
5. add 12; 52, 64 **7.** add $\frac{1}{2}$; $4\frac{1}{4}$, $4\frac{3}{4}$ **9.** 29.6 **11.** geometric sequence; 1,296, 7,776 **13.** arithmetic sequence; 52, 65
15. Sample answer: 1, $2\frac{1}{4}$, $3\frac{1}{2}$, $4\frac{3}{4}$, … **17.** 4(x) − 3; Sample answer: The values 1, 5, 9, 13, and 17 increase by 4, so the rule includes 4(x). When the input is 1, the output is 1, which is 3 less than 4. So, the rule is 4(x) − 3.

Page 446 Lesson 6-2 Multi-Step Problem Solving

19. 34 **21.** 11

Page 451–452 Lesson 6-3 Independent Practice

1. $y = 6(x)$

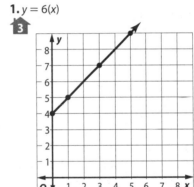

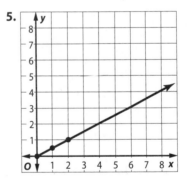

7.

Input (x)	1	2	3	4
Output (y)	5	10	15	20

; $y = 5(x)$

9. Sample answer: Ray is saving $7 per week to buy a new DVD player. The variable y represents the total amount he has saved. The variable x represents the number of weeks.
11. $y = 2x + 1$

13. B   **15.** 0.3

17.

Width (x)	Length (y)
4	11
5	10
8	7

; The equation is $y = 15 - x$. Sample ordered pairs are shown in the table.

1. 35 cubes   **3.** 50 and 36

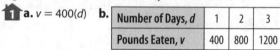 **a.** $v = 400(d)$ **b.**

Number of Days, d	1	2	3
Pounds Eaten, v	400	800	1200

c.

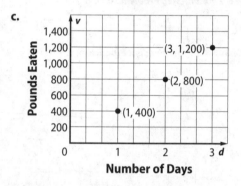

The graph is a line because with each day the amount of vegetation increases by 400. The independent quantity is d, the number of days. The dependent quantity is v, the number of pounds eaten.   **3 a.** $t = 1.75c$; where t represents the total earned and c represents the number of chores

b.

Number of Chores, c	1	2	3
Total Earned ($), t	1.75	3.50	5.25

c.

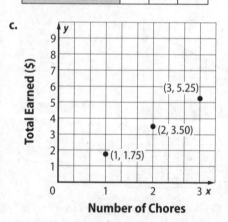

d. $8.75   **e.** The independent quantity is the number of chores and the dependent quantity is the total earned.
5. no; The graphs of the lines will never meet other than at zero hours.   **7.** $c = 25 + 2m$, where c represents the total cost and m represents the number of movies rented.

9. C   **11.** 21

1 no; Sample answer: The differences between each x- and y-value are not consistent, so it cannot be written in the form $y = x + a$.   **3** yes; Sample answer: Since each output is 4 more than the input, the relationship can be written as $y = x + 4$.   **5a.**

Number of Laps Anne Ran (x)	1	2	3
Number of Laps Kelly Ran (y)	3	4	5

5b.

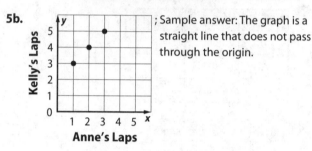

; Sample answer: The graph is a straight line that does not pass through the origin.

5c. $y = x + 2$ **5d.** Sample answer: Kelly ran 2 more laps than Anne.   **7.** yes; Sample answer: Since each output is 6.75 more than the input, the relationship can be written as $y = x + 6.75$.
9. yes; Sample answer: Each y-value is 0 more than each x-value. The equation can be written as $y = x + 0$.

11. B   **13.** $40   **15.**

; $8

1 yes; Sample answer: Since each output is 1.5 times the input, the relationship can be written as $y = 1.5x$.
3a.

Kodi			
Number of Dozens (x)	1	2	3
Cost ($) (y)	15.99	31.98	47.97

Shellie			
Number of Dozens (x)	1	2	3
Cost ($) (y)	15.99	16.99	17.99

3b.

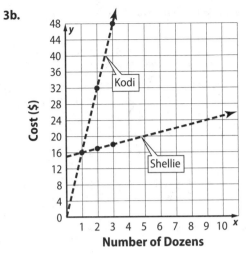

Number of Dozens

Sample answer: Each graph appears to lie in a line. The graph for Kodi passes through the origin while the graph for Shellie does not.
3c. Kodi: $y = 15.99x$; Shellie: $y = x + 14.99$; The equation for Kodi shows a multiplicative relationship. The equation for Shellie shows an additive relationship. **3d.** Sample answer: The cost of Kodi's cupcakes is $15.99 times the number of dozens of cupcakes. The cost of Shellie's cupcakes is $14.99 more than the number of dozens of cupcakes. **5** Sample answer: For every lap of a track that William runs, Patrick runs 1.5 laps; $y = 1.5x$ **7.** Sample answer: The graph of $y = 3x$ will be steeper than the graph of $y = \frac{1}{3}x$. The two graphs will only intersect at the origin.

Pages 481–482   Lesson 6-6   Multi-Step Problem Solving

9. B   **11.**

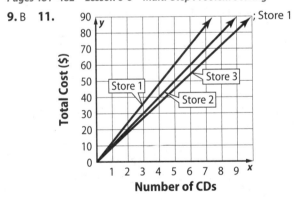

Number of CDs

13. When two baskets are purchased, the price would be the same. A table can be made for each store to find when the price is the same, or analyzing a graph will also find the number of baskets when the price is the same.

Page 489   Chapter Review

1. term   **3.** sequence   **5.** additive   **7.** independent quantity

Page 490   Chapter Review

1. 24   **3.** geometric   **5.** additive relationship

Page 491   Chapter Review

7. yes; Sample answer: She decorates 6 cupcakes in 15 minutes. So, in 15 × 4 or 60 minutes, she decorates 6 × 4 or 24 cupcakes. She has already decorated 48 cupcakes. So, she still needs to decorate 150 − 48 or 102 cupcakes. That will take her 102 ÷ 24 or 4.25 hours. Since 4.25 < 5, she will make her goal.

Chapter 7 Algebraic Expressions

Page 496   Chapter 7   Are You Ready?

1. 343   **3.** 6,561   **5.** $1\frac{5}{9}$ **7.** $\frac{1}{20}$

Pages 507–508   Lesson 7-1   Independent Practice

1. 6^2 **3.** 5^6 **5** 27^4 **7** $6 \times 6 \times 6 \times 6$; 1,296
9 $\frac{1}{8} \times \frac{1}{8} = \frac{1}{64}$ **11.** 1.0625   **13.** 1,100.727

15a.

Powers of 2	Powers of 4	Powers of 10
$2^4 = 16$	$4^4 = 256$	$10^4 = 10,000$
$2^3 = 8$	$4^3 = 64$	$10^3 = 1,000$
$2^2 = 4$	$4^2 = 16$	$10^2 = 100$
$2^1 = 2$	$4^1 = 4$	$10^1 = 10$
$2^0 = 1$	$4^0 = 1$	$10^0 = 1$

The next values are found by dividing the previous power by 2.
15b. The next values are found by dividing the previous power by 4.   **15c.** The next values are found by dividing the previous power by 10.   **15d.** Any number with an exponent of 0 has a value of 1.   **17.** $(-3)^2 = (-3)(-3) = 9$; $(-3)^3 = (-3)(-3)(-3) = -27$; When the exponent is even, the product is positive. When the exponent is odd, the product is negative.

Page 510   Lesson 7-1   Multi-Step Problem Solving

19. C   **21.** $256

Pages 515–516   Lesson 7-2   Independent Practice

1 prime   **3.** composite   **5.** neither   **7.** $2 \times 3 \times 11$
9 $-1 \times 2^4 \times 3$ **11.** $-1 \times 2 \times 3^2 \times 7$ **13.** $2^2 \times 3 \times 5^2$
15. 7, 11, 19; The numbers 7, 11, and 19 are all prime and their sum is 37.

17.

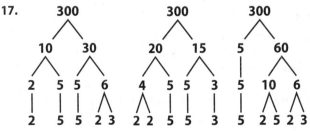

19. 3 and 5, 5 and 7, 11 and 13, 17 and 19, 29 and 31, 41 and 43, 59 and 61, 71 and 73

21a. 3^{14} **21b.** 3^{20}

Power	Value	Prime Factorization
9^1	9	3×3 or 3^2
9^2	81	$3 \times 3 \times 3 \times 3$ or 3^4
9^3	729	3^6
9^4	6,561	3^8

Page 518   Lesson 7-2   Multi-Step Problem Solving

23. 3   **25.** 18,000 ft²; $2^4 \times 3^2 \times 5^3$; 3

Pages 523–524   Lesson 7-3   Independent Practice

1. 8   **3.** 61   **5** 39   **7.** 79   **9.** $5 \times \$9 + 5 \times \$6 + 5 \times \$4$; \$95
11 $3 \times 10 + 2 \times 5$; 40 rolls   **13a.** $(34 - 12) \div 2 + 7$
13b. Sample answer: $34 - (12 \div 2) + 7 = 34 - 6 + 7 = 28 + 7 = 35$ **15.** $4 \times 5 + 9$; The other expressions have a value of 27.

Pages 525–526   Lesson 7-3   Multi-Step Problem Solving

17. D   **19.** \$1,086   **21.** 3; Sample answer: Use the order of operations to determine the numerator and denominator. The value of the numerator is 39. The value of the denominator is 13. Divide $39 \div 13 = 3$.

Pages 531–532   Lesson 7-4   Independent Practice

1. 12   **3.** 18   **5.** 1   **7** 20   **9.** $\frac{1}{8}$ m³   **11** \$415.80   **13.** 29
15. 7 ft²   **17.** Sample answer: Both numerical expressions and algebraic expressions use operations, for example $6 + 7$ and $8 \div n$. An algebraic expression, such as $6 + a$, includes numbers and variables, where a numerical expression, such as $6 + 3$, only includes numbers.

Pages 533–534   Lesson 7-4   Multi-Step Problem Solving

19. 140
21. 48 in²; $4(12 \cdot 1)$ **23.** The perimeter would be $d + a + e + 2c + f + b + g + (a + b)$, or $d + a + e + c + c + f + b + g + (a + b)$. The missing side length was found using parallel side lengths of a and b in the figure.

Pages 543–544   Lesson 7-5   Independent Practice

1. w = the width; $w - 6$ **3** t = Tracey's age; $t - 6$
5 s = the number in the Senate; $4s + 35$; 435 members
7. $2.54x$; 30.48 cm
9. m = Marcella's age; $\frac{1}{3}m + 2$; Justin is 23 years old and Aimee is 42 years old.   **11.** c = total customer order; $2 + 0.2c$
13. Sample answer: A photographer charges \$10 per person plus \$45 for the photo session. Let p represent the number of people. $10p + 45$

Pages 545–546   Lesson 7-5   Multi-Step Problem Solving

15. C   **17.** 0.8b; \$640   **19.** $fa + cd - gh$

Page 549   Focus on Mathematical Processes

1. Team 3   **3.** 352 people

Pages 555–556   Lesson 7-6   Independent Practice

1. yes; Associative Property   **3** no; The first expression is equal to 17 and the second is equal to 1.   **5.** no; The first expression is equal to 32, not 0.   **7** $75,000 \cdot 5$ and $5 \cdot 75,000$ **9.** r **11** 3   **13.** Sample answer: $12 + (8 + 5)$ and $(12 + 8) + 5$ **15.** Sample answer: $24 \div 12 = 2$ and $12 \div 24 = 0.5$ **17.** Sample answer: $48 + 82$ can be rewritten as $48 + (52 + 30)$. By using the Associative Property, $48 + (52 + 30) = (48 + 52) + 30$. So, $48 + 82 = 130$.

Page 558   Lesson 7-6   Multi-Step Problem Solving

19. B   **21.** 48

Pages 563–564   Lesson 7-7   Independent Practice

1. $9(40) + 9(4) = 396$ **3** $7(3) + 7(0.8) = 26.6$ **5.** $66 + 6x$
7 $6(43) - 6(35) = 6(43 - 35)$; 48 mi   **9.** $6(9 + 4)$ **11.** $11(x + 5)$
13. $7(11x + 3)$ **15a.** $x(7.00 + 7.50)$ and $x(7) + x(7.50)$
15b. It is cheaper to pay regular admission. The total cost for one person is \$13.50 versus \$14.50 on Family Night.
17. Sample answer: $3(4.8)$ and $3(4) + 3(0.8)$ **19.** Sample answer: The Distributive Property combines addition and multiplication. The expression $3(5x)$ is one term with three factors. So, $3(5x) = 15x$.

Page 566   Lesson 7-7   Multi-Step Problem Solving

21. A   **23.** 4

Pages 573–574   Lesson 7-8   Independent Practice

1. $11x$ **3** $-45x$ **5.** $21x + 35y$ **7** $6(4x + 3y)$ **9.** $4(x + 6) + 4x$; $\$8x + \$24$ **11** $6(3t + 2c) = 18t + 12c$ **13.** 9
15a. $3(x + 0.75) + 2x$; $\$5x + \$2.25$ **15b.** $6(x + 3.00) + 2x$; $\$8x + \$18.00$ **15c.** $2(x + 1.50) + 3x$; $\$5x + \$3$ **17.** Sample answer: The expressions are equivalent because they name the same number regardless of which number stands for y.
19. $6x + (-21)$ or $6x - 21$

Pages 575–576   Lesson 7-8   Multi-Step Problem Solving

21. B   **23.** 7   **25.** $0.30x + 0.10x = 0.15x + 0.25x = 0.40x$

Page 579   Chapter Review

1. algebraic   **3.** perfect square   **5.** like terms
7. powers   **9.** base   **11.** variable   **13.** coefficient

Page 580   Chapter Review

1. $12x + 12$ **3.** $3x - 6$ **5.** $2(x + 3)$

Chapter 8 Equations and Inequalities

Page 586   Chapter 8   Are You Ready?

1. 1.11   **3.** 2.69   **5.** $\frac{1}{3}$ **7.** $\frac{13}{40}$ mi

Pages 593–594   Lesson 8-1   Independent Practice

 25   **3.** 5   **5.** 13   **7.** −11   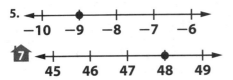 $10   **11.** Sample answer:
11 + 5 is a numerical expression. 11 + 5 = 16 is a numerical
equation.   **13.** 10.3 minutes per mile   **15.** Sample answer: m
$+ 8 = 13$ **17.** true; Since $m + 8$ is not equal to any specific
value, there are no restrictions placed upon the value of m.

Pages 595–596   Lesson 8-1   Multi-Step Problem Solving

19. A   **21.** $35.75
23. $r = 8$; He ate 1 cup of rice.

r	$12 - r = 4$	Are Both Sides Equal?
5	$12 - (5) = 4$ $7 \neq 4$	No
6	$12 - (6) = 4$ $6 \neq 4$	No
7	$12 - (7) = 4$ $5 \neq 4$	No
8	$12 - (8) = 4$ $4 = 4$	Yes

Pages 601–602   Lesson 8-2   Independent Practice

1. Let a = the height of the antennas; $441 + a = 546$ 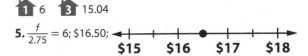 Let
t = the number of hours the temperature dropped; $-3t = -51$

5.

-10 -9 -8 -7 -6

-7-

45 46 47 48 49

9. Sample answer: Stephanie walked on her treadmill every
day for a week. Each day she walked the same distance for a
total of 17.15 kilometers. How far did she walk each day?
11. Let s = the original cost of the sweater; $s + 7.35 =$
25.65   **13.** Let g = the number of pounds Gabrielle picked;
$g + 4.4 = 7.2, 7.2 - g = 4.4$ **15.** Sample answer: Using fact
families, I know that $-17 - (-8) = -9$. So, $x = -8$. To
represent the solution, draw a number line and locate the
number -8.

-10 -9 -8 -7 -6

Pages 603–604   Lesson 8-2   Multi-Step Problem Solving

17. C   **19.** $-9.50 + x = 16.25$; $25.75

20 22 24 26 28 30

21. $5 + x = a - b$;
$0.2a = 3; b \div \frac{1}{2} = 4; x = 8$

Pages 613–614   Lesson 8-3   Independent Practice

 3   **3.** 7.9   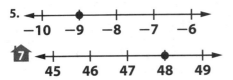 $d - 7.55 = 14.95$; $22.50   **7a.** $30 + p = 50$;
20 points   **7b.** $36 + p = 50$; 14 points   **9.** $\frac{1}{3}$ **11.** $x - 56 = 4$;

$60   **13.** 0, 1, 2   **15.** Sample answer: I have d dollars. After
paying my sister $32.73, I have $64.31 left. How much money
did I have to start with?

Pages 615–616   Lesson 8-3   Multi-Step Problem Solving

17. B   **19.** $20   **21.** $\frac{5}{24}$; Jen had less than a pound of
sunflower seeds. After she ate $\frac{1}{8}$ pound of seeds, she had $\frac{1}{12}$
pound left. How many pounds of sunflower seeds did she
have to begin with?

Pages 625–626   Lesson 8-4   Independent Practice

 6   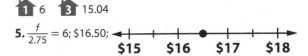 15.04

5. $\frac{f}{2.75} = 6$; $16.50;

$15 $16 $17 $18

7a. $20 = 5x$; 4 books   **7b.** $\frac{x}{5} = 7$; 35 points   **9.** $\frac{1}{2}$ **11.** He did
not divide each side by 5; $x = 15$ **13.** $4b = 7$; The solution for
the other equations is 4.   **15.** Sample answer: $\frac{x}{7} = 6$

Pages 627–628   Lesson 8-4   Multi-Step Problem Solving

17. B   **19.** $8g = p$; 5.3   **21.** $\frac{140}{4} = x$; $4x = 140$; $x = 35$;
Division Property of Equality

Page 631   Focus on Mathematical Processes

1. five problems worth 2 points each and two problems worth
4 points each   **3.** $3 \times 4 + 6 \div 1 = 18$

Pages 639–640   Lesson 8-5   Independent Practice

 5   **3.** yes   **5.** flying, stand up, or suspended   Jan.
and Feb.; $0.75   **9.** Sample answer: 0, 1, and 2   **11.** $a > c$;
Sample answer: If $a > b$, then it is to the right of b on the
number line. If $b > c$, then it is to the right of c on the number
line. Therefore, a is to the right of c on the number line.
13a. 5 and 6   **13b.** $-3, -2$, and -1 **13c.** 4   **13d.** none

Page 642   Lesson 8-5   Multi-Step Problem Solving

15. C   **17.** 4

Pages 647–648   Lesson 8-6   Independent Practice

1. $p \leq 35$ 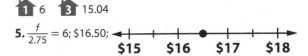 $p < 437$
5.

0 1 2 3 4 5 6 7 8 9 10 11

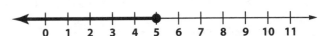 Sample answer: A rewritable compact disc must have less
than 20 songs on it.

13 14 15 16 17 18 19 20 21 22 23 24

9. She used the incorrect symbol. "At least" means the values
will be larger than 10, but include 10; $c \geq 10$ **11.** Sample
answer: When an inequality uses the greater than or less than
symbols, it does not include the number given. So, $x > 5$ and

$x < 7$ do not include 5 or 7, respectively. When the greater than or equal to and less than or equal to symbols are used, the given numbers are included. So, $x \geq 5$ and $x \leq 7$ include 5 and 7, respectively. **13a.** $x \geq 3$ and $x < 6$ **13b.** $x > -10$ and $x < -5$

Pages 649–650 Lesson 8-6 Multi-Step Problem Solving

15. D **17.**
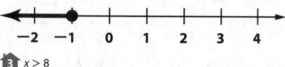

Pages 657–658 Lesson 8-7 Independent Practice

1. $y \leq -1$

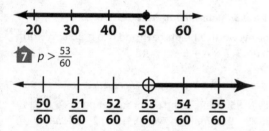

 $x > 8$

5 Sample answer: A company charges $0.10 for each engraved letter. Bobby plans to spend no more than $5.00 on the engraving of a jewelry box. What is the maximum number of letters he can have engraved? $x \leq 50$

7 $p > \frac{53}{60}$

9. Sample answer: An airplane can hold 53 passengers and there are currently 32 passengers on board. How many more passengers can board the airplane? **11.** yes; Sample answer: $x > 5$ is not the same relationship as $5 > x$. However, $x > 5$ is the same relationship as $5 < x$. **13.** Sample answer: $7x \geq 49$

Page 660 Lesson 8-7 Multi-Step Problem Solving

15. $45 + 9.99 + 10.50x \leq 100.25$; 4
17. $2x \geq 40$; 20;

Page 663 Chapter Review

1. expression **3.** addition property **5.** equal sign
7. equation

Page 664 Chapter Review

1. $x = 16$ **3.** $x = -24$ **5.** $x > 68$

Page 665 Chapter Review

7. $60

Chapter 9 Represent Geometry with Algebra

Page 670 Chapter 9 Are You Ready?

1. 23 **3.** 20.5 **5.** 3.6 **7.** $17x = $96.56; x = 5.68

Pages 677–678 Lesson 9-1 Independent Practice

1. adjacent, complementary **3.** adjacent **5** $90° + x° + 45° = 180°; x = 45$ **7.** $140° + (2x)° = 180°; x = 20$ **9** always; Sample answer: Supplementary angles have a sum of 180°. Since right angles are 90°, two right angles have a sum of 180°. **11.** never; Sample answer: A pair of angles cannot have a sum of 90° and 180°. **13.** 120° **15.** 30° **17.** 60° **19.** They are congruent; Sample answer: If two separate angles each make a sum of 90° with a third angle, then those two angles must have the same degree measure. **21.** no; Sample answer: Acute angles have degree measures less than 90°. In order for an acute angle to be one of the angles in a pair of angles that are supplementary, the other angle must be obtuse. **23.** Sample answer: Complementary angles have a sum of 90°. Obtuse angles have measures that are already greater than 90°, so they cannot have a complement.

Pages 679–680 Lesson 9-1 Multi-Step Problem Solving

25. D **27.** 72 **29.** 149°

Pages 689–690 Lesson 9-2 Independent Practice

1. right, scalene **3.** obtuse, scalene **5** $x° + 114° + 37° = 180°; x = 29$ **7** acute, isosceles; 40° **9.** $57.1° + 88.4° + x° = 180°; x = 34.5$ **11.** right scalene; 30°, 60°, 90° **13.** $x = 159$ **15.** true; Sample answer: If the sum of two of the angles of a triangle is less than 90°, then the third angle must be greater than 90°, or an obtuse angle. **17.** Sample answer shown.

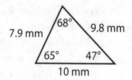

Page 692 Lesson 9-2 Multi-Step Problem Solving

19. B **21.** 153

Pages 697–698 Lesson 9-3 Independent Practice

1 $1.5x = 60; x = 40; y + 3.4 = 7.1; y = 3.7$ **3** $x + 3.8 = 13; x = 9.2$ **5.** $2.5x = 60; x = 24$; The sum of the angles of a regular hexagon is 120° × 6, or 720°. **7.** Sample answer: The two congruent angles are $\angle S$ and $\angle R$, not $\angle S$ and $\angle Q$. The congruent angles are opposite the congruent sides. $180° - 70° = 110°$ and $110° \div 2 = 55°$. So, $m\angle S = 55°$. **9.** Sample drawing shown.

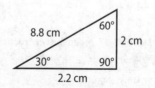

Sample answer: A scalene triangle has three sides of different lengths and three angles of different measures. The angle opposite the longest side has the greatest angle measure. **11.** sometimes; Sample answer: An isosceles triangle with angle measures of 100°, 40°, and 40° is obtuse. An isosceles triangle with angle measures of 90°, 45°, and 45° is right. An isosceles triangle with angle measures 70°, 55°, and 55° is acute.

Page 700   Lesson 9-3   Multi-Step Problem Solving

13. 44.25   **15.** 150

Pages 707–708   Lesson 9-4   Independent Practice

1. no; $2.1 + 4 \not> 7.9$ **3** yes; each inequality is true   **5.** $\overline{VW}$, $\overline{WX}$, $\overline{VX}$ **7.** The triangle cannot be made since $8 + 8 \not> 20$. **9** Her locker is closer to the cafeteria. Sample answer: The angle at her English class is less than the angle at the cafeteria, so the side opposite English is shorter.   **11.** cabin directly to the firepit; Sample answer: The side opposite the 90° angle is the longest side of the triangle. So, the other two sides must have a sum greater than that side. So, the path from the cabin to the firepit is shorter than the other path.
13. Sample answer shown.

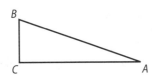

15. 37 units; Sample answer: The third side cannot be greater than or equal to 19 units long or the two sides shown would not meet to form a triangle. The greatest length the third side can be is 18 units. So, the greatest perimeter is $11 + 8 + 18$, or 37 units.

Pages 709–710   Lesson 9-4   Multi-Step Problem Solving

17. C   **19.** Combination D; 20.75   **21.** $\overline{AD}$, $\overline{AB}$, $\overline{BD}$, $\overline{CD}$, $\overline{BC}$; Order the sides of each triangle separately. Side $\overline{BD}$ is the shortest side of △ABD and the longest side of △CDB. List the sides of △ADB in order first, followed by the sides of △CDB.

Page 713   Focus on Mathematical Processes

1. 25 balloons   **3.** 272 customers

Pages 719–720   Lesson 9-5   Independent Practice

1 $A = 9 \cdot 20$; $A = 180$ in^2 **3.** $A = 7\frac{1}{2} \cdot 3\frac{1}{4}$; $A = 24\frac{3}{8}$ ft^2
5. $A = (28)^2$; $A = 784$ in^2 **7** 63 ft^2 **9.** 108 in^2 **11.** 60 ft^2
13. $120 = 12 \cdot w$; $w = 10$ m   **15.** Sample answer: 5 m × 8 m; 2 m × 20 m   **17.** 1.5 ft^2

Pages 721–722   Lesson 9-5   Multi-Step Problem Solving

19. C   **21.** 17.82 mm^2 **23.** about 324,000 cm^2; Sample answer: If the length is about 7.2 m, divide by 1.6 to get the width. The width is about 4.5 m. In centimeters, these dimensions are 450 and 720. The area is 450 × 720, or 324,000 cm^2.

Pages 731–732   Lesson 9-6   Independent Practice

1. 12 units^2 **3** 80.04 cm^2 **5.** $166\frac{1}{2}$ ft^2 **7** No; in order for the area of the first floor to be 20,000 ft^2 and the base 250 feet, the height must be $20,000 \div 250$ or 80 feet.
9a. Sample answers are given.;

Base (cm)	Height (cm)	Area (cm^2)
1	4	4
2	4	8
3	4	12
4	4	16
5	4	20

9b.

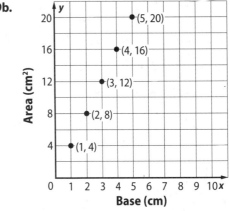

9c. It appears to form a line.   **9d.** $y = 4x$ **9e.** multiplicative relationship; Sample answer: Since the equation can be written in the form $y = ax$, it is a multiplicative relationship.   **11.** Sample answer: Both parallelograms and rectangles have bases and heights. So, the formula $A = bh$ can be used for both figures. The height of a rectangle is the length of one of its sides while the height of a parallelogram is the length of the altitude.

Page 734   Lesson 9-6   Multi-Step Problem Solving

13. D   **15.** 20.5 ft

Pages 743–744   Lesson 9-7   Independent Practice

1. 24 units^2 **3** 747 ft^2 **5.** $256.5 = \frac{1}{2}(27)(h)$; $h = 19$ cm
7 **a.** $\frac{5n}{2}$ or $\frac{1}{2}(5)(n)$

b.

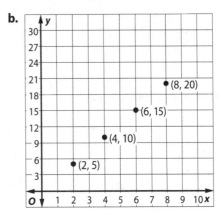

c. The points appear to form a line.   **9.** The formula is $\frac{1}{2}bh$, not bh. $100 = \frac{b \cdot 20}{2}$, $b = 10$ m   **11.** Sample answer: Area of first triangle is 24 cm^2; Area of second triangle is 48 cm^2; 1:2 or $\frac{1}{2}$.

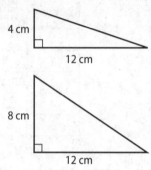

Pages 745–746   Lesson 9-7   Multi-Step Problem Solving

13. B   **15.** 20.25 mi^2 **17.** 111 sq in.

Pages 755–756   Lesson 9-8   Independent Practice

1. $178\frac{1}{2}$ yd^2 **3.** 112 m^2 **5.** $h = \frac{2(402.8)}{14.6 + 35.4}$; $h = 16.112$ m   **7. a.** 7,000 ft^2 **b.** 4 bags   **9.** $A = 9$ cm^2;

11. The lengths of the bases can be rounded to 20 m and 30 m, respectively. The area can be rounded to 250 m^2. Divide 250 by $\frac{1}{2}(20 + 30)$ or 25. The height h is about 10 m.   **13.** 6 in. and 12 in.

Pages 757–758   Lesson 9-8   Multi-Step Problem Solving

15. C   **17.** 13 m   **19.** The area will be multiplied by 9.

Pages 763–764   Lesson 9-9   Independent Practice

1. 132 m^3 **3.** 171 in^3 **5.** 17 m   **7.** $109.2 = 7(w)(5.2)$; $w = 3$ mm   **9. a.** $50\frac{5}{8}$ in^3 **b.** $16\frac{7}{8}$ in^3 **c.** 75%   **11.** No; the volume of the figure is 3^3 or 27 cubic units. If the dimensions doubled, the volume would be 6^3 or 216 cubic units, eight times greater.   **13.** Sample answer: A gift box is 7 inches long, 9 inches wide, and 4 inches tall. What is the volume of the gift box? 252 in^3

Page 766   Lesson 9-9   Multi-Step Problem Solving

15. D   **17.** 38.14 ft^3

Page 769   Chapter Review

1. height   **3.** base   **5.** congruent

Page 770   Chapter Review

1. $A = \frac{1}{2}h(b_1 + b_2)$ **3.** $A = \frac{1}{2}(9.8)(7 + 12)$ **5.** $A = 93.1$

Page 771   Chapter Review

7. 4 in. and 6 in.; Sample answer: Make a table for possible dimensions that have a product of 24. Then find the perimeter.

Width (in.)	Length (in.)	Area (in^2)	Perimeter (in.)
2	12	24	28
4	6	24	20
3	8	24	22

Chapter 10 Statistical Measures and Displays

Page 776   Chapter 10   Are You Ready?

1. 68.75   **3.** $21.60   **5.** 24.20   **7.** 115.2 miles

Pages 787–788   Lesson 10-1   Independent Practice

1. 66.2; The data are centered around 66.2 stories.   **3.** $25   **5.** 88   **7.** Sample answer: pages read: 27, 38, 26, 39, 40   **9.** 203.7 lb

Pages 789–790   Lesson 10-1   Multi-Step Problem Solving

11. 3

13. $13.75   **15.** Sample answer: 14, 20, 22, 24, 30, 31, 33, 34; $14 + 20 + 22 + 24 + 30 + 31 + 33 + 34 = 208$; $208 \div 8 = 26$

Pages 795–796   Lesson 10-2   Independent Practice

1. 89; none; There is no mode to compare.   **3.** The values are close. The median and mode are equal, 44 mph, and the mean, 45.58 mph, is slightly more. The data follows the measures of center in that they are close to the measures of center.   **5.** mode; The mode of the temperatures in Louisville is 70° and the mode for Lexington's temperatures is 76°. Since $76° - 70° = 6°$, the mode was used to make this claim.   **7.** $21   **9.** Sample answer: The median or mode best represents the data. The mean, 8, is greater than all but one of the data values.

Pages 797–798   Lesson 10-2   Multi-Step Problem Solving

11. A   **13.** 8.5   **15.** Miles per Gallon dot plot; The mode is 36, which is a lot higher than the rest of the data. In game scores, the mode and median are both more similar to the mean.

Pages 803–804   Lesson 10-3   Independent Practice

1. a. 1,028   **b.** 923.5; 513; 1,038   **c.** 525   **d.** none   **3.** median: 357.5; Q_1: 298; Q_3: 422; IQR: 124   **5.** range: 63; median: 7.5; Q_3: 30.5; Q_1: 0.5; IQR: 30; Sample answer: The number of moons for each planet varies greatly. The IQR and range are both large.   **7.** Sample answer: The median is correct, but Hiroshi included it when finding the third and first quartiles. The first quartile is 96, the third quartile is 148, and the interquartile range is 52.   **9.** Sample answer: The third quartile is the median of the upper half of the data and the first quartile is the median of the lower half of the data. **11.** Sample answer: The range of each data set are the same; $21 - 1$, or 20. The IQR of Data Set A is $6 - 2$, or 4. The IQR of Data Set B is $18 - 17$, or 1. The IQR tells more information, specifically that the middle half of the data in Set B are closer together than the middle half of the data in Set A.

Page 806   Lesson 10-3   Multi-Step Problem Solving

13. 6   **15.** 38 (any number 38 or greater)

Pages 811–812   Lesson 10-4   Independent Practice

1 median: 7.5; mode: 7; range: 7; no outlier; There are a total of 18 summer camps represented. The median means that one-half of the summer camps are longer than 7.5 days and one-half are less. More camps are 7 days than any other number of days.

Length of Summer Camps

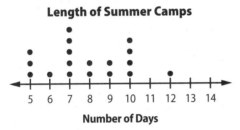

Number of Days

3 Sample answer: There are 15 play lists represented. mean: 40; median: 40; modes: 40 and 42; So, the majority of the data is close to the measures of center. Q_1: 38; Q_3: 42; IQR: 4, which means half the playlists have between 38 and 42 songs; there is an outlier at 25.   **5.** 11   **7.** The outlier of the data set is 29°F, not 20°F.   **9.** 24 cm   **11.** mode; Sample answer: With the four values, the mean is 61.36, the median is 62, and the mode is 56. Without the four values, the mean is 63.5, the median is 63.5, and the modes are 62, 65, and 68. Not including the four values changes the mode more drastically.

Page 814   Lesson 10-4   Multi-Step Problem Solving

13. B   **15.** 10

Pages 819–820   Lesson 10-5   Independent Practice

1   Wait Time (min)

Stem	Leaf
5	5
6	
7	0 0 1 5 6 9
8	0 1 3 5
9	0 2 9
5	5 = 55 minutes

3. The range of points is 37. The median score is 74 and there is no mode. Most of the scores were in the 70s and 80s. **5** Sample answer: More of the wind speeds for Strayer are in the 10–19 interval. The median wind speed for Eaton is 20 mph while the median for Strayer is 19.   **9.** Sample answer: If a stem-and-leaf plot has a leaf of 0, then there is a data value with 0 in the least place value. If there are no leaves for a specific stem, then there are no data values with that specific value as the greatest place value.   **11.** Sample answer: If the data set has a large range, then a dot plot may not be the most appropriate representation of the data.

Page 822   Lesson 10-5   Multi-Step Problem Solving

13. B   **15.** 2

Page 825   Focus on Mathematical Processes

1. 42 customers   **3.** 6 students; 10 students

Pages 831–832   Lesson 10-6   Independent Practice

1. Sample answer: 24 cyclists participated. No one finished with a time lower than 60 minutes.   **3** 60–64

5.

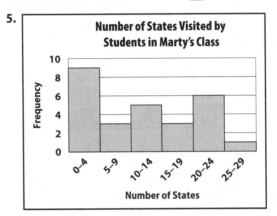

7 6th grade   **9.** Sample answer: ages of students at summer camp: 3, 4, 5, 7, 7, 8, 8, 10, 10, 11, 13, 14, 15, 15   **11.** Sample answer: One set of intervals would be from 0 to 45, with intervals of 5. Another set would be from 0 to 50 with intervals of 10. If smaller intervals are used, less data values will be in each interval, therefore the bars of the histogram will be shorter.

Page 834   Lesson 10-6   Multi-Step Problem Solving

13. 35.5%   **15.** 5 parks

Pages 839–840   Lesson 10-7   Independent Practice

1

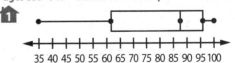

3 a.   **Length of Coastline (mi)**

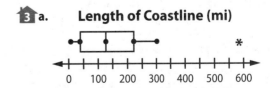

b. 127 mi   **c.** Sample answer: The length of the box plot shows that the number of miles of coastline for the top 25% of states varies greatly. The number of miles of coastline for the bottom 25% of states is concentrated.   **5a.** The median number of students in a homeroom in seventh grade is 24, which is more than the median number of students in a homeroom in sixth grade which is 19.   **5b.** The range of students in homerooms for both grades is 14.   **5c.** The middle 50% of the homerooms in seventh grade have between 22 and 26 students in each while the middle 50% of homerooms in sixth grade is more spread out, having between 18 and 24 students.   **5d.** Sample answer: Seventh grade homerooms generally have more students in them as 75% of the homerooms have between 22 and 29 students while 75% of sixth grade homerooms have between 18 and 26 students. In sixth grade, the same number of homerooms have 18 or 19 students as those that have between 19 and 24 students.
7. Sample answer: {28, 30, 52, 68, 90, 92};

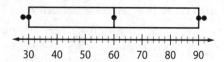

9. Sample answer: The median is the average of the least and greatest values.

Page 842   Lesson 10-7   Multi-Step Problem Solving

11. B   **13.** 3

Pages 847–848   Lesson 10-8   Independent Practice

1 Sample answer: The shape of the distribution is not symmetric. There is a cluster from 1–79. The distribution has a gap from 80–199. The peak of the distribution is on the left side of the data in the interval 20–39. There is an outlier in the interval 200–219.   **3a.** median and interquartile range; Sample answer: The distribution is not symmetric.
b. Sample answer: The data are centered around 23.5 text messages. The spread of the data around the center is about 3 text messages.   **5a.** Sample answer: The lengths of each box and whisker are not equal.   **5b.** skewed left; Sample answer: The data are more spread out on the left side due to the long left whisker.   **5c.** Sample answer: Use the median and interquartile range to describe the center and spread since the distribution is not symmetric. The data are centered around 40 feet. The spread of the data around the center is 10 feet.   **7.** Sample answer: The distribution is symmetric. The appropriate measure to describe the center is the mean. A box plot shows the location of the median and interquartile range but it does not show the location of the mean.

Pages 849–850   Lesson 10-8   Multi-Step Problem Solving

9. C   **11.** range and median; 112.5   **13a.** range = 8, mean = median = 64;   **13b.** range = 8, mean = median = 65

Pages 857–858   Lesson 10-9   Independent Practice

1 More people chose path, so path is the mode.   **3.** track: 25%; path: 34.4%; treadmill: 14%; gravel: 3.1%; sidewalk:

23.4%   **5** Sample answer: Almost half the time is spent at practice. About 40% of the time is spent doing homework.
7. Sample answer: By determining the relative frequencies, it is easier to determine the part of the whole set that each category represents.   **9.** Sample answer: The table shows the number of students who participate in various clubs.

Club	Number of Students	Relative Frequency
Art	16	32%
Debate	8	16%
Pep	19	38%
Spanish	7	14%

Students in Each Club

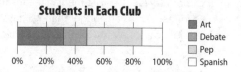

Page 860   Lesson 10-9   Multi-Step Problem Solving

11. A   **13.** 31.6%

Pages 865–866   Lesson 10-10   Independent Practice

1 histogram; The histogram shows how many counties are in each interval. By counting the number of counties in each interval, you can determine the number of counties with 3 or less trails.   **3** box plot; A box plot easily displays the median.

7.   **Number of Legs**

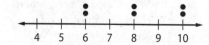

Sample answer: The dot plot allows you to easily see how many animals have various numbers of legs. The bar graph, however, allows you to see the number of legs of individual animals.   **9.** Sample answer: dot plot; You can easily locate the values with the most dots to find the mode.

Pages 867–868   Lesson 10-10   Multi-Step Problem Solving

11. A   **13.** histogram; 4 days

Page 873   Chapter Review

1. mode   **3.** range   **5.** interquartile range

Page 874   Chapter Review

1. 505; 53   **3.** 249; 281   **5.** 138   **7.** 691   **9.** 96   **11.** 8312; 83

Page 875   Chapter Review

13. Write and solve an equation to find the number of cans x.

$$\frac{45 + 50 + 48 + 60 + x}{5} = 55$$
$$x = 72$$

Chapter 11
Personal Financial Literacy

Page 880 Chapter 11 Are You Ready?

1. $48 **3.** −$19 **5.** $61,100

Page 883 Lesson 11-1 Independent Practice

1 ; 185.20

Check No.	Date	Transaction	Withdrawal	Deposit	Balance	
	1/02	paycheck		$460.00	$ 549	25
880	1/08	cell phone bill	$65.00		$ 484	25
881	1/11	groceries	$134.05		$ 350	20
	1/17	paycheck		$460.00	$ 810	20
	1/29	transfer from savings		$75.00	$ 885	20
882	1/31	rent	$700.00		$ 185	20

3 Main Street Bank; Main Street Bank would charge him $4.99 + (20 − 10)$0.15, or $6.49 per month while First City Bank would charge him $9.99 per month. **5.** First City Bank; Main Street Bank would charge him $4.99 + (45 − 10)$0.15, or $10.24 per month while First City Bank would charge him $9.99 per month.

Page 884 Lesson 11-1 Multi-Step Problem Solving

7. D

Page 887 Lesson 11-2 Independent Practice

1 Sample answer: If Shannon uses a credit card, she can make payments over time, but may have to pay interest. If she uses her debit card, she will have a penalty fee because she does not have enough in her checking account. **3.** Yes; If they do not pay off the entire balance, they will owe interest fees on their next statement.

Page 888 Lesson 11-2 Multi-Step Problem Solving

5. A

Page 891 Lesson 11-3 Independent Practice

1 M. Caprette and H. Bixler; They have the highest credit scores. **3** Making payments on time will raise M. Lombardo's credit score. Borrowing more than he can repay will lower F. Johnson's credit score. Making 6 late payments in one year will lower R. Garrett's credit score. The negative actions will usually remain in the report for 7 years. **5.** Sample answer: Borrowers need a positive credit report to obtain a loan. Lenders need to know if a borrower can repay the loan on time and this information is noted in the credit report. **7.** false; Sample answer: My credit report will most likely affect my future ability to obtain a loan. **9.** true

Page 892 Lesson 11-3 Multi-Step Problem Solving

11. B

Page 895 Lesson 11-4 Independent Practice

1 $21,800 **3.** $4,500 **5** Sample answer: A student loan requires repayment, usually with interest. A grant does not require repayment, but Mei-Ling would have to apply for a grant. It is often easier to obtain a student loan than a grant.

Page 896 Lesson 11-4 Multi-Step Problem Solving

7. C

Page 899 Lesson 11-5 Independent Practice

1 A travel agent earns $1,274,800 in lifetime income. A real estate agent earns $1,704,000 in lifetime income. A real estate agent earns $429,200 more in lifetime income than a travel agent. **3** A high school teacher earns $1,863,050 in lifetime income. A librarian earns $1,907,500 in lifetime income. A librarian earns $44,450 more in lifetime income than a high school teacher.

Page 900 Lesson 11-5 Multi-Step Problem Solving

5. C

Page 901 Chapter Review

1. scholarships **3.** credit card **5.** lender **7.** withdrawal **9.** grants

Page 902 Chapter Review

1.

Credit Cards and Debit Cards

Compare

Sample answer: Both credit cards and debit cards are methods of payment for goods and services.

Contrast

Sample answer: Debit cards immediately remove money from a linked account. Credit cards allow a buyer to put off repayment, usually with interest.

Page 902 Chapter Review

3. 8 years

Index

Mm

Qq

Rr

Ss

Tt

Uu

Index

Name _____

Cut out each parallelogram. Decompose and rearrange it to compose a rectangle as indicated.

Then determine the area of each parallelogram.

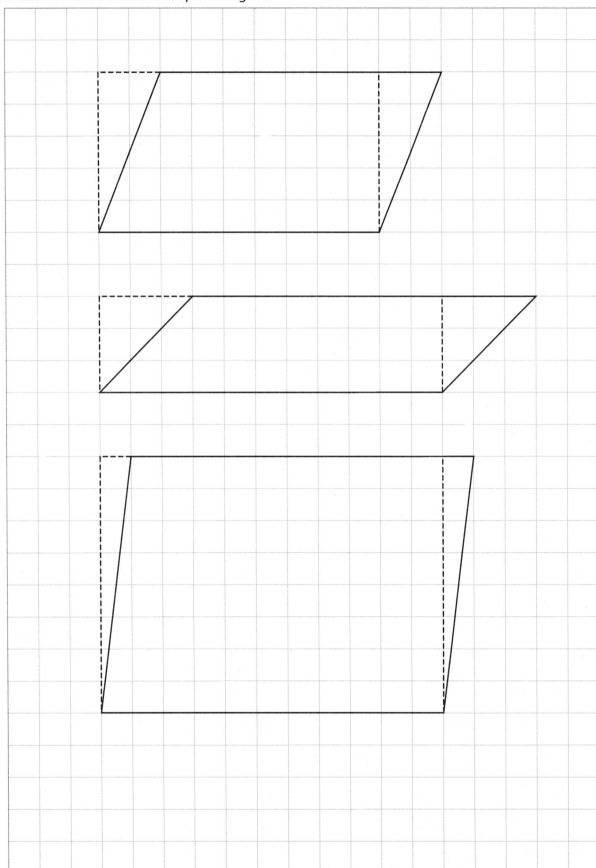

Cut out each parallelogram. Decompose and rearrange it to compose two triangles as indicated.

Then determine the area of each triangle.

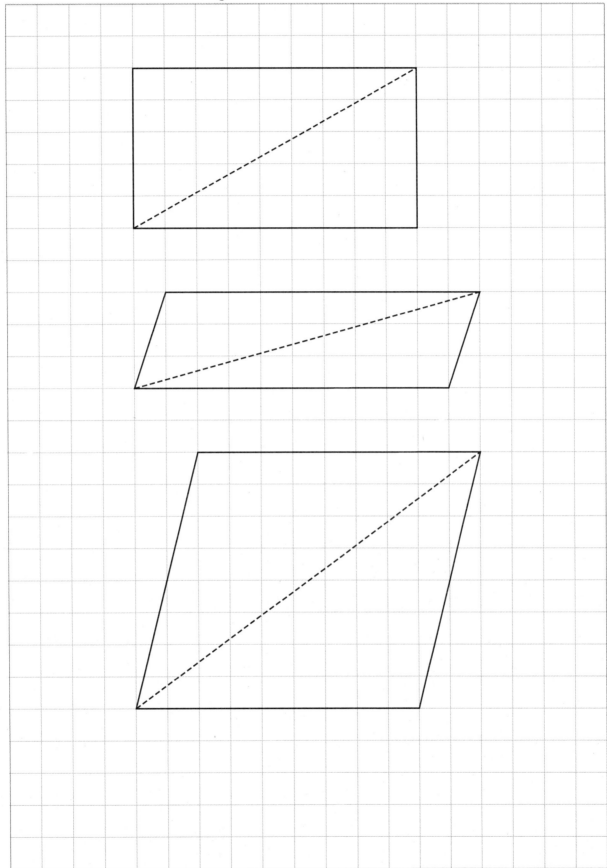

Name _____

Cut out each trapezoid. Rearrange each set of identical trapezoids to compose a parallelogram.

Then determine the area of each trapezoid.

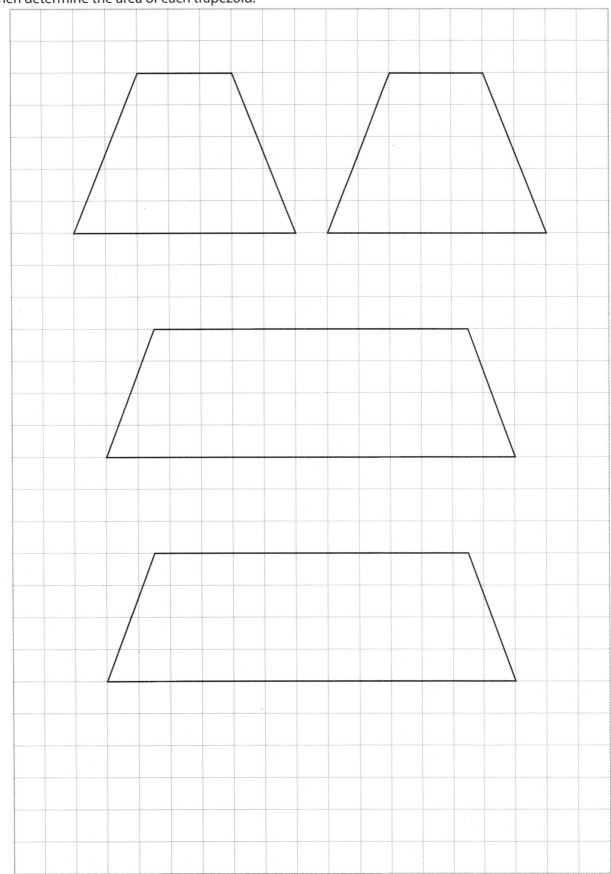

What are VKVs® and How Do I Create Them?

Visual Kinethestic Vocabulary Cards® are flashcards that animate words by focusing on their structure, use, and meaning. The VKVs in this book are used to show cognates, or words that are similar in Spanish and English.

Step 1

Go to the back of your book to find the VKVs for the chapter vocabulary you are currently studying. Follow the cutting and folding instructions at the top of the page. The vocabulary word on the BLUE background is written in English. The Spanish word is on the ORANGE background.

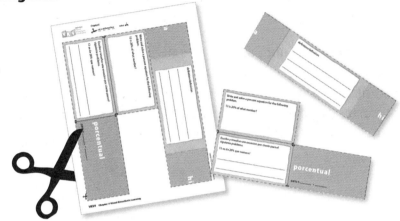

Step 2

There are exercises for you to complete on the VKVs. When you understand the concept, you can complete each exercise. All exercises are written in English and Spanish. You only need give the answer once.

Step 3

Individualize your VKV by writing notes, sketching diagrams, recording examples, and forming plurals.

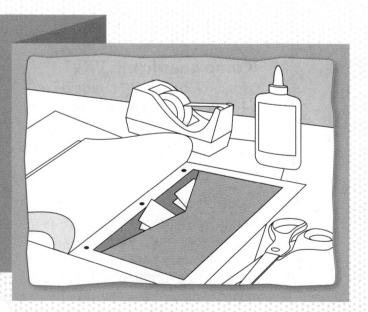

How Do I Store My VKVs?

Take a 6" x 9" envelope and cut away a V on one side only. Glue the envelope into the back cover of your book. Your VKVs can be stored in this pocket!

Remember you can use your VKVs ANY time in the school year to review new words in math, and add new information you learn. Why not create your own VKVs for other words you see and share them with others!

Las tarjetas de vocabulario visual y cinético (VKV) contienen palabras con animación que está basada en la estructura, uso y significado de las palabras. Las tarjetas de este libro sirven para mostrar cognados, que son palabras similares en español y en inglés.

Paso 1

Busca al final del libro las VKV que tienen el vocabulario del capítulo que estás estudiando. Sigue las instrucciones de cortar y doblar que se muestran al principio. La palabra de vocabulario con fondo AZUL está en inglés. La de español tiene fondo NARANJA.

Paso 2

Hay ejercicios para que completes con las VKV. Cuando entiendas el concepto, puedes completar cada ejercicio. Todos los ejercicios están escritos en inglés y español. Solo tienes que dar la respuesta una vez.

Paso 3

Da tu toque personal a las VKV escribiendo notas, haciendo diagramas, grabando ejemplos y formando plurales.

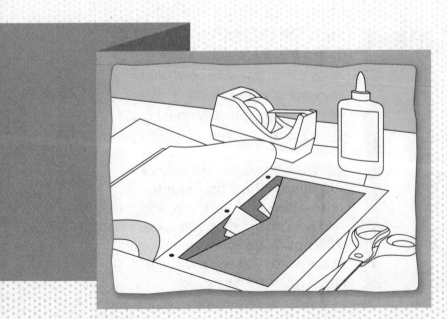

¿Cómo guardo mis VKV?

Corta en forma de "V" el lado de un sobre de 6" X 9". Pega el sobre en la contraportada de tu libro. Puedes guardar tus VKV en esos bolsillos. ¡Así de fácil!

Recuerda que puedes usar tus VKV en cualquier momento del año escolar para repasar nuevas palabras de matemáticas, y para añadir la nueva información. También puedes crear más VKV para otras palabras que veas, y poder compartirlas con los demás.

✂ cut on all dashed lines

▱ fold on all solid lines

geometric sequence

aritmética

Circle the correct word. (Encierra en un círculo la palabra correcta.)

An arithmetic sequence uses (addition/multiplication). (Una sucesión geométrica usa la (adición/multiplicación).)

Dinah Zike's
VKV
Visual
Kinesthetic
Vocabulary®

Chapter 6

✂ cut on all dashed lines

▭ fold on all solid lines

secesión geométrica

arithmetic

Dinah Zike's
Visual
Kinesthetic
Vocabulary

Circle the correct word. (Encierra en un círculo la palabra correcta.)

A geometric sequence uses (addition/multiplication). (Una progresión aritmética usa la (adición/multiplicación).)

Dinah Zike's
V K V Visual
Kinesthetic
Vocabulary ®

Chapter 6

✂ cut on all dashed lines

▭ fold on all solid lines

linear relationship

A linear relationship is a relationship that (Una relación lineal es aquella que)

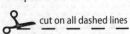
Dinah Zike's
**Visual
Kinesthetic
Vocabulary** ®

✂ cut on all dashed lines   ✂▭ fold on all solid lines

relación lineal

Write an equation to represent the relationship.
(Escribe una ecuación que represente la relación.)

Input (x)	0	1	2	3	4
Output (y)	0	4	8	12	16

Dinah Zike's
V K V Visual
Kinesthetic
Vocabulary®

Chapter 7

✂ cut on all dashed lines

▭ fold on all solid lines

Define properties. (Define propiedades.)

Evaluate 12*m* if *m* = 3. (Evalúa 12*m* si *m* = 3.)

Define coefficient. (Define coeficiente.)

properties

evaluate

coefficient

Dinah Zike's
VKV
Visual
Kinesthetic
Vocabulary®

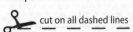

✂ cut on all dashed lines

◻ fold on all solid lines

iciente

r

iedades

Name the property that is shown in each example. (Nombra la propiedad que se muestra en los siguientes ejemplos.)

$56 + 0 = 56$

_____

$12 \cdot 5 = 5 \cdot 12$

_____

$3 + (6 + 4) = (3 + 6) + 4$

_____

What information do you need to be able to evaluate $6x + 3$? (¿Qué información necesitas para evaluar la ecuación $6x + 3$?)

Circle the coefficients in the expressions below. (Encierra en un círculo los coeficientes de las siguientes expresiones.)

$6x + 3 = 21$

$m - 3y$

$15 - 2p$

$24 + 3a = 9$

Dinah Zike's
VKV Visual
Kinesthetic
Vocabulary ®

Chapter 7

✂ cut on all dashed lines

▭ fold on all solid lines

Rewrite the expression $3x + x + x$ so that it has only one term. (Reescribe la expresión $3x + x + x$ de manera que tenga un único término.) _____

expression

term

numérica

Simplify each numerical expression. (Simplifica las siguientes expresiones numéricas.)

$3 + 12 - (2 \times 3) =$ _____

$15 \div 3 + 20 - 8 =$ _____

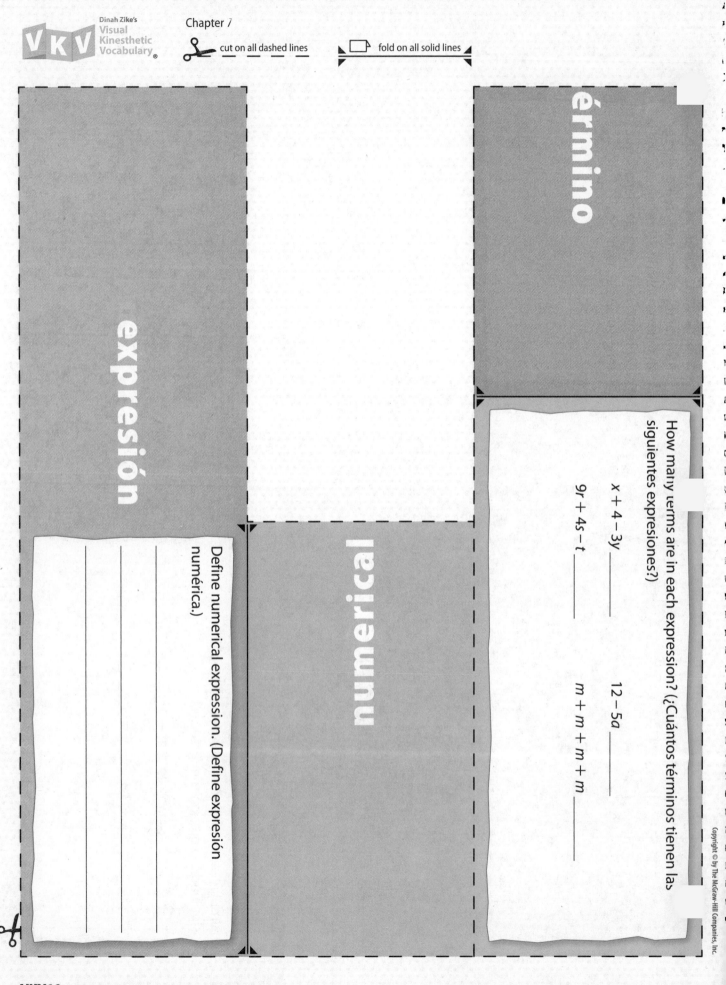

término

expresión

numerical

How many terms are in each expression? (¿Cuántos términos tienen las siguientes expresiones?)

$x + 4 - 3y$ _____

$12 - 5a$ _____

$9r + 4s - t$ _____

$m + m + m + m$ _____

Define numerical expression. (Define expresión numérica.)

_____
_____
_____
_____
_____

Dinah Zike's
VKV
Visual
Kinesthetic
Vocabulary ®

Chapter 8

✂ cut on all dashed lines

▭ fold on all solid lines

Define equation. (Define ecuación.)

Circle the solution to each equation. (Encierra en un círculo la solución de las siguientes ecuaciones.)

$27 - y = 9$	14	16	18
$x + 52 = 100$	47	48	49
$36 \div m = 12$	2	3	4

What is the inverse operation of division? (¿Cuál es la operación inversa de la división?)

equation

solution

inverse operations

What is the inverse operation of addition? (¿Cuál es la operación inversa de la adición?)

Dinah Zike's
Visual
Kinesthetic
Vocabulary®

Chapter 8

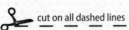

✂ cut on all dashed lines   ▭ fold on all solid lines

inversas

ción

cuación

operaciones

Solve each equation using inverse operations. (Utiliza las operaciones inversas para resolver las siguientes ecuaciones.)

$x + 12 = 25$

$x = \underline{\hspace{2cm}}$

$16 = y - 3$

$\underline{\hspace{2cm}} = y$

Define solution. (Define solución.)

Aiden bought 24 marbles for $6. Write and solve an equation to show how much each marble cost. (Andrés compró 24 canicas en $6. Escribe y resuelve una ecuación que muestre cuánto costó cada una.)

cut on all dashed lines

fold on all solid lines

rhombus

Define rhombus. (Define rombo.)

____

____

____

____

Circle the formula that represents the area of a parallelogram. (Encierra en un círculo la fórmula que representa el área de un paralelogramo)

$A = b^2 + h^2$ $A = 2(b + h)$ $A = bh$

parallelogram

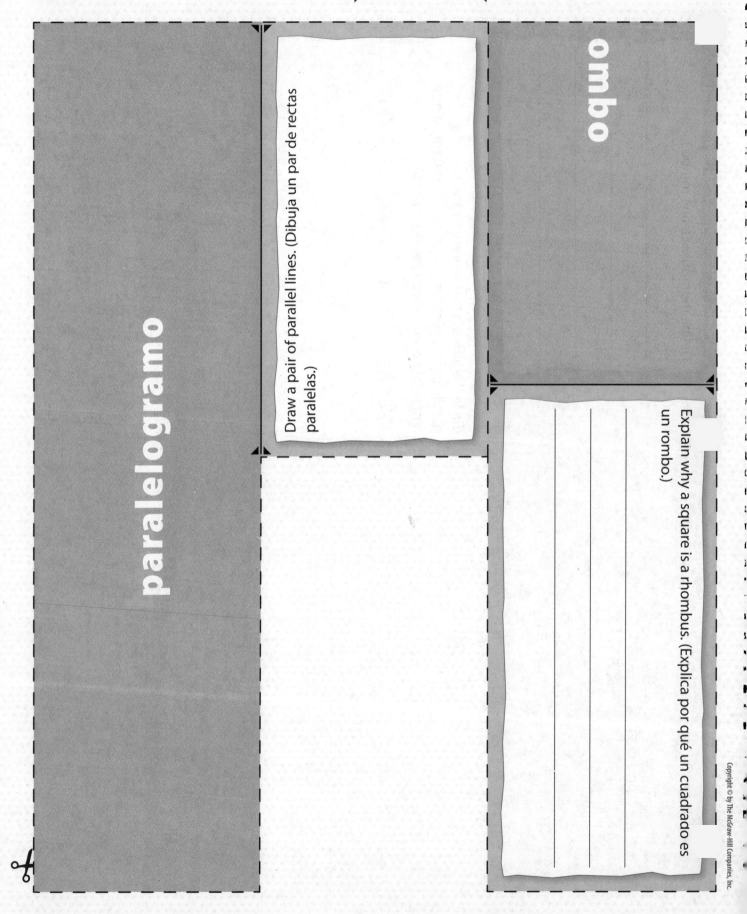

paralelogramo

Draw a pair of parallel lines. (Dibuja un par de rectas paralelas.)

ombo

Explain why a square is a rhombus. (Explica por qué un cuadrado es un rombo.)

Dinah Zike's
**Visual
Kinesthetic
Vocabulary**®

Chapter 10

✂ cut on all dashed lines

▭ fold on all solid lines

How is the median of a data set different from the mean? (¿Cuál es la diferencia entre la mediana y la media de un conjunto de datos?)

Define range. (Define rango.)

Define mode. (Define moda.)

median

range

mode

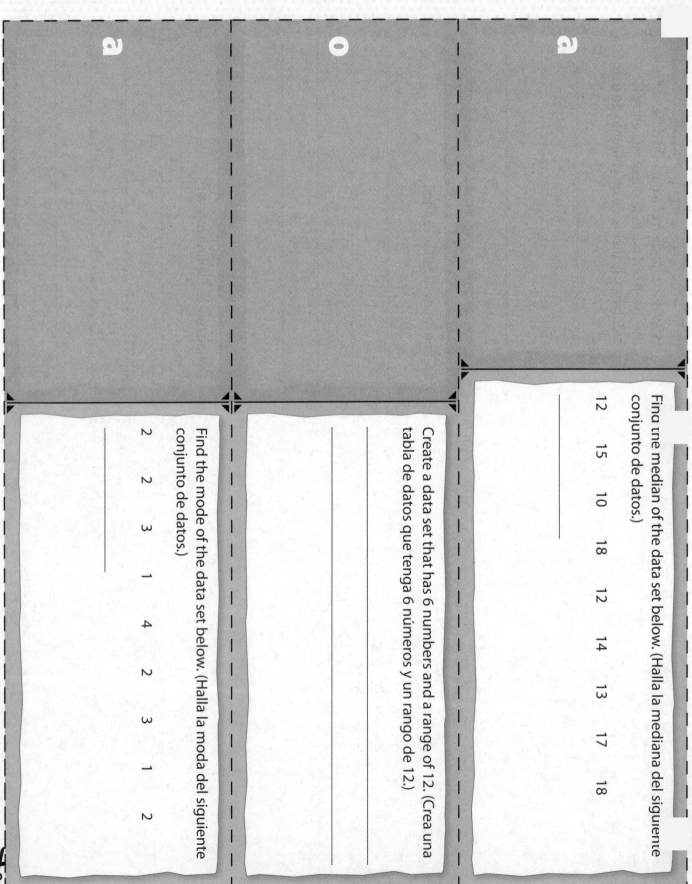

a

o

a

Find the median of the data set below. (Halla la mediana del siguiente conjunto de datos.)

12 15 10 18 12 14 13 17 18

Create a data set that has 6 numbers and a range of 12. (Crea una tabla de datos que tenga 6 números y un rango de 12.)

Find the mode of the data set below. (Halla la moda del siguiente conjunto de datos.)

2 2 3 1 4 2 3 1 2

Dinah Zike's
V K V Visual
Kinesthetic
Vocabulary ®

Chapter 10

✂ cut on all dashed lines

▱ fold on all solid lines

interquartile

What is the interquartile range of the data set below?
(¿Cuál es el rango intercuartil del siguiente conjunto
de datos?)

4   4   5   6   6   6   7   8   8   8   8

Dinah Zike's
**Visual
Kinesthetic
Vocabulary** ®

Chapter 10

✂ cut on all dashed lines

▭ fold on all solid lines

inercuartile

Circle the first and third quartiles in the data set below.
(Encierra en un círculo el primer y el tercer cuartiles en el
siguiente conjunto de datos.)

4   4   5   6   6   6   7   8   8   8

Dinah Zike's
Visual
Kinesthetic
Vocabulary®

Chapter 10

✂ cut on all dashed lines   fold on all solid lines

frequency distribution

Write about a time when it might be useful to know the frequency distribution. (Escribe acerca de una situación en la cual podría ser útil conocer la distribución de frecuencias.)

distribución de frecuencias

Define distribution. (Define distribución.)

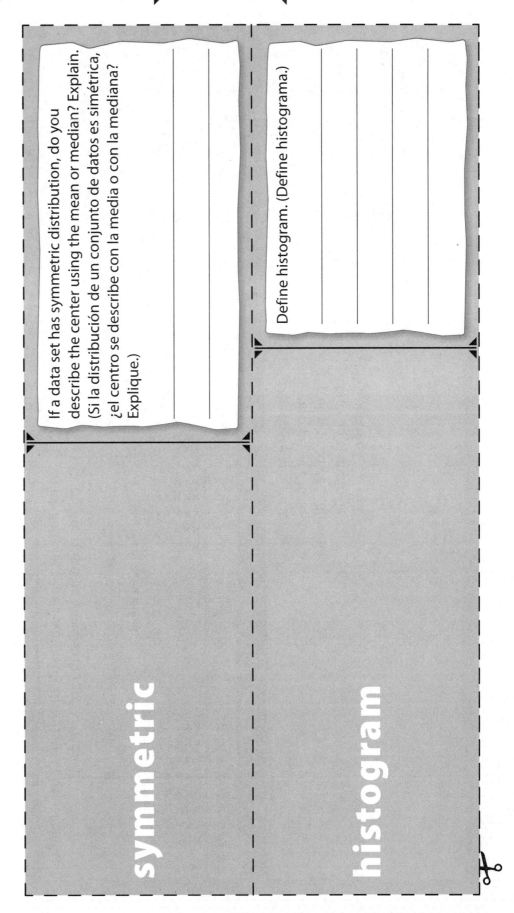

If a data set has symmetric distribution, do you describe the center using the mean or median? Explain. (Si la distribución de un conjunto de datos es simétrica, ¿el centro se describe con la media o con la mediana? Explique.)

Define histogram. (Define histograma.)

symmetric

histogram

Dinah Zike's
Visual
Kinesthetic
Vocabulary®

✂ cut on all dashed lines

⬜ fold on all solid lines

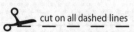

a

imétrico

In the space at right, draw an example of a histogram. (En el espacio de la derecha dibuja un ejemplo de histograma.)

Which line plot shows symmetric distribution? (¿Cuál gráfica de puntos presenta una distribución simétrica?)

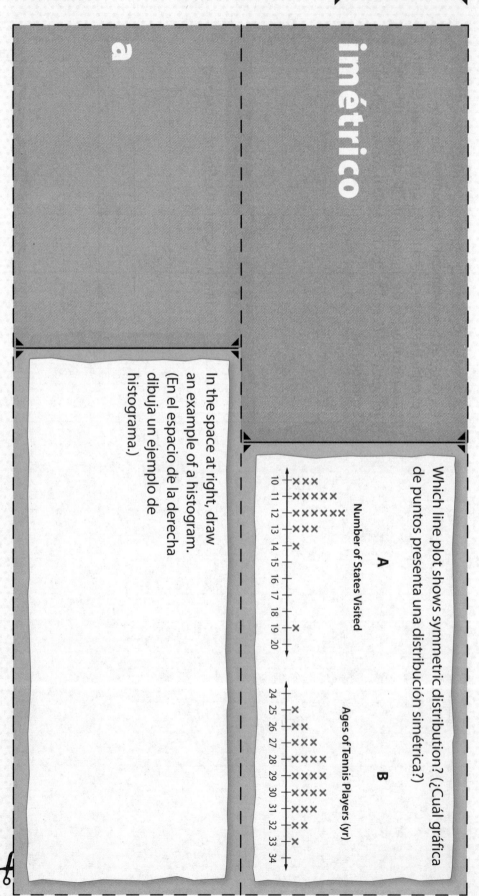

A

Number of States Visited

10 ×××
11 ×××××
12 ××××××
13 ×××
14 ×
15
16
17
18
19 ×
20

B

Ages of Tennis Players (yr)

24
25 ×
26 ××
27 ×××
28 ××××
29 ××××
30 ××××
31 ×××
32 ××
33 ×
34

Grade 6 Mathematics Reference Materials

LENGTH

Customary			Metric		
1 mile (mi)	=	1,760 yards (yd)	1 kilometer (km)	=	1,000 meters (m)
1 yard (yd)	=	3 feet (ft)	1 meter (m)	=	100 centimeters (cm)
1 foot (ft)	=	12 inches (in.)	1 centimeter (cm)	=	10 millimeters (mm)

VOLUME AND CAPACITY

Customary			Metric		
1 gallon (gal)	=	4 quarts (qt)	1 liter (L)	=	1,000 milliliters (mL)
1 quart (qt)	=	2 pints (pt)			
1 pint (pt)	=	2 cups (c)			
1 cup (c)	=	8 fluid ounces (fl oz)			

WEIGHT AND MASS

Customary			Metric		
1 ton (T)	=	2,000 pounds (lb)	1 kilogram (kg)	=	1,000 grams (g)
1 pound (lb)	=	16 ounces (oz)	1 gram (g)	=	1,000 milligrams (mg)

Inches
0
1
2
3
4
5
6
Inches

AREA

Triangle	$A = \dfrac{bh}{2}$	or	$A = \frac{1}{2}bh$
Rectangle or Parallelogram			$A = bh$
Trapezoid			$A = \frac{1}{2}(b_1 + b_2)h$

VOLUME

Rectangular Prism	$V = Bh$